MORAL DILEMMAS
AND MORAL THEORY

MORAL DILEMMAS
AND MORAL THEORY

EDITED BY

H. E. Mason

New York   Oxford
OXFORD UNIVERSITY PRESS
1996

Oxford University Press

Oxford   New York
Athens   Auckland   Bangkok   Bogota   Bombay
Buenos Aires   Calcutta   Cape Town   Dar es Salaam
Delhi   Florence   Hong Kong   Istanbul   Karachi
Kuala Lumpur   Madras   Madrid   Melbourne
Mexico City   Nairobi   Paris   Singapore
Taipei   Tokyo   Toronto

and associated companies in
Berlin   Ibadan

Copyright © 1996 by Oxford University Press, Inc.

Published by Oxford University Press, Inc.
198 Madison Avenue, New York, New York 10016

Oxford is a registered trademark of Oxford University Press

Library of Congress Cataloging-in-Publication Data
Mason, H. E.
Moral dilemmas and moral theory / H. E. Mason.
p.   cm
Includes bibliographical references and index.
ISBN 0–19–509681–9
1. Ethics.   2. Dilemma.   3. Decision-making (Ethics)
I. Title.
BJ1031.M32   1996
170—dc20   95–16122

9 8 7 6 5 4 3 2 1

Printed in the United States of America
on acid-free paper.

To the memory of
ALAN DONAGAN

Acknowledgments

A number of the essays included in this collection were originally presented at a conference on moral dilemmas held at the University of Minnesota in April 1991. That Conference was made possible by the generous support of the College of Liberal Arts, the Department of Philosophy, the Graduate School, the Hubert H. Humphrey Institute of Public Affairs, and the Carlson School of Management, all at the University of Minnesota. In the preparation of the collection, the chair of the Department of Philosophy, William Hanson, has been very supportive. I must give special thanks to Ruth Anne Allen and Jean Borgwardt of the Department's staff for their generous help in preparing the collection for submission to the publisher. My colleagues Norman Dahl, Joseph Owens, Michael Root, and Jasper Hopkins have on numerous occasions offered helpful advice. Joan Mason's careful reading and thoughtful judgment have been indispensable.

Two of the essays included in the collection have been previously published. Alan Donagan's essay was included in the memorial issue of *Ethics* in his honor. It is included in this collection with the consent of Barbara Donagan and the permission of the editors of *Ethics* and of the University of Chicago Press. I am particularly grateful to Barbara Donagan, and to Barton Schultz, who edited the memorial issue. David Brink's essay was published in the *Philosophical Review* 103 (1994). I am grateful to David Brink and to Cornell University for their permission to reprint the essay in this collection. Finally I must thank the editors at Oxford University Press, and in particular Robert Dilworth and Grace Elaine Suh, for their welcome help.

Contents

Contributors

Simon Blackburn is Edna J. Koury Distinguished Professor of Philosophy, University of North Carolina at Chapel Hill.

David O. Brink is Associate Professor of Philosophy, University of California at San Diego.

Norman O. Dahl is Professor of Philosophy, University of Minnesota.

Alan Donagan was Doris and Henry Dreyfuss Professor of Philosophy, California Institute of Technology.

Christopher W. Gowans is Professor of Philosophy, Fordham University.

Thomas E. Hill, Jr., is William Rand Kenan, Jr., Professor of Philosophy, University of North Carolina at Chapel Hill.

Ruth Barcan Marcus is Halleck Professor of Philosophy and Senior Research Scholar, Yale University, and Distinguished Visiting Professor of Philosophy, University of California at Irvine.

H. E. Mason is Professor of Philosophy, University of Minnesota.

Terrance C. McConnell is Professor of Philosophy, University of North Carolina at Greensboro.

Mary Mothersill is Professor of Philosophy Emeritus, Barnard College, and Senior Scholar, Columbia University.

Peter Railton is Professor of Philosophy, University of Michigan at Ann Arbor.

Walter Sinnott-Armstrong is Professor of Philosophy, Dartmouth College.

Introduction

H. E. MASON

Moral conflict has long been recognized as a fundamental fact of moral life, but the full implications of the possibility of conflict within the moral consciousness of a conscientious person exhibited in a moral dilemma have only recently engaged moral philosophers. The perspicuous specification of a moral dilemma is a matter of philosophical controversy, but generally speaking, a person can be said to face a dilemma in a situation in which compelling moral considerations favor each of the courses of action open to him. Suppose that a person in a position of responsibility must decide how to respond to terrorists holding a number of hostages. If he deals with them, he may win the release of the hostages but encourage the practice; if he refuses to deal with them, he may risk the lives of the hostages. Or suppose that a military commander must either withdraw air support from an exposed unit under his command or risk substantial losses to the balance of his troops. Whatever he does he will bear some responsibility for the attendant loss of life, and he may in retrospect carry the burden of that responsibility whatever course of action he might have taken. Not all dilemmas are as dramatic as these. Dilemmas take many forms, arise in a wide variety of circumstances, and appear to arise in the context of widely differing moral and ideological systems.

At a practical level moral dilemmas call out for resolution. Facing a difficult situation, a person is bound to seek a sound and reliable way through the difficulty. But in the most difficult cases of dilemma, that appears to be out of the question. Reasonable grounds of resolution will presumably have been exhausted. This possibility tends to arouse philosophical perplexity. How is it possible, one may feel inclined to ask, that moral considerations should run out, leaving a conscientious person with no clear practical guidance? Does the possibility of dilemma merely signal a rare anomaly, or is it a sign of some underlying misconception? Does the thought that we might face a genuine dilemma call for fundamental reconsideration, or is it a fact to live with and to work through?

These questions about the possibility of moral dilemmas arise with some urgency for philosophers attracted by the project of normative moral theory crafted to serve practice. Those theories commonly undertake a systematization and critical reconstruction of moral thought with the aim of serving practical moral deliberation. The possibility that there may be situations in which decisive moral considerations require incompatible courses of action appears to thwart that project. Some philosophers have argued that accepting the possibility of moral dilemma exhibits an inconsistency in the principles constituting a governing moral view. Others have argued that the project of normative moral theory is threatened by the prospect of paradox, where paradox arises from the assumption that there may be genuine moral dilemmas conjoined with principles of deontic logic commonly employed in moral reasoning. Because the project of normative moral theory seems a reasonable development of common moral practice, it is a natural philosophical reaction to doubt the possibility of moral dilemmas, taking the sense of their possibility as no more than an expression of ill-considered intuitions. As a result, the controversy over dilemmas brings into play both general philosophical considerations and more particular intuitions growing out of moral practice, and the requirements of theory tend to be pitted against common practice.

The line of thought I have sketched lies behind a lively philosophical controversy that may be initially perplexing, but goes to the heart of some fundamental questions about morality. A number of the papers in this collection address the controversy fairly directly, and others turn to somewhat independent questions about moral dilemmas and their place in moral practices. The papers speak for themselves, but because they are a diverse lot, I will say a word about several of the overlapping topics, with some indication of the place of particular papers. I will first describe briefly the recent history of the controversy.

In a pair of influential articles published in the sixties, Bernard Williams argued that it is "falsifying of moral thought" to represent its logic as conforming to that appropriate to beliefs. Williams phrased his argument in terms of opposing *ought*-statements: a person experiencing moral conflict is disposed to accept a pair of conflicting moral judgments expressed in opposing *ought*-statements. He argued that it is a peculiarity of such conflicts that even when the conflict is resolved with the acceptance of one of the conflicting judgments, the other may continue to stand, its standing acknowledged in the agent's regret and other dispositions appropriate to moral failure of a sort. Williams cited tragic conflicts in which an agent's regret is understandably exhibited whatever course might have been taken. That regret Williams took to show that, having acted in a situation of conflict, an agent may without inconsistency believe that he ought to have taken the course he didn't take, and may respond appropriately to his failure to take that course, even while believing that he did in fact take the right course. Allowing the appropriateness of those responses, Williams suggested, requires an account of consistency and inconsistency peculiarly applicable to *ought*-statements. He also suggested that an adequate account will have meta-ethical implications, supporting a non-realist interpretation of *ought*-statements.

It is worth noting that, in raising these questions about the logical peculiarities of *ought*-statements, Williams cited signal features of their use within moral practices, features markedly present in the examples he offered. The plausibility of the attitudes and responses exhibited in the examples are crucial to Williams's contentions, and to the cogency of his questions about the logical peculiarities and the semantic interpretation of *ought*-statements.

Discussion of the issue phrased in this way has taken several directions. Some philosophers have argued that it is apparent that there are moral dilemmas, and in defense of that line of thought, they have taken up the analytic tasks posed by Williams's arguments. Others have argued that on a reasonable understanding of a moral obligation no moral predicament could pose a genuine moral dilemma. Both Alan Donagan and R. M. Hare have taken that tack, but from quite different theoretical standpoints. Both have argued that carefully formulated and cogent moral principles pertinent to problematic situations will show the dilemmas to be only apparent. Other prominent contributors to the literature have argued that while there are genuine moral dilemmas, they do not necessarily have the consequences Williams alleged. Philippa Foot, for example, allows the possibility of both resolvable and irresolvable dilemmas, and argues that their possibility is not only compatible with realistic interpretations of the judgments forming the dilemmas, but in fact depends upon realistic interpretations.

It is a common view, assumed in many discussions of moral dilemmas, that the existence of moral dilemmas is evidence of inconsistency in the principles or obligations giving rise to the dilemmas. Alan Donagan, for example, contended that the generation of moral dilemmas is to moral rationalism what the generation of self-contradictions is to theories generally: an indispensable sign that a particular theory is defective. In a very influential paper, Ruth Marcus challenged that view. In defense of the possibility of genuine moral dilemmas, she offered an interpretation of consistency for moral principles or rules in the light of which their consistency does not entail that moral dilemmas are resolvable in the sense that acting in accord with one horn of a dilemma "erases the original obligation with respect to the other." In her view, establishment of a consistent set of moral principles or a moral code is not in itself an effective way of avoiding the possibility of genuine dilemmas. The dilemmas we face may have a contingent origin in the circumstances of our lives and do not necessarily point to a failure of our moral views or principles. In her contribution to this volume, Marcus discusses the attitude toward consistency of principles taken in a number of earlier accounts of moral dilemmas, and elaborates her own account. She discusses implications of that account for moral philosophy and for deontic logic. She also develops some of her earlier remarks about the dynamic force of the recognition of the reality of moral dilemmas, and makes some suggestive remarks about the relationship of that idea to some of Kant's views.

The prospect of paradox, where the assumption that there may be genuine moral dilemmas is conjoined with various deontic principles commonly employed in moral reasoning, raises the question of consistency in a more general way. In his contribution to this volume, David O. Brink explores three paradoxes said to follow from the assumption of moral dilemmas in conjunction with deontic principles variously supposed to be central to moral and deliberative reasoning. He argues that two of the three paradoxes create fairly substantial difficulties for anyone inclined to accept the possibility of moral dilemmas. He discusses the costs of rejecting the principles in question in favor of allowing the possibility of dilemmas, and concludes that the costs would be substantial. Brink also offers an argument against the possibility of moral dilemmas independent of the deontic paradoxes he discusses. That argument turns on his specification of a moral dilemma as a conflict of overriding all-things-considered obligations.

In several previous papers on the possibility of moral dilemmas, Terrance C. McConnell has argued that it is a condition of adequacy for a moral theory that it not allow the possibility of genuine moral dilemmas. In his contribution to this volume, he addresses those phenomenological arguments in favor of dilemmas that cite various residual responses supposed to exhibit an agent's recognition of the standing of a rejected alternative in an apparently dilemmatic situation. In each case, he offers an alternative account of the residual response compatible with denial of the possibility of moral dilemma, and supports the account with realistic examples. In the case of residual feelings of guilt and remorse, for example, he offers an account of those feelings making them appropriate responses in the absence of actual moral failure. He supports that account with a case in which feelings of guilt and remorse might be an appropriate retrospective response to conduct not reasonably blameworthy. He offers similar objections to other commonly cited phenomenological arguments, and argues that the psychological phenomena normally cited in favor of dilemmas can in some instances be as well or even better explained on the contrary view. Among other contributors to the volume, Marcus, Thomas E. Hill, Jr., and Simon Blackburn also give some attention to the interpretation of the phenomenological considerations cited by Williams.

Supposing that general difficulties in the way of allowing the possibility of moral dilemmas can be overcome, the question of whether a specific normative theory can allow dilemmas depends on the details of the theory. It tends to be commonly assumed that neither Kantian nor utilitarian theory can accommodate dilemmas. Peter Railton argues that, contrary to common philosophical opinion, a Millian form of utilitarianism can accommodate dilemmas, and will in fact have good reason to do that. In a wide-ranging discussion of Kantian theory, Thomas E. Hill, Jr., introduces the notion that a substantive moral theory may be silent on some deliberative questions, and may in that respect have "gaps." He places that possibility in an interesting light with some reflections on the moral advantages of a theory that is silent on some practical deliberative questions. In his view, Kantian theory can in fact be interpreted as having such gaps: there may be instances in which difficult, even tragic, decisions may be unavoidable, even for a faithful Kantian. In the course of his discussion, he takes up Alan Donagan's arguments to the effect that, while Kantian theory cannot generally be said to allow moral dilemmas, it may do so in the instance that an agent comes to face a dilemma in virtue of prior moral failure. Hill offers reasons for rejecting that opening for dilemmas. Hill also considers in some detail the question what place a reasonable Kantian could give to the various feelings commonly thought appropriate in the wake of moral failure.

In a probing paper, Alan Donagan raises the much more general question of what sort of moral theories can allow dilemmas. He argues that those theories which treat moral questions as resting on expectations or commands, whether divine or social, can obviously allow the possibility of moral dilemmas. Where authoritative commands are the final word, there is no telling what difficulties might be imposed upon willing subjects. Should such command theories not seem a likely basis for moral judgment, Donagan cites contemporary cases in which the expectations of the scientific community function in just that way. Rationalist theories like that of Aquinas and Kant, however, cannot consistently allow dilemmas. Because they treat moral requirements as imposed by practical reason, consistency is an overriding constraint, and any apparently conflicting requirements are subject to critical revision. Donagan also offers an historical speculation in explanation of the recent tendency of philosophers to acknowledge the possibility of moral dilemma.

Norman O. Dahl carries the discussion a step farther by asking which conceptions of morality can countenance moral dilemmas. Supposing that, in a case of dilemma, deciding considerations must have run out, he asks on which general views of morality, substantive or meta-ethical, that could be possible. He allows that on both constructivist views of morality and ideal utilitarian views, considerations may well be judged to have run out. That may not be true in the case of realistic views, or for that matter, quasi-realist views. His survey leads him to conclude that so long as there is some question of which conception of morality to adopt, the possibility of moral dilemmas is an open question. Dahl also questions the notion of moral requirement prominent in the controversy over the possibility of moral dilemmas. He discusses a number of the views curently held, and offers an account in terms of a kind of appropriateness of feelings of guilt in the instance of failure.

In these discussions, both the notion of a moral dilemma and the terms used to specify it have become terms of art. Acknowledging that, Walter Sinnott-Armstrong offers a range of definitions of a moral dilemma, all employing the notion of a moral requirement, but varying with their susceptibility to being overridden by other obligations or requirements. In his view, philosophically interesting questions of the possibility of genuine moral dilemmas are questions of the possibility of conflicts of non-overridden moral requirements. Dubbing such dilemmas "moderate dilemmas," he offers some reasons for accepting their possibility, those reasons resting for the most part on the plausibility of examples of moderate dilemmas. In that light, he undertakes a broad discussion of the possibility of dilemmas arising over questions of rights, considering a variety of cases of conflicting rights. His paper exhibits the diversity and the logical complexity of conflicts reasonably described as moral dilemmas.

Christopher W. Gowans regards the controversy over the existence of dilemmas as dominated by a pair of opposed philosophical styles: rationalist and experientialist, the former exhibited in a penchant for abstract theory, the latter in the tendency of those favoring dilemmas to appeal to moral experience of one sort or another. In his view, a readiness to countenance the possibility of dilemmas stems from a sense of our responsibility to those other humans affected in one way or another by our actions. That sense of responsibility is nurtured by our experience of others as intrinsically and irreplaceably valuable, and stands opposed to more abstractly motivated theoretical considerations.

It is a striking feature of the controversy over the possibility of moral dilemmas that specific examples of conflict tend to be offered to counter the aspirations of moral theory. Mary Mothersill casts a quizzical eye on the controversy. She expresses perplexity over the commonly accepted terms of the controversy, and raises questions about both the plausibility and argumentative force of the examples cited, and the conceptions of moral theory in question. Noting similarities with G. E. Moore's proof of an external world, she finds the citation of particular examples in favor of dilemmas unconvincing. She notes that many of the cases most commonly cited tend to involve cruel coercion, and she asks why responses to circumstances of that sort should be taken as paradigmatic for thoughtful and responsible responses to morally difficult situations. Moreover, the cases tend to be fictional cases, leaving little place for realistic consideration of alternative possible responses. Mothersill also expresses doubts about rationalistic arguments offered against the possibility of dilemmas. She offers some doubt of the standing of those axioms of deontic logic supposed to entail contradiction when conjoined with the supposition that there are genuine dilemmas. In her view, their bearing on everyday moral reasoning has yet to be made out. She is also skeptical of the conception of moral theory assumed by those rationalists dubious of the possibility of dilemmas. Moral theory, she suggests, seems to be thought of as a kind of ideal adviser, standing at our sides to tell us what to do in any difficult situation. She argues that no ethical theory promises a unique solution to every moral problem.

Simon Blackburn places philosophical questions about moral dilemmas in the more general context of the quandaries commonly encountered in any sort of practical reasoning. He describes quandaries in which no practical investigation could be reasonably expected to settle a choice among realistically presented alternatives as stable agent's quandaries, and argues that moral dilemmas are stable quandaries. As in the case of other stable quandaries, an agent facing a moral dilemma must ultimately *plump* for one of the alternatives: a quandary only occurs when available rational considerations have run out. Noting that philosophers tend to describe moral dilemmas in terms of *requirements,* he expresses some doubt about the notion that a requirement can be identified independently of the verdict a person comes to in the face of a quandary, and on that basis questions the perspicuousness of the notion that there might in the case of moral dilemmas be *matched* requirements. Blackburn questions the notion, common in the literature, that the residual regret or remorse sometimes appropriately experienced by an agent exhibits the agent's recognition that he has failed to fulfill a requirement. Blackburn concludes that moral dilemmas are better conceived simply as stable agent's quandaries, in which moral considerations favor or stand in the way of each alternative equally. Because the judgment that a quandary could not be resolved by any line of thought open to us is a defeasible judgment, it is not surprising that a person in a quandary might find himself wondering whether he is in the grip of misconception. In Blackburn's view, that response is understandable, but no sign of warranted philosophical perplexity.

The controversy over moral dilemmas is marked by the opposition of particular cases to more general philosophical considerations. That is particularly apparent in Peter Railton's paper. In his initial discussion, he offers an account of moral dilemmas designed to show their compatibility with utilitarianism. In the expansion of that paper, he discusses a wide array of cases of moral conflict exhibiting both the variety of moral considerations that engender conflict and the hazard of conceptions of moral conflict ruled primarily by the prospect of their bearing on moral theory. The range of considerations and circumstances exhibited in the cases he discusses cast a very different light on the issue. They cast doubt on both the common philosophical understanding of moral dilemma and on its implications for moral theory. In the course of his discussion, he considers in some detail the meta-ethical dimensions of the controversy over moral dilemmas, giving some attention to various implications for moral realism and for various anti-realist views. He concludes with a rather speculative account of a moral order, giving a realistic standing to a full range of morally relevant considerations.

In my own paper, I do not address the controversy over moral dilemmas directly. I attempt instead to discuss the sources in our moral practices of those conflicts commonly said to be dilemmas. To that end I take up conflicts of common responsibilities, and discuss in some detail how they arise and what light they cast on moral conflict generally. I consider a number of examples of moral dilemma, personal and public, and I offer in conclusion some rather skeptical observations about the common aspirations of moral theory.

This volume grew out of a conference on moral dilemmas held at the University of Minnesota in the spring of 1991. Alan Donagan offered the lead paper in that conference, and he was, as always, a very active participant in the discussions. Much to our sadness, his untimely death came less than a month later. His broad learning, his enthusiasm for philosophy and commitment to it, and his human warmth are missed by all who knew him. This volume is dedicated to his memory.

1

Moral Dilemmas, Genuine and Spurious:
A Comparative Anatomy

ALAN DONAGAN

"If one were to publish two volumes, the first containing the entire preceding philosophical literature concerning [moral dilemmas], broadly construed, from Plato to W. D. Ross, . . . while the second was devoted to the publications of the last thirty years, the second volume would be by far the larger."[1] So Alasdair MacIntyre, in a recent paper. The implied change in philosophers' interests is remarkable, and presumably has an explanation. What is it?

Two tempting answers are false. The first is that developments in modern culture, especially in the technology of medicine and warfare, have presented moralists with many new cases, about which traditional moral opinions yield conflicting answers. Moral theory, however, is no more completable than law. That moral theory at a given time yields conflicting answers to new cases implies no more than that it is incomplete, not that it cannot be developed to treat those cases satisfactorily. The second is that, in the past half century, rebellious groups hitherto repressed in western civilization (for example, blacks and women) have exposed conflicts in its moral practices by showing that they are inconsistent with certain of its professed principles. Such conflicts, however, are not moral dilemmas, but symptoms of moral progress: as the rebellious groups point out, they vanish when the morally indefensible practices are abandoned.

MacIntyre's proposal—it is not an answer—is more promising. It is that moralists are now more interested in moral dilemmas than they used to be because of developments in "large-scale moral theory." He therefore recommends us, if we wish to advance beyond the substantial achievement of recent work, to shift the focus of our attention. "It is where we stand on issues of large-scale moral theory," he writes, "that will determine our characterization of the relevant facts concerning moral dilemmas. The issues concerning moral dilemmas cannot be treated in independence of the larger issues on which they bear and which bear on them."[2] In this article, I shall try to redirect my attention as he recommends.

I. What a Moral Theory Is a Theory of and What Moral Dilemmas Would Be if There Were Any

Any and every predicament in which there are moral considerations both for and against a proposed course of action may be called a 'moral dilemma' in today's free and easy usage. Thus, on a recent *McNeil-Lehrer News Hour,* after listing reasons for and against intervening militarily to defend the Kurds, a respected newspaper editor described our situation in Iraq as a 'dilemma'. So understood, moral dilemmas would be a rag-bag class of objects about which nothing useful could be said. Unfortunately, although no philosopher takes them to be merely situations in which it is hard to say what is morally required, not all take them to be the same things. I therefore begin with what I take them to be, which I know is not peculiar to myself, but which I also know is not what every philosopher does. I do so not to claim that everybody should mean by it what I do, but to avoid making what I or anybody else means by it a matter of dispute.

I begin with the word 'moral'. One way in which social groups are distinguished from one another is by differences of *mores,* ways in which their members expect one another to conduct themselves, on pain of disapproval by their fellows if they do not. To the extent that a social group is well defined, so are its *mores;* and with respect to any one of its *mores,* if any member asks, "And what if I do not observe it?" the answer is that he or she will incur the kinds of social disapproval that have so far deterred most others in that group from not observing it. Although members of such groups will employ general words like 'right', 'wrong', 'virtuous', and 'vicious', or more specific ones, in expressing disapproval of conduct contrary to the group's *mores,* they do not thereby imply that their disapproval is more than socially sanctioned. They can imply that only if they have adopted the additional *mos* of disapproving certain kinds of conduct in whatever social group they are found, and the disapproval they express is because of that *mos.*

By adopting that additional *mos,* they implicitly recognize that observance of certain *mores* may be required, not simply by membership of whatever social groups have adopted them, but by something that holds for human beings whatever their social group—even if they have none. They also implicitly recognize that members of other social groups that have adopted this same additional *mos* may in following it disapprove some of the *mores* of their group. Both Xenophon and Plato depict Socrates' vain efforts to persuade Athenians to ask themselves whether non-Athenians might not reasonably disapprove some Athenian *mores.* Are the *mores* of Sparta, he invited them to consider, to be preferred in some respects, even by Athenians, to those of their own *polis?* Are even Hellenes to modify the *mores* they all share in the light of what non-Hellenes reasonably think of them? I take asking and answering questions like these to be moral inquiry, and morality to be that set of possible *mores* which human beings of any social group or none can be expected, simply as human beings, to observe. Such a set of possible *mores* would rest on a set of principles that members of any social group could find out, if they had learned to think in a sustained way and were accustomed to doing so. Those principles would be the true principles of morality, and morality could also be described as the set of requirements on human conduct derivable from those principles. Of course, it may be a delusion that there is such a set of principles. And, even if it is not a delusion, it does not follow that whoever is both qualified to inquire what that set is and does so will find it, although it would be astonishing if, after almost two and a half millennia of effort in the western world alone, considerable progress had not been made.

Given what morality is, what would a moral dilemma be, if there were such a thing? A common answer—indeed, the one that immediately comes to mind—is that it would be a situation in which, according to the true principles of morality, a moral agent was obliged both to perform an action of a specified kind and not to perform it. Anybody who believes himself or herself to be in such a situation, MacIntyre has implied, would be "at least confronted with an ineliminable blank contradiction in his or her moral thought."[3]

Aquinas, I believe, has shown that this answer oversimplifies, although Mac-Intyre does not read him as I do. On my reading, Aquinas distinguishes two sorts of situation in which you might think yourself morally obliged both to do and not to do some specified kind of action: (1) those that would not have come about except as a direct causal consequence of some violation by you of your moral principles; and (2) those that would have come about even though no violation by you of those principles was among its direct causes. By a 'direct causal consequence' I mean one that is not a free action, or the consequence of a free action; and by a 'direct cause', one among whose effects free reactions and their consequences are not counted.[4] Given this distinction, Aquinas holds that, although the true principles of morality must be such that, if you always observe them, you can never find yourself in a situation which they oblige you both to do and not to do some specified action, it is not *inconveniens* that violating them should put you in a situation in which you cannot avoid further violations.[5] He therefore distinguishes two ways in which, according to your moral principles, you can be in a dilemma (what he calls 'perplexed'): either *secundum quid,* that is, conditionally on your having violated those principles, or *simpliciter,* that is, even though you have not violated them. Your moral principles can allow you to be in a dilemma *secundum quid* without being inconsistent. For example, if your moral principles are Christian, and you have wrongly promised marriage to two prospective spouses, you cannot fail to commit a further wrong to at least one of them whether you break your promise or keep it to the extent you can, by going through the ceremony of marriage twice. But it does not follow that your moral principles are inconsistent, for they forbade you to make the second of your two promises, and you need not have made it.

Among our contemporaries, R. M. Chisholm has usefully discussed the logical questions raised by the 'contrary-to-duty imperatives' that tell you, in such cases, which wrong you should do.[6] Dilemmas *simpliciter,* or those not directly caused by the wrongdoing of those in them, are another matter. I shall hereafter refer to them simply as 'dilemmas'. Aquinas, for example, holds that any moral theory that generates such dilemmas must be inconsistent and so false, and he denies that Christian moral theory generates them. But even if he is right about Christian moral theory, was he right that any and every kind of moral theory whose principles generate such dilemmas must be inconsistent?

The answer will turn on what the theory in question asserts about the principles it specifies and the code derivable from them. A moral theory is not the same thing as the code it endorses; for, as Sidgwick demonstrated in his *The Methods of Ethics,* given suitable metaphysical assumptions (e.g., the existence of a benevolent divine creator), moral principles as radically distinct as those of egoism and utilitarianism would yield exactly the same moral code. Indeed, as Ruth Marcus has shown, since moral codes, or sets of moral rules or precepts, are not sets of propositions, they cannot be inconsistent or consistent in the sense in which the propositions composing a set are, namely, that their conjunction is or is not logically false. Nothing forbids us to define a set of rules as consistent if and only if there is a possible world in which all of them can always be obeyed, whether or not that world is actual. However, it will not follow, because the code derivable from a moral theory is consistent in this sense, that the theory itself is: whether it is or not will depend on what it asserts about that code. A moral theory is a set of propositions, with supporting reasons; and it will be inconsistent or consistent in the same sense as the propositions composing any set are.

The large-scale issues MacIntyre recommends us to investigate if we are to find out whether or not there are genuine moral dilemmas seem to be two. They are: (1) Of the various moral theories taken seriously by philosophers, do some consistently allow moral dilemmas, and others not?[7] and (2) Of the various rationally defensible moral theories, can any consistently allow moral dilemmas? It is of the first importance that these questions not be confounded. To the first, the correct answer seems to me to be yes, and to the second, no.

II. The Possibility of Moral Dilemmas According to Classical Moral Theories

Let us begin with the first of these questions. Of the various moral theories taken seriously by philosophers, do some consistently allow moral dilemmas and others not?

It is not difficult to show that there is a large class of such theories that do not, namely, rationalist ones, like those of Aquinas and Kant. Such theories hold: (1) that the principles of morality are comparatively few; (2) that each states, as required by practical reason, some 'side-constraint' (in Robert Nozick's useful term)[8] on what human beings can in fact do in the kind of world they inhabit; (3) that what the more specific requirements of morality are cannot be deduced from its principles alone, as from a set of axioms; but (4) only from them together with an indefinite number of additional premises, each specifying further some constraint already shown to be required; and (5) both principles and additional premises are adopted on the basis of informal dialectical reasoning.[9] Some critics have confounded rationalist moral theories with would-be axiomatic systems, and others with 'foundationalist' deductive theories that purport to begin with principles that are self-evident. Doing either is a disabling mistake. Rationalist moral theories, although not empirical, are developed much as physical theories are. The deductive form in which they may be set out (like that of Newton's *Principia*) neither exhibits the steps by which they were arrived at nor is meant to: it is the form most convenient both for applying them and for testing them. Any formulated rationalist theory is put forward as open to criticism, whether internal (e.g., that it gives rise to inconsistencies or paradoxes, or that its parts are badly articulated) or external (e.g., that it fails to account for features of other moral theories that appear not to be irrational); and whether a criticism is to be accepted, modified, or rejected will depend on its relation to the whole body of provisional beliefs and questions within which it arises.

Rationalist theories cannot allow moral dilemmas because of what they assert about the moral codes they endorse. Each principle and each derivative proposition of a rationalist theory asserts, of some rule or precept that it assumes all human beings can observe in all situations to which that rule or precept applies, that practical reason requires them all to observe it. If, therefore, any such theory were to assert that practical reason requires any human being in any situation to observe a set of precepts that cannot all be observed in it, it would contradict itself; for it would assert that set of precepts not to be what it also asserts or assumes them to be. Hence, if it should turn out that an accepted rationalist moral theory yields assertions of the form, "In situations of kind S, which have not arisen because you have earlier violated one of its principles, practical reason requires you neither do nor not do an action of kind K," then it is inconsistent, and must be repaired or discarded. On the other hand, moral rationalists have no more reason to abandon their project because a particular theory turns out to be inconsistent than, say, set theorists did in a like case. The generation of moral dilemmas is to moral rationalism what the generation of self-contradictions is to theories generally: an indispensable sign that a particular theory is defective.[10]

Although the rationalist ones are a large class of moral theories that cannot consistently allow dilemmas, there is a second large class that can: namely, that of command theories. The divine command theory is the best known of them, because it has been embraced by many Jews, Christians, and Muslims. According to all forms of the divine command theory, the principles by which human beings everywhere are to regulate their conduct have been promulgated by God, the almighty creator of the natural universe, through revelations to prophets. Such theories characteristically offer no proofs either that the God they postulate exists, or that the prophets to whom he revealed the principles of morality were in fact prophets: the alleged external history of revelation and the nature of the principles revealed are taken to establish both without strict proof.

Those who accept some form of revealed monotheism as beyond criticism, and with it a set of moral principles as divinely commanded, may find themselves, as William E. Mann contends in a recent paper, without having violated any of the moral principles they have accepted, in situations analogous to that of Jephthah, as reported in Judges 11.[11] Jephthah had vowed to God, permissibly, according to Mosaic Law as he understood it, that if he should be granted victory over the Ammonites he would, on his return, offer as a burnt sacrifice the first living creature that should leave his doors to greet him. On his return after winning the victory, his daughter was the first living creature to leave his doors to greet him. By Mosaic Law as Jephthah understood it, he was morally bound on one hand not to break his vow, and on the other not to commit murder—that is, not to kill the innocent: in other words, to kill his daughter and not to kill her.¹² Yet although the revealed moral law he accepted made it possible for him, without having broken it, to be in a situation in which it would condemn him whatever he did, Jephthah could not reject as self-contradictory his belief in the validity of the Mosaic Law as he understood it. He did not contradict himself by believing both (1) that the divine creator of the natural universe revealed to Moses the law as he understood it, and (2) that that law permits binding vows to be made the keeping of which would violate other provisions of it.

The only ground on which those in situations like Jephthah's could reasonably challenge the validity of the revealed moral principles that impose conflicting commands on them would be that there is some independent principle by which, if putatively revealed moral principles impose conflicting commands, they cannot have been divinely revealed. Yet the very idea that morality is ultimately a matter of divine command excludes the possibility of such an independent principle. That is why monotheists like Aquinas, who hold both that God did reveal the moral law to Moses on Mount Sinai and that the moral law is an expression of God's infinite rationality, are not divine command theorists: they believe that the moral law has been divinely commanded, but that its essence is its rationality, not that it is commanded. As rationalists, Thomists can argue that a set of putatively revealed moral principles that generates moral dilemmas cannot in fact have been divinely revealed. Pure command theorists cannot.

Not all pure command theories are religious: communitarian theories of morality are examples. Some who despair of the evils of societies like ours—that is, of societies culturally varied but more or less 'formally' free, both politically and economically—have concluded that those evils can only be remedied if those who are fit to form true communities do form them, a community being an organized body of fit persons such that both the laws of that body and the weight of public opinion in it are true indexes of morality. As with true revealed religions, so with true communities—there are no applicable criteria of what constitutes a fit person or a proper organization: the real thing is supposed to be recognizable when it appears. The example now most popular is the ancient Greek *polis,* as Hegel imagined it rather than as Thucydides described it. Rousseau was the founding father of such theories, and among his progeny are Hegelians both of the Right and of the Left, Marxists, Fascists, and Guild Socialists. The attitudes of communitarians to the principles of the communities they recognize to be such resemble those of divine command theists to God: although they hold that a community's will is the true will of its fit members, and purportedly accord them a part of determining it, when a community rejects what a member wills as merely individual, they acknowledge no external standard by which that rejection may be judged. A member's relation to his community resembles Abraham's to God over the destruction of Sodom: he or she is permitted to supplicate that something proposed not be enacted, but not to question what in the end is enacted.

Since neither divine command theorists nor communitarians can permit the source of moral legislation to be questioned by those for whom it legislates, neither can call in question principles of conduct that spring from such a source, even if situations can and do occur in which people who have not violated those principles find themselves divinely or socially commanded both to do something and not to do it. I used to believe that a theory according to which the ultimate moral authority gives commands that cannot all be obeyed (as distinct from ones that can each be obeyed by itself) "conceives the moral universe as analogous to the U.S.S. Caine in Hermann Wouk's *The Caine Mutiny,* and the moral authority as analogous to Captain Queeg"—who was a paranoid lunatic.[13] I overlooked the fact that, on any form of command theory, moral life is obeying a set of principles which normally can be lived by, and which it is deeply repugnant to violate. Moreover, violations are punished by the moral authority, whether God or the community. Such a set of commanded principles can win acceptance even though on some important occasions it generates dilemmas. Jephthah's horrible predicament may well have increased his contemporaries' fear of disobeying God's commands. Those occasions, however, can only be rare and terrifying. Commanded principles that must every day be disobeyed cannot inspire the awe that on all command theories they must. Nobody will believe that human beings as such are obliged to obey principles laid down by a paranoid lunatic.

No sets of principles advanced as commanded by a credible God or community can therefore generate conflicts in the normal run of things, and most will resemble those put forward in rationalist theories. They will not be barbarous or mad. Yet it may credibly be believed that there are large and good purposes which a moral authority would best promote by commanding, on pain of punishment, that everybody obey rules that, in exceptional situations, cannot all be obeyed. Those who complacently imagine otherwise should consider the rules of professional ethics reportedly advocated by some respected scientists in a recent case. In 1986 a postdoctoral fellow at a highly respected university was driven out of scientific employment for four years, and is not in academic employment even now, for questioning, through the recognized 'chain of command', certain experimental results reported by her superiors. The scientific community proclaims such questioning as a duty; and according to a recent National Institute of Health report, it would have been promptly established that in this case the questioner was right, if her superiors had not prevented it. Yet, according to an article in the *New York Times,* that has not deterred a distinguished scientist from declaring that it would have been better if the matter had been dropped—that is, if the postdoctoral fellow had continued to be punished for both doing her scientific job and failing to avoid embarrassing a superior who had, at best, not done hers.[14] He is quoted as saying, "I don't want to be quoted as saying that sloppiness or fraud is O.K., but it might be better to tolerate a low level of that rather than create an inhibitory atmosphere in science."

It may indeed be that scientific progress would be well served if scientists were professionally required both to report results that fail to confirm those of their superiors and to refrain from embarrassing those same superiors, even though, on occasion, those requirements would confront professional innocents with dilemmas. Such occasions would be rare, because most scientists who discovered mistakes in their superiors' work would (not without chagrin) be thanked rather than penalized. But even though a few would be penalized for doing their job, it might well be that the harm of that to science would be outweighed by the benefit that an inhibitory atmosphere had not been created. In short, whatever may be thought of command theories of morality that generate dilemmas in exceptional cases, they are neither inconsistent nor need they lack coherent purpose.

III. Moral Dilemmas in Recent Moral Philosophy

Why has work on moral dilemmas flourished in the last thirty years as never before? The tempting answer, that it is because the classical theories that countenanced them—the command theories—have displaced the rationalist theories that did not, is easily shown to be false. As we have seen, serious command theories, while allowing that moral dilemmas are possible, take care that they are rare; the recent view of them, however, is that they are common. In discussing the subject, one becomes accustomed to being told things like this: "One of my stronger intuitions in ethics is that there are genuine moral dilemmas. I did not come to have this intuition as a reaction to moral theory; it seems to have predated my philosophical career and not to have been erased by it. I believe that moral dilemmas are not all that rare; many of them are, fortunately, fairly trivial (that may explain why we tend to overlook the fact that they are nevertheless dilemmas)."[15] Such opinions at first bewildered me, although they were advanced as obvious.

There were two chief reasons for this. The first was that the examples of dilemmas offered arise only in moral codes I considered barbarous or barbarously interpreted. Agamemnon's dilemma (that Iphegenia be both sacrificed and not sacrificed) is an example of the former, and Jephthah's of the latter. Alleged dilemmas like that presented in William Styron's novel *Sophie's Choice* seemed to me spurious: while agonizing in practice, Jewish studies of resistance to tyranny, both rabbinic and recent, seemed to me to have treated them correctly.[16] The second reason was that I could not understand how the new view of dilemmas could have arisen, as it did, out of the theories dominant in the fifties and sixties—utilitarianism and the various forms of Ross's neo-intuitionism—for those theories seemed to me not only to have excluded the possibility of moral dilemmas, but to have been in part designed to do so.

Although the first of these reasons still seems to me strong, the second has vanished. I believe that I can now explain how the anti-dilemmatic theories of the mid-century have been transformed into the pro-dilemmatic ones of today. The peculiar nature of Ross's theory is the key. It is best exhibited by tracing its descent from Henry Sidgwick's treatment of the 'methods' of commonsense intuitionism and utilitarianism in the third and fourth books of *The Methods of Ethics*.[17]

Utilitarianism, as Sidgwick conceived it, is essentially a refinement and correction of the 'intuitional' morality of common sense—the intuitively sanctioned moral rules that children are brought up to regard as binding. The justification of observing these rules is twofold: that without some system of teachable rules that are generally received as self-evidently binding, people generally would be less happy, and that those accepted in the late-nineteenth-century western world on the whole promoted the general happiness better than those of previous ages. However, what these rules require in many cases is unclear, and in some they generate dilemmas. This compels moralists to regard them as inexact and not wholly true, and to look for an exact and wholly true principle to guide conduct in cases in which they fail to, a principle they find in the utilitarian 'greatest happiness' principle, according to which no action is to be done unless it would produce as much happiness as can be produced. The rules of intuitional morality are therefore to be acted on except when what they require is either unclear or inconsistent; but then what is to be done must be directly calculated from the utilitarian principle itself. R. M. Hare refined and developed this approach by distinguishing two stages in sophisticated moral thinking: an intuitive one that in most cases is both necessary (for economy of thought) and sufficient (as yielding correct conclusions); and a critical one, at which the shortcomings of the intuitive stage for complex and difficult cases are removed by recourse to utilitarian calculation.

Although formally Sidgwick's and Hare's utilitarianism excludes moral dilemmas, it does not exorcize their ghosts. Both concede that the moral code of any society must consist of specific rules that its members are taught to think of as self-evident, although they are also to be taught, in the rare cases in which their application is obscure or generates a dilemma, to resolve it by recourse to the greatest happiness principle. However, those brought up to think of the specific rules of the code as self-evident can be expected to have serious qualms when they must override any of them, especially as calculations of what the greatest happiness principle requires in a given case in which the specific rules are obscure or in conflict will usually be disputable. True, the theory unambiguously lays it down that conflicts between these qualms and confidence in utilitarian calculation are to be decided in favor of the latter. There is no intellectual conflict, only emotional discomfort.

It is to this condition that Ross's theory of prima facie duties brings relief. It begins by abolishing the separation of the commonsense intuitional stage in moral thinking from the utilitarian one, by degrading the utilitarian principle to an intuitional rule on the same level as the commonsense ones. Of course, if the theory were to stop with that, it would be flagrantly inconsistent; but it does not. It proceeds to remove any inconsistency by degrading the entire set of intuitional rules, the utilitarian principle among them, as 'prima facie' only: that is, as not actual rules of duty, but merely potential ones. Rules of prima facie duty are rules not in the sense that it is morally required to observe each of them but only in the sense that it would be morally required to observe each of them, provided only that observing it would not conflict with observing any of the others. In Ross's view, it is a matter of intuition not only whether a putative rule of prima facie duty is genuine or spurious, but also, when more than one such rule applies in a given situation, what the comparative weights of the prima facie duties are to which each gives rise in that situation. Intuitions of the former sort he considered relatively uncontroversial; the latter he acknowledged to be less so.

Here example is more illuminating than exposition. If you have made an appointment to meet somebody at a certain time and place, the intuitive rule that promises are not to be broken will, as Ross understands it, prima facie oblige you to keep that appointment; but it does not thereby follow that you are under any actual obligation to keep it. For, if, on your way to your appointment, you pass the scene of a traffic accident and the paramedics taking care of the injured beg you to help, then your situation falls under a second prima facie rule, that help is to be given to others who urgently need it. But here, too, it does not follow that you are under any actual obligation to give it. Ross believed that anybody with a civilized elementary education is capable of intuiting what rules of prima facie duty apply in any situation he or she may encounter. But that is not enough. Each kind of prima facie duty in a given situation has a certain potential weight, which need not be the same as the potential weight it has in another; and your actual obligation in any situation is determined by the greatest potential weight of prima facie duty you can discharge. This also is a matter of intuition, but intuitively assigning comparative potential weights is less certain than intuitively recognizing the various kinds of prima facie duty. In the case imagined, if you can both help the injured and keep your appointment, you have no difficulty. Since the weight of both together must be greater than that of either singly, then you are actually obliged to do both. If, however, you can do one but not the other, you must intuit as best you can which potential duty has the greater potential weight, for you are actually obliged to do whichever that is. In such cases, while intuitions mostly agree, in some they do not.

The crucial point in Ross's theory is that the prima facie duty with the lesser potential weight has no actual weight at all: you have no actual obligation to do what you promised (although you may, depending on the case, have an obligation to compensate whomever you have disappointed). Because of this, not only do you have no conflict of duties, you do not even have the ghost of a conflict. If the person you have disappointed complains, you can dismiss the complaint as morally uninformed. Even in the cases in which there is disagreement about which applicable prima facie duty has the greater potential weight there is no dilemma: the possibility of moral error is not a conflict of duties.

According to Ross's theory, no question of the form, "In situation *S,* either an action of kind *F* violates the principles of morality, or an action of kind *G* does, but which?" would be dilemmatic, because it would simply call for a determination of which of the two prima facie duties, not to do *F* or not to do *G,* which cannot both be done, is the weightier, and so actual and not merely potential. At the same time, it is not difficult to see that a change in the theory would transform every such question into a dilemma: *no more is needed than to consider prima facie duties as not potential but actual, although capable of being overridden.* Since a Rossian prima facie duty that remains potential is not an actual duty at all, it cannot be in conflict with the weightier prima facie duty that is actualized by defeating it; for it presents nothing to be overridden. Whether they noticed it or not, as philosophers came more and more to speak of weighing actual reasons for conflicting courses of action rather than of weighing prima facie duties for them, they were more and more treating situations calling for such weighings not, as Ross did, as ones in which it is hard to say what is morally required, but as dilemmas in which whatever is decided will have something wrong about it.[18]

Yet how did a distinction that, in Ross's theory, is as clear as any technical distinction can be, come to be overlooked? Part of the answer is that, as Ross's ideas became common property, his exposition of them ceased to be studied, and their relation to Sidgwick's views was forgotten too. In Sidgwick, it should be remembered, an intuitional moral rule is neither exact nor strictly true: it is an approximation to the truth that can be taught to children and can come to seem self-evident, but which they also learn must be corrected in certain difficult cases according to a higher principle that few ever try to formulate exactly, but which some should. Ross, as far as I can tell, did not investigate Sidgwick's predecessors: neither Whewell, whom Sidgwick detested and misrepresented,[19] nor Kant in his systematic *Metaphysik der Sitten*. If he had, he would have found that Whewell did not confine intuitional morality to the commonplaces children are taught but regarded it as a systematic study in which those commonplaces are given exact senses, and in which their exact applications to difficult cases are worked out. Kant, it is well known, did not speak of 'intuitional' morality at all, but also took it to be the task of a philosophical moralist to work out an exact system of specific moral rules. Between 1850 and 1950, philosophers came either to forget that they had ever considered it their business systematically to work out what morality specifically requires or to dismiss without argument the feasibility of attempting it. There was, indeed, a class of exceptions: philosophers in the then intellectually segregated Catholic institutions went on with the traditional project, and some of them—Germain Grisez, for example—still do.

If, as Sidgwick assumed, systematic investigations of the specific content of morality can result in nothing more accurate than a highly abstract first principle and a set of inexact commonplaces that can be taught to children (or, as Hare sometimes says, to 'proles'), then not only did Ross have a case for degrading those commonplaces to the status of merely prima facie rules, and leaving us to intuit our way among them, but his successors also had a case for demurring, and concluding that those commonplaces cannot be merely prima facie but must have some real weight. And if they have real weight, then conflicts between them are authentic dilemmas. In my opinion, the entire line of thought from Sidgwick through Ross to those who think that moral deliberation is largely about moral dilemmas is an aberration from the true line, whose last great representative was Kant. Whether this line of development explains the phenomenon I have tried to explain, I of course do not know. In this murky region of our subject, I am confident only of two things: that the phenomenon needs explanation, and that the true explanation will throw a flood of light on both the present and the future of moral philosophy.

Notes

1. MacIntyre (1990), p. 367. I owe too much, not only to this paper, but to the body of MacIntyre's work on moral philosophy, to be able to estimate how much. The bibliography of Christopher W. Gowans's representative collection bears out the observation here quoted. Cf. Gowans (1987).

2. MacIntyre (1990), p. 382.

3. MacIntyre (1990), p. 380.

4. I have explored the concept of what I here call the 'direct consequences' of an action in Donagan (1977b), pp. 37–52. There I refer to direct consequences as 'causal consequences', and to consequences, whether direct or indirect, as 'consequences' simply. I owe the distinction to H. L. A. Hart and A. M. Honoré (1959), and in particular to their treatment of the concept of a *novus actus interveniens*.

5. St. Thomas Aquinas, *De Veritate*, 17, 4 *ad* 8. Cf. his remark that 'Sicut in syllogisticis, uno inconvenienti dato, necesse est alia sequi, ita in moralibus, uno inconvenienti posito, ex necessitate alia sequuntur' (*Summa Theologiae* I–II, 19, 6, *ad* 3).

6. Chisholm (1963) was the pioneering article.

7. Among the recent writers represented in Gowans (1987), R. M. Hare, Philippa Foot, Terrance McConnell, and Earl Conee, from different points of view, take this position, as Aquinas and Kant had before them.

8. Nozick (1974). However, while the only side-constraints Nozick appears to recognize as valid are those Kant would call 'perfect duties to others', I think there are valid side-constraints of all four Kantian kinds: perfect duties to oneself (not to harm oneself) and imperfect duties both to others and to oneself (to act within reasonable plans of promoting others' happiness and one's own self-improvement).

9. This analysis of rationalist moral theory modifies one in Donagan (1984) in the light of MacIntyre (1990), pp. 372–73. As MacIntyre observes (p. 272, note 10), the two analyses are compatible.

10. MacIntyre (1990) not only makes this point forcibly, but adds that 'the occurrence of inconsistencies plays a central role in the moral life' (p. 375).

11. Mann (l991). Mann kindly both sent me an early draft of his article, and discussed it in correspondence.

12. 'It is possible to interpret the Hebrew text as implying that Jepht[ha] meant to sacrifice a beast; but in any case (as the sequel discloses) he must have included human as well as animal life in his vow. Some think he made the vow by special inspiration; but it is perhaps the better opinion that it was a vow sinful in itself, but prompted (as an act of supreme devotion) by an erroneous conscience' (*The Holy Bible*, trans. Ronald Knox [London: Burns & Oates, 1963], p. 213).

13. Donagan (1984), p. 299.

14. Hilts (1991).

15. Quoted from a private letter, not because what was written is in any way exceptional, but because I feared that I would garble things that have been said to me in trying to recollect them.

16. See Daube (1965) for a contemporary analysis of the rabbinic treatment; and any of the numerous studies of the part played in the Holocaust by compromises with Nazism for recent ones. In Styron's novel, Sophie's decision to make a choice saved neither of her children.

17. Sidgwick (1907).

18. The first book I remember studying that spoke of good reasons rather than of prima facie duties was Toulmin (1950), and the second was Baier (1958). However, in neither are the two assimilated. Their assimilation, I suggest, was gradual and unnoticed.

19. Sidgwick's debt to Whewell has received belated justice in Schneewind (1977). I have argued that even Schneewind has accepted too much of Sidgwick's version of their relation in Donagan (1977a) and Donagan (1980).

2

More about Moral Dilemmas

Ruth Barcan Marcus

In "Moral Dilemmas and Consistency,"[1] I argued that moral dilemmas need not signify an inconsistency in the set of principles under which we define our obligations. I also argue that consistency of principles does not entail that dilemmas are resolvable in both a weak and a strong sense. The weak sense is that even where principles, including priority principles, favor one alternative in a dilemma, the original obligation with respect to the other is not erased. The strong sense is that there is no reason to suppose that any set of moral principles will be sufficient to provide grounds for making a choice in every case of conflict. In so claiming, I am not also claiming that there *is* a right choice to be arrived at, by intuition independent of principle or the like. I am claiming that there may be cases of dilemma for which there is no morally justified resolution at all. As explained below, there may be non-moral grounds for choosing. I do not count tossing a coin or using a lottery as clearly *morally* justified grounds for choice.

The existence of dilemmas in the strong and weak sense suggests a second-order principle: that as rational agents we ought to arrange our lives and institutions with a view to reducing such conflicts.

I want in this paper to clarify some of the original arguments, to modify some of my earlier claims, and to elaborate on some of the consequences.[2] But, first, a review of the arguments.

I

It is assumed that a moral principle is one that applies to all moral agents in a moral community. A moral code is a set of moral principles. To count as a principle, a precept must be of a certain generality, and not tied to specific individuals, times, or places, except that on any occasion of use it takes the time of that occasion as a zero coordinate and projects into the future. It proscribes or prescribes action. For the discussion here, no distinction need be drawn between categorical and conditional principles. We may think of categorical moral principles as imposing obligations on an agent by virtue of his being a person and a member of a moral community. In the conduct of our lives, circumstances arise or are brought about in which our code mandates a course of action. Sometimes, as in dilemma, incompatible actions x and y are mandated, where doing x precludes doing y. Indeed, y may consist of refraining from doing x.

Dilemmas are usually presented as a predicament for an individual, such as Plato's case, in which the return of weapons has been promised to one who, intent on mayhem, comes to claim them. But they need not be so confined. In the case of Antigone and Creon, Antigone's sororal obligations conflict with Creon's obligation to keep his word and preserve peace. Creon's meeting his obligations precludes Antigone's meeting hers and the converse, under shared principles. Of course, if one of their shared principles is the principle of respect for the obligations of others, then the dilemma could be viewed as an individual predicament for each of them.

We will say that denial of the reality of moral dilemmas consists in claiming that, in every situation where the moral code applies, there is only one right choice in accordance with the code, and on making that choice there is no residue. Doing the right thing cancels other apparent conflicting obligations.

Kant[3] denied the reality of moral dilemmas. He says, categorically, "Because however duty and obligation are in general concepts that express the objective practical necessity of certain actions . . . it follows that a conflict of duties is inconceivable (*obligationes non colliduntur*)." His account of what for him would be apparent dilemmas is notoriously deficient.

W. D. Ross also denied the reality of moral dilemmas but takes pains to give us an account of them. He proposed that principles that in *particular cases* generate conflicting obligations are insufficient. In cases of conflict, they do not yield a *final* basis for decision. Ross, like Kant, argues that there is always one morally right choice, but, unlike Kant, he claims that right choices in cases of conflict need not be wholly mandated by our prima facie principles. Although Ross recognizes that estimates of the stringency of different prima facie principles will permit some ordering of priorities in situations of conflict, the ultimate determination is a matter of intuition, albeit some kind of rational intuition. For Ross, the locus of the apparent dilemma is in the agent's uneasiness. For, he says, "Where a possible act is seen to have two characteristics in virtue of one of which it is prima facie right and in virtue of the other prima facie wrong, we are well aware that we are not *certain* whether we ought or ought not to do it. Whether we do it or not, we are taking a moral risk."[4] Dilemmas are seen to generate uncertainty. They are not evidence of inconsistency.

There are those who do view dilemmas as evidence for inconsistency. John Lemmon,[5] citing instances of dilemma, says, "This moral situation merely reflects an implicit inconsistency in our existing moral code; we are forced if we are to remain both moral and logical, by the situation, to restore consistency to our code by adding exception clauses to our present principles or by giving priority to one principle over another, or by some such device. The situation is as it is in mathematics; there if an inconsistency is revealed by derivation, we are compelled to modify our axioms; here if an inconsistency is revealed in application, we are forced to revise our principles."

For philosophers like those to whom Lemmon refers, such as Hare, and to some extent Rawls, dilemmas aren't, or at least may not be, quite "real." Hare supposes that amplifying a code with exception clauses, priority rules, and the like will dispel dilemmas and yield a resolution in all possible cases. Rawls early on supposed that there would always be a "lexical ordering." I will not review the many arguments against such implausible proposals since my claim is that dilemmas are not evidence for inconsistency of a code.

Donald Davidson[6] is another who views dilemmas as evidence for inconsistency. He says, "Unless we take the line that moral principles *cannot* conflict in application to a case, we must give up the concept of the nature of practical reason we have so far been assuming. For how can premises all of which are true (or acceptable) entail a contradiction? It is astonishing that in contemporary moral philosophy this problem has received little attention and no satisfying treatment."

Until the recent revival of interest, philosophers who addressed the question of moral dilemmas seemed to agree, to the extent that I can determine, that dilemmas, whether real or apparent, have their initial source in the plurality of principles. They believed that if there were a single rule or maxim, conflicts would not arise. It is perhaps such a belief that accounts for Kant's inattention to the problem. It is surprising that philosophers concerned with practical reasoning persisted in that view despite its obvious falsehood. (I'm thinking here, for example, of remarks of Thomas Nagel[7] and Charles Fried.[8]) Promise-keeping defines a non-controversial moral principle, yet I might make two promises in all good faith and reason that they will not conflict, but then find that they do as a result of circumstances that are unpredictable and beyond my control. If all other considerations balance out, we have a dilemma in the strongest sense. There may be no *moral* reasons in favor of keeping one promise over the other. The examples can be multiplied.

It is true that unqualified act utilitarianism with a procedural tie-breaker is a plausible candidate for a moral system free of dilemma, but not only because it is a single principle. It is rather that for the utilitarian only consequences of an action count. It is not particular features of the agent and the act per se that determine its rightness or wrongness. For the utilitarian, the valuation is computational, and where conflicting courses of action have the same utility it is open to him to adopt a computational procedure for deciding, such as tossing a coin. Computation is what yields reasons for the utilitarian. It is clear that for dilemmas to arise some deontological principle is required—a principle that proscribes or commends certain clearly specified intentional actions toward others, without regard to wider consequences. Intentional actions such as violating another's rights, lying, or killing an innocent person are familiar proscriptions. Keeping promises and respecting the rights of others are familiar prescriptions, along with those that come with certain roles, such as that of parent, public official, and the like. These are actions in which the moral features, including intentions, circumstances, and immediate outcomes, are incorporated in the description of the action. In that respect the attributive content of that description is like an essential property—a property that the action has in all possible circumstances, or, if you like, in all possible worlds. Lying is an action in which an individual tells what she believes to be a falsehood with intention to deceive another, and it is wrong in accordance with a principle independent of any further consequence. It is this sense in which the prohibition against lying is absolute.

There has been a tendency to confute two quite different senses of absolute—one in which it means essential and the other in which it means has priority under all circumstances. If an agent has among his principles a deontic principle about lying as well as a utilitarian principle, even though lying is essentially bad, it need not be the case that it overrides *all* utilitarian considerations. There may be some priority principle that specifies conditions under which utilitarian considerations override deontic considerations.

Dilemmas therefore would seem to require that a code have at least one deontic principle. If one also has a utilitarian principle in one's code, one might resolve all dilemmas by adopting an ordering that says that all deontic principles override the utilitarian principle and that only in cases of strong dilemma is the utilitarian principle to be applied. But that would be false to the moral facts for those who are not absolute deontologists. Our usual principles are such that the most familiar dilemmas are often generated by a conflict *between* deontic and utilitarian principles. For most of us with mixed principles, which include a principle of utility, there may be bad consequences of sufficient magnitude to justify a killing or telling a lie.

Of contemporary moral philosophers, Bernard Williams[9] is the one who has noted the contingent origin of dilemmas and seen most clearly that there should be a way of squaring dilemmas with consistency of moral codes. He sought to do that by seeing whether there were principles of deontic logic which, if rejected, would secure consistency despite dilemmas. Familiar systems of deontic logic are not only obscure in many respects, they apply to worlds that are doubly perfect; to worlds where not only is it *possible* always to act in accordance with duty, but where everyone always acts in accordance with duty. Indeed, *all* of the early standard postulates of deontic logic are met in such doubly perfect worlds. What one wants is a definition of consistency independent of controversial systems of deontic logic. Such a definition might, of course, have consequences for deontic logic.

II

Consistency, as generally defined, is a property of a set of propositions such that it is possible for all the members of the set to be true, in the sense that a contradiction would not be a logical consequence of supposing each member of the set true. *Grass is white* and *snow is green* is a consistent set of propositions. Analogously, we define a set *of rules* as consistent if there is some possible world, some alternative set of circumstances, in which they are all *obeyable*. In such a world persons bent on mayhem have not been promised or do not simultaneously seek the return of a cache of arms. Sororal obligations do not conflict with obligations to keep one's word or preserve the peace. Agents may still fail, through an imperfect will, to fulfill their obligations.

Consider, for example, a silly two-person card game.[10] The deck is shuffled and divided equally, face down between two players. Players turn up top cards on each play until the cards are played out. Two rules are in force: black cards trump red cards, and high cards (ace high) trump lower-valued cards without attention to color. Where no rule applies, e.g., two red deuces, there is indifference and the players proceed. We could define the winner as the player with the largest number of tricks when the cards are played out. There is an inclination to call such a set of rules inconsistent. For suppose the pair turned up is a red ace and a black deuce; who trumps? This is not a case of rule indifference, as in a pair of red deuces. Rather, two rules apply, and both cannot be satisfied. But, on the definition here proposed, the rules are consistent in that there are possible circumstances where, in the course of playing the game, the dilemma would not arise and the game would proceed to a conclusion. It is possible that the cards be so distributed that, when a black card is paired with a red card, the black card happens to be of equal or higher value. Of course, with shuffling, the likelihood of dilemma-free circumstances is very small indeed. But we could have invented a similar game where the likelihood of proceeding to a conclusion without dilemma is greater. Indeed, a game might be so complex that its being dilemmatic under any circumstances is very small and may not even be known to the players. On the proposed definition, rules are consistent if there are possible circumstances in which no conflict will emerge. By extension, a set of rules is *inconsistent* if there are *no* circumstances, no possible world, in which all the rules are satisfiable.

A pair of offending rules that generates inconsistency provides *no* guide to action under any circumstance. Choices are thwarted whatever the contingencies. Well, a critic might say, you have made a trivial logical point. What pragmatic difference is there between the inconsistent set of rules and a set, like those of the game described above, where there is a likelihood of irresolvable dilemma? A code is, after all, supposed to guide action. If it allows for conflicts without resolution, if it tells us in some circumstances that we ought to do x and we ought to do y even though x and y are incompatible in those circumstances, that is tantamount to telling us that we ought to do x and we ought to refrain from doing x and similarly for y. The code has failed us as a guide. If it is not inconsistent, then it is surely deficient, and, like the dilemma-provoking game, in need of repair.

But the logical point is not trivial, for there are crucial *disanalogies* between games and the conduct of our lives. It is part of the canon of the family of games of chance, such as the game described, that the cards must be shuffled. The distribution of the cards must be "left to chance." To stack the deck, like loading the dice, is to cheat. But, presumably, the moral principles we subscribe to are, whatever their justification, not justified merely in terms of some canon for games. Granted, they must be guides to action and hence not totally defeasible. But consistency in our sense is surely only a necessary but not a sufficient condition for a set of moral rules. Presumably, moral principles have some ground; we adopt principles when we have reasons to believe that they serve to guide us in right action. Our interest is not merely in having a playable game, whatever the accidental circumstances, but in doing the right thing to the extent that it is possible. We may want to ensure that we can act in accordance with each of our rules. To that end, our alternative as moral agents, individually and collectively, as contrasted with the card game players, is to try to stack the deck so that dilemmas do not arise or that their likelihood is reduced.

Given the complexity of our lives and the imperfection of our knowledge, the occasions of dilemma cannot always be foreseen or predicted. In playing games, when we are faced with a conflict of rules, we abandon the game or invent new playable rules; in the conduct of our lives, in contrast, we do not abandon action, and there may be no justification for making new rules to fit. We proceed with choices as best we can. Priority rules and the like assist us in those choices and in making the best of predicaments.

The foregoing analysis of consistency reveals the sources of confusion in Lemmon's and Davidson's claim about dilemma's being evidence for inconsistency. They fail to attend to the obvious assymetries between deductive reasoning in the sciences and "deductive" reasoning, in which principles mandate future courses of action. In a dilemma, in the absence of a lexical ordering, we may choose each of the two courses of action. But we cannot meet both conflicting obligations. We cannot simultaneously return and fail to return a cache of arms to a person at a given place and time. Even if one wanted to keep the deontic principle of factoring—that if x ought to do A and x ought to do B, then x ought to do A and B—no *contradiction* is generated. There is no *contradiction* in recommending that someone do the impossible, although it might create considerable anxiety in the agent (the double bind). A contradiction, if we include factoring, does arise if we accept the principle that ought implies can.

Whether one adopts one or the other claim or neither requires independent justification. Considerations of consistency alone will not settle the matter. The simple response to Davidson's question is that where our principles have the consequence that they mandate conflicting courses of action in a particular case, we need not, as in the sciences, alter our principles; we may seek to change the world so that such conflicts do not arise. To allow that it is likely that we cannot wholly succeed is to acknowledge the reality of evil.

Our analysis of consistency as it applies to moral principles sheds light on the Kantian precept "Act so that thou canst will thy maxim to become a universal law of nature." As Kant understood laws of nature, they are universally and jointly applicable in *all* particular circumstances. It is that analogy with universal laws of *nature*, laws about what is rather than what we ought to do, that is the source of Davidson's and Lemmon's remarks about consistency. But, counter to Kant's ostrich-like stance, however perfect our will, circumstances may defeat such universal applicability. However, Kant's principle may be viewed as a second-order principle, and in fact a peculiar *consequentialist* rather than deontic principle. To will maxims to become universal laws of nature one must will the means. Those means are not confined to specific acts toward other persons, but they include arranging our lives and institutions, bringing about certain consequences that will help to ensure that moral principles are universally applicable. Of course there is no reason to suppose that we can always succeed in such an effort. The world may defeat us. Still, in troublesome dilemmas we often wish we could have avoided the emergence of such a predicament, and we often do take steps, to the extent that it is possible, to avoid them in the future. But as a general principle of action, that second-order principle is, like unmitigated utilitarianism, burdensome and seemingly supererogatory. Furthermore, it generates another deep dilemma: not a moral dilemma but one that creates a tension between our pursuit of what we may regard as a good and rich or fulfilling life and our pursuit of a life without moral conflicts.[11] The principle may also, as it often does, deter morally conscientious persons from assuming roles in which their participation would be for the greater good, such as politics. In political life, dilemmas may be virtually certain to occur and dirty hands may be an inevitability. Of course, that tension is partly a function of what we count as moral principles. Those extreme libertarians who urge that moral principles be confined to *minimal negative* deontic obligations, such as not interfering with the rights of others and the like, have much greater latitude in pursuing life goals without encountering dilemmas as compared with those whose range of principles includes positive deontic, egalitarian, and consequentialist principles. Stoicism, asceticism, and the like can also be seen as at least in part a response to this tension.

III

I should like to talk about the consequences of our analysis for deontic logic. One may think of the deontic operator 'O' as applying to descriptions of particular actions where those actions fall under a moral rule. So, if there is a general rule about promise keeping, then O (Sally keeps her promise to Bill). The systems of deontic logic like that proposed by Chellas[12] are inadequate. Indeed, the basis for such familiar systems of deontic logic may be reduced to one axiom and a rule. The rule says that from the material conditional

$$A_1 \mathbin{\&} A_2 \ldots A_n \longrightarrow B$$

it follows that

$$OA_1 \mathbin{\&} OA_2 \ldots OA_n \longrightarrow OB$$

The axiom says

1. $-(OA \mathbin{\&} O-A)$

The axiom makes invalid the situation of moral dilemma and hence must be rejected.

The rule, a rule of closure for the ought operator, is also implausible. Suppose as a matter of fact that, in this world, whenever someone keeps a promise, he raises his eyebrows. Then from that rule it follows from the obligation to keep promises that we have an obligation to raise our eyebrows.

Nor does strengthening the conditional to a causal conditional improve matters. Here we would have a rule of closure over the causal conditional. But (utilitarianism aside) obligatoriness characterizes an action that falls under a kind (see above). It is not the actions that are its causal consequences that are being prescribed and proscribed. One imagines that, in worlds with different physical laws, actions that are essentially right and wrong under a system of moral rules would remain so, although actions that are causal consequences of those actions may shift. Suppose that under some set of psychological laws and conditions of upbringing, when Sally does the right thing, it always causes Sally to applaud. Applauding is an action that does not fall under a moral principle.

Nor does the rule hold where the conditional is strengthened to entailment. Recall that, for deontologists, ought is supposed to operate on action descriptions in which the action is, according to the normative principle, essentially right. But action descriptions that mention all relevant factors *entail* action descriptions that do not mention all relevant factors. Keeping a promise entails doing something or other. So keeping a promise to return a cache of arms to Sam entails giving something to Sam. But giving something to Sam has none of the features of an action description that falls under a normative principle. And what of the entailment from the troublesome law of addition? Returning a cache of arms to Sam entails returning a cache of arms to Sam or killing Sam. Ought, like some other intensional operators, is not closed under logical consequence. "Believes" and "desires" are among such operators.

There are, of course, no grounds for demanding that standard deontic systems fit the moral facts, devised as they were for a kingdom of ends. In deontically perfect worlds, there is no need for principles such as ought implies can, since there are two senses in which everything that ought to be done can be done. Contingent circumstances do not present us with symmetric moral choices in which choosing one alternative precludes choosing the other, nor do agents ever suffer failures of will.

The minimal system[13] of deontic logic also retains closure under logical consequence but has only the axiom

2. $$-O(A\&-A)$$

In such a system, dilemmas are not ruled out as they are by 1. Nor is the factoring principle for ought derivable as a theorem, as it is in standard deontic logic. One cannot, as in Plato's case, go from

$$OA \ \& \ O-A$$

to

$$O(A\& -A)$$

—which contradicts the axiom of this minimal system. Indeed, the axiom of this minimal system may be seen as a very *weakened* ought implies can. Such 'acts', if we may by extension call them that, which are the doing and refraining from doing A, fall under no normative principle.

But the minimal system still has as its only rule closure under implication, and we have seen that even closure under *known* entailment will fail. Questions of closure reflect deep difficulties we encounter with the semantics of so-called opaque contexts.

I do not wish here to elaborate on further modifications to arrive at an appropriate system, if that is possible. But a satisfactory system will be very complicated indeed. It will require some very non-standard assumptions to cope with the difficulties of closure. An adequate semantical base for a theory of obligation will require a semantical theory in which sentences designate possible states of affairs. It will also need to include modal operators (logical and metaphysical), temporal operators, and operators for physical modalities, for the latter is required for a proper treatment of the more general ought implies can.

In my previous paper I defended the principle of ought implies can, but I would like to qualify that defense.[14] In the principle ought implies can, 'can' is not used merely in the purely logical sense. It is supposed to include physical possibility. Obligations often require plans and arrangements if one is to discharge them. Something goes wrong when, for example, I promise to meet someone for lunch, deliberately go on a trip at a great distance, and plead that I could not return in time. One needs a condition that says at least that if an agent ought to do x and if he does nothing to thwart the doing of x, then he can do x. But even here the question remains. Even in the case in which an agent didn't thwart the doing of x, in which his car broke down, for example, the agent is *not* exactly in the same position as someone who said he *might* be at lunch and failed to appear. The agent who promised will still make explanations and excuses, and may even resolve to have his car checked more regularly to avoid such predicaments in the future. In other words, he behaves in *some* respects like someone who had failed to meet an obligation simpliciter—who simply failed to act responsibly. Indeed, that view of the matter is more in keeping with my more general reflections on the reality of dilemmas. Such a case is not exactly like a case of dilemma in which one in fact *could* have met either of the competing obligations, taken separately, although one could not meet them both. Intuitively, in the case of dilemma, remorse seems more appropriate when what is done and what fails to be done are, before the actual choice, among the irreconcilable alternatives *each* of which is within the agent's range of choices. Regret seems appropriate when, owing to circumstances beyond control and despite all reasonable precaution and planning, an agent cannot meet an obligation—when what thwarts it is not a conflicting obligation but a straightforward physical impossibility. In both cases, explanations are required. The agent who incurred *no* obligation need not explain.

Given the character of deontic principles that define rightness in terms of the essential character of the act, it is perhaps more appropriate to adopt the principle that what is deontically prescribed is never annulled, but that when, through no deliberate scheme of his own, an agent cannot meet his obligation, he cannot be *blamed*. Here, as elsewhere, deontic principles diverge from consequentialist ones. For if what makes an action right is only its consequences, then if through no contrivance of the agent it cannot be done, it cannot be viewed as an obligation. What cannot be done has no consequences and there *are* no other features of the act that make it right or wrong.

IV

In his analysis of moral sentiments, Rawls[15] says that it is an essential characteristic of such a feeling that an agent "invokes a moral concept and its associated principle. His (the agent's) account of his feeling makes reference to an acknowledged right or wrong." "When plagued by feelings of guilt . . . a person wishes to act properly in the future and strives to modify his conduct accordingly. He is inclined to admit what he has done, to acknowledge and accept reproofs and penalties." In the case, for example, of a person of stern religious upbringing to whom theater-going had been forbidden, and who claims to feel guilty when attending the theater although he no longer believes it wrong, Rawls wants to say that he is mistaken in so claiming. The agent may have sensations of uneasiness that are like those one has when he feels guilty. But according to Rawls, *moral* sentiments such as feelings of guilt are not merely sensations, not *merely* psychological, but, like other attitudes toward states of affairs, a complex involving—along with diffuse feelings—beliefs, acknowledgments, and states of affairs. In the case of the uneasy theater-goer, the essential feature is absent: no moral concept or associated moral principle is invoked. The agent consequently is not apologetic, does not resolve to absent himself from the theater, does not regard himself as blameworthy or deserving of reproof. His sensations resemble feelings of guilt. It is the non-moral ground of his feelings that needs to be explained or excused, not his action.

Rawls's account suggests a finer-grained analysis of moral sentiments such as guilt, in which an agent acknowledges a moral principle in accordance with which he has failed to act. When, out of a failure of will, an agent fails to discharge a moral obligation that he acknowledges under a principle and that he could have discharged, all of the features *appropriate* to guilt feelings may be present. Nor does he absolve himself when, through cunning, he arranges his life so as to make it impossible to discharge his obligation. In both cases, he is appropriately distressed by guilt feelings. When he has such feelings, the moral agent wishes to act properly in the future, acknowledging his *own* failure and blameworthiness.

Where an agent fails to discharge an obligation when through no failure of his own he can't discharge it, such as the doctor who is prevented by a hurricane from seeing a critically ill patient, he acknowledges his obligation, but he has acted properly, and no future modification of his action is required. In the strong sense, he could not have done otherwise; his feeling is closer to that of regret. He does not acknowledge that reproofs and penalties are deserved. Explanations and excuses are appropriate.

In the case of dilemma in both the weak and the strong sense, the agent *could* have done otherwise with respect to each of the obligations. Through no fault of his own, he could not fulfill *both* of them. In such cases, particularly the strong cases of dilemma in which the choices are absolutely symmetrical, although he may have acted as properly as he could under the circumstances, excuses and explanations such as those appropriate to the doctor impeded by a hurricane are seen as insufficient. In cases of dilemma, the agent may be profoundly apologetic; he may impose on himself reproofs and penalties. He may even be inclined to accept some reproofs and penalties. Regret, here, as above noted, is too weak a description of the accompanying moral sentiment. Something closer to remorse is more appropriate. In Sartre's[16] case in which an agent struggles with a choice between joining the Free French and caring for an aged mother, it is more than regret he feels for the unmet obligation. Of course, our analysis suggests that Sartre was wrong in concluding that therefore "No rule of general morality can show you what you ought to do." Rules of general morality have shown the agent in question what to do in *each* case. In the absence of a conflict, he would have been obliged to do one or the other or both under those rules.

We see here the source and dynamic force of the second-order principle. There *is* a sense in which someone who has failed to discharge the obligation that was one horn of a dilemma may wish to act properly in the future and modify his actions accordingly. Here it is not a case of striving to meet those obligations that through a failure of will were not met on a given occasion. Rather, the agent may strive to arrange his own life and encourage institutional arrangements that would prevent, to the extent possible, future conflicts. To deny that the feelings that follow upon choice in a dilemma are inappropriately described as guilt feelings is to weaken the impulse to make such arrangements. Such considerations are particularly appropriate to the question of the inevitability of dirty hands in public life. We want in public life those who are moved by such feelings and who would therefore try to avoid such conflicts, yet who are willing to take the moral risk of entering into public life. It is in such cases that we see the tension between life choices and moral risk.

V

I have argued that there is no reason to suppose on considerations of consistency that there *must* be principles that, on moral grounds, will provide a sufficient ordering for deciding all cases of dilemma. But, it may be argued, when confronted with what are *apparently* symmetrical choices undecidable on moral grounds (dilemma in the strong sense), agents do, finally, choose. That is sometimes understood as a way in which, given good will, an agent makes explicit the rules under which he acts. It is the way an agent discovers a priority principle under which he orders his actions. That may sometimes correctly describe the case. But I should like to question the generality of such a claim.

A frequently quoted remark of E. M. Forster's is "If I had to choose between betraying my country and betraying my friend, I hope I should have the courage to betray my country."[17] One could, of course, read that as if Forster had made manifest some priority rule: that certain obligations to friends override obligations to nation. But consider a remark by A. B. Worster: "If I had to choose between betraying my country and betraying my friend, I hope I should have the courage to betray my friend." Both recognize a dilemma, and one can read Worster as subscribing to a different priority rule and, to that extent, a different set of rules from Forster's. But is that the only alternative? Suppose Forster had said that, morally, Worster's position is as valid as his own—that there was no moral reason for generalizing his own choice to all, and that there was disagreement between them not about moral principles but rather about the kind of persons they wished to be and the kind of lives they wished to lead. Forster may not want Worster for a friend; a certain possibility of intimacy may be closed to them that Forster perhaps requires in a friend. Worster may see in Forster a sensibility that he does not admire. But there is no reason to suppose that such appraisals are or must be moral appraisals. Not all questions of value are moral questions, and moral dilemmas in the strong sense may be "resolved" by principles for which no *moral* justification can be given.

The latter conclusion is one I believe of important consequence for moral philosophy. One of the most difficult questions in ethics is what falls within the sphere of *moral*. If we insist that, whenever we make a choice in a moral dilemma, we always invoke a further *moral* principle, then, as in Forster's case, Forster would be said to have adopted a general principle that makes loyalty to friends a moral principle that overrides, for all, loyalty to nation. That, it seems to me, is a wrong and dangerous conclusion. For one can see how that might bring virtually all action into the moral sphere. As Thomas Nagel[18] points out, there are, independent of pure self-interest, other values that guide action, such as commitments to personal goals (in which those goals may even be seen as contrary to self-interest) and commitments to advancing ends that are thought of as good in themselves, such as the advancement of knowledge, art, and the like.

Nagel classifies five fundamental types of value distinct from self-interest, which he calls obligations, rights, utility, perfectionist ends, and private commitments. Rights may be seen as generating 'categorical obligations'—obligations one has, as a *person,* to act or refrain from acting in certain ways toward others. The other obligations are proscriptions and prescriptions on action toward others one incurs or assumes by virtue of a more special role. For the strict deontologist, such obligations make up the only sphere of the *moral*. It is what lies behind libertarian ethics.

For moral philosophers like Rawls, when egalitarianism is more than everyone having certain rights, and when consequentialist considerations about improving the material lot of others enter into a determination of right action, then the sphere of the moral has been enlarged—perhaps constrained by the difference principle, but nevertheless enlarged. When, however, as in versions of virtue ethics or many religious moralities, some view of what counts as a good, or valuable, or desirable life is generalized to all, then all determinations of value are open to *moral* scrutiny. That is a conclusion I, for one, would not want to accept.

VI

This paper is not about conflicts between moral and non-moral values, but conflicts within the moral sphere. It also supposes that not all questions of value are moral questions and that the choices one makes may reflect other values. That conclusion poses some interesting questions about legal decision making.

Ronald Dworkin[19] has argued that there is *always* a right answer in a legal disagreement; that, implicitly, the law is *complete,* and that judges are not creating but discovering law. Here the arguments against that likelihood are like those I have offered against the necessity of *moral principles* settling all moral disputes. But it is a peculiar feature of our legal system that with some singular exceptions judges must rule in favor of one of the litigants' claims. Among singular exceptions are, for example, a judge's being exempt from ruling which of two creditors ought to be paid when a debtor has legal obligations to both. A bankruptcy law permits a distribution to all creditors. But those are the exceptional cases. In being *forced to rule,* a judge, given the role of precedent in our legal system is, contra Dworkin, creating law. Furthermore, in those areas of the law that are supposed to reflect moral commitments, a judge, being *forced* to a decision in hard cases, may be making legal, or illegal, actions for which no analogous *moral* resolution *would* have been available. In that way, the judge or legislator may be constraining our choice of action in non-moral spheres. He may be legislating about lifestyles; about what are, to use Nagel's terminology, considered perfectionist ends and private commitments.

Notes

1. Marcus (1980). Many passages in the present paper are repetitions of passages in the original paper. Versions of the present paper have been circulating (and sometimes referred to) since October 1980.

2. Some of the modifications and elaborations are a result of comments of Joel Feinberg, Paul Benacerraf, Walter Sinnott-Armstrong, and a study of Thomas Nagel's *Mortal Questions* (1979), as well as close reading of Bernard Williams's "Ethical Consistency" (1965).

3. Kant (1965), p. 24.

4. Ross (1930), p. 30.

5. Lemmon (1965), pp. 39–61.

6. Davidson (1970), p. 105.

7. Nagel (1979), footnotes on p. 74 and p. 114.

8. Fried (1978), p. 16.

9. Williams (1965).

10. One could devise an equally silly one-person game of solitaire.

11. A point made by Paul Benacerraf. Still, such a second-order principle was regarded by Rousseau as "the only one perhaps which is of practical use: to avoid situations which place duties in opposition to our interests." Rousseau (1958), pp. 62–63. Peter Railton pointed out this quotation to me.

12. See Chellas (1980).

13. See Chellas (1980).

14. I am indebted to Walter Sinnott-Armstrong for pointing out these difficulties with the principle ought implies can, and for suggesting alternatives.

15. Rawls (1971), pp. 481–83.

16. Sartre (1956), pp. 295-98.

17. Forster (1939).

18. See Nagel (1979).

19. Dworkin (1978).

3

Moral Residue and Dilemmas

Terrance C. McConnell

A moral dilemma is a situation in which each of two things ought to be done but both cannot be done. Restricted to single agents, a dilemma is a situation in which a person ought to do A, ought to do B, and cannot do both A and B.[1] In order for a moral conflict to count as a genuine dilemma, the conflicting obligations or moral requirements[2] must at least be such that neither overrides the other. If one moral requirement does override another, we have a resolvable conflict but not a dilemma.[3] But in a genuine dilemma, not only must the conflicting requirements both be non-overridden, they must also both issue in ought-all-things-considered moral judgments.[4] Also, genuine moral dilemmas are ontological, not merely epistemic; the truth of the conflicting ought-statements is independent of the agent's beliefs.

I have argued elsewhere that an adequate moral theory must exclude genuine moral dilemmas.[5] In this essay I shall critically assess one type of argument advanced by those who support the view that moral theories must allow for dilemmas. I shall call the view to be assessed the "moral residue argument." Three types of moral residue are said to support the reality of dilemmas: the remorse or guilt that agents experience after acting in conflict situations; the duty to apologize or to make amends that arises after acting in a conflict situation; and the second-order moral requirement to structure one's life so as to minimize conflicts between basic rules and principles. Here I shall argue that foes of dilemmas can adequately explain these residues; ironically, in some cases they can explain them better than can friends of dilemmas. Before discussing this, however, let me put the debate in perspective.

I. The Debate about Moral Dilemmas

There are two main arguments against moral dilemmas. One of these—the conceptual argument—tries to show that moral dilemmas are impossible because affirming their existence commits us to a contradiction. One version of the conceptual argument appeals to two principles: that "ought" implies "can" and that if an agent ought to do each of two acts then he ought to do both acts.[6] A second version appeals to the principle that an agent ought to do an act if and only if refraining from doing that act is impermissible.[7] Normally the principles appealed to in these arguments are said to be conceptually true, and so it is concluded that dilemmas are conceptually impossible. As one would expect, defenders of dilemmas have challenged the truth of the principles utilized in these arguments. Walter Sinnott-Armstrong, for example, tries to refute all three of the principles just cited.[8] Not surprisingly, then, the adequacy of the conceptual argument turns on the plausibility of the principles utilized.

The second argument against moral dilemmas is phenomenological. It claims that agents facing moral conflicts typically engage in certain types of behavior, that this behavior is reasonable, and that its reasonableness can be accounted for only on the assumption that there are not genuine dilemmas.[9] This argument too has been criticized,[10] and its plausibility hinges on the claim that proponents of dilemmas cannot adequately explain the phenomena in question.

The main arguments against moral dilemmas claim, in part, that common sense and the way we use moral terms support the position that an adequate moral theory must eliminate dilemmas. Because these arguments have been challenged and because many think that the arguments from moral residue show that common sense and ordinary moral discourse are on the side of friends of dilemmas, it is important to investigate them.

II. Conflicts and Moral Emotions

Perhaps the most common argument in favor of the reality of moral dilemmas appeals to the moral emotions that agents experience when acting in such situations. Let us begin with a familiar example. A young Frenchman whose brother had been killed in the German offensive of 1940 believes that there are morally compelling reasons for him to join the Free French forces in England. But his mother lives alone with him and is wholly dependent on him. His disappearance or death will undoubtedly plunge her into despair. So he has morally compelling reasons to stay with his mother.[11] Since he ought to join the Free French forces and ought to stay with his mother, but cannot do both, he seems to be in a moral dilemma.

Now suppose that this man joins the Free French forces. It is likely that he will experience remorse or guilt for having abandoned his mother. And not only will he experience these emotions, but it is appropriate that he do so. Yet, had he stayed with his mother and not joined the Free French forces, he also would have appropriately experienced remorse or guilt. Remorse or guilt are appropriate only if the agent properly believes that he has done something wrong (or failed to carry out an all-things-considered ought-judgment). So, no matter what course of action he takes, this man will fail to do something that he ought to do.[12]

Many cases of moral conflict are in crucial respects similar to this example. In these cases, proponents of the argument from moral residue claim that four things are true: (1) when the agent acts, she experiences remorse or guilt; (2) that she experiences these emotions is appropriate; (3) had the agent acted on the other of the conflicting obligations, she would also have experienced remorse or guilt; and (4) in the latter case these emotions would have been equally appropriate. In these situations, then, remorse or guilt will be appropriate no matter what the agent does and these emotions are appropriate only when the agent has done something wrong. Therefore, these situations are genuinely dilemmatic.

Although this argument has persuaded many, I shall raise two objections against it. The first of these objections has been stated previously,[13] although here I shall put it in a slightly different way. Even if opponents of dilemmas must grant that *if* remorse is appropriate no matter what the agent does, the agent is in a dilemma, they can still plausibly deny the antecedent.[14]

What is uncontroversial is that some bad feeling or other is called for when an agent is in a situation like that of Sartre's student. But the negative moral emotions are not limited to remorse and guilt. Among these other emotions, let us consider regret. An agent can appropriately experience regret even when she does not believe that she has done some wrong. For example, a parent may appropriately regret that she must punish her child even though she correctly believes that the punishment is deserved. Her regret would be appropriate because a bad state of affairs would have been brought into existence (say, the child's pain), even when bringing this state of affairs into existence was morally required. Regret can be appropriate even when one has had no causal connection at all with the bad state of affairs. It is appropriate for me to regret the damage that a recent fire has caused to my neighbor's house, the pain that severe birth defects cause in infants, and the suffering experienced by a starving animal in the wilderness.

With remorse (guilt), at least two components are present: the *experiential* component, namely, the negative feeling that the agent has, and the *cognitive* component, namely, the belief that the agent has done something wrong and takes responsibility for it. Although this same cognitive component is *not* part of regret, the negative feeling is.[15] And the experiential component alone cannot serve as a gauge to distinguish regret from remorse, for regret can range from mild to intense, and so can remorse.[16] In part, what distinguishes the two is the cognitive component. But now when we examine the case of an alleged dilemma, such as that of Sartre's student, it is question-begging to assert that it is appropriate for him to experience remorse no matter what he does. No doubt, it is appropriate for him to experience *some* negative feeling. To say, however, that it is remorse that is called for is to assume that the agent appropriately believes that he has done something wrong. Since regret is warranted even in the absence of such a belief, to assume that remorse is appropriate is to *assume*, not argue, that the student's situation is genuinely dilemmatic. Opponents of dilemmas can say that one of the obligations overrides the other, or that the student faces a disjunctive obligation, and that regret is appropriate because even when he does what he ought to do, some bad results. Either side, then, can account for the appropriateness of some negative moral emotion. To get more specific, however, requires more than is warranted by the present argument. Therefore, this appeal to moral residue does not establish either the reality or possibility of moral dilemmas.

Although I think that this criticism alone shows that appeals to remorse and guilt cannot be used with much success by friends of dilemmas, I want to develop a second objection, one that will demonstrate that matters are even murkier than they now seem. There are cases in which the value of an agent's experiencing remorse can be explained even when that agent has no good reason to believe that what he has done is wrong.[17] Let us consider a specific case. It concerns a middle-aged man, Bill, and a seven-year-old boy, Johnny. It is set in a midwestern village on a snowy December day. Johnny and several of his friends were riding their sleds down a narrow, seldom used street, one that intersects with a busier, although still not heavily traveled, street. Johnny, in his enthusiasm for sledding, was not being very careful. During his final ride he skidded under an automobile passing through the intersection and was killed instantly. The car was driven by Bill. Bill was driving safely, had the right of way, and was not exceeding the speed limit. Moreover, given the physical arrangement, it would have been impossible for Bill to have seen Johnny coming. Bill was not at fault, legally or morally, for Johnny's death. Yet Bill experienced what can only be described as remorse or guilt about his role in this horrible event.

There are several things to be said about this case. At one level, Bill's feelings of remorse or guilt are not warranted. Bill did nothing wrong. One might even recommend that Bill seek therapy. But this is not all to say. There is certainly a sense in which one understands Bill's response. From Bill's point of view, the response is not inappropriate, not irrational, not uncalled-for. To lend credence to this, imagine that Bill had had a very different response. Suppose that Bill had said, "I regret Johnny's death. It is a terrible thing. But it certainly was not my fault. I have nothing to feel guilty about and I don't owe his parents any apologies." Even if Bill is correct intellectually, it is hard to imagine someone being able to achieve that sort of objectivity about his own behavior. When human beings have caused great harm, it is natural—and so in a sense not inappropriate—for them to wonder if they are at fault, even if to outsiders it is obvious that they bear no moral responsibility for the damage. Human beings are not so finely tuned emotionally that when they have been *causally* responsible for harm, they can easily turn remorse on or off depending on their degree of *moral* responsibility.[18] And this may not be a bad thing; for it may make agents more cautious about their actions and more sensitive about their responsibilities.

The point is this. There may be situations in which we will say that an agent's remorse is not inappropriate even though we think that the agent is not warranted in believing that he has done something wrong. Because of this, and because in any given situation the appropriate response may be regret and not remorse, the argument for dilemmas that appeals to the moral emotions is unconvincing.

III. Conflicts and Duties to Apologize

Suppose you promised to meet Juan at a given time and Helga at the same time. Because you promised to meet Juan in one place and Helga in another, you cannot meet both as promised. You seem to be in a moral dilemma. If you decide to meet Juan, surely you ought (at least) to apologize to Helga for failing to keep your promise to her. And if you decide to meet Helga, you ought to apologize to Juan for not keeping your promise to him. That you ought to apologize is evidence that you have done something wrong. Since in this case no matter what you do you ought to apologize to someone (if you meet neither Juan nor Helga, you ought to apologize to each), then no matter what you do you will have failed to do something you ought to have done. The duty to apologize is moral residue, and in a case like this provides evidence of a genuine dilemma.

Foes of dilemmas are apt to respond that in cases like this, one obligation overrides or defeats the other, and fulfilling that obligation is what the agent ought, all things considered, to do. The defeated requirement, often said to be a prima facie obligation, is nevertheless real; it is an objective feature of the situation that exerts moral force.[19] And it is this moral force that generates the obligation to apologize.

Defenders of dilemmas are apt to find this line of reasoning unconvincing, and they might plausibly respond as follows: "You [opponents of dilemmas] say that the agent has acted on the more important obligation, yet still has an obligation to apologize. But this does not make sense. There is a duty to apologize only when one has done something wrong. And if the agent is so situated that she will have a duty to apologize no matter what she does, then you will have to admit that she is in a moral dilemma."

This reply shows that this version of the moral residue argument is important. Since there surely are situations in which an agent will have an obligation to apologize (or something akin to this) no matter what she does, foes of dilemmas will have to explain how such an obligation can arise. Before embarking on this task, however, it is worth showing how one very prominent opponent of dilemmas is unable to handle this objection.

Alan Donagan eschews any talk about prima facie obligations. Instead, he argues that the rules that characterize the Hebrew–Christian moral tradition, such as the rule that one ought to keep one's promises, hold absolutely.[20] Any time that someone makes such a claim, critics delight in producing counterexamples to the rules. Typically, they point to cases in which complying with the rules will lead to very bad consequences. Thus, concerning the rule about keeping one's promises, critics make the familiar point that one is not required to keep one's promises in certain extreme circumstances, for example, when one must break a promise in order to save a person's life.

Donagan, of course, is aware of this sort of objection. He responds by claiming that those who argue this way do not understand the nature of moral rules. The rule requiring one to keep one's promises must be understood to contain built-in conditions. Donagan puts the point this way:

> If a man accepts an invitation to dinner, it would be absurd for his host to understand him as having promised not to prevent a serious accident, or not to bring relief to victims of one, if to do these things would prevent him from dining. It is a promiser's duty to express any condition to his promise which the promisee might misunderstand; but there would be no misunderstanding in such a case, and to demand that the promiser stipulate all the emergencies

on which his obligation would be annulled would be vexatious as well as superfluous. To any relatively trivial promise there are a host of tacit conditions, all of which will normally be satisfied, which both the promiser and the promisee must and do understand; and when, as occasionally happens, such a condition is not satisfied, the promiser treats his obligation to the promisee as annulled. He has no need to consider himself as having a responsibility to fulfil it that is outweighed by a heavier responsibility.[21]

According to Donagan, then, in these extreme cases one need not say that one has a prima facie obligation to keep the promise and that this obligation has been overridden by a stronger one; that is, one is not forced to admit that there are exceptions to the rule. Rather, there is no obligation to keep the promise because one of the tacit conditions for being so obligated is not satisfied.

To evaluate this response, let us contrast the case that Donagan mentions with one in which the conditions attached to a promise *are* stated explicitly. Suppose that you invite me to dinner. In response, I say, "I accept your invitation and I shall join you for dinner unless I am making significant progress on my book; then I shall continue working." Now let us suppose that I do not join you for dinner. It will be quite natural for you to assume that I am making progress on my book and so have decided to keep writing. As an author yourself, you will understand and will not expect me to offer any explanation or apology; and, indeed, if I am working on my book I will feel no need to explain my activities to you, although the next time we meet I may confirm what we both take for granted.

Contrast this with the case in which the promiser states *no* explicit conditions on his promise. Suppose, again, that the promiser fails to keep his dinner invitation, but his reason for doing so is that he has stopped to help an accident victim. In this case, the promisee surely will expect an explanation, and it is plausible to say that the promiser has an obligation to explain his absence. There is, then, an important difference between cases in which the conditions are stated explicitly and those in which the conditions are said (by Donagan) to be tacitly understood. In the former case, one who fails to keep the promise has no additional obligation; in the latter case, however, failure to keep the promise leaves one with moral residue, even when one is justified in not keeping the promise.

Consider again the case in which the conditions are stated explicitly. Suppose that I am not making significant progress on my book and therefore I decide to join you for dinner. On my way to your home, however, I encounter an accident victim and stop to help her, thereby missing my dinner date. In this case I ought to explain my absence to you. Notice that if I fail to offer you an explanation and if later one of your friends reports having seen me going for a drive on the night in question, you will rightly feel indignant. This suggests that the moral residue is present unless one's reason for failing to keep the promise is that the *explicitly* stated condition was not satisfied.

If this is correct, then Donagan's response to the familiar objection is inadequate. If, in the case in which one saved the accident victim, the obligation to keep the promise were completely annulled, as Donagan maintains, it is difficult to see why one would be required to explain one's actions to the promisee. The view Donagan presents cannot account for this moral residue. From this we can learn that any adequate answer to this version of the moral residue argument must allow that the defeated (or overridden) obligation is still applicable to the situation and so exerts some moral force.

In showing how opponents of dilemmas can respond to the argument that appeals to the obligation to apologize, let me begin by making a small point. The argument actually shows too much; for, if successful, it even shows that the case in which one obligation clearly overrides the other must also be counted as a genuine dilemma. Consider again the case in which one must break a relatively trivial promise in order to save the life of an accident victim. Even in this case the promiser owes the promisee an explanation of his absence. Yet this is not a moral dilemma because there is a uniquely correct resolution to the conflict.[22] So if the argument is to be convincing, it must be qualified in some way.

Proponents of this argument say that agents in these conflict cases have a duty to compensate or to apologize to those disadvantaged by their decisions. And there can be no obligation to compensate or to apologize unless wrongdoing has occurred. There are at least two ways to respond to this contention. One is to deny that there can be no obligation to compensate in the absence of wrongdoing. This line of reasoning is pursued by both Joel Feinberg and Judith Jarvis Thomson.[23] They cite cases in which agents in dire straits are *permitted* to use the property of others, but ought to compensate the owners for that use. If Feinberg and Thomson are correct, the conditional appealed to by defenders of dilemmas is false.

Without judging the adequacy of the claim advanced by Feinberg and Thomson, I shall develop a different response to the argument. For the cases in question, it is doubtful that it is correct to describe these agents' additional obligations as obligations to apologize or to compensate victims. A more plausible characterization of the requirements is that these agents have an obligation to *explain* their behavior to the affected parties. And an obligation to explain one's behavior need not presuppose wrongdoing, as I shall show.

Those who endorse the "apology" instantiation of the moral residue argument for dilemmas typically describe the options available to agents in situations of conflict in a way that is too limited. Thus, in the standard case, they suppose that there are only two options: the agent must either break his promise and save the accident victim, or he must keep his promise and allow the victim to die. And in the earlier case of conflicting promises, your options are either to meet Juan and break your promise to Helga, or to meet Helga and break your promise to Juan. This is too simplistic, however; the options are richer. The agent has good moral reason to consider not just isolated options, but scenarios of actions available to him. For example, one attractive option in the former case is for the agent to save the accident victim, to contact the promisee and explain his absence, and to make alternative arrangements (if possible) to do what he promised.[24] In the latter case, you may resolve to meet Juan, call Helga and explain your decision, and then make arrangements to meet her later. And in each of these cases, even if the agent cannot later do what he promised, there are still good moral reasons to explain one's absence to the promisee.

To see this, we should focus on the agent's decision at that point when he recognizes the conflict.[25] What the agent should do at that point is to initiate (and carry out) the morally best scenario of actions available to him. Let us suppose that act-utilitarianism is the correct moral theory. From this perspective, presumably saving the life of an accident victim is more important than keeping a trivial promise (on any plausible theory of the good). Yet the interests of the promisee count too. A promise has been made and will be broken. Expectations have been created and they will be frustrated. Given this, there are good utilitarian reasons to minimize these frustrations. Since the promiser's explaining his absence to the promisee will (likely) achieve this end, he has an obligation to do so, an obligation that in no way presupposes wrongdoing. And one need not be an act-utilitarian for reasoning of this sort to make sense. Suppose that the fundamental moral precept is always to act so as to respect persons. Arguably, saving a life better promotes respect for persons than does keeping a trivial promise. Yet to ignore the promisee after the fact is surely to manifest disrespect for her. In this case, respect for persons is best achieved by saving the accident victim and (at least) explaining one's behavior to the promisee. I speculate that similar reasoning can be applied to other examples and with other moral theories.

Many of the examples of moral conflicts purported to be genuine dilemmas involve promises. And in most of these cases if the agent breaks his promise, there are additional things that he ought to do for the promisee. Friends of dilemmas describe these additional requirements as obligations to apologize or to compensate the victim. I have told a different story. To lend credence to the account that I have given, let us consider another example, one that does not involve promising. Suppose that upon reflection I have concluded that I ought to visit my friend tonight because she has been depressed recently. I think that it is important that I visit her now. On the way, I encounter an accident victim whose life I can save. I do this, and am thus unable to visit my friend tonight. This conflict is as plausible as any offered by proponents of dilemmas. Yet clearly in this case there is no obligation to apologize to the friend or to explain why one did not visit her. This is *not* because there is no prima facie obligation to visit her; it is rather because she had no expectations that I would do so on this occasion. The force of the overridden prima facie obligation is still at work, however; for what I ought to do is visit her the next day, or as soon as possible. This additional obligation is not evidence that I faced a dilemma or that I engaged in wrongdoing; this obligation cannot plausibly be described in terms of compensation or making amends. Instead, the obligation is most plausibly explained in terms of doing that which will best promote the values of one's system, whether this is act-utilitarianism, respect for persons, or something else.

One other consideration shows that the remainder cited in this instantiation of the moral residue argument does not support the reality of moral dilemmas. Return again to the agent who chooses to break the promise in order to save the accident victim. Suppose now, however, that the agent fails to save the victim and is himself injured or killed. Suppose further that you are a bystander and you are aware of the agent's promise. Given your knowledge, among other things, you have a moral reason to inform the promisee about the situation. But your obligation is not evidence that you were in a dilemma, is not due to your wrongdoing, and is not to be explained in terms of compensation. Instead, your obligation is based on the promotion of fundamental values, such as minimizing unhappiness and showing respect for persons.

The residual obligations cited in the previous two paragraphs clearly are not evidence for the reality of moral dilemmas. Friends of dilemmas do *not* have to say that *any* residual obligation provides such evidence; but they must distinguish cases that do provide such evidence from those that do not. The account that I have given on behalf of opponents of dilemmas can adequately explain all of these residual obligations within the same general framework. This is an advantage. For the phenomena here are diverse, and some do not lend even initial credence to the claim that there are dilemmas. Foes of dilemmas have a unified way of handling these residual obligations; defenders of dilemmas, by contrast, must scramble to explain why only some of these support their hypothesis.

IV. The Requirement to Minimize Conflicts

One other kind of moral residue has been cited as evidence of the reality of moral dilemmas. This argument originated with Ruth Marcus.[26] It is desirable morally for agents to avoid (when possible) conflicts of the sort cited herein. But unless these conflicts are genuinely dilemmatic and involve inevitable wrongdoing, agents have no moral motivation to avoid them. After all, if there is a resolution to these conflicts and the agent plans to act properly, there is nothing to fear in facing these situations. Acknowledging the reality of moral dilemmas, then, "motivates us to arrange our lives and institutions with a view to avoiding such conflicts."[27]

One cannot plausibly deny that it is morally desirable for agents to minimize the conflicts they face. If foes of dilemmas are to answer Marcus's argument, then, they must show that they can affirm this datum while denying the reality of dilemmas. The framework employed above can be used to demonstrate that they can do this.

Consider again your promises to Juan and Helga. Suppose that when you made the second of these promises, you knew that they conflicted. In that case, the very act of making the second promise was wrong—wrong in part because it deliberately created a situation in which someone's expectations would be frustrated. Still, at this point, you must ask, "What should I do now that I have done something wrong?"[28] To this point, all parties to the dispute can agree. What is at issue is whether you must do some *additional* wrong now that you have (culpably) made the conflicting promises. Opponents of dilemmas *deny* that *additional* wrongdoing is inevitable.[29] You are now in a new situation; you are required to assess each of the options and choose the best (where, again, the all-things-considered obligation may be a disjunctive act). Some may claim that breaking the promise to (say) Helga must be an additional wrong because we cannot explain what has gone awry in this situation absent her frustration. But that is not correct. Even if Helga were to die before the time you promised to meet her (and so no one's expectations must be frustrated as a result of your promises), that you made the conflicting promises was still wrong—wrong because in so acting you showed disrespect for Juan and Helga. Because it is wrong knowingly to create conflicting obligations, it is *wrong not to take due care* to avoid such situations.

This obligation to take due care is binding even if there is an *obviously correct* resolution to the conflict. The agent who breaks a trivial promise to one person in order to save another's life has done the right thing. But had he foreseen the accident, he would have been required not to make the promise, for in such a case, making the promise would demonstrate disrespect to the promisee. Thus opponents of dilemmas can explain why agents are bound by a second-order moral requirement to avoid conflicts whenever they can. This rationale to support the obligation to take due care presupposes the reality of moral conflicts; but it does not necessitate the endorsement of irresolvable dilemmas. The most obvious way for supporters of dilemmas to block this argument is to claim that *every* moral conflict is a genuine dilemma. If that were the case, then the rationale just sketched to establish the obligation to take due care would presuppose the existence of genuine dilemmas and so could not be used by opponents of dilemmas. Perhaps it is no accident, then, that Marcus has such an inclusive definition of 'moral dilemma'.[30]

V. Conclusion

As I noted at the outset, there are two main arguments against moral dilemmas: the conceptual argument and the phenomenological argument. These arguments are designed to show, among other things, that common sense and our understanding of moral concepts favor the position that an adequate moral theory must exclude the possibility of moral dilemmas. And even though criticisms of these arguments seem answerable, recently momentum has been on the side of those who claim that common sense supports friends of dilemmas. One of the more powerful arguments in favor of this position claims that the various kinds of moral residue can be adequately explained only if moral dilemmas are real. Three kinds of moral residue are prominent: the remorse that agents experience after acting in conflict cases; the obligation to apologize or explain one's behavior to those adversely affected; and the second-order requirement to structure one's life so as to minimize conflicts.

In this essay I have argued that opponents of dilemmas can explain the first and third kinds of residue as well as proponents of dilemmas can. With regard to these phenomena, there is a standoff. Concerning the second type of residue, I have argued that opponents of dilemmas actually have an advantage; for there are a rich variety of phenomena to be accounted for here, and the explanation available to those who deny dilemmas better fits these. If I have been successful, momentum is again on the side of foes of dilemmas.

Notes

I thank Michael J. Zimmerman for comments on an earlier version of this essay, and Gene Mason for detailed suggestions on the penultimate draft.

1. For a discussion of multi-person dilemmas and an argument that they represent rather different challenges, see McConnell (1988).

2. I use the expressions "duty," "obligation," and "moral requirement" interchangeably, and let each designate an act that an agent ought to perform. For one who disavows the interchangeability of such terms, see Sinnott-Armstrong (1988), ch. 1, esp. pp. 29–30.

3. Marcus counts even resolvable conflicts as genuine dilemmas. Cf. Marcus (1980). For one who criticizes her on this point, see Greenspan (1983), p. 117.

4. Sinnott-Armstrong defines dilemmas in terms of non-overridden moral requirements. Sinnott-Armstrong (1988), ch. 1. For a defense of my way of defining them, see McConnell (1993).

5. McConnell (1978).

6. McConnell (1978).

7. Conee (1982) and McConnell (1978).

8. Sinnott-Armstrong (1988), ch. 4 and 5.

9. McConnell (1978).

10. Lebus (1990), esp. pp. 113–14.

11. Sartre (1956), pp. 295–96.

12. Among the proponents of this argument are Williams (1965); Marcus (1980), pp. 130–32; and Sinnott-Armstrong (1988), ch. 2. Sinnott-Armstrong acknowledges (p. 53) that this argument alone does not show that moral dilemmas are possible.

13. McConnell (1978), pp. 277–80, and Conee (1982), pp. 89–92.

14. Here one might also challenge the entire conditional by distinguishing different senses of 'remorse' or 'guilt'. See Conee (1982), pp. 91–92, and Zimmerman (1987), pp. 201–202.

15. I am not claiming that there are no other differences between remorse and regret. One important difference is that remorse is *necessarily* self-referential and regret is not. Regret *can be* self-referential, however, and that is enough for the modest claims that I make here.

16. It is possible that no experiential component common to remorse and regret can be *independently* identified, and that instead each notion involves a *family* of attitudes with some similarities and some differences. But unless the differences between the two are clear in the contested cases, it will not help proponents of the argument from the emotions.

17. Sinnott-Armstrong (1988), p. 48, acknowledges this possibility, but gives a reason rather different from the one that I develop.

18. Michael J. Zimmerman makes a similar point, distinguishing between the *intrinsic* appropriateness and *extrinsic* appropriateness of an agent's remorse. Discussing someone who faultlessly causes another's death, Zimmerman says that "it is unlikely that anyone in such a position can turn remorse off in a manner that is intrinsically appropriate to the circumstances." Zimmerman (1988), pp. 134–35.

19. W. D. Ross (1930) expresses regret that the phrase "*prima facie*" "suggests that one is speaking only of an appearance"; Ross insists, however, that as he uses that expression it designates "an objective fact involved in the nature of the situation" (p. 20).

20. According to Donagan, in order for a promise to impose an obligation it must be freely made and involve something that is morally permissible to do. Donagan (1977b), p. 92.

21. Donagan (1977b), p. 93. Donagan (1984) makes a similar point in arguing that rationalist moral systems can exclude moral dilemmas.

22. As mentioned in note 3, among proponents of dilemmas only Marcus counts cases to which there is a clearly correct resolution as genuine dilemmas.

23. See Feinberg (1980), pp. 229–32 and Thomson (1986), pp. 66–77.

24. If the facts of the case were different, it is easy to see how some other scenario would be preferable. For example, if the accident victim were not in immediate peril, perhaps what the agent ought to do is to call the emergency squad (so that qualified professionals can assist the victim) and then continue to meet the promisee, even if belatedly.

25. The idea that an agent's obligations change as the circumstances change, and change even because of his own wrongdoing, is defended by a number of philosophers. See, for example, Goldman (1976) and Zimmerman (1990).

26. Marcus (1980), pp. 133–34.

27. Marcus (1980), p. 121.

28. The need for moral theories to answer questions like this is the main point in Chisholm (1963).

29. Not all opponents of dilemmas deny that wrongdoing is inevitable in situations like this. This situation is an example of what Donagan calls perplexity *secundum quid*—a dilemma conditional upon the agent's misdeed. See Donagan (1977b), pp. 144–45.

30. See note 3.

4

Moral Dilemmas and Rights

Walter Sinnott-Armstrong

It is pointless to argue about whether moral dilemmas are possible unless the arguers agree about what a moral dilemma is. It doesn't help to define moral dilemmas in terms that are unclear or disputed. It also doesn't help to ask which definition of "moral dilemma" is the correct one: "Moral dilemma" is a technical term in these contexts, and different philosophers use it to refer to different kinds of situations. Thus, the only reasonable approach is to construct a series of definitions and ask which of these kinds of situations are possible. That is what I will do here. I hope that we will find general agreement on which kinds of situations are possible. If so, then we can move beyond verbal disputes and ask more interesting questions about whether and how the possibilities that do exist are important for moral theory.

I. Moral Requirement Conflicts

In order to construct my definitions, I will start with examples that should not be controversial. It is morally wrong to kill or maim a person just for fun or just because you hate that person. It is also morally wrong to break a promise just because you don't feel like keeping it. And it is morally wrong to lie and cheat just to get ahead in your career. If no such judgments are granted, it is hard to see how to get any moral theory off the ground.

What makes these acts morally wrong? Although much could be said, what is crucial here is the structure of the examples. They have two stages. First, these acts are of certain kinds (killing, maiming, promise-breaking, lying, and cheating) that create a presumption against them, so they need an adequate justification. Second, there is no adequate reason for acts of these kinds when the only reason to do them is that the agent will have fun or hates the victim or feels like doing the act. These kinds of reasons are not enough to overcome the presumptions against such acts.

In order to capture this kind of moral presumption, I will say that:

An agent violates a *moral requirement* when the agent does an act that it would be morally wrong for the agent to do if the agent had no moral reason to do the act.

48

For example, I violate a moral requirement if I kill a person even when this is necessary to prevent him from killing me, since my act *would* be morally wrong if I *did not* have this reason to kill him. Counterfactuals are tricky, but the idea here is simply to ask whether the act would be morally wrong in a situation as much like the present one as possible, except that all positive moral reasons for the act are removed. This counterfactual will hold when the act is of a kind such that acts of that kind are morally wrong unless they are justified. An act of such a kind violates a moral requirement even when it is justified.

The term "requirement" might seem too strong. If so, just substitute "obligation" or "duty" or "constraint." Some of these terms are relational, so substituting them will require grammatical changes, but it will not affect my main points. What matters is not the word but the definition. The point of defining requirements by what would be wrong is to distinguish moral requirements from other moral reasons, such as a moral reason to contribute to a specific charity, to which it would not be morally wrong for an agent to fail to contribute, even without a moral reason to do so.[1] Moral theorists often disagree about which facts are moral reasons and which facts create moral requirements, but there are some clear cases, and every plausible substantive moral theory must assign these roles to some facts.[2]

This definition of a moral requirement is the main tool that we need to construct a series of definitions of moral dilemmas. First:

A *weak moral dilemma* is any situation in which the agent cannot avoid violating some moral requirement or other.

A situation fits this definition if each available alternative would be morally wrong if the other alternatives were not also problematic, so each has the kind of feature that I defined as a moral requirement. It is not always clear *which* situations are weak moral dilemmas, but it is clear that *some* situations are. Just consider the proverbial runaway trolley: the driver will kill one innocent bystander if she turns the trolley and another innocent bystander if she does not turn the trolley. Either act would be wrong if the other track were clear. Conflicting promises also fit the bill. So nobody could reasonably deny that weak moral dilemmas are possible.

Since moral requirements can conflict, we sometimes have to ask whether either moral requirement overrides the other in a morally relevant way. Roughly:

One moral requirement *overrides* another if and only if they conflict and the first is morally stronger.

Judgments about what overrides what are often controversial, but some obligations do clearly override others. For example, if I have to drive my car into a pedestrian in order to pick up my kids on time, the moral requirement for me not to run into the pedestrian overrides the moral requirement for me to pick up my kids on time. Such situations are still weak moral dilemmas, but they are resolvable.

A more restrictive definition of moral dilemmas would exclude resolvable conflicts of moral requirements:

> A *strong* moral dilemma is any situation in which the agent cannot avoid violating an overriding moral requirement.[3]

For a situation to fit this definition, every available alternative would have to violate a moral requirement that is overriding. However, if one requirement is morally stronger, the other is morally weaker, so it cannot also be morally stronger. Since terms like "stronger" and thus "overriding" refer to asymmetric relations, strong moral dilemmas are obviously impossible.

The only real controversy lies between weak and strong moral dilemmas. There are several intermediate possibilities, but the most prominent and important one is this:

> A *moderate moral dilemma* is any situation in which the agent cannot avoid violating a non-overridden moral requirement.[4]

A moderate moral dilemma can also be described as an unresolvable conflict of moral requirements.

This moderate kind of moral dilemma is what most defenders of moral dilemmas want to defend. Opponents often deny this, however, so it is worth quoting a few official definitions of moral dilemmas by their defenders: Thomas Nagel defines moral dilemmas as situations in which "there is decisive support for two or more incompatible courses of action or inaction . . . since either choice will mean acting against some reasons without being able to claim that they are *outweighed*."[5] Similarly, Bas van Fraassen defines a moral dilemma as "a conflict between what ought to be for one reason and what ought to be for another reason, which cannot be resolved in terms of one reason overriding another."[6] Third, Bernard Williams calls a moral conflict tragic when "an agent can justifiably think that whatever he does will be wrong: that there are conflicting moral requirements, and that neither of them succeeds in overriding or outweighing the other."[7] These quotations show that other defenders of moral dilemmas also have in mind moderate moral dilemmas.

So, are moderate moral dilemmas possible? It is usually hard to prove that a moral conflict cannot be resolved, but there are some ways to rule out any overriding. For example, a trolley driver might run over one person if she keeps pressing down on a lever and another person if she lets up on the lever. (The lever ensures that both alternatives are positive actions.) No resolution is possible because there is no morally relevant difference between the alternatives. Such symmetrical cases are rare, but asymmetrical cases can also be unresolvable. For example, suppose that a group wants to hold a protest in a small town, and the town clerk must decide whether to issue a permit. It would be morally wrong for the clerk to refuse to issue the permit if the clerk had no reason to refuse, so there is a moral requirement for the clerk to issue the permit. However, it would also be morally wrong for the clerk to allow a clear and present danger in the town if the clerk had no reason to allow it, so there is a moral requirement for the clerk not to allow the clear and present danger. Which of these moral requirements overrides? That depends on the degree of danger. The moral requirement to issue the permit overrides when the danger is small. But, if the danger to the town is clear, present, and large enough, then the moral requirement not to allow it overrides. Different people will disagree about how much danger is needed to override, but everyone should admit that sometimes it is too dangerous to issue the permit. Now, since each moral requirement overrides at one end of the continuum of dangers, there must be at least one point in the middle where neither moral requirement overrides. People might disagree about where such a point is, but there must be some such point. At that point, the conflict is unresolvable.[8]

This conclusion is controversial. Many opponents insist that the agent in such a situation is not morally required to adopt either alternative alone but is morally required only to adopt the disjunction: either one alternative or the other. This is correct in a way. In an unresolvable conflict, the agent does not have an overriding moral requirement to adopt either alternative alone but does have an overriding moral requirement to adopt the disjunction. However, that shows only that the situation is not a strong moral dilemma. It does not show that the agent cannot have a non-overridden moral requirement to adopt each alternative separately, which is all that is necessary for the situation to be a moderate moral dilemma.

There are also formal arguments that try to derive a contradiction from the definition of moral dilemmas. Here's one:

$$(1.1)\quad \blacksquare A \ \& \ \blacksquare B \ \& \ \sim\!Can(A \ \& \ B)$$
the definition of a moral dilemma

$$(1.2)\quad (\blacksquare A \ \& \ \blacksquare B) \longrightarrow \blacksquare(A \ \& \ B)$$
the agglomeration principle

$$(1.3)\quad \blacksquare(A \ \& \ B) \longrightarrow Can(A \ \& \ B)$$
"$\blacksquare$" implies "can"

$$(1.4)\quad Can(A \ \& \ B) \ \& \ \sim\!Can(A \ \& B)$$
from (1.1)–(1.3)

"A" and "B" are action sentences; "Can(A)" stands for "The agent can make 'A' true"; and "&", "~", and "⟶" stand for conjunction, negation, and material conditional, respectively. This makes the argument form valid, but whether the premises are true depends on what "$\blacksquare$" stand for. What is in the black box? If "$\blacksquare$" is replaced by "there is a non-overridden moral requirement," then agglomeration or (1.2) fails. To see this, consider a runaway trolley that will run over a father, a mother, and their ten children if the driver does nothing, will run over only the father if the driver turns left, and will run over only the mother if the driver turns right. These are the only alternatives, and the brakes fail. On my definition, the driver has a moral requirement not to turn right and a moral requirement not to turn left, since to turn either way would be morally wrong if another track were clear. And neither requirement is overridden by the other, assuming there is no morally relevant difference between the mother and the father. Nonetheless, even if there is a moral requirement to do the conjunction (not to turn right *and* not to turn left), this moral requirement is overridden by the larger number of lives that would be lost by not turning either way. Thus, there is no *non-overridden* moral requirement to do this conjunction, so agglomeration (1.2) fails.[9] Of course, agglomeration fails in this case only because the moral requirements conflict, so (1.2) cannot fail in this way if "■" stands for overriding moral requirements. Thus, this argument rules out strong moral dilemmas but not moderate moral dilemmas, even if (1.3) is granted.

A second formal argument uses something parallel to the claim that "ought" implies "not ought not" or "permitted":

(2.1)	■A & ■B & ~Can(A&B)	the definition of a moral dilemma
(2.2)	[■B & ~Can(A&B)] ⟶ ■~A	closure principle
(2.3)	■A ⟶ ~■~A	"■" implies "~■~"
(2.4)	■A & ~■A	from (2.1)–(2.3)

This argument form is valid, but whether the premises are true depends on what "■" stands for. Again, what is in the black box? If "■" stand for "there is an overriding moral requirement," then (2.3) has to be true, since there cannot be both an overriding requirement for A and also an overriding requirement for ~A. Nonetheless, if "■" is replaced by "there is a non-overridden moral require-ment," then (2.3) fails, since there *can* be a non-overridden moral requirement for A and also a non-overridden moral requirement for ~A, as in symmetrical trolley cases.[10] Consequently, this argument, like the previous ones, rules out strong but not moderate moral dilemmas. Since there are no good arguments against moderate moral dilemmas, and many examples seem to be moderate moral dilemmas, I conclude that moderate moral dilemmas are possible.

So what? What does this possibility show? Some philosophers try to use moral dilemmas to argue that morality is irrational in some way that rules out moral theory in general. Strong moral dilemmas would show this, since they would introduce contradictions, which would imply every moral judgment and its denial. But moderate moral dilemmas do not imply anything this extreme, since they do not imply any contradiction or detrimental kind of inconsistency.[11] To this extent, my position is deflationary. Moral dilemmas are not as revolutionary as some have claimed them to be.

Nonetheless, moderate moral dilemmas do have important implications.[12] The most important here is that they limit the aspirations of moral theory. Some moral theorists seek completeness in the sense of univocal advice in each situation to which morality is relevant.[13] This kind of completeness is unattain-able if moderate moral dilemmas are possible. But that doesn't show that there is anything wrong with moral theory. Some might like a moral theory to give univocal advice in every conflict, but the lack of univocal advice is not a defect if the demand for such advice is unreasonable. A moral theory that gives no univocal advice in unresolvable conflicts is no worse than an aesthetic theory that does not pick one novel as the best when one novel is more profound but another is more fun to read, or an economic theory that does not say which investment is better when one investment has a low chance of a high return and another has a high chance of a low return. Such theories are not useless or defective just because they do not resolve every conflict.

Besides, a moral theory that includes unresolvable conflicts can in principle still be complete in a different way: it can capture every moral truth. Such a moral theory can still say when we have moral requirements, when they conflict, and when conflicts are resolvable or not. Of course, no actual theory could in practice capture every moral truth, but the point here is just that the lack of resolution in some conflicts need not be a failure to include any true moral judgment, so a moral theory that includes unresolved moral conflicts is in no worse position to capture truths than any other moral theory.

In fact, there would be something wrong with a moral theory that *did* resolve conflicts like those above. When moral requirements are symmetrical or incomparable, neither is overriding, so a moral theory that favored one of the requirements would fail to capture the truth about the relative strength of the conflicting moral requirements. Constructivists might object that there are no truths about the strengths of moral requirements apart from their rankings in an ideal moral theory. However, defenders of moral dilemmas can still argue that an ideal moral theory would not rank either moral requirement above the other when they are symmetrical or incomparable. One reason is that, in order to resolve such conflicts, moral theorists would have to resort to arbitrary and artificial devices. This arbitrariness would cast doubt on the whole theory, or even on the whole enterprise of moral theory. That makes it better for a moral theory to admit its own inability to resolve all conflicts. So both realist and constructivist friends of reasonable moral theory can and should be friends of moderate moral dilemmas.

II. Moral Wrongs Dilemmas

Critics sometimes respond that there is more to moral dilemmas than just conflicts of non-overridden moral requirements. In particular, moral dilemmas are often defined directly in terms of "wrong":

> A moral *wrongs* dilemma is a situation in which the agent cannot avoid doing something morally wrong.

Is this kind of moral dilemma possible?

That depends on how "wrong" is used here. If the term "wrong" is used so that an act is morally wrong only when it violates an overriding moral requirement, then moral wrongs dilemmas are the same as strong moral dilemmas, so they are impossible for the same reasons. In contrast, if the term "wrong" is used so that an act is morally wrong whenever it violates a non-overridden moral requirement, then moral wrongs dilemmas are the same as moderate moral dilemmas, and they are possible for the same reasons.

Which use is correct? Ordinary speakers usually reserve the term "wrong" for acts that violate overriding requirements, but they also often say things like "There is something wrong about that" or even "Sometimes you should do what is wrong," and they talk about wronging someone or doing someone a wrong. In such contexts, the term "wrong" does not seem to be restricted to violations of overriding requirements. So common usage is not determinate enough to settle this uncommon issue. And philosophical usage in discussions of moral dilemmas is not much more determinate.

Of course, those who insist on denying the possibility of moral wrongs dilemmas can always formulate another definition of "wrong" that makes them impossible. For example, Foot argues against moral wrongs dilemmas on the grounds that "'wrong' as understood in moral contexts applies to actions that count against a person's *goodness.*"[14] I doubt that "wrong" is always used as Foot claims, but this might be how some people use it in the definition of moral wrongs dilemmas. If so, unresolvable moral wrongs dilemmas are impossible, since an agent in an unresolvable conflict always can violate one non-overridden moral requirement in order to fulfill another, and that action would not count against the agent's goodness (although it might count against her goodness that she got herself into the dilemma). This impossibility does show something about conflicts among moral judgments about persons, or even about blame and virtue, but it does not show anything about conflicts among moral requirements, which are about acts rather than persons. Consequently, a defender of moderate moral dilemmas should simply agree that moral wrongs dilemmas are impossible on such uses of "wrong" and then go on to show why other kinds of moral dilemmas are still important.[15]

III. Moral Residue Dilemmas

When critics claim that there is more to moral dilemmas than to unresolvable conflicts of moral requirements, they might not just rely on terms like "wrong." Instead, their point might be that each act in a moral dilemma is supposed not only to violate a non-overridden moral requirement but also to leave some moral residue. Much of the debate about moral dilemmas has been concerned with moral residue or remainder, which includes moral remorse or guilt feelings, as well as obligations to apologize, explain, or compensate after the act, or to seek a release in advance. However, moral residue is normally used as *evidence* for moral dilemmas[16] rather than as part of a *definition* of moral requirements, wrongs, or dilemmas. Nonetheless, the notion of residue could instead be built into a definition of moral dilemmas.[17] One way to do so is this:

> A moral *residue* dilemma is a situation in which an agent cannot avoid doing something that will justify some moral residue.

Other possibilities are to add a clause about justified residue to any of the previous definitions of moral dilemmas.

Such definitions in terms of residue would not be equivalent to any of the previous definitions, since, as opponents of moral dilemmas often point out, moral residue is not owed or even appropriate after *every* violation of a moral requirement. Suppose that I promise to meet you for a casual lunch, but I break my promise in order to save someone's life. Later you tell me that, if we had met, we would have both been killed by a bomb in the restaurant. It would then be odd for me to feel bad about breaking my promise or to say, "I'm sorry. I'll make it up to you." So I grant that some violations of moral requirements leave no moral residue. Indeed, even some unresolvable conflicts of moral requirements will not be moral residue dilemmas. Thus, the possibility of moderate moral dilemmas does not imply the possibility of moral residue dilemmas.

So, are moral residue dilemmas possible? It seems so. Suppose that Ginny's daughter cuts herself so badly that Ginny needs to take her to a doctor. The only way to get there soon enough is to drive, but the driveway is blocked by construction, so Ginny has to drive over one neighbor's flower garden or another neighbor's flower garden. She has seen both neighbors work long and hard on their gardens, both entered a flower show next week, and both have told Ginny many times not to let her child play close to their flowers. But Ginny must get her daughter to the hospital, so Ginny drives over the garden to the left. Afterward, she seems at least justified in feeling remorse. She also seems to owe an apology and some compensation to her neighbor. Since the situation is symmetrical, the same responses are justified if she drives over the other garden to the right. So this moderate moral dilemma is also a moral residue dilemma.

Critics often respond that it is not remorse but only regret that is justified in such cases. That depends on what you mean by "regret" and "remorse." Ginny is *not* justified in feeling remorse if remorse implies a belief that she violated an overriding moral requirement or that she is a bad person. In contrast, Ginny *is* justified in feeling remorse if remorse implies only a belief or a quasi-belief[18] that she chose to violate a moral requirement (or a non-overridden moral requirement). Ginny does believe that it would have been morally wrong for her to drive over her neighbor's garden if she had had no justification—if her child had not needed a doctor. Her neighbor did not give her permission to drive over the garden (and possibly would not have given permission if asked). And Ginny also has no excuse, since she was able to drive the other way, was not forced or coerced to drive the way she did, and knew the effects of her choice. That is why she should feel more than an uninvolved stranger who feels bad just to see the ruined garden. For these reasons, the appropriate feeling for Ginny is not just regret. If we cannot call it "remorse," we need a new term. Marcus reports that Rawls once suggested "regorse." But I prefer to continue to call it "remorse," and just explain what I mean by "remorse" here, namely, the kind of bad feeling that results from one's belief or quasi-belief that one chose to violate a moral requirement.

Another way around this problem is to turn to other kinds of moral residue. If the neighbor calls and asks Ginny what happened, she should not say just, "I drove over your garden." She at least ought to tell her neighbor *why* she drove over the garden. She also seems to owe an apology and some compensation. If Ginny does not compensate, her neighbor ends up paying the costs of getting Ginny's child to the doctor. This shift in costs is unfair, and that is why Ginny has to compensate.[19] The same holds if she drives over the other garden, but not if she is a mere bystander. So there is *some* moral residue, whichever garden she destroys. That is enough to establish the possibility of moral residue dilemmas, whatever one thinks about remorse.

IV. Rights

How does all of this apply to rights? Moral rights are among the most important moral requirements, so it is also important to determine whether moral rights can conflict. This issue turns out to be very complex.

In general, moral rights conflict when someone has no alternative that does not infringe either one moral right or another. Such conflicts make up a new kind of moral dilemma:

> A moral *rights* dilemma is a situation in which the agent cannot avoid infringing some moral right.[20]

A moral rights dilemma is then unresolvable when neither of the conflicting moral rights is overridden.

Not all moral requirement conflicts are moral rights conflicts. The reason is simple: not all moral requirements involve moral rights. Some acts (such as cheating on taxes) violate moral requirements and are morally wrong, even though they do not violate any moral rights of any specific individual. Consequently, even if some moral requirements can conflict, as I argued, those moral requirements that involve moral rights still might not be able to conflict. The possibility of moderate moral dilemmas does not imply the possibility of moral rights dilemmas.

So, are moral rights dilemmas possible? People often talk about conflicts of rights, but such common talk might be loose or mistaken, so we need to look at arguments. In order to show that (unresolvable) moral rights dilemmas are impossible, one would have to point to some special feature of moral rights that prevents them from conflicting (unresolvably). There are two main candidates for this role. First, rights are supposed to have a special strength. Second, rights are often supposed to imply clusters of duties for different people. I will look at these two features in turn. I will focus on concrete moral rights, since these are the kinds of rights that conflict in moral rights dilemmas.

The Strength of Rights

First, it is common to claim that rights are especially strong in that rights override other kinds of requirements, utility in particular, except possibly in extreme cases.[21] If rights are strong in this way, then some or all conflicts between rights and mere utility are resolvable. However, this tells us nothing about what happens when rights conflict with other rights, since then we have especially strong requirements on both sides.

The only way to rule out all conflicts between moral rights would be to claim that all concrete moral rights are absolute. Some do seem to go this far. For example, Benditt claims, "*if* the right exists at [time] *t*, then it cannot be overridden, or non-accorded, or in any way made inoperative except as the right-holder wishes not to act, or insist on it. . . . And this means, I think, that a right that one has at time *t* is absolute."[22] Benditt infers that concrete moral rights cannot conflict.

But can absolute rights conflict? That depends on what "absolute" means. There can *not* be conflicts among rights that are absolute in the sense that they override everything that they conflict with. Such conflicts would be strong moral dilemmas and so impossible. However, sometimes, as in the above quotation from Benditt, rights are called "absolute" because they cannot be overridden. Two rights that are absolute in this sense *could* conflict. Neither would be overridden, but that only shows that the conflict is unresolvable, and we have already seen how unresolvable moral conflicts are possible. Thus, the only way to rule out all conflicts between moral rights would be to claim that all moral rights are absolute in the sense of overriding.

There is no reason to accept that strong claim, and there are plenty of reasons to deny it. Thomson argues against absoluteness with a simple example: "Let us suppose that A owns some land and that he has not . . . given B permission to enter any part of it. . . . Suppose now that B's child falls seriously ill, and that by far the shortest way from B's house to the hospital lies across a corner of A's land."[23] In this case, according to Thomson, A still has a right against B that B not enter A's land, but this right does not override (and, indeed, is overridden by) B's moral requirement to help his child. So not all rights are absolute in the sense of overriding.

In response, Benditt denies that A has any right that B not enter A's land under these circumstances. However, Thomson argues that B does have (1) a duty to ask A for permission to cross the land if B can ask without cost, as well as (2) a duty to rectify or compensate for any harm done to A's property in crossing it; and the best account of why B has these subsidiary duties (1) and (2) is that B still violates a right of A even when that right is overridden. Benditt tries instead to explain such duties of compensation by "the having, using, destroying, depriving, or whatever of another's property, so long as nothing in the affair made it yours or made it cease to be his."[24] However, to say that something is "another's property" is not to describe physical possession but is instead to ascribe certain rights to him. And no permission need be sought or compensation paid if the property does not include a right to prevent the relevant use by others, such as when B has a right of way to cross A's land. Thus, Benditt's explanation in terms of property does not really avoid referring to rights that are overridden. This leaves no reason to believe that all moral rights are absolute or that unresolvable conflicts between such rights are impossible.

Claims, Privileges, and Powers

Even though the strength of rights does not exclude unresolvable conflicts, something else in the nature of rights still might exclude conflicts or ensure resolution. One possibility is that rights involve complex clusters of duties of and to different people.

In his justly famous discussion of rights,[25] Hohfeld distinguishes claims, privileges, and powers. Since Hohfeld defines these categories in terms of duties rather than requirements, I will do so too.

The first category is claims:

X has a *claim* against Y that Y do A =
Y is under a duty to X to do A.

For example, Nick has a claim against Kalleen that Kalleen teach Nick if and only if Kalleen is under a duty to teach Nick.[26]

The second category is privileges:

X has as regards Y a *privilege* of doing A =
X is not under a duty to Y not to do A.

For example, Tom has a privilege as regards Susan to stay in bed if and only if Tom does not have a duty to Susan not to stay in bed.[27]

Privileges are defined negatively, whereas claims are defined positively. And claims are defined by duties of Y, the claim-owner, whereas privileges are defined by duties of X, the privilege-owner. Despite these differences, claims and privileges are closely related. X has a claim against Y that Y do A if and only if Y does not have privilege as regards X that Y does not do A.[28]

The third category is powers:

X has a *power* over a claim or privilege = X has the ability to do a certain kind of act that will alter that claim or privilege.

For example, if Frances has the ability to sell her car to George, then she has the power to destroy her claim against George that he stay out of the car, to give George a claim against her that she stay out of the car, and thereby to destroy her privilege with regard to George that she enter the car. The ability to promise also confers moral powers.

These three categories are basic, but more notions can be defined by reference to them. For example, an immunity is simply the negation of a power, so it is an inability to alter claims and privileges.

There are also more complex clusters of claims and privileges and their negations. One important case is liberties:[29]

X is at *liberty* with regard to Y that X does A =
X has a privilege as regards Y that X does A, and
X has a claim against Y that Y not interfere in a certain range of ways with X's doing A.

For example, Joe is at liberty with regard to Ken to go to the church of his choice when not only does Joe have no duty to Ken not to go to that church, but Ken also does have a duty to Joe not to interfere in some ways with Joe going to that church. Of course, Ken has no duty to Joe not to buy the church and then lock the door, or not to refuse to let Joe borrow his car, even when these acts would interfere with Joe's going to church. That is why the definition of a liberty refers to "a certain range of ways."

Many more examples can be analyzed as clusters of claims, privileges, powers, and their negations. It is not clear whether all rights can be understood in terms of these three basic categories. Thomson finds this idea "very plausible,"[30] and I can't think of any counterexamples. All possibilities seem to be covered, since claims, privileges, and powers include duties, denials of duties, and changes in duties for the affected parties.

Conversely, it is not clear whether all of these categories are rights. Hohfeld claimed, "The term 'rights' tends to be used indiscriminately to cover what in a given case may be a privilege, a power, or an immunity, rather than a right in the strictest sense."[31] This seems to suggest that the term "right" changes its meaning for each different kind of cluster. Such extreme ambiguity in common language should be hard to stomach.

A simpler view would look for a common core to all rights. My hypothesis is that rights are claims that others not interfere in certain ways.[32] To say that George has the right to sell his car is to say that others have a duty not to interfere in certain ways with his selling it. George might also have a privilege and a power to sell his car. But that is not what we directly refer to when we say he has a right to sell it.

Why? Because a claim against interference is the only thing that is common to all rights. Not all rights imply powers: I can have a moral right not to be enslaved even if I lack any power to change or alienate this right in any relevant way.[33] Similarly, not all rights imply privileges: Even if one has a moral right to vote for a Nazi, since others should not interfere in certain ways, one still might have a moral duty to those others not to vote for the Nazi if one's vote increases the chances that the Nazi will harm those others. But all rights do imply claims that others not interfere in certain ways.

This might seem wrong in some cases. For example, we can say that Joe has a right to park in the last empty spot in a parking lot. It might seem that others have no duty not to interfere, for Ken also has a privilege to park in the same spot, and Ken's parking will interfere with Joe's parking. But this is too quick. Ken may interfere in some ways but not others. He may not call a truck to tow Joe's car out of the spot or threaten to harm Joe if he does not move his car or lock the gate to the lot, if the lot is public. Thus, Joe does have a claim that Ken not interfere *in certain ways*. If Joe did not have this claim, Joe would not have any right to park there. If the parking lot is private, and Ken owns it, then Ken may lock the gate or call a tow truck, and then Joe does not have any right to park in the last spot. Rights can vary in the kinds of interference that are excluded, as well as in the range of people who have duties not to interfere. And rights can still cluster together with other claims, privileges, and powers. But the minimum required for there to be any right at all is that there be some claim against interference. So this is what makes rights rights.

Even though privileges, powers, and some claims are not rights, it is still interesting to ask, Which of these can conflict, and how? For the sake of simplicity, I will discuss only claims and privileges but not powers. Powers are defined by abilities rather than duties, and the discussion will be complex enough without them.[34]

First, claims. The simplest way to define conflicts between claims is parallel to my definition of weak moral dilemmas:

A *moral claims dilemma* is any situation in which an agent cannot avoid infringing some moral claim.

For example, Zack is in a moral claims dilemma if Xavier has a claim against Zack that Zack not kill Xavier, and Yancy has a similar claim, but Zack cannot avoid killing at least one of them (as in a trolley case). Since moral duties are a kind of moral requirement, moral claims dilemmas are weak moral dilemmas. Since not all rights or claims are overriding, moral claims dilemmas are possible for the same reasons as weak moral dilemmas. And there is no more reason to think that all moral claims dilemmas are resolvable than to think that all moral requirement conflicts are resolvable.

However, this definition seems too narrow. For example, hate speech is often said to create a conflict of rights, because people are supposed to have one claim against others not to interfere with their speech and another claim against others not to be deprived of equal opportunity, but hate speech can be so demeaning and obstructive as to prevent equal opportunity. Nonetheless, there might be no agent who cannot avoid infringing a claim, since the speaker can avoid infringing any claim just by not using hate speech. What makes this a conflict of rights is instead that the exercise of one right infringes another right.

Such cases still fit under my definition of moral claims dilemmas if some third party has a duty to protect the infringed right. If the speaker and the target of the hate speech are students, the school administration might have a duty to the target to prevent interference with an equal education. Then the administration cannot avoid infringing either one student's claim to equal education (if it does not interfere with the hate speech) or another student's claim to free speech (if it does interfere with the hate speech). However, there is not always a third party with a duty to protect the infringed right. In an election, hate speech can reduce a candidate's opportunity to be elected, but there might be no third party who has a duty to prevent such interference, and thus no agent who cannot avoid infringing a moral claim. If so, such cases still do not fit under the above definition of moral claims dilemmas, but the definition could be expanded to include them, if so desired.

Whether or not they count as moral claims dilemmas, such situations are possible. Critics might deny that there is any moral right to use hate speech. However, I already argued that a moral right can be overridden and that a moral right to do something does not imply that it is morally right to do it. These qualifications make it more plausible to claim that the general right to free speech includes a right to hate speech, at least in political contexts, even if this right is overridden and morally wrong to exercise. There is then no reason to deny that some people can have moral rights whose exercise would infringe or even violate other people's moral rights.

What about privileges? Can they conflict? It makes no sense to say that a privilege is infringed, but we can say that a privilege is exercised when the agent does what she or he has no duty not to do. Then:

A *moral privileges dilemma* is any situation in which an agent cannot exercise all of his or her privileges.

For example, if Joe has a privilege to park his only car in either of two spots in a parking lot, but he cannot park it in both, then he is in a moral privilege conflict. We can also say that Joe and Ken are in an interpersonal moral privileges conflict if each has a privilege to park in the last spot. Since privileges are defined as negations, these kinds of conflicts are obviously possible. In fact, each of us is in a moral privileges dilemma at every waking moment.

It is more interesting to ask whether privileges can conflict with claims:

A *moral claim/privilege dilemma* is any situation where
1. X has a moral claim against Y that Y do A,
2. Y has a moral privilege as regards X that Y do B, and
3. Y cannot do both A and B.

This kind of situation is not possible. X's claim implies that Y has a duty to X to do A. If Y cannot do both A and B, then Y's doing B will prevent Y from doing A. So Y has a duty to X not to do B.[35] But Y's privilege means that Y does not have a duty to X not to do B. Since their definition implies a contradiction, moral claim/privilege dilemmas cannot ever happen.

An example should make this clear. Suppose a landlord wants to inspect one of his apartments at 6 A.M. If the tenant has a moral claim against the landlord that the landlord not annoy her, and if inspecting the apartment at 6 A.M. will annoy her, then the landlord has a moral duty not to inspect the apartment at 6 A.M. But this means that the landlord cannot have a moral privilege as regards the tenant to inspect the apartment at 6 A.M. Thus, it is not possible that the tenant has a claim against the landlord while the landlord has a privilege as regards the tenant if the exercise of the privilege would infringe the claim. Of course, the landlord can still have other privileges, such as to inspect the apartment later. He can also have a privilege as regards other people, such as his wife, since he has no duty to his wife not to inspect the tenant's apartment at 6 A.M. All that is excluded is one person's claim against another person that the latter do what the latter has a privilege as regards the former not to do.

These possibilities can be diagrammed as follows:

Can they conflict?	Y's privilege as regards X that Y not do A	Z's claim against Y that Y not do A
X's claim against Y that Y do A	NO (claim/privilege dilemma)	YES (claims dilemma)
Y's privilege as regards X that Y do A	YES (privileges dilemma)	YES (none of the above)

What about clusters? There are too many possibilities to discuss them all here. But one general principle seems plausible: Whether and how clusters of claims, privileges, and powers can conflict depends only on whether their component claims, privileges, and powers can conflict. For example, if a landlord is at liberty to inspect one of his apartments at 6 A.M., this liberty consists of a privilege of inspecting it at 6 A.M. plus a claim against others not to interfere in certain ways with his inspecting it at 6 A.M. If the others include the tenant, and if the certain ways include new locks, then the tenant cannot have a privilege of putting a new deadbolt on the only door without giving the landlord a key. Liberties and privileges can conflict in other ways, but not if the liberty includes the very claim that the privilege denies. Similarly, liberties also cannot conflict with claims if the liberty includes a privilege that denies the claim, as in the claim/privilege dilemma above. In general, any combination is ruled out as impossible if and only if the conflicting elements include or imply a contradiction, such as the assertion and denial of the very same duty.

Of course, there are many more possibilities. It would be a massive (even infinite) task to explore all of the ways in which claims, privileges, powers, and clusters can conflict. This exploration would be fascinating, but I will not attempt it here. All I can hope to have done is lay some of the groundwork for understanding some kinds of conflicts of rights.

What all of this shows is that there are many different kinds of moral dilemmas with very different logical structures. Although some kinds of moral dilemmas *are* possible, other kinds are *not* possible. In order to determine whether a particular kind of moral dilemma is possible, one cannot appeal to any claim as general as that moral dilemmas are possible. There is no substitute for a careful analysis of the particular kind of moral judgment and the particular kind of situation at issue.

Notes

I am grateful to Gene Mason and Ann Bumpus for very helpful comments on earlier versions, and to audiences at Tufts, the University of Massachusetts at Amherst, and the University of Maryland at College Park for stimulating discussion.

1. This distinction clears up some supposed counterexamples to my definition of (moderate) moral dilemmas. Earl Conee writes, "Suppose that you owe a favor to each of two friends. Today you can get just one ticket to a concert that each of the two would like to attend. You foresee that tomorrow you will be able to do something equally nice for either friend. You have no other pressing moral responsibilities that conflict with these opportunities today and tomorrow to repay your debts of gratitude to these two friends, and you have no special commitment to repay either friend today. It would be wrong not to give each of these friends the ticket today, unless you have a good excuse. So you are subject to what Sinnott-Armstrong calls 'moral requirements' to give each friend the ticket." Conee (1989), p. 134. I disagree. It would *not* be morally wrong not to give the ticket to either friend, since it is your ticket, and you can and may repay your debts to your friends in other ways in the future. What you "owe" is *some* favor but not any specific favor, so you can choose which favor to do. And if you choose not to give the ticket to either friend, it would not be appropriate to punish or condemn you, as long as you repay your debt in another way. Thus,

there is no moral requirement to give the ticket to either friend, so this case is not a (moderate) moral dilemma on my definitions. A similar case is given by Philip Quinn (1991), p. 695, but in Quinn's case the ticket is to a dinner, and the potential recipients are "deserving . . . poor folk." If these folk are not too hungry, I think it still would not be morally wrong for me to refuse to give the ticket to either, for the same reasons as above. In contrast, if these poor folk are starving, it would be morally wrong for me to refuse to give the ticket to either. But *then* I see nothing counterintuitive about counting this situation as a (moderate) moral dilemma.

2. Even Alan Donagan, who is one of the strongest opponents of moral dilemmas, speaks of "grounds of obligation" and explains them by counterfactuals, for example, in Donagan (1984), in Gowans (1987), p. 287. See also Donagan (1977b), p. 72, where he describes his procedure as starting with kinds of acts that it is impermissible to do at will.

3. A moral requirement is *overriding* not when it overrides *some* moral requirement that conflicts with it but when it overrides *every* moral requirement that conflicts with it.

4. In his paper in this volume, Brink concludes that non-overridden requirements are not all-things-considered requirements when he writes, "an all-things-considered obligation . . . must be overriding." However, his preceding sentence says, "An all-things-considered moral obligation is what one ought to do in light of all morally relevant factors." One must consider all morally relevant factors in order to determine whether a moral requirement is non-overridden. For this reason, it is not clear why non-overridden moral requirements should not count as all-things-considered moral requirements. But this issue is just terminological.

5. Nagel (1979a), in Gowans (1987), p. 175 (Nagel's emphasis).

6. van Fraassen (1973), in Gowans (1987), p. 141.

7. Williams (1979), p. 74.

8. These moral requirements are also not equal, since, if two things are equal, adding to one will destroy the equality, but a slight increase in the danger will not make that requirement override. This makes the requirements incomparable. See Sinnott-Armstrong (1988), p. 67.

9. It might seem that the antecedent of (1.2) is not true in my example because the moral requirement not to turn right is weaker than the moral requirement not to do the conjunction of not turning right *and* not turning left, but the former is still non-overridden, because these two requirements do not conflict; and the same goes for the moral requirement not to turn left. For more counterexamples to agglomeration, see Sinnott-Armstrong (1988), pp. 129–34.

10. (2.3) corresponds to Brink's "weak obligation principle" in his paper in this volume. He calls it "especially uncontroversial" and argues, "If I'm obligated not to kill my neighbor, then surely it's not the case that I'm obligated to kill him." But this is "sure" only if "obligated" refers to overriding obligations. It fails in unresolvable conflicts if "obligated" refers to non-overridden obligations (or to all obligations). (2.3) is sometimes supported by claiming (2.3.1) "■A ⟶ Permitted (A)" and (2.3.2) "Permitted (A) ⟶ ~■~A", or equivalents, such as Brink's "weak impermissibility" and "correlativity" principles in this volume. However, the argument applies to moderate moral dilemmas only if "■" stands for "non-overridden moral requirement," and it is natural to read "Permitted (A)" as "there is no overriding moral requirement not to do A," but then (2.3.2) fails in symmetrical trolley cases. If one redefines "Permitted (A)" as "there is no non-overridden moral requirement not to do A," then (2.3.1) fails in symmetrical trolley cases. So the argument is not strengthened by interjecting the notion of permission.

11. See Sinnott-Armstrong (1988), ch. 6, on kinds of inconsistency.

12. Further implications for prescriptivism, moral realism, and tolerance are discussed in Sinnott-Armstrong (1988), chs. 6, 7, and 8, respectively. These implications are what justify my definition of moderate moral dilemmas, since technical definitions should be judged by their usefulness.

13. The notion of univocal advice is not as clear as some assume, but I will not question it here. See Sinnott-Armstrong (1988), pp. 182ff.

14. Foot (1994), p. 126 (Foot's emphasis).

15. Similarly, Conee says, "An act is absolutely morally obligatory only if it is done in every life that is as nearly ideal as the person is able to attain." Conee (1989), p. 137. This definition runs into several problems. First, it conflates obligations with ideals and thus makes it absolutely morally obligatory to contribute to many charities. Second, this account assimilates (1) a trolley driver who avoids a crowded track by turning onto a less crowded track and thereby killing many people to (2) a different trolley driver who avoids a crowded track by turning onto an empty track and killing no one. Neither act violates an absolute moral obligation in Conee's sense, but they are still very different morally. Third, Conee argues that his definition is important because by fulfilling absolute moral obligations "the person falls no farther short of perfection than is avoidable." Conee (1989), p. 137. This shows that Conee, like Foot, is concerned with judgments of the person rather than of the act. Nonetheless, Conee's definition does make it obvious that absolute moral obligations in his sense cannot conflict. So my main response is just that his definition does nothing to show that other kinds of conflict are not possible or not important.

16. See Sinnott-Armstrong (1988), pp. 44–53.

17. I am grateful to Norman Dahl for suggesting this kind of definition.

18. Greenspan (1988) and Roberts (1988) argue that emotions do not imply beliefs but only quasi-beliefs or construals. This issue does not affect my point here.

19. This argument is derived from Thomson (1990), p. 100 (note).

20. Following Thomson, I will say that an agent infringes a right when the agent does what someone has a right that the agent not do, even if doing it is adequately justified. An infringement of a right is then called a violation if and only if it is not adequately justified.

21. See the references to Dworkin, Nozick, Williams, and Feinberg in Decew (1988), pp. 64–65. The most detailed account of the strength of rights is Thomson (1990), ch. 6. These accounts and my discussion in this section apply to rights that are claims, as defined in the next section.

22. Benditt (1982), p. 40. See also pp. 11, 36.

23. Thomson (1990), p. 98. Thomson makes the same point with an example of symmetrical contracts on pp. 92–93. Another example occurs in Feinberg (1978), p. 102, and is discussed by Thomson (1986), p. 66.

24. Benditt (1982), p. 62.

25. Hohfeld (1919). My discussion simplifies Thomson's schema in (1990), which simplifies Hohfeld's schema, but these simplifications do not affect the issues of conflicts or resolvability.

26. Thomson's definition of claims in (1990), p. 41, allows claims of X against Y that P even if "P" does not refer to any action by Y or anyone. But nothing important here is lost by considering only claims that someone else do something. Also, notice that to have a claim is not the same as to make or assert a claim (verbally), although having a claim might be necessary in order to make a legitimate claim.

27. As before, Thomson's definition of privileges in (1990), pp. 44–45, allows privileges of X as regards Y that P, where "P" does not refer to any act by X or by

anyone. This leads to odd results if "P" = "the sky is blue." And nothing important here is lost by considering only privileges to do an act.

28. See Thomson (1990), p. 66.

29. Hohfeld (1919), p. 42, quoted at Thomson (1990), p. 53, identifies liberties with privileges, as do others, but Thomson (1990), pp. 53–56, argues that a liberty is more than a privilege. I don't know whether Thomson is right about the common use (if any) of "privilege," "liberty," and "at liberty," but her distinction is useful, so I will use it here.

30. Thomson (1990), p. 67.

31. Hohfeld (1919), p. 36. Thomson agrees in (1990), p. 59.

32. Rights of X that Y do an act are a limiting case where for Y to interfere is simply for Y not to do the act.

33. I can destroy my right not to be enslaved by killing myself if nobody has a duty not to enslave me after I am dead. But this does not count as a power over my right any more than my ability to kill you would give me a power over your right to vote. That is why my definition of a power refers to "a certain kind of act."

34. Sometimes an agent cannot exercise all of her powers, but it is not as clear whether powers of different people can conflict. If a husband has the power to sell a house, and his wife also has the power to sell the same house, what if they try to sell it at the same time to different people? They cannot transfer full and exclusive rights of ownership to different people, so it seems impossible for both to have the power to sell the house *simpliciter*, although each can still have a conditional power to sell the house *if* the other person does not do so.

35. This argument assumes a principle of closure which I defend in (1988), pp. 146–55, and (1992).

5

The Moral Dilemmas Debate

MARY MOTHERSILL

I

The question under debate is whether there *are* any moral dilemmas, that is, any "real" or "genuine" ones as distinct from those that are "merely apparent." Some—call them the "pro-Ds"—say that there are and draw the consequences for ethical theory; others say that there are not—call them the "rationalists"[1]—and draw a different set of consequences. The question itself, with its epistemological overtones, may strike us as odd. A stick that is really straight is one that would look bent in water even if it is never put in water. A genuine dilemma is one that, given the right conditions, would appear to be . . . appear to be *what?* Neither the pro-Ds nor the rationalists put the question quite this way: they start from the appearances and go on to present their respective views about whether there is, so to speak, such a thing as the genuine article. We should begin by asking what it takes to be as much as a candidate, that is, what we understand by "moral dilemma." Everyone agrees on certain requirements: an agent in a dilemma has to choose between conflicting obligations, each of which is supported by strong, ordinarily decisive reasons. He cannot discharge both obligations, but failure on either count would be morally wrong.

Some of the disputants want to extend this definition by having it cover not just apparently undecidable choices but every case of moral conflict. Plato's example is often cited: a person leaves a weapon with you for safekeeping but when he returns to claim it, you observe that he has become demented and has murderous intentions. The moral is said to be that it would be wrong to give it back to him even though to refuse means breaking a promise. But if this is supposed to be a judgment in which all right-thinking people concur, I don't see why it should be called a dilemma. A further proposed extension: Ruth Marcus, a pro-D representative, thinks that restriction to a single agent is a matter of convenience, and writes:

> The one-person case may be seen as an instance of the n-person case under the assumptions of shared principles. Antigone's sororal (and religious) obligations conflict with Creon's obligations to keep his word and preserve the peace. Antigone is obliged to arrange for the burial of Polyneices; Creon is obliged to prevent it. Under generality of principles they are each obliged to respect the obligations of the other.[2]

Here we have opposition and interpersonal conflict generated by conscientious motives, but where is the dilemma? The "obligation to respect the obligations of others" is a liberal sentiment that, as far as I remember, the text does not ascribe either to Antigone or to Creon. It could be added by stipulation, but then surely it would be better to speak of two dilemmas rather than of one two-person dilemma. (Is a departmental wrangle a ten-person dilemma?)

The most extreme case is one that extends the term "dilemma" to any contentious social issue. Christopher Gowans, for example, writes:

> A moral dilemma is a situation in which Agent S ought morally to do A and morally ought to do B but cannot do both either because B is just not-doing A or because some feature of the world prevents doing both. That there are cases of *apparent* dilemmas can hardly be denied. Contemporary work in applied ethics has shown that compelling arguments can be given for incompatible positions on a variety of topics: abortion, euthanasia, capital punishment, preferential treatment and censorship are but a few examples.[3]

The pros and cons of abortion may figure in the dilemma of someone deliberating about whether to have an abortion or about how to cast a deciding vote on the issue in a judicial or legislative context. But if a dilemma is a difficult and conflicted choice, then those who do not face a choice or have no conflicts do not qualify. Abortion is not a dilemmatic topic for Cardinal O'Connor or (presumably) for those who think that the Court made the right decision in *Roe v. Wade*.

In short, it seems to me that if there is anything interesting to be learned by studying moral dilemmas, it will be more likely to emerge if we stand by our pretheoretical ideas and say of a moral dilemma that it is a crisis of conscience for a particular individual, occasioned by his perception first that a decision is mandated, and second that of the options available to him none is morally permissible. The rationalists claim that, so understood, all dilemmas are "merely apparent": the pro-Ds, that at least some are genuine. Ruth Marcus (for the pro-Ds) goes farther: having rejected the utilitarian thesis, according to which even the most difficult decisions can be rationalized in the light of estimated consequences, she writes:

> I would like to claim that it is a better fit with the moral facts that all dilemmas are real, even where the reasons for doing x outweigh, and in whatever degree, the reasons for doing y. That is, wherever the circumstances are such that an obligation to do x and an obligation to do y cannot as a matter of circumstance be fulfilled, the obligations to do each are not erased, even though they are unfulfillable.[4]

The distinction between a genuine and an apparent dilemma is assumed by both parties to be obvious—at any rate, it is rarely explained. Terrance McConnell (a rationalist) is an exception in that although he takes the contrast to be intuitively clear—clear enough, at least, to figure in an argument—he does raise what one would think to be a crucial question. He asks whether the pro-D advocate has "a criterion (in the epistemic sense) for distinguishing situations that are truly dilemmatic from those that erroneously appear so," and continues:

Notice that if [the pro-D] did have a plausible criterion he would, in effect, have a straightforward argument (for his pro-D thesis). I know of no such criterion, however. In fact, it seems reasonable to assume that there is no such criterion; even [the pro-D advocate] can and must grant this.[5]

Perhaps McConnell is right; but before looking for "a criterion" ("in the epistemic sense") don't we need a better idea of what it is that the criterion will enable us to identify? One possibility is suggested by Walter Sinnott-Armstrong, an uncompromising pro-D, who writes:

A moral dilemma is any situation where at the same time: (1) there is a moral requirement for an agent to adopt each of two alternatives, (2) neither moral requirement is overridden in any morally relevant way, (3) the agent cannot adopt both alternatives together, and (4) the agent can adopt each alternative separately. . . . So defined, almost everyone admits that some situations appear to be moral dilemmas. But the issue is not about appearances. The issue is whether or not there really are or can be situations that fit the definition of moral dilemmas.[6]

This seems straightforward enough: any "situation" that fails to meet one or more of the four conditions will be a dilemma that is "merely apparent." What are the possibilities of error? An agent might be mistaken in thinking that she was morally required to adopt either or both alternatives, or mistaken in thinking that the alternatives were exhaustive, or mistaken in thinking that neither "moral requirement was overridden in any morally relevant way," or mistaken in thinking that she could not adopt both, or mistaken in thinking that she could adopt either. (Also, presumably, she could be in error about one or more of the relevant facts or circumstances.) In any case, if what she believes, with or without reason, on any of the four points is false, then however she may view her predicament, she is mistaken in taking it to be a genuine moral dilemma. On this interpretation, the rationalist position emerges as something akin to Humean skepticism: it is not that every agent's beliefs are necessarily false, but rather that no agent has any defensible ground for thinking them true. (This fits in with McConnell's point about there being no epistemic criterion for drawing the line.) Then the opinion of the pro-Ds, whose case rests less on argument than on counterexample, would be analogous to that of G. E. Moore, who professed to have refuted skepticism about the external world by holding up his hands and saying, "There are at least two physical objects."[7]

The trouble with this interpretation is that there is no evidence that rationalists support any such general thesis. Indeed, they seem to need some non-skeptical epistemological assumptions in order to make out their main point, which is that there is a correct and morally defensible solution, if only one can find it, to every apparent dilemma. There may be fraudulent solutions to genuine problems, but what would it mean to find a genuine solution to what, for all one knows, may be a fraudulent problem?

As I look again at Sinnott-Armstrong's formulation, it occurs to me that the only condition that the rationalist really cares about is (2), which says that "neither requirement is overridden in any morally relevant way." The rationalists' thought is that this condition either is never met or that, if it is met, the agent can never know that it is. Their main thesis that although an agent assumed to be a reliable judge of conditions (1), (3), and (4) may sincerely believe that of two moral requirements neither overrides the other, his belief is always open to question. In an apparent dilemma, we convince ourselves that we are ineluctably stuck, that our predicament is morally hopeless; but this is never the case. There is always one option that is preferable to another—it may be bad, but the alternative is worse.

What reason does the rationalist have for insisting that there are no genuine moral dilemmas? There are, after all, lots of questions for which there is no hope of an answer. Prehistoric folk talked before history was recorded, no doubt before writing was invented. What were the favorite topics of conversation in the caves or around the campfires? How many blades of grass were there in Central Park an hour after it was open to the public? Why should we resolve to discount the testimony of someone who says, in a particular situation, "Show me a way out. I have to do something and anything I *can* do would violate one of my deepest moral commitments?"[8] If an agent finds herself in a situation in which no option seems morally defensible, why should she be bullied ? What, in short, is it that fuels the rationalist preoccupation with dilemmas? An answer is suggested by two different arguments, one that draws on the resources of deontic logic and a second that turns on a traditional conception of the role of ethical theory. Both depend on premises that, if true, are a priori truths; both fit the pattern of *reductio* arguments. Both show an affinity with Kant, a rationalist avatar whose oft-cited argument (or perhaps it should be called a pronouncement) is as follows:

> A *conflict of duties* would be a relation of duties in which one of them would annul the other (wholly or in part). But a conflict of duties and obligations is inconceivable. For the concepts of duty and obligation as such express the objective practical necessity of certain actions and two conflicting rules cannot both be necessary at the same time: if it is our duty to act according to one of these rules, then to act according to the opposite one is not our duty and is even contrary to duty.[9]

Kant's view does not admit of counterexamples, and neither does the position of latter-day rationalists. But counterexamples are the stock and trade of the pro-Ds. Their response to Kant would be that (1) a conflict of duties is not only conceivable but a fact of life to be reckoned with; (2) where such a conflict occurs, one duty does not "annul" the other—both remain in force; and (3) on occasion the claims of conflicting duties have equal weight, in which case the agent confronts genuine moral dilemma in which none of the options open to him is morally permissible.

Today's rationalists do acknowledge the need for argument but express views in an apodictic and Kantian idiom. Alan Donagan, for example, writes, "The problem of moral conflict is dismissed by rationalists as spurious, root and branch."[10]

And what are the arguments? There are two. The first is that the pro-D thesis, conjoined with two axioms of standard deontic logic, entails a contradiction. Those rationalists who take deontic logic as authoritative, for example

Terrance McConnell and Earl Conee,[11] point out that consistency can be preserved by dropping the supposition that there are genuine dilemmas. But since consistency can also be preserved by dropping one of the axioms, the deontic argument cuts across party lines. Indeed, its current form was introduced by Bernard Williams, an early pro-D, in 1965.[12] Williams cites two axioms. The first, which he christens "the agglomeration principle," holds that it follows from "A is obligatory" and "B is obligatory" that "A and B are obligatory." The second is a formalized version of the Kantian adage that "ought" implies "can." When the two axioms are conjoined with the pro-D thesis—namely, that an agent may be bound by two equally stringent obligations although he cannot discharge both—what is entailed is a contradiction. Since Williams, for independent reasons, accepts the pro-D thesis, he argues that what should be dropped is the agglomeration principle. Ruth Marcus, a fellow pro-D, argues that the genuineness of moral dilemmas poses no threat to the consistency of ethical reasoning, but she differs from both the rationalists and fellow pro-Ds in focusing not on deontic logic but on what she calls "moral codes."

What should we make of the deontic logic argument? It tells against the pro-D thesis only for someone who takes the two deontic principles to be true or, at any rate, more plausible than the thesis itself. But is there any reason to think that they *are* true? They may not be entirely arbitrary, but my impression is that they are adopted as axioms with a view to exploring their consequences—to discovering what theorems can be derived from them. The idea of a systematic deontic theory depends on a supposed analogy with modal logic: "obligatory" and "permissible" are supposed to parallel "necessary" and "possible." What bearing the axioms of deontic logic have on everyday moral reasoning has, in my opinion, yet to be made out. Why, for example, should we accept the agglomeration principle? At this very moment there are at least five things I ought to be doing instead of writing this paper, but it does not follow that I ought to be doing all five things and also writing this paper. In rejecting agglomeration, do I rely on the "ought" implies "can" principle? Yes, but I don't take *it* as a principle *either*, but only as an occasionally relevant reminder. There is no point, for example, in telling someone what she ought to do, if doing what she ought to do requires her to be in two places at the same time. Apart from such commonplaces, the notion of what is or is not possible for some agent varies with the context, and the "ought" that figures in "ought to do" is treated differently from the "ought" that figures in "ought to be," "ought to feel," "ought to have realized," and so on. Besides, implication is a relation that is intelligible only when there is a system in place—quantification theory or the sentential calculus—not when a system is, as appears to be the case with deontic logic, under construction. Hence, on my view, the deontic logic argument cuts no ice and does not persuade me that there are no genuine dilemmas. Moreover, there is a sense, admittedly not very clear, in which the pro-Ds *need* the two deontic principles. As remarked earlier, they rely on dramatic examples, and those that they favor are examples of *tragic* conflict as opposed to humdrum dithering. That one cannot be in two places at once may be regrettable, but how much more poignant the conflict if what is demanded violates not just the constraints of space and time but the constraints of logic. If my obligation comprises doing A and also not doing A, then I am truly stuck.

The second rationalist argument mentioned earlier is one that is seldom made explicit but draws on assumptions shared by Thomas Aquinas, John Stuart Mill, W. D. Ross, and a number of moralists in the "non-cognitivist" tradition. The general idea is that to acknowledge genuine dilemmas is to entertain the possibility that ethics is an empty and pointless exercise. (An analogy: If there are uncaused events, then perhaps the onset of cancer or AIDS is among them. If such a view came to be widely accepted, medical researchers, after expending a certain amount of time and effort, would be justified in simply giving up.) The argument against moral dilemmas might run as follows.

Ethics is a practical science: its aim is to guide the deliberation of a conscientious agent by making clear and explicit the principles that determine a particular decision or action as morally right or wrong. Given the complexities of everyday life, it would be too much to ask of an ethical theory that it provide a unique solution to every moral problem, but that is the ideal that it approaches as a limit. To an agent faced with what she takes to be a dilemma, the ethical theorist will recommend a reexamination of the data. She should ask, for example, whether the principles that support each alternative may not admit of exceptions. Lying is wrong, yes, but only "under conditions of free communication where violence is neither done nor threatened to anyone."[13] She should ask whether the relevant principles may not be subject to priority ranking, whether, for example, it is not more important to save a life than to keep a luncheon engagement. She should ask whether there is not some second-order, across-the-board principle—the principle of utility is often cited—that can be invoked as a tie-breaker. If, as the pro-Ds claim, there is a permanent possibility of moral conflict in which, of the reasons supporting incompatible alternatives, neither overrides the other, then this procedure is stalemated and the main task of ethical inquiry nullified.

Is this a good argument? Two observations: First, it requires not only that neither of the competing reasons be overridden but that the agent in question *knows* that this is so. Otherwise she would have no reason not to continue the inquiry recommended by the ethical theorist with the hope of discovering suitable qualifications, or priority rankings or some overarching second-order principle. But the rationalist can argue that such knowledge presupposes that the agent has to hand a reliable procedure for sorting out the real from the apparent. This was the point of McConnell's observation, quoted earlier, to the effect that the pro-D needs but lacks a criterion for distinguishing the apparent from the real. If the pro-D claims that no criterion is needed and that it is a matter of intuitive certainty, then, as McConnell goes on to note, it will be hard for him to explain why the agent in conflict should experience doubts, and why, in particular, he should seek advice: nobody can tell him anything he doesn't know, namely, that he is in an impossible situation—so what is the point of his asking?[14]

On the face of it, the rationalist argument is persuasive: even if there are genuine dilemmas, the agent, supposing she does not know that her predicament qualifies, must proceed as if it were an apparent dilemma and look for an escape route. And how, after all, could one come to *know* that (in Sinnott-Armstrong's terms) "neither requirement is overridden in any morally relevant way"? How, when it comes to that, could one know that it *was* overridden? But this difficulty, if it is a difficulty, tells as much against the rationalist as against his opponent. Admittedly, the whole notion of one reason or principle "overriding" another[15] is obscure. Metaphors abound: one reason is "more pressing," has "greater weight," or is "more binding" or "more stringent" than another. Perhaps advances in theory of action or moral psychology will lead to a more perspicuous account, but in the meantime rationalists, pro-Ds, and the rest of us are in the same boat. To the extent that we know what it means, at least in the particular case, to say that one consideration overrides another, there can be no special objection to the claim that of two considerations neither overrides the other. This weakens if it does not rebut the rationalist's objection. There is, moreover, a different line that the pro-D can take. Thomas Nagel, for example, believes in genuine dilemmas that arise not because the conflicting obligations are perceived as being of equal stringency but because the moral values that generate them are "incommensurable." He writes:

> There can be cases where, even if one is fairly sure about the outcomes of alternative courses of action, or about their probability distributions, and even though one knows how to distinguish the pros and cons, one is nevertheless unable to bring them into a single evaluative judgment, even to the extent of finding them evenly balanced. An even balance requires comparable quantities.
>
> The strongest cases of conflict are genuine dilemmas, in which there is decisive support for two or more incompatible courses of action or inaction. In that case, a decision will be necessary, but it will seem necessarily arbitrary. When two choices are evenly balanced, it does not matter which choice one makes, and arbitrariness is no problem. But when each seems right for reasons that appear decisive and sufficient, arbitrariness means the lack of reasons where reasons are needed, since either choice will mean acting against some reasons without being able to claim that they are *outweighed*.[16]

Would Nagel's view, if accepted, lighten the task of the pro-Ds? Some of the rationalists' prescriptions are ruled out: there will be "no clear set of priorities" and no possibility of appeal to "a single, reductive method."[17] When an agent opts for one alternative over another, her decision will seem "necessarily arbitrary," since by hypothesis she can give no reason for it. The incommensurability thesis perhaps does better than the equal-weight conception in capturing the *aporia* and sense of paralysis an agent feels in the face of an apparent dilemma, but it remains open to rationalist objections. If, in a state of conflict, I cannot justify my belief that competing obligations have equal weight, how can I have any confidence in my intuitive finding that competing obligations are incommensurable? If the rationalists' epistemological challenge tells against one version of the pro-D thesis, it tells equally against alternative versions. The problem, as noted earlier, is that systematic skepticism with respect to knowledge of which of one's obligations is or is not overridden would have as corrosive an effect on the rationalist view as on the pro-D thesis. If that is so, then, in the lack of a systematic account of moral knowledge in general, the answer to the central question is: perhaps there are genuine moral dilemmas and perhaps not; we shall never know.

What about the larger claims of the traditional rationalist position sketched above? Is the mere *possibility* of genuine dilemmas enough to subvert the aims of ethical theory? An answer: If the focus of ethical theory is the deliberation of an individual agent in particular circumstances, if the aim is to provide him with the means of resolving conflicts in a morally justifiable way, then the occurrence of unresolvable conflicts would mean that some such projects would necessarily fail. On the other hand, if, as on the present supposition, neither the agent nor his advisers nor the ethical theorist is able to distinguish the genuine dilemmas from those that are merely apparent, then there is no point at which the theorist need admit failure; given patience and sufficient attention, the right solution may always be forthcoming. But the rationalists want something more— something like a guarantee. What is it? No ethical theory promises a unique solution to every moral problem. Kantian ethics, in its appeal to the notion of perfect duties, places strict limitations on entertainable options but nonetheless leaves open a wide range of permissible choices. Even utilitarianism, the leading candidate when it comes to providing an "ultimate" criterion for moral decision, allows lots of slack. John Stuart Mill, for instance, rebutting the accusation that "the greatest happiness principle" affords excuses for acting on selfish motives, writes:

> [Is] utility the only creed which is able to furnish us with excuses for evil-doing, and means of cheating our own conscience? They are afforded in abundance by all doctrines which recognize as a fact in morals the existence of conflicting considerations; which all doctrines do, that have been believed by sane persons. It is not the fault of any creed, but of the complicated nature of human affairs, that rules of conduct cannot be so framed as to require no exceptions, and that hardly any kind of action can safely be laid down as either always obligatory or always condemnable. There is no ethical creed that does not temper the rigidity of its laws by giving a certain latitude, under the moral responsibility of the agent, for accommodation to peculiarities of circumstance; and under every creed, at the opening thus made, self-deception and dishonest casuistry get in. There exists no moral system under which there do not arise unequivocal cases of conflicting obligation. . . . With respect to such conflicts, if utility is the ultimate source of moral obligations, utility may be invoked to decide between them when their demands are incompatible. Though the application of the standard may be difficult, it is better than none at all; while in other systems, the moral laws all claiming independent authority, there is no common umpire entitled to interfere with them. . . . We must remember that only in . . . cases of conflict between secondary principles is it required that first principles should be appealed to.[18]

Although Mill's sensible and moderate statement offers no guarantee that appeals to utility, although the "ultimate standard" will resolve all conflicts, I wonder whether the perennial attraction of utilitarianism does not depend on an assumption that, were it not for what Mill calls "the complicated nature of human affairs," it *would* be sufficient, and would give us an algorithm for dealing with apparent dilemmas. If that thought is in the offing, then Mill belongs squarely with the rationalists in holding that we would be *better off* with a tie-breaking theory (provided it was tenable) than without one. That seems to be Alan Donagan's suggestion when he writes:

> I do not think that Davidson, or Williams, or Marcus, or any of the phalanx of distinguished contemporary philosophers who, by maintaining the reality of moral conflict implicitly reject the possibility of an acceptable rationalist moral theory, would deny that such a theory would be desirable if it were possible.[19]

Nobody believes in what is deprecated as a "mechanical" procedure for making hard decisions, but perhaps something equally untenable and primitive is at work. I have been speaking as if ethical theory and friendly "advisers" were parallel resources for the troubled agent. Maybe we imagine an ethical theory as personified—Socrates' *daimon*, but more forthcoming; the voice of conscience, only more intelligent and discursive. Mill speaks revealingly of the principle of utility as an "umpire," not as an umpire's rule book. So maybe what we fantasize is some ideal adviser who, in any difficult situation, will say: "Here is *exactly* what you must do, given that you want to do the right thing." But this *is* a fantasy: doing as you are told is following orders, which is not an aid to moral judgment but a substitute. We did not need to wait for Kant and the elevation of "moral autonomy" to understand the difference between making a decision and implementing one. If the gods unanimously decide that it is Euthyphro's duty to bring criminal charges against his father, we want to know what their reasons are. Either the gods have reasons or they do not: if they do, then their reasons can be made explicit. They are then like ordinary non-divine advisers. If they have or offer no reasons, then why should we listen to them? The gods cannot *make* a course of action into a duty just by declaring it to be such. The upshot is that if the pro-D belief in genuine dilemmas—conflicts that neither god nor man can resolve—serves to discourage authoritarian fantasies, then even if it is not provable, it is all to the good.

A related observation: What Edmund Pincoffs referred to as "quandary ethics"[20] is a relatively recent development and does not hold a patent. Moral philosophy need not be conceived as a project that stands or falls on its success in resolving individual problems of conscience. As appears from the work of Aristotle, Hume, John Dewey, and current practitioners of "virtue ethics," there are quite different questions to be explored about the aims of moral education, for example. What kinds of skills, emotions, and habits need to be cultivated if a child is going to become a person who can deal in a rational way with dilemmas, real or apparent, when they arise?

The pro-Ds' case rests largely on examples designed to counter the a priorist thesis in the way, as noted above, that G. E. Moore sought to confound the skeptic by displaying his two hands as instances of physical objects that exist. Among the pro-D examples, here are three that are most frequently cited. (1) Agamemnon, leader of the Achaean naval force dispatched to attack Troy, is becalmed at Aulis; the goddess Artemis, through the medium of a seer priest, tells him that the only way he can get a favorable wind is by sacrificing his daughter Iphigenia. Agamemnon kills his daughter.[21] (2) Sartre tells of a student in occupied France who came to him in a state of perplexity, asking whether it was his duty to join the Free French and avenge his brother's death or to stay at home and take care of his dependent mother. Sartre famously said, "You are free, therefore choose—that is to say invent." We are not told what the outcome was.[22] (3) In William Styron's novel *Sophie's Choice,* Sophie is forced by a concentration camp guard to decide which of her two children is to be killed and which to be spared, with the proviso that, should she refuse to make the choice, both will be killed. She decides that the younger one should die.[23]

These are offered as examples of genuine dilemmas. What should we think of them? It is perhaps important that two of three involve cruel coercion. The impermissible alternatives forced on the agents are not merely exclusive but exhaustive; they are given only two options and a limited time to decide. The agents themselves are not—initially, anyway—at fault; have not, for example, made incompatible promises. As depicted, they are not deliberating agents but victims, torn by conflicting emotions and personal loyalties. We can imagine Buridan's rational ass taking his own good time to decide which of the two bales of hay looks the tastier; not so with Agamemnon and Sophie, who are in no position to undertake a cost-benefit analysis. Their situations are more like that of a downhill skier who has the choice between skiing over a precipice and being buried by an avalanche. The perplexities of Sartre's student are explicitly ethical (as the plight of Agamemnon or Sophie is not) but do not require an on-the-spot life or death decision. The moral of Sartre's (unhelpful) advice is, I suppose, that attempts to weigh the pros and cons are to no avail—perhaps because the alternatives are "incommensurable"—and that the rationalist search for qualifications or priority rankings is futile; the choice required must be made in a void. Hence the need to "invent."

A second observation: The examples are drawn from fiction. (Sartre's student may have existed but could just as well be a figment invented in order to give Sartre an opening for his little homily.) In all three examples, the genuineness of the dilemma is, as it were, built into the story and the story (including its fictional context, if we happen to know it) is all there is. Fictional contrary-to-fact conditionals are empty.[24] With this point in mind, a rationalist critic might regard the pro-D examples as tendentious: the sort of questions that he would like to raise are automatically ruled out of order. Did it, for example, never occur to Agamemnon that he might negotiate a compromise with Artemis, offering to sacrifice a bullock or his favorite hound instead of Iphigenia? Sophie had seduced others before; did she make a real effort to work her wiles on the sadistic guard? Could Sartre's student have joined a local chapter of the Free French and stayed at home, or perhaps persuaded his mother to enlist along with him and become a comrade in arms? The rationalist might reasonably complain that by resting his case on examples from literary fiction in which what is given and inalterable is confrontation with a genuine dilemma, the pro-D has tacitly begged the question or at any rate stacked the deck. But the pro-D has an answer: in the passage cited earlier, Sinnott-Armstrong observes that "[the] issue is not about appearances. The issue is whether there are *or can be* situations that fit the definition of moral dilemmas.[25]

The pro-D could argue that all that has to be shown is that genuine dilemmas are not impossible and that his examples, free as they are from references to square circles and the like, are not even indirectly question-begging. Since the most the rationalist can claim is that, at least in real-life situations, a solution to a dilemma is always *possible,* this would put the pro-D and the rationalist on the same footing. But now what is taken to be the central issue of the debate seems to dissolve. For any arbitrarily chosen case of moral conflict, we may ask whether it is or is not a genuine dilemma, but neither rationalists nor pro-Ds are able to offer us anything beyond their respective intuitive findings. I think we must conclude that although it is possible that all dilemmas are merely apparent, it is also possible that some dilemmas are genuine. This is not a very interesting outcome. Can we perhaps reformulate the issue in a way that would allow both parties to say what they want to say without ending up in a trivial impasse? In the following section I offer a tentative suggestion.

II

My initial inclination was to take a moral dilemma as a crisis of individual conscience occasioned by the need to choose between conflicting and equally stringent obligations. Like the pro-Ds, I took a dilemma to be a situation in which, morally speaking, one's hands are tied. But then, in line with the rationalists, I recognized that whatever the conflicted agent does, whether it is to decide on one or the other alternative or to discover some third option,[26] what she does will be subject to moral evaluation, and at least in some cases it will be reasonable to say that she has solved her dilemma. My present proposal is to extend this scope and to count as a dilemma every conflict of duties or obligations. Many of the disputants do that anyway, which shows that they are not fixated on the question of resolvability—the question that, as we have seen, leads to a dead end. Furthermore, if we talk about conflicts in general, it is harder to drive a wedge between the apparent and the genuine. When it comes to inner turmoil, *esse est percipi* is the order of the day. This is not to say that I am an infallible authority. The causal origins of my uneasiness may be inaccessible to me: unconscious wishes, self-deception, and just ordinary mistakes may all be operative. Still, my quandary, like my headache, is *mine,* and even if, as some would hold, it is a mistake to speak of my awareness as "knowing that" (something is the case) it would require special circumstances to justify your saying to me, "You think you're worried about what you ought to do but you really aren't."

The proposed move will not get us very far if it leads us to underline the term "moral" in "moral conflict," since there are as many disputes about what qualifies a reason or principle as "moral" as there are about what qualifies a dilemma as "genuine." This point is relevant because rationalists often say that their thesis, namely, that obligations never collide, applies only to conflicts that are "moral" and that these have to be marked off from problems that are "practical." Donagan, for example, claims that moral considerations rarely suffice to answer the question, "What shall I do?" when the relevant considerations are "irreducibly multiple," and he adds that most practical questions including many of those we think about hardest and find it hardest to decide on (such as those raising questions like, Shall I rebuild my house on Malibu beach? Shall I abandon the program in Assyrian and apply to business school? Shall I propose marriage to Bathsheba?) have little or nothing to do with morality.[27]

My suggestion is that rather than trying to find an acceptable criterion for a principle's being "moral" we leave that stone unturned. Both rationalists and pro-Ds seem content with traditional examples: one should tell the truth, keep one's promises, relieve suffering, and so forth: nothing controversial. None of the disputants is a Nietzschean, nor, aside from a common preoccupation with the plight of Sartre's student, does any of them show sympathy with an existential ethic. Since we have dropped (or bracketed) the question of whether moral conflicts are or are not resolvable, we can bypass the question of what exactly makes a conflict "moral." That leaves us with the claim that there are often reasons pro and con with respect to a particular projected action, and that moral conflicts are sometimes resolved and sometimes not resolved, the latter being cases in which the agent can offer no reasons for his decision except that he had to do *something*. Both parties could accept such minimal assumptions; how could they not?

Given this common ground, what is it that the pro-Ds want to establish? I draw on the work of two authors here, Bernard Williams and Ruth Marcus. Both attach importance to the idea that when an agent in conflict makes up his mind and elects one alternative, then whether his decision is based on reasons— he finds one obligation more stringent than the other—or whether, as Nagel puts it, his decision seems arbitrary, he may well, after the fact, experience feelings of regret, remorse, or guilt. Two questions present themselves. (1) Given either that he chose what he believed to be the better course or that, finding nothing to choose between them and being forced to decide, he chose at random, are his retrospective negative emotions evidence of irrationality? (2) If the answer is no—if it makes sense to feel bad about having failed to fulfill one of the competing obligations (call this the "moral remainder thesis")—then what consequences does the thesis have for ethical theory and for conscientious practice?

Both Williams and Marcus endorse the remainder thesis. Williams takes it to support his claim that moral conflict, given due weight, generates the "inconsistent triad" discussed above and hence requires an emendation of the principles of deontic logic. He also believes that the remainder thesis provides grounds for holding that so-called "cognitivist" ethical theories are inadequate. Marcus, on the other hand, believes that the remainder thesis creates no logical difficulties for ordinary moral reasoning but that it gives us a reason to plan our lives, individual and collective, in ways that will minimize situations of moral conflict.

Some comments: As for the remainder thesis itself, the question of whether post-dilemmatic feelings of regret or remorse are "rational" depends on the circumstances of the particular case. If the conflict is serious then the overridden obligation must have the status of what W. D. Ross dubbed a "prima facie duty," a requirement that in the absence of countervailing considerations provides a decisive reason for action. Prima facie duties are contrasted with "all-things-considered duties," or, as Ross sometimes says, "absolute," "actual," or "duties *sans phrase*."[28] Williams and Marcus are correct in observing that where an all-things-considered decision precludes the discharge of a prima facie obligation, the latter is not thereby erased. If I have a duty to support my aged parents but if, because of peculiar circumstances, it is outweighed by my duty to support my aged children and I cannot do both, then my obligation to my parents, though unfulfilled, remains standing. How should I *not* feel regret and remorse? Williams is also correct in saying that someone who lacked the capacity for such feelings would be morally defective. Imagine an Agamemnon who thought, "Too bad about Iphigenia, but I had no choice. After all, my responsibilities as a commander had to come first." Guilt, perhaps, is a different matter; attracted by the legal model, we tend to think that feeling guilty about having done what one decided was the morally required thing to do *is* irrational. Maybe so, and yet it is a commonplace that, just as a person may be anxious without being able to identify any threat, she may suffer pangs of guilt without being able to identify any crime, still less to identify herself as the criminal. (Neurosis is as common as grass.)

Ruth Marcus expresses doubts about the coherence of doctrines such as "original sin" that find it appropriate to judge a person guilty because of the past actions of others. But Marcus correctly points out that moral conflicts are different. She writes:

> Where moral conflict occurs, there is a genuine sense in which both what is done and what fails to be done are, before the actual choice among irreconcilable alternatives, within the agent's range of options. But, as the saying goes—and it is not incoherent—you are damned if you do and you are damned if you don't.[29]

(True enough, but, given the frequency with which an agent fails to fulfill either one of two conflicting obligations, so is the obverse: you get moral credit if you do and moral credit if you don't.)

But surely there are cases in which not only guilt but even regret is out of place. In a good discussion of this issue, Philippa Foot offers an example. She writes:

> One has promised to meet someone but must instead take an accident victim to hospital. . . . We shall suppose that things turn out splendidly all around; the promisee does not have a moment's annoyance, and meets his future beloved, or someone who offers him a job, while standing at my door. Are we to say that nevertheless in the general rejoicing there should be an element of distress (moral distress) because after all a promise was broken and that is something bad and therefore regrettable? To this suggestion one hardly knows what to reply. . . . Someone who . . . felt distress would seem to some of us rather foolish.[30]

I conclude that the remainder thesis sometimes holds and sometimes does not: it depends on the circumstances. In what is technically a case of moral conflict, the correct solution may be overwhelmingly obvious—as some people think it is in Kant's example of lying to a would-be murderer about the whereabouts of his intended victim—subsequent remorse would be irrational. Indeed, one could say, as Williams says of the *absence* of remorse under certain conditions, such feelings, when misplaced, are not only "foolish" but the sign of moral defect.

Thinking just of those cases (whichever they may be) in which the moral remainder thesis is true, let us consider question (2), that of what consequences for theory or for practice ensue. I argued above that Williams's claim about the "inconsistent triad," namely that given the occurrence of moral conflict, we must drop either the agglomeration principle or the "ought implies can" principle, is likely to convince only those inclined to take the deontic principles seriously. Since I see no reasons to take them as "principles" of any kind rather than as informal, vague, and only occasionally appropriate maxims, I am not impressed by the alleged paradox. There is a further difficulty that deserves mention: a description of moral conflict in conjunction with the two deontic principles is supposed to yield a contradiction: the agent ought to do A and it is not the case that the agent ought to do A. But if the conflicting obligations are prima facie obligations—those that present the agent with a choice—no contradiction ensues. In the light of one set of reasons he ought to do A and in the light of another, it is not the case that he ought to do A. It is only if we suppose that his deliberations terminate in a decision that *all things considered* he ought to do A and also that *all things considered* it is not the case that he ought to do A that his reasoning leads him to a contradiction. But since anyone with the wit to deliberate at all will see the difference between acknowledging conflicting obligations and coming to a decision about what, in the light of his circumstances and of the conflict, he *must* do, I find it hard to imagine the train of reasoning that would lead someone to assent to the contradiction that the alleged paradox requires. Deontic logic is out of touch with ordinary moral reasoning.

Marcus claims that the remainder thesis plays an important role on a practical level. She writes:

> Although dilemmas are not settled without residue, the recognition of their reality has a dynamic force. It motivates us to arrange our lives and institutions with a view to avoiding such conflicts. It is the underpinning for a second-order principle: that as rational agents with some control of our lives and institutions, we ought to conduct our lives and arrange our institutions so as to minimize predicaments of moral conflict.[31]

To grasp her point, we need to understand her primary argument, which is designed to show that the occurrence of dilemmas, that is, such conflicts as leave a residue,

> need not and usually does not signify that there is some inconsistency (in a sense to be explained) in the set of principles, duties, and other moral directives under which we define our obligations, either individually or socially.[32]

At first one assumes that, like van Fraassen, Williams, and many of the rationalists, Marcus proposes to address the question of the "inconsistent triad," but this turns out not to be so. What she is concerned with is what she calls a "moral code." She writes, "To count as a principle in such a code, a precept must be of a certain generality; that is, it cannot be tied to specific individuals at particular times and places."[33] She does not give examples, but, taking the line recommended above, I will assume that "Tell the truth," "Keep your promises," and "Do not cause unnecessary pain" would qualify as principles of a moral code. Conflicts arise, she notes, when a moral code mandates actions that are incompatible. Philosophers who take such conflicts as evidence of inconsistency assume that "a code is consistent if it applies without conflict to all actual—or, more strongly—to all possible cases."[34]

This notion strikes me as odd. Consistency I take to range over sentences and, following the line that Marcus later seems to adopt, may be extended to prescriptions or "ought" statements on the basis of the sentences that would have to be true if a particular "ought" statement is satisfied or a prescription carried out. So, taking the three examples cited above as a miniature moral code, the principles will be consistent, because the sentences "A promise is kept," "The truth is told," and "Unnecessary pain is avoided" are themselves consistent. No reference to "conflicts" is required. A moral code would be inconsistent just in case we added to the three principles a fourth such as "Break your promises." To try to act on such a code would indeed lead to conflict, not only in the actual but in all possible worlds except those in which nobody made any promises.

A further question: Who are those who claim that the occurrence of moral conflict signifies inconsistency in our moral code? Williams and others who plead the case of the "inconsistent triad" are not among them, if only because the principles they invoke are, if anything, meta-ethical. The principle of agglomeration, or the "ought" implies "can" principle, are not what one learns at one's mother's knee, not of the same order as "Tell the truth" and "Keep your promises." Marcus, of course, is aware of the deontic logic arguments but deals with them summarily. Like Williams, she proposes to drop the agglomeration principle but to keep "ought" implies "can," although she observes (correctly) that it applies in some cases and not in others. She writes:

> If we interpret the 'can' of the precept as "having the ability in this world to bring about," then . . . in a moral dilemma 'ought' *does* imply 'can' for *each* of the conflicting obligations, *before* either one is met. And after an agent has chosen one of the alternatives, there is still something which he ought to have done and could have done and which he did not do.[35]

On the other hand, for the "regulative principle," the one that enjoins planning with a view to avoiding moral conflicts, "ought" does *not* imply "can." (What she means is not that we can't make an all-out effort but that we can't hope that our effort will be completely successful.)

> There is no reason to suppose, this being the actual world, that we can, individually or collectively, however holy our wills or rational our strategies, succeed in foreseeing and wholly avoiding . . . conflict. It is not merely failure of will or failure of reason, which thwarts moral maxims from becoming universal laws. It is the contingencies of the world.[36]

It is perhaps this passage that Alan Donagan (for the rationalists) has in mind when he observes that moralists confronted by moral conflicts have always been tempted to find fault with the contingencies of the world rather than with their moral thinking.

> When Cicero lamented to Atticus that Cato seemed to think that he lived in Plato's republic, and not in the cesspool of Romulus, he was objecting not to Cato's principles, but to his rustic notion that principles were to be acted on. . . . Like Cato, rationalists have always rejected this position. Morality, as they conceive it, is a system of precepts defining the limits imposed on human action by practical reason; and human action takes place in the actual world—in Cicero's cesspool of Romulus.[37]

Marcus defines consistency for a set of rules on analogy with consistency for a set of sentences: sentences are consistent when it is possible, that is, when no contradiction follows, from the supposition that each member of the set is true, and adds:

> We can define a set of rules as consistent if there is some possible world in which are all obeyable in all circumstances in *that* world. (Note that I have said "obeyable" rather than "obeyed" for I want to allow for the partition of cases where a rule-governed action fails to be done between those cases where the failure is a personal failure of the agent—an imperfect will in Kant's terms— and those cases where "external" circumstances prevent the agent from meeting conflicting obligations. To define consistency relative to a kingdom of ends, a deontically perfect world in which all actions that ought to be done are done, would be too strong; for that would require both perfection of will *and* the absence of circumstances that generate moral conflict. In such a world [i.e. the world where all rules are obeyable] persons intent on mayhem have not been promised or do not simultaneously seek the return of a cache of arms. Sororal obligations such as those of Antigone do not conflict with obligations to preserve the peace and so on. Agents may still fail to fulfill obligations.[38]

Marcus asks us to imagine a two-person card game in which the deck is shuffled and divided equally face down. Players turn up the top cards until the cards are played out. Two rules are in force: black cards trump red cards and high cards trump cards of lower value. The winner is the one who has the most tricks by the end of the game.

> There is an inclination to call such a set of rules inconsistent. For suppose the pair turned up is a red ace and a black deuce; who trumps? . . . two rules and both cannot be satisfied. But on the definition here proposed, the rules are consistent in that there are possible circumstances where, in the course of playing the game, the dilemma would not arise and the game would proceed to a conclusion. . . . On the proposed definition, rules are consistent if there are possible circumstances in which no conflict will emerge. By extension, a set of rules is inconsistent if there are *no* circumstances, no possible world, in which all the rules are satisfiable. . . .
>
> A pair of offending rules which generates inconsistency as *here* defined provides *no* guide to action under any circumstance. Choices are thwarted whatever the contingencies.[39]

The parallel Marcus offers between the principles of a moral code and the card-game rules strikes me as not quite right. Unlike "Keep your promises" and

"Tell the truth," the game rules lay down priorities and are inconsistent (as I understand the term) in that both priorities cannot be satisfied. The proper analogy would be two moral directives that specify exemptions, as, for example, (1) "Tell the truth unless in doing so you break a promise," and (2) "Keep your promises unless in doing so you tell a lie." As we saw earlier, moralists (except Kant) agree that no substantive moral principle—I mean to exclude, for example, "Do what is morally right"—is "absolute," that is, holds without exception. A particular conflict situation may lead us to hedge our obligations by introducing escape clauses. Thus it is wrong to lie unless (the Kantian example again) by lying one can prevent a murder. A principle, no matter how heavily qualified, remains a principle. (In high school you learn Boyle's Law, and in college you learn the many conditions under which it does not hold.) But a moral code does not append to each principle a list of exceptions—and for good reason. It is not just that it would be hard to teach to children; it is that there is no limit to the list of exceptions. Moral principles hold ceteris paribus, which is to say that they hold unless (for some good reason) they do not hold. The idea that moral principles can be progressively defined, slightly modified with each new case, is like the idea that prima facie obligations can be lexically ordered on the basis of relative stringency: both are attractive to theorists, but neither seems at all promising.

It appears to me, therefore, that anything that we would count as a moral code will be consistent in my sense and, since it will not include priority principles analogous to the defective game rules cited by Marcus, in her sense as well. It follows that although she is correct in claiming that moral conflict does not threaten the consistency of moral codes, she does nothing, beyond adverting to "circumstances," to explain the genesis of moral conflict, and this omission is serious. The essential facts are pretty clear: moral principles prescribe or forbid actions under certain descriptions, for example, "truth-telling," "promise-keeping," and so on. In general, every action, every event, like every individual, is the topic of indefinitely many true descriptions. A conflict arises when a projected action satisfies a description under which it is enjoined by one moral principle and also satisfies a description under which it is forbidden by another moral principle. Imagine a particular speech act, a remark, let us say, that I make in public. Without any great strain, we can suppose that it is a case of truth-telling (good) and also a case of promise-breaking (bad) and furthermore that it is the cause of pleasure to most of my audience (good) but a cause of pain to a minority (bad). It would be possible (although tedious) to continue, running through the duties of my office, special obligations, long-range consequences, and so forth. So it was not that Agamemnon's moral *code* was inconsistent; it was that one and the same action, under the description "killing Iphigenia," was mandated by one principle and forbidden by another.

If my account is plausible, then there are difficulties for the Marcus conception of a possible world in which, as it happens, no moral conflicts arise and, although not all obligations are actually discharged—weakness of the will, personal failure stand in the way—all moral principles are obeyable. Duties may conflict with inclinations but not with other duties. What would such a world be like? (The question is interesting in view of the second-order regulative principle proposed by Marcus, the one that tells us to plan our lives and institutions with a view to minimizing moral conflict. The possible world that she envisages would be the limit at which our endeavors aim.) It would be a world with a moral code, let us say, our moral code. It would be a world in which people, for example, made remarks in public. Such remarks would either satisfy or fail to satisfy such descriptions as "telling the truth," "keeping a promise," "causing unnecessary pain," and so forth. But it would be a world in which no making of a remark would qualify under more than one description. But how could that be? I have no strong convictions about the limits of possibility, but it does seem to me that the only world that could satisfy the Marcus conditions would be a world without agents, without moral principles—indeed, without language users—a world, as might be, of trilobites.

(Come to think of it, the Marcus proposal suggests an argument in favor of the original pro-D thesis: given a world close enough to the actual world to be interesting—a world in which there is a moral code and in which people do things such as making remarks and murdering their daughters—conflicts of obligation are bound to arise, and hence one does not need, as the rationalists claim, an "epistemic criterion" in order to claim that moral dilemmas are not merely apparent but real.)

Consider, finally, the claim that it is desirable at least to eliminate where we can the possibility of moral conflict. Marcus writes:

> Although dilemmas are not settled without residue, the recognition of their reality has a dynamic force. It motivates us to arrange our lives and institutions with a view to avoiding such conflicts. It is the underpinning for a second-order principle: that as rational agents with some control of our lives and institutions, we ought to conduct our lives and arrange our institutions so as to minimize predicaments of moral conflict.[40]

It seems to me first that in attempting to justify some action of mine, it is never enough to say, "I did it in order to avoid moral conflict." If I take steps, perhaps by keeping a diary or an engagement book, to ensure that I do not make conflicting promises, it is not, surely, with a view to avoiding subsequent dilemmas—although that might be a secondary gain. I try to be careful because it is important to me to *keep* my promises. As for what Marcus refers to as "arranging our institutions" with a view to minimizing conflicts, I am not sure I know what that means. It sounds odd to ask someone to compare, for example, Columbia University with IBM with respect to their success in forestalling moral conflicts. Perhaps something like having a reasonable parental-leave policy that would not force employees to choose between their careers and child care would be counted.[41] Even here, though, the main point is something different, such as, for example, treating others like ends in themselves. I do agree that the desire to manipulate and coerce other people provides a motive for devising situations that *will* be dilemmatic for them and that this is morally indefensible. (This was the point I wanted to make about the pro-Ds' "tragic" examples.)

A more general point: One way of avoiding moral conflict is to cut down on the number of one's obligations or to resolve to worry less about what precisely they are. The analogue would be the person whose concern with cognitive certainty leads him to become a skeptic or who, with a view to achieving peace of mind, concentrates on ridding himself of desires and passions. In a good, although inconclusive, discussion of this point, Bernard Williams writes:

> I think that morality emerges as different from both belief and desire. It is not an option in the moral case that possible conflict should be avoided by way of scepticism, or the pursuit of *ataraxia*—in general, by indifference. The notion of a moral claim is of something that I may not ignore: hence it is not up to me to give myself a life free from conflict by withdrawing my interest from such claims.[42]

In summary: I have argued that although the moral dilemmas debate hinges on a question that, beyond a certain point, is not a topic for profitable discussion, at least some of the issues can be reformulated in an interesting way, and that in the course of exploring some of the consequent questions, we encounter neglected and philosophically important issues.

Notes

This essay was inspired by a conference on moral dilemmas held at the University of Minnesota in 1991. Several of the authors I discuss were participants, but since their papers have not yet appeared in print, I draw from their contributions to an excellent anthology, *Moral Dilemmas*, edited by Christopher Gowans (1987). I owe a debt of gratitude to Gisela Striker and John Lad for their critical comments on an earlier version of this paper.

1. The term was coined by Alan Donagan. Cf. Donagan (1984), in Gowans (1987), p. 281. Donagan counts himself as a rationalist and cites Aquinas and Kant as his forebears. As we shall see, there are a number of other philosophers, traditional as well as contemporary, who seem to meet the requirement.

2. Marcus (1980), in Gowans (1987), p. 188ff.

3. Gowans (1987), p. 3.

4. Marcus conflates moral dilemmas with conflicts of obligation in general. Many of the authors on both sides do this—one thing that makes it difficult to get a fix on the central question.

5. McConnell (1978), in Gowans (1987), pp. 167ff.

6. Sinnott-Armstrong (1988), p. 29.

7. Moore (1962), p. 126.

8. McConnell's answer is that it is not incumbent on the rationalist "to supply the correct moral answer to every apparent quandary" and he continues:

> In other areas of inquiry, for example, history or physics, there may be some evidence supporting one hypothesis and some evidence supporting a conflicting hypothesis. That one does not know which hypothesis is correct does not by *itself* cast doubt on the claim that there is a uniquely correct answer. McConnell (1978), in Gowans (1987), p. 162.

9. Kant (1965), p. 24.

10. Donagan (1984), in Gowans (1987), p. 274.

11. Conee (1982), in Gowans (1987), p. 239.

12. Williams (1965), in Gowans (1987), p. 115.

13. See Donagan (1984), in Gowans (1987), p. 273.

14. McConnell (1978), in Gowans (1987), p. 167.

15. The examples come from W. D. Ross, who evinces some uneasiness about terminology and at one point allows himself to speak of one duty being "more of a duty" than another. Cf. Ross (1930), in Gowans (1987), pp. 83ff.

16. Nagel (1979a), in Gowans (1987), p. 175.

17. Nagel (1979a), in Gowans (1987), p. 174.

18. Mill, in Gowans (1987), p. 54.

19. Donagan (1984), in Gowans (1987), p. 281.

20. Pincoffs (1971).

21. Doubtless the Agamemnon example has been used before, but in the current debate it was introduced by Bernard Williams.

22. Sartre (1956).

23. Styron (1980). The Sophie example was introduced by Patricia Greenspan. Greenspan (1983). It is a good example, partly because of its symmetry and I am struck by the number of authors who make use of it without credit to Greenspan. (Some do not even bother to footnote Styron.)

24. Janet Malcolm, reflecting on the hazards of writing biography, writes as follows:

> In a work of nonfiction we almost never know the truth of what happened. The ideal of unmediated reporting is regularly achieved only in fiction. When Henry James reports in *The Golden Bowl* that the Prince and Charlotte are sleeping together, we have no reason to doubt him, or to wonder whether Maggie is "overreacting" to what she sees. The facts of imaginative literature are as hard as the stone that Dr. Johnson kicked. We must always take the novelist's word or the poet's word, just as we are almost always free to doubt the biographer's or the autobiographer's or the historian's or the journalist's. In imaginative literature we are constrained from considering alternative scenarios—there are none. This is the way it is. Malcolm (1993).

25. Sinnott-Armstrong (1988), p. 29 (emphasis added).

26. Anna Karenina, unable to give up either her lover or her son, was driven to kill herself. Whether suicide can be counted as a "solution" is problematic. At any rate it is not an option available to all, e.g., not to Hamlet, whose dilemma turned on the question whether or not to commit suicide.

27. Donagan (1984), in Gowans (1987), p. 288.

28. Cf. Ross (1930), in Gowans (1987), p. 86ff.

29. Marcus (1980), in Gowans (1987), p. 194.

30. Foot (1983), in Gowans (1987), p. 258.

31. Marcus (1980), in Gowans (1987), p. 188.

32. Marcus (1980), in Gowans (1987), p. 190.

33. Marcus (1980), in Gowans (1987), p. 190.

34. Marcus (1980), in Gowans (1987), p. 190.

35. Marcus (1980), in Gowans (1987), p. 199.

36. Marcus (1980), in Gowans (1987), p. 199.

37. Donagan (1984), in Gowans (1987), p. 281.

38. Marcus (1980), in Gowans (1987), p. 195.

39. Marcus (1980), in Gowans (1987), p. 195.

40. Marcus (1980), in Gowans (1987), p. 188.

41. I owe this suggestion to Gene Mason.

42. Williams (1965), in Gowans (1987), p. 128.

6

Morality, Moral Dilemmas, and Moral Requirements

NORMAN O. DAHL

There are at least two issues that are central to determining whether genuine moral dilemmas exist. The first is whether moral considerations are bound to "run out" in certain situations, leaving an agent with conflicting moral requirements. The second is what notion of *requirement* it is that, if a person were faced with conflicting requirements, would be enough all by itself to place the person in a genuine moral dilemma. I shall not try to settle the first of these issues. Rather, I shall call attention to a question that needs to be answered to settle it, a question whose importance has not always been recognized. I shall, however, offer a suggestion as to how the second issue should be settled.

I

As anyone who is familiar with the literature on moral dilemmas is aware, there are some who approach this topic with the intuition that there clearly are genuine moral dilemmas, and there are others who approach it with the intuition that there are no genuine moral dilemmas. In his contribution to this volume, Alan Donagan[1] asks which traditional moral theories countenance genuine moral dilemmas. Since he finds no such theory to be plausible, he goes on to ask why people have nevertheless thought that moral dilemmas exist. I want to take the inquiry Donagan has begun one step farther and ask what conception of *morality* would lead a person to affirm or deny the existence of genuine moral dilemmas. I shall focus on a question whose relevance for the existence of moral dilemmas has not always been recognized. Is morality something about which more could always be *discovered* or *understood,* this further discovery or understanding then being something that could be used to resolve apparent moral dilemmas, or is morality the sort of thing whose full resources we can expect to have at hand in at least some situations of conflict?

There is no doubt that people are faced with situations that from their point of view appear to be moral dilemmas. A person may be faced with two actions, each of which she thinks she ought to do, and both of which she knows she can't do. Given her moral beliefs, there may be nothing that warrants her saying that only one of these actions ought to be done (and, if so, which one), or that it is morally indifferent which of the two actions she performs. If everything that is morally relevant to her situation turns up in the content of her moral beliefs, then morality lacks the resources to resolve her conflict. Things are the way they appear to her, and she is in a genuine moral dilemma. On the other hand, if there is more that could be discovered or understood that is morally relevant to her situation, then her dilemma may only be apparent. Although it appears to her as if there are two actions, each of which she ought to do and both of which she can't do, it may turn out that there is really only one action that, all things considered, she ought to do, or it may turn out that it is morally indifferent which of the two actions she does. The question I am interested in is, Why adopt the former view about some apparent dilemmas, rather than taking the latter view about all such cases? What is it about morality that would lead one to expect that one could have all of its resources at hand in at least some cases of conflict, resources that are then bound to run out in some of these cases, rather than expecting it to be something about which more could always be discovered or understood, this further understanding then being something that could be used to resolve any such conflict?

One conception of morality that leads to the former view is that morality is, or essentially involves, something that is socially constructed or socially constructible. Either morality is itself a social practice, or it essentially involves something that is socially constructible in the way that social practices are constructed.

For example, morality might itself be taken to be a social practice, one that is designed to assess social *mores* and other more specific social practices, and to adjudicate the various and conflicting claims that arise from other social practices. Here one might think of morality as a higher order social practice designed to assess and place priorities on the demands of more specific, lower order practices. Despite this higher order function, however, this practice, like any other social practice, will have only the resources that come with its current level of development. Given these limits together with the complexities of moral life, one would expect the resources of morality to run out in certain situations. No social practice can anticipate all the demands that life may place on it, and this includes the practice of morality itself. As a result, one would expect that a person faced with a conflict could have at hand all the resources morality has to offer, and these would be insufficient to resolve his conflict. That is, one would expect there to be genuine moral dilemmas.[2]

In her well-known paper on moral dilemmas, Ruth Barcan Marcus points out that there is nothing impossible or incoherent about a situation in which the rules of a game yield conflicting directions.[3] Even if discovering such a situation would motivate one to change its rules to eliminate the source of this conflict, it would still be true that when the situation arose the rules of the game did yield conflicting directions. If morality is itself a social practice, then the analogy with games seems an apt one. As with social practices that are games, there will be nothing incoherent or impossible about a situation arising in which the rules that constitute morality yield conflicting directions. In fact, given the complexities of moral life, one would be surprised if such situations didn't arise. Furthermore, even if, having found such conflicts, society would feel the need to modify the practice of morality to remove them, it would still be true that morality did give rise to irresolvable conflicts. And even if morality were modified to eliminate previously discovered conflicts, there would still be no guarantee that new ones wouldn't arise for the modified practice. Indeed, given the complexities of moral life, one would be surprised if new irresolvable conflicts didn't arise. Again, one would expect there to be genuine moral dilemmas.

Another way in which morality might involve something socially constructible is exemplified by the kind of ideal utilitarianism Peter Railton refers to in his paper in this volume.[4] According to this form of utilitarianism, an action is morally required if a code that sanctions it by attaching negative opinion or guilt to its non-performance, would maximize utility when compared with other moral codes that might be taught, adopted, or become current in that society. According to this view, moral requirements are to be understood in terms of something that is socially constructible—an ideal moral code. Given the limits that come with what allows such a code to be taught and adopted, together with the complexities of moral life, and given that what justifies such a code is the comparative consequences of its being taught or adopted, it should come as no particular surprise if there are situations in which such a code would yield conflicting requirements. It seems perfectly possible that part of what allows such an ideal code to lead to those consequences that justify its adoption is that in some situations it will attach social or internal sanctions to an agent's action, no matter what the agent does. This may be one of the costs that has to be borne if a society is to have all of the value that can be provided by the adoption of the moral code that is ideal with respect to it in this way. Again, on such a view the existence of moral dilemmas would not be particularly surprising.

On the other hand, if one takes morality to have certain affinities with empirical science, one would not expect to be able to have the full resources of morality at hand when facing situations of conflict. Like the subjects of the various sciences, one would expect that there could always be more that could be discovered about morality, including considerations that would ultimately resolve apparent moral dilemmas.

Take, for example, the kind of externalist, realist[5] view of morality discussed by David Brink in his contribution to this volume.[6] If there are properties of actions that carry moral forces of various weights with them, and if moral requirements or obligations are determined by the vector sum of all of the relevant moral forces on a given action, then there may be a good deal that can still be discovered about the morality of various actions. Not only could one discover new properties of actions that carry moral forces with them, there may be more to learn about what specific weights different moral forces have in particular situations, and thus more to learn about what their weighted sum would be in a given situation. In short, when faced with an apparent dilemma, there is no guarantee that one will have exhausted the resources of morality in trying to resolve it. What appear to be dilemmas may in fact be resolvable after all.

The idea that morality is the sort of thing about which a good deal can yet be discovered or understood is not confined to externalist, realist views of the sort I just mentioned. It also fits certain quasi-realist views, including certain forms of internalism,[7] according to which moral features have certain affinities with secondary qualities.

Suppose that an action ought to be done if anyone with full knowledge of the circumstances surrounding the action would, when considering the action from a detached or impartial point of view, approve of it. Or suppose that an action ought to be done if anyone who had all of the knowledge that someone in the circumstances of the action could be expected to have, would, upon reflection from an appropriately detached point of view in circumstances like those facing the agent, be more strongly motivated to perform that kind of action than any other kind of action open to that agent. According to each of these views, what ought to be done is a function of a certain response that anyone would have toward various actions under certain idealized circumstances. The morality of actions, thus, is a function of a certain aspect of human nature, the one that gives rise to just that sort of response. According to this way of conceiving of morality, one would expect there to be a good deal that could still be discovered or understood about morality.

For example, one could discover new features of actions that, under the appropriate conditions, would give rise to the relevant response. Or one could develop a more sensitive response of the relevant sort. To press the analogy with secondary qualities a bit, just as experience, reflection, and feedback can lead one to recognize differences in shades of colors, or differences in the pitch or quality of sounds that one had not previously recognized, so one could develop a more sensitive response of the sort that gives rise to moral judgments, now recognizing morally relevant differences where previously one saw none. It might be more natural to describe this latter development as having acquired a deeper understanding of certain aspects of morality rather than having discovered something about morality or the sort of response that gives rise to moral judgments. But a development of either of these two sorts could lead one to change one's mind about what ought or ought not be done in a particular situation, including cases of apparent dilemmas. According to this conception of morality, one could always discover or understand more about morality that could then allow one to resolve apparent moral dilemmas.

There is, however, a version of this last way of conceiving of morality that carries with it certain limits to what can be relevant to the morality of particular actions, limits that might then lead one to think that the resources of morality can be expected to run out in some apparent dilemmas. Since this is a picture of morality to which I am attracted, I want to say something about whether it should be taken to carry this expectation with it.

The version in question is that what a person ought to do is what the person has reasons to do of such strength that failure to act in accord with them would leave the person open to charges of practical irrationality. It also takes what a person has a reason to do to be what she would be motivated to do from an appropriate impartial or detached point of view. According to this way of understanding morality, moral behavior turns out to be a species of rational behavior.

What gives rise to the suggestion that on such a view the resources of morality will run out in at least some situations of conflict is that what a person has reason to do is constrained by what he can be reasonably expected to know or believe. Features that I cannot reasonably be expected to be aware of are not features that can determine whether what I do is rational or not. For example, it cannot be irrational for me to fail to guard against consequences that I am unable to foresee. Given the conception of morality under consideration, this feature of rational action imposes a limit on what can be relevant to what I ought to do in any particular situation. What is morally relevant will be limited to what I can reasonably be expected to know or believe about the situation. This limit might then be thought to guarantee that the resources of morality will run out in at least some apparent dilemmas. As long as it is possible to know everything that one could reasonably be expected to know about a particular situation, it looks as if it will be possible to know everything that is morally relevant about a particular situation, including apparent moral dilemmas. But then it looks as if one can have the full resources of morality at hand when faced with an apparent dilemma, and, thus, that the resources of morality will run out in at least some of these situations.

However, I do not think that this latter suggestion is correct.[8] It may be that, according to this way of conceiving of morality, there will be a limit to the features of any action that can be relevant to whether it ought to be done. But it does not follow from this that there is a limit to what can be discovered or understood about the relevance of any one of these features. This latter will be determined by the particular motivation people will have toward actions with these features when they consider them from the appropriate point of view. Assuming that there is such a motivation, there is no guarantee that we have understood everything about morality that this motivation allows us to understand. If we can sometimes be mistaken about whether we have succeeded in adopting the appropriate detached point of view, or if we could always develop a still more sensitive motivation of the relevant sort, one would expect that there is a good deal that we can yet learn about morality, including just what difference the morally relevant features of an action make to whether we ought to perform it or not. If this is right, then this is still a conception of morality according to which there is always more that could be discovered or understood about morality that could then be used to resolve apparent moral dilemmas.

In keeping with my claim that the last general conception of morality that I have been discussing is compatible with certain forms of quasi-realism, I should point out that it makes no difference to the points I have been making whether one accepts a cognitivist or a non-cognitivist account of moral judgments in connection with this conception of morality. As the example of a judge's verdict shows, utterances that are neither true nor false can still be *correct* or *incorrect*, where correctness and incorrectness share certain formal properties with truth or falsity. As long as there is an analogous way for moral judgments to be correct or incorrect, one will be able to say the same sorts of things about morality and moral dilemmas that one can say if moral judgments turn out to be true or false.

Take, for example, the simplest way in which moral judgments could be correct or incorrect without being true or false. Suppose one accepts the sort of conception of morality that I have been discussing and one takes moral 'ought'-statements to express the feeling or motive one would have were one to take the appropriately detached point of view. Since expressions of feelings are neither true nor false, moral 'ought'-statements will have a component that is neither true nor false. Nevertheless, one could still take such 'ought'-statements to be correct just in case one would have the relevant feeling or motive, were one to adopt the appropriate point of view.[9] Given some such way in which moral 'ought'-statements can be correct or incorrect, one can say whatever needs to be said about morality and moral dilemmas in terms of the correctness of 'ought'-statements about various actions.

For example, a person will be in a moral dilemma if the person is faced with two actions, of each of which it would be correct to say in the appropriate sense of 'ought' that it ought to be done, and both of which the person can't do. A dilemma will only be apparent, if it turns out that it is correct to say of only one of the two actions in question that it ought to be done, or if it is only correct to say that the agent ought to perform one or the other of the two actions, it not being correct to say that the agent ought to perform each of them. The resources of morality will run out in an apparent dilemma if there is nothing more that could be discovered or understood about what it is correct to say about the situation that would lead one to say that the dilemma is only apparent. Something more can be discovered or understood about morality if there is something more that can be discovered or understood about what it is correct to say ought or ought not to be done in certain situations.

Thus, even if one accepts a non-cognitivist version of the conception of morality that I have been discussing, it still makes sense to talk about the possibility of discovering or understanding something about morality that might lead to the resolution of any apparent moral dilemma. This should make it clear that taking morality to be something about which such discoveries could always be made is not restricted to certain forms of moral realism.

In what I have said so far I have not tried to canvass all of the conceptions of morality that a person might accept. Nor do I want to claim that accepting any one of the conceptions that I have discussed is sufficient all by itself to determine one's position on the existence of moral dilemmas. For example, one could maintain that there is always more that could be discovered about morality, and still maintain that one of the things that we have discovered or will discover is that there are genuine moral dilemmas.[10] I also see nothing incoherent in the claim that something socially constructed has, over the years, acquired the resources to deal with any apparent dilemma that might face human beings, even if this doesn't turn out to be a particularly plausible claim. I do want to maintain, however, that accepting any one of the conceptions of morality that I have discussed will strongly influence one's stance on the existence of moral dilemmas.[11] An important part of a person's stance on moral dilemmas will be shaped by her conception of morality. As a result, it is likely that a full defense of the existence or non-existence of moral dilemmas will rest in part on a defense of a certain conception of morality.

If I am right about this, then one won't simply be able to cite the existence (or non-existence) of moral dilemmas as a datum against which to assess particular moral theories. Looking at their stance on the existence of moral dilemmas may well be a useful way to assess particular moral theories. But if the existence (or non-existence) of moral dilemmas depends in part on a certain conception of morality being correct, any such assessment may need to be supplemented with a defense of the relevant conception of morality.

There is, of course, nothing novel in the suggestion that adopting a certain conception of morality will influence one's stance on the existence of moral dilemmas. A number of years ago Bernard Williams argued that the existence of moral dilemmas is incompatible with moral realism.[12] What I have been arguing, however, is that the important contrast for moral dilemmas is not between whether one is a moral realist or not. It is between whether or not one can defend a conception of morality according to which there is always more that could be discovered or understood about morality that could then lead to a resolution of apparent dilemmas. At best, moral realism is only one of the forms that this latter conception of morality can take.

II

I now want to take up the second question I raised at the beginning of this paper. What notion of *requirement* is it that, if a person were faced with conflicting requirements, would be enough all by itself to place the person in a genuine moral dilemma?

The first thing to say is that it is not the notion of requirement that holds simply in virtue of a person's being under an obligation in one familiar sense of 'obligation'. A number of years ago H. L. A. Hart pointed out that there is an ordinary notion of obligation that typically presupposes a social practice, arises in virtue of some prior committing action, and the non-fulfillment of which usually carries with it the threat of a sanction.[13] Examples of such obligations include the obligation to keep promises and the obligations one incurs when one takes an oath of office. A person can be under conflicting requirements of this sort without being faced with a genuine dilemma.

One reason for this is that there is more that can be morally required of people than what arises from this kind of obligation. Obligations of this sort do not exhaust the field of what one ought to do. A second reason is that such obligations can be overridden by other considerations, including other such obligations. As a result, one can always ask whether all things considered one ought to fulfill any such requirement. Since this is so, a person can fail to fulfill such a requirement without thereby doing something that all things considered is wrong. However, as I understand moral dilemmas, one is in a moral dilemma only if one is in a situation in which, no matter what one does, one will do something that all things considered is wrong.[14] Thus, the existence of conflicting requirements of this sort is not all by itself enough to place a person in a genuine moral dilemma.

There are two reasons that it is important to recognize this notion of requirement. The obvious one is to recognize that it will not be enough to support the existence of moral dilemmas simply to note that people can be faced with conflicting moral requirements of this sort. Since in principle any such requirement could fail to be one that all things considered a person ought to fulfill, being faced with conflicting requirements of this sort will not by itself be enough to place a person in a genuine moral dilemma. Of course, there is also no guarantee that a person faced with such conflicting requirements *won't* be in a genuine moral dilemma. Nothing that has been said so far rules out the possibility that all things considered a person ought to fulfill each one of two such conflicting requirements. But it will take more to argue for this last possibility than to point out that people can be faced with conflicting requirements of this sort.[15]

The second reason has to do with an equally unsuccessful way of arguing that moral dilemmas do not exist. Each obligation of the sort I have been talking about is defeasible. There are circumstances in which the kind of committing action that normally gives rise to such an obligation won't create an obligation. For example, a promise that has been extracted by means of coercion doesn't create an obligation to keep that promise, and a promise to do what all parties in advance know is immoral doesn't seem to create a binding obligation. Given this, one might think that the defeasibility of such obligations is unlimited, so that if there are moral grounds for not fulfilling such a requirement, these grounds provide reasons for thinking that there really is no such requirement. But in fact the defeasibility of such obligations is not unlimited. Such obligations can and do exist even when there are moral grounds not to fulfill them. As a result, the requirements they give rise to can and do come in conflict with one another without disappearing.[16] Of course, given what I have said above, the existence of these sorts of conflicts is not enough to show that there are genuine moral dilemmas. But it also won't be enough to deny the existence of moral dilemmas to argue that such requirements can't ultimately conflict with one another because the obligations on which they rest are defeasible. It will take more than the defeasibility of such obligations to show that moral dilemmas do not exist.

But if this is not the notion of requirement that is sufficient by itself to place one in a genuine moral dilemma, then what is the relevant notion of requirement? An obvious answer is that it is the notion of a requirement that all things considered it would be wrong to fail to fulfill. A moral dilemma is not just a situation in which one has equally strong reasons for performing each of two actions, both of which one can't do. It involves more than a disjunctive obligation to perform one or the other of two such competing actions. And it involves more than what Simon Blackburn has called an objective moral quandary.[17] It must also be true that all things considered it would be wrong not to perform each of these actions. Each action must be one that all things considered one ought to do *and* one that all things considered one ought not to do. As David Brink[18] (along with a number of others) has pointed out, it is this notion of a moral dilemma that raises the problems that have led a number of philosophers to deny their existence. As a result, it seems to be the notion that should be used when the existence of moral dilemmas is controversial.

Unfortunately, this answer isn't very helpful in settling the question of whether genuine moral dilemmas exist. One seems in no better position to determine whether there are situations in which, no matter what one does, one will have done something that all things considered is wrong, than one is to determine whether there are situations in which there are two actions, each of which all things considered one ought to do and both of which one can't do. What one would like is a criterion, or some identifying marks, of this notion of moral requirement. One might then be able to argue either that moral dilemmas exist because there are situations in which there are two conflicting actions, each of which bears these marks, or that moral dilemmas do not exist, because the nature of these marks shows that there can't be conflicting requirements of this sort. A number of such marks have been proposed. For example, it has been suggested that such a requirement exists if failure to fulfill it makes it morally appropriate or incumbent on the agent to compensate others for her failure, or to apologize for that failure, or to feel guilt, remorse, or regret for her failure.[19] I shall concentrate on the last of these suggestions—in particular, on the appropriateness of feeling guilt for such a failure.

There is a common problem that arises for all of these suggestions. Situations exist in which these marks are present but the agent has not done what all things considered is wrong. Take, for example, actions for which compensation is owed. There are situations in which what all things considered a person ought to do involves the infringement of someone else's rights. That is, there are occasions on which the infringement of someone's rights is justified. This can be most readily seen if the rights in question are what have been called special rights (e.g., property rights, or rights that issue from a binding contract) rather than general or human rights. However, infringements of rights are typically the sorts of things for which people ought to be compensated. Since they are, there will be situations in which compensation is owed for what a person has done, but in which the person has not done what all things considered is wrong. Whether one owes compensation for what one has done thus fails to be a mark of the sort of requirement that would be sufficient to place a person in a genuine moral dilemma. Similar things can be said about the need for a person to apologize for what he has done.[20]

The same problem arises for the criterion I want to discuss—the appropriateness of guilt feelings for what a person has done. Take, for example, the often-discussed case of a driver who, through no fault of her own, strikes and kills a child.[21] She had been driving carefully and responsibly. The child was hidden from view, and suddenly darted in front of her car, leaving her no time to stop. In such a case there would be something wrong with the driver if she didn't experience some sort of guilt for what she had done. Failing to feel guilty under these circumstances would betray a lack of sensitivity to the importance of human life, especially a life with so much of its future in front of it. Thus, this is a situation in which feelings of guilt would be morally appropriate. But it is not a situation in which the person in question did anything wrong. She may have been driving as carefully as could have been expected of anyone.

It is important to recognize that the feelings that are morally appropriate in such a situation are feelings of guilt, and not some lesser feeling or emotion such as regret. One way of accounting for this is to acknowledge two kinds of guilt—one resting on the belief that one is at fault or has done something wrong, the other requiring only that one respond as if one had done something wrong.[22] One could then argue that it is the second kind of guilt that would be morally appropriate in these circumstances. However, I think that the same thing could be said even if one recognizes only one kind of guilt, taking guilt always to carry with it the belief that one was at fault or had done something wrong. This would mean that there would be a sense in which the guilt feelings felt by such a driver would be irrational; for, if she were to reflect on her situation, she would recognize that she hadn't done anything wrong and wasn't at fault. If under these circumstances she still felt guilty, she would find herself with inconsistent beliefs. But I see no reason why one shouldn't say that under circumstances such as these it would be morally appropriate for her to have such irrational feelings of guilt and that there would be something morally amiss with her if she didn't have them. A number of things might be suggested to explain why this should be so.

For example, it may be that people can't achieve a fine enough control over their feelings and emotions that, if they are disposed to feel guilty in situations in which they have done something wrong and are at fault, they won't be able to prevent themselves from feeling guilty in comparable situations in which they are not at fault. Or perhaps such guilt feelings are the other side of the coin of the kind of optimism that we need if we are to try to eliminate injustices and rectify wrongs in circumstances in which it seems almost impossible that we will be able to do so, an optimism that prevents us from feeling that these evils are unpreventable.[23] If it is appropriate to feel the kind of optimism that allows us to continue to try to eliminate such evils when it seems almost impossible that we shall succeed, then it may also be true that, when a tragedy of the sort we have been talking about occurs, we will continue to believe that there is something we could have done to prevent it, and thus that we were to some extent at fault for its occurrence. Whatever the reason, it does seem morally appropriate for the driver in the case under consideration to experience some guilt for what she has done. There would be something morally amiss with her if she didn't.

However, since she didn't do anything wrong in this situation, the appropriateness of such guilt feelings can't serve as a mark of the notion of moral requirement with which we are interested.

Nevertheless, I think this criterion can be amended so that it will serve as such a mark. Even though it would be morally appropriate for the driver in the case discussed above to feel guilty for what she did, it is not true that she *deserves* to feel guilty for what she does. She would have deserved to feel guilty if she had been in any way at fault in the death of the child. But, under the circumstances, she was not at fault. The suggestion I want to put forward is that if a person *deserves* to feel guilty for what she has done, then she has failed to fulfill the kind of requirement that, were conflicting requirements to exist, would be sufficient to place her in a genuine moral dilemma. The case of the driver shows that there is more than one way in which it can be morally appropriate for a person to feel guilty, and that one of these can't serve as a mark of the appropriate notion of moral requirement. What I am suggesting is that another of these ways can serve as such a mark. In particular, if a person *deserves* to feel guilty for what she has done, then she has failed to fulfill the sort of requirement that, if she were faced with conflicting requirements of this sort, would be enough all by itself to place her in a genuine moral dilemma.[24]

It might be thought that this suggestion is of no help at all. If one asks what the conditions are under which a person deserves to feel guilty for what he has done, the natural answer seems to be that he must have done something wrong for which he is at fault. That is, he must have done something wrong without being able to plead one or more of an identifiable set of excuses. This means that in order to determine whether a person deserves to feel guilty for what he has done, one must determine whether or not he has done something wrong. But isn't that just what we wanted a criterion to help us discover in the first place? Why doesn't this suggestion put us right back where we started, still needing a criterion that we can use to show that a certain kind of requirement exists that, if a person were faced with conflicting requirements of this sort, would leave him in a genuine moral dilemma?

I think it would be premature to conclude that we are right back where we started. If the suggestion I have offered is correct, then what the circle we seem faced with shows is that there is a mutual dependency between what people are morally required to do and what they deserve to feel guilty for failing to do. A full understanding of what people are morally required to do will involve understanding what people deserve to feel guilty for failing to do and why they deserve to feel guilty for failing to do it. And a full understanding of why people deserve to feel guilty for failing to do certain actions will involve understanding what people are morally required to do. But this *mutual dependency* can be used to shed light on the kind of things people can be morally required to do.

What this mutual dependency means is that any theory of what people are morally required to do must be developed in tandem with a theory of when and why people deserve to feel guilty for what they have done. Taking guilt to be a form of self-blame, it means that any theory of what people are morally required to do must be developed in tandem with a theory of when people are morally blameworthy for what they have done.[25] What people can be blameworthy for doing puts constraints on what people can be morally required to do, and vice versa.[26] However, if this is right, then the criterion for the existence of moral requirements that I have suggested *can* be used to shed light on the existence of moral dilemmas. Taken together with different bases for holding people blameworthy, this mutual dependency can yield different answers to the question of what people can be required to do, including whether they can be faced with the kind of conflicting requirements that would place them in a genuine moral dilemma.

Take, for example, the kind of ideal utilitarianism discussed in the first section of this paper. This theory exemplifies the kind of connection I have suggested holds between what people are morally required to do and blameworthiness. According to this theory, an action is morally required if a code that sanctions it by attaching negative opinion or guilt to its non-performance would maximize utility when compared with other moral codes that might be taught, adopted, or be current in that society. Taking these external and internal sanctions to be forms of blame, and taking a person to be blameworthy when such sanctions would be justified, this theory takes a person to be required to do what she would be blameworthy for failing to do. If one adds to this a utilitarian approach to blameworthiness, one arrived at by emphasizing the deterrent aspect of the sanctions that constitute blame, then I think it would come as no surprise if it turned out that people can be faced with the kind of conflicting requirements that constitute genuine moral dilemmas. One of the consequences that might well contribute to a particular moral code's being ideal in this way for a given society is the deterrent effects that would be achieved by taking people in certain situations to be blameworthy no matter what they ended up doing. Accepting the kind of connection between moral requirements and blameworthiness that I have suggested and taking a utilitarian approach toward blameworthiness might well provide a basis for arguing that genuine moral dilemmas do exist.

On the other hand, if one were to accept the kind of connection I have suggested and were to adopt an approach toward blameworthiness more closely connected with certain deontological theories of what people are morally required to do, one might end up with a basis for denying the existence of moral dilemmas. Suppose, for example, that one takes autonomy to be something whose promotion or preservation is of such great importance that it is not to be sacrificed simply for the sake of better consequences. Suppose further that one takes a person to be autonomous to the extent to which he can determine what happens to him by means of his own decisions or choices, decisions or choices that are in turn determined by his own conception of the good. If one takes the extent to which a person is blamed, including both the negative attitudes of others and his own internal feelings of guilt, to be among the things that happen to him that should be tied to his own decisions or choices, then it looks as if one will end up with a rather different picture of when people will be blameworthy from the one that results from the utilitarian view sketched just above. In fact, taken together with the connection between moral requirement and blameworthiness that I have suggested, this link between blameworthiness and autonomy provides grounds for denying the existence of any moral dilemmas that are not a result of the agent's own actions.[27] Given the connection between moral requirements and blameworthiness that I have suggested, taking a person to be in a dilemma that didn't result from his own action would amount to an infringement of that person's autonomy. If blameworthiness is tied to the restriction that a person's being blamed should be determined by his own decisions or choices, then there should be no situation in which a person will be blameworthy no matter what he might have chosen or decided to do. Since that is just the sort of situation a person would be in if there were genuine moral dilemmas, and the connection between moral requirements and blameworthiness that I have suggested holds, this approach to moral blameworthiness could provide moral grounds for denying the existence of genuine moral dilemmas.

It is, of course, beyond the scope of this paper to try to defend a theory of blameworthiness that, when tied to the connection between moral requirements and blameworthiness I have suggested, would yield grounds for affirming or denying the existence of genuine moral dilemmas. But if anything like what I have been saying is correct, there is a second avenue, the exploration of which may shed light on the existence of moral dilemmas. Besides determining whether morality is the sort of thing about which more could always be discovered or understood that could then resolve apparent dilemmas, developing an adequate theory of blameworthiness that satisfies the connection between moral requirement and blameworthiness that I have suggested may also put one in a position to determine whether moral dilemmas exist or not. Indeed, a full defense of the existence or non-existence of genuine moral dilemmas may require both a defense of a certain conception of morality and a defense of a theory of blameworthiness.

Notes

I am grateful to Carl Brandt, Martin Gunderson, Thomas Hill, Jr., Gene Mason, Terrance McConnell, and Henry West for their comments on earlier drafts of this paper.

1. See Donagan's paper in this volume.

2. This will be true even if morality is taken to be as complex and historically rooted a social practice as are particular languages. Just as the need to develop new technical vocabulary shows that there are situations in which the current resources of a particular language have run out, so one would expect there to be situations in which the resources of morality will run out. If these turn out to be situations of conflict, then there will be genuine moral dilemmas.

3. In fact, she offers an account of consistency according to which the rules of such a game can be consistent. A set of rules is consistent if there is a possible world in which the rules in question are all obeyable in all circumstances in that world. Marcus (1980), p. 128.

4. See pp. 143–5.

5. By externalism I mean the view that there is no necessary connection between a person's recognizing, fully understanding, accepting, or sincerely believing that he ought to do something and his having a motivation to do it. I am less sure how to characterize moral realism. But I take it essentially to be the view that the moral features of actions are independent of the mental states of any second party who might ascertain their presence. I take a view that regards moral features to have the status of primary qualities to be one clear form of moral realism.

6. See Brink's paper in this volume.

7. By internalism I mean the view that there is a necessary connection between what people ought to do and their being motivated to do it, such that necessarily, if a person recognizes, fully understands, believes, or sincerely accepts that she ought to do something, she will have a motivation to do it.

8. It would be more than ironical if it were correct. Almost certainly, the most prominent historical opponent of moral dilemmas is Kant. As I understand Kant, he subscribes to the conception of morality under discussion.

9. For a more sophisticated account of how moral statements could express feelings and still be assessed in terms that share certain formal properties with truth and falsity, see Blackburn (1984), ch. 6.

10. See also Mason's paper in this volume. According to the view of morality Mason sets out, there may always be something that one could discover about the particular kinds of obligations or responsibilities one might have in a given situation. However, since there are no more general features or principles of morality that could be discovered that could be used to compare the relevant strengths or weights of such particular obligations or responsibilities, one would still expect there to be genuine moral dilemmas.

11. For example, if one accepts a conception of morality according to which

there is a good deal that could yet be discovered about morality, and one takes it to be the function of morality to provide guidance in situations of conflict, then I think one's natural response to apparent dilemmas would be to suppose that there is more that could be discovered that would resolve them, rather than that they constitute genuine moral dilemmas.

12. Williams (1965) and (1966). For a critical response to Williams, see Foot (1983).

13. Hart (1958).

14. This conception of moral dilemmas is not shared by everyone. (See, e.g., Marcus [1980] and Sinnott-Armstrong [1988].) However, as I point out below, it is this conception of moral dilemmas that raises the problems that have led a number of philosophers to deny their existence. As a result, this seems to be the conception one should use when the existence of moral dilemmas is taken to be controversial.

15. For one attempt to provide these additional considerations, see Mason's paper in this volume.

16. For more on this issue, see McConnell's paper in this volume, pp. 39–44.

17. See Blackburn's paper in this volume.

18. See Brink's paper in this volume.

19. See, e.g., Williams (1965), pp. 110–15; Marcus (1980), pp. 126–27, 130-31; and Sinnott-Armstrong (1988), pp. 39–53.

20. See, e.g., McConnell's paper in this volume, pp. 39–44.

21. See, e.g., McConnell's paper in this volume, p. 39, for a discussion of this kind of case that draws a similar conclusion to the one I draw just below.

22. See, e.g., Greenspan (1992).

23. Such feelings may be a holdover from a religious view according to which God would not allow such unpreventable evils. But there may also be reason to hang on to such optimism even if we have given up its religious underpinnings. Without it, we might fail to act when in fact our action could prevent such evils.

24. Thus, I suggest that we take the notion of a moral dilemma whose existence is controversial to be what Sinnott-Armstrong in this volume, pp. 53–55, would describe as a moral wrongs dilemma, understood as a specific sort of moral residue dilemma. So understood, there is no initial guarantee that moral dilemmas do or do not exist. But, as I point out below, understanding moral dilemmas in this way does open up a line of argument that could determine whether they exist or not.

25. One might resist this last move, arguing that because guilt and blame are distinct phenomena, so are deserving to feel guilty and being blameworthy. For example, it might be argued that guilt is a feeling or emotion, while blame is an action, so that deserving guilt and deserving blame amount to deserving two different things. Furthermore, as cases like that involving the driver show, guilt can be appropriate even when a person is not at fault and thus isn't blameworthy. Thus, it is a mistake to tie actions for which people deserve to feel guilty to actions for which they are blameworthy.

I grant that blame and guilt are distinct phenomena. But I deny that they are so distinct that it can't be true that the actions for which people deserve to feel guilty are actions for which they are blameworthy, and vice versa. Blame certainly has a wider scope than does guilt. I can blame others for their actions, but I can't feel guilty for their actions, unless perhaps I instigated them. It is also true that guilt is a feeling, attitude, or emotion, while blame can be an action. But blame can also be a feeling, attitude, or emotion. For example, it is quite all right for someone to say, after witnessing an angry flare-up, "I didn't realize it, but he has blamed her all along for the breakup of their marriage," in which during the period of time in question the subject of this remark hadn't engaged in any overt acts of blaming. Acts of blame and attitudes of blame are also intimately connected; acts of blame typically express feelings or attitudes of blame. Furthermore, the connection I have drawn between guilt and blameworthiness only requires one to take feeling guilty to be a form of *self*-blame. The most that it requires in the case of others is that if they are blameworthy, then they deserve to feel guilty for what they have done. Finally, even though there are situations in which it would be morally appropriate for people to feel guilty but aren't blameworthy for what they have done, this does not show that people can *deserve* to feel guilty for what they have done without being blameworthy for what they have done. As the case of the driver shows, not every case in which it would be morally appropriate for a person to feel guilt is a case in which the person deserves to feel guilty for what she has done. It is only the latter kind of case with which I am concerned.

If guilt is a form of self-blame, then it does seem true that if a person deserves to feel guilty for what she has done, then she is blameworthy for what she has done. (She at least deserves that kind of self-blame that is guilt.) And if it is true that self-blame will be warranted if any kind of blame is warranted, then it looks as if a person who is blameworthy deserves to feel some degree of guilt for that for which she is blameworthy. This is all that is needed to support the suggestion I am offering here.

26.   There is a tradition in moral philosophy that denies the existence of any such connection between what people ought to do and blameworthiness. It standardly rests on one or more of two bases. The first takes blame to be an action, assimilates blame to punishment, and takes acts of blame to be justified by their effects, usually their deterrent or reformative effects. Since such acts can be directed against someone who has failed to do what he ought to have done without having the desired reformative or deterrent effects, a person can fail to do what he ought to do and not be blameworthy. The second basis maintains that moral worth, including both moral praiseworthiness and moral blameworthiness, depends on the motives from which a person acts, whereas what a person ought to do or is morally required to do is independent of any such motives. As a result, a person who acts from a morally good motive can fail to do what he is morally required to do but not be blameworthy.

However, the first of these two bases is faulty. Blame is not just an action. It is sometimes an attitude or a feeling. Blame also serves more functions than simply to reform or deter. For example, it serves important expressive and educative functions. Furthermore, it is by no means clear that blame is justified solely in virtue of its consequences, especially if these consequences are restricted to its reformative or deterrent effects.

As for the second of these two bases, I have argued elsewhere (Dahl [1986]) that even though there is a sense in which what people ought to do is independent of the motives from which they would do it, there is still an important connection that holds between what people ought to do and when they are morally praiseworthy that allows one to argue from premises about the latter to conclusions about the former. I see no reason why a similar argument couldn't be forthcoming in the case of what people ought to do and moral blameworthiness. Besides, although it may be true that people can be blameworthy for acting from bad motives even if they haven't done anything wrong, what I am concerned with is when people are blameworthy for their actions. One of the circumstances in which people seem to be blameworthy for their actions is when they have failed to fulfill some moral requirement. And unless their having a good motive is an indication that they can plead an excuse such as ignorance or coercion, the most such a motive seems to do is to mitigate the degree to which these people are blameworthy. It does not eliminate their blameworthiness altogether.

Of course, it would help if we had a more precise statement of the connection that allows conditions under which people are blameworthy to put constraints on what people can be morally required to do. Although it may not ultimately hold up, the obvious thing to say is that what a person is morally required to do is what, in the absence of some specifiable excuse such as ignorance, coercion, duress, or provocation, the person would be blameworthy for failing to do.

27. As a candidate for a dilemma that is a result of the agent's own actions, consider someone who has made two promises, both of which he knows he can't keep. For independent reasons for marking off dilemmas that are a result of one's own actions from those that are not, and taking only the latter to be genuine moral dilemmas, see Donagan's paper in this volume, pp. 13–14.

7

Moral Conflict and Its Structure

David O. Brink

It is commonly thought that there might be conflicts of obligations or moral dilemmas and that their existence would have serious implications for moral theory, metaethics, or deontic logic. Some alleged implications of moral dilemmas depend upon their *frequency*. On one such view, the fact that moral dilemmas are so common places severe constraints on the prospects for a systematic moral theory and on the possibility of moral knowledge.[1] But a more common view is that something about the *structure* of a moral dilemma generates troublesome or paradoxical implications. On this view, the important question is whether there are or could be any moral dilemmas; their frequency is of little or, at most, secondary importance. Indeed, if we understand 'moral dilemmas' univocally in both contexts, then the question of their existence must be prior to the question of their frequency. In any case, I shall focus on this second, structural issue.

Before we debate whether there are moral dilemmas, we need to know what sort of conflict is necessary to produce trouble or paradox in ethical theory. In fact, it will be useful to reserve the expression 'moral dilemma' as a term of art that refers to conflicts with such consequences. When the nature of these conflicts and their consequences are clear, we can ask whether it is reasonable to suppose that there are moral dilemmas.

I. Prima Facie and All-Things-Considered Obligations

A moral dilemma involves some kind of conflict of obligations or duties. (I shall not distinguish between obligations and duties. Moreover, I shall assume that both duties and obligations are ascribed using the moral "ought.") If an agent is faced with a moral dilemma, he has an obligation to do A and an obligation to do B, but can't do both. This much is clear.[2] But we need to know more about the structure of these obligations. It is common and, I believe, important to distinguish between *prima facie* and *all-things-considered* obligations or duties. For, I shall argue, it is a conflict of all-things-considered, and not merely prima facie, duties that is required to generate a moral conflict that would have serious implications for ethical theory.

I propose to understand the distinction between prima facie and all-things-considered obligations in the way that I think W. D. Ross understood his distinction between prima facie and *sans phrase* obligations.[3] A prima facie obligation to do x means that there is a moral reason to do x or that x possesses a right-making characteristic. But prima facie obligations can be, and often are, defeated by other, weightier obligations, individually or in concert. A prima facie obligation to do x that is superior to all others constitutes an all-things-considered obligation to do x. An all-things-considered moral obligation to do x means that on balance, or in view of all morally relevant factors, x is what one ought to do or that x is supported by the strongest moral reasons.

If prima facie obligations correspond to the presence of morally relevant factors or right-making characteristics, and an all-things-considered obligation is an undefeated prima facie obligation, then a natural way to understand a prima facie obligation to do x is as the claim that, ceteris paribus, x is all-things-considered obligatory. The fact that x is prima facie obligatory results from x's possessing some morally relevant factor F and can be derived from the fact that x is F, together with the generalization that F-ness makes actions prima facie obligatory. This generalization should itself be understood as the claim that, ceteris paribus, F-ness makes actions all-things-considered obligatory. All else will be equal only if the moral factor F is *undefeated*. F will be undefeated if

1. there are no competing moral factors,
2. there are competing factors that cancel each other out, or
3. competing factors not canceled out do not override F's support for x.[4]

On this account, we treat prima facie obligations as moral factors or forces that interact so as to determine all-things-considered obligations. To determine all-things-considered obligations we must do *moral factor addition*. It is not essential to the factor addition model that we always be able to assign precise numerical values to the various moral forces present in a situation. What is important is that the moral status of an act *sans phrase* results from adding the moral forces, positive and negative, contributed by the various morally relevant factors; the act with the highest moral total is all-things-considered obligatory.[5] This, I believe, is a fairly traditional account of prima facie and all-things-considered obligations that would have appealed to Ross.

Some writers think that prima facie obligations are not genuine obligations and that all genuine obligations are all-things-considered obligations.[6] This tendency may be reinforced by the fact that the standard principles of deontic logic using the operator for obligation—'O'—signify an all-things-considered obligation. This claim is harmless if it simply expresses our intention to call only all-things-considered moral requirements "duties" or "obligations" and to treat 'prima facie obligation' as a technical term. But I think that more than this is usually intended by those who deny that prima facie obligations are genuine obligations, and their denial rests on a misunderstanding of prima facie obligations that it is important to avoid.

These writers sometimes say that prima facie obligations are merely *apparent* obligations such that they have no moral force if overridden.[7] But this does not fit our understanding of prima facie obligations, or Ross's. As Ross points out, we should not understand prima facie obligations as the *epistemic* claim that certain things appear to be obligatory that may not prove to be.[8] This reading does not imply that there is any moral reason supporting x corresponding to the prima facie obligation to do x. Rather, prima facie obligations should be given a *metaphysical* reading that recognizes prima facie obligations as moral forces that are not canceled by the existence of other moral forces even if the latter override or defeat the former.[9]

Now Ross does say that prima facie duties are conditional duties and not duties proper.[10] This, I believe, reflects only his decision to reserve the terms 'duty' and 'obligation' for all-things-considered moral claims. If we concede this to him, then we can explain most of his claims about prima facie obligations on our model. Prima facie obligations are *conditional* (all-things-considered) duties in the sense that if all else is equal, then there is not only a prima facie obligation to do x but also a genuine or all-things-considered obligation.

Sometimes Ross says that prima facie obligations refer to features of an act that *tend* to make acts of that type (all-things-considered) obligatory.[11] This claim admits of a *purely statistical* reading: although there may be nothing about this token act that makes it obligatory, it belongs to a type or class of acts many of whose tokens are (all-things-considered) obligatory.[12] But we can and should avoid this purely statistical reading of Ross's tendency claims.

Suppose that we have a prima facie obligation to do anything that is F and that we analyze this as the generalization that, ceteris paribus, F-ness makes actions all-things-considered obligatory. Suppose also that all else is usually, but not always, equal. If so, the statistical claim is true. But it says nothing about F's contribution to the rightness of right acts that are F or about F's role in situations in which other things are not equal. But F does have a role and exerts a moral force in every situation in which it is present. In this way, the metaphysical reading of prima facie obligations explains why the statistical claim is true when it is true and implies reasonable claims that the statistical claim does not; so the statistical claim cannot exhaust our account of prima facie obligations.

Consider this parallel. We might analyze the claim that Bonny is a valuable player as the claim that she tends to help her team win games. But this should not be analyzed as the purely statistical claim that when she plays her team usually wins. This does not convey the idea that she helps *produce* their victories or the idea that she is a positive force even in the games they lose. We must understand her role as a positive factor when she's on the field, whether the outcome is a win or a loss. This is how we must analyze the tendency for her to win games if this claim is to be an analysis of her being a valuable player.

If so, we must reject the purely statistical reading. Indeed, Ross himself explains the tendency claims with an analogy between the way in which the interaction of prima facie obligations determines all-things-considered right conduct and the way in which vector addition determines the trajectories of physical objects in motion.[13] This is precisely the "moral forces" interpretation of prima facie obligations.[14]

II. Soluble and Insoluble Conflicts and Regret

What does this account of prima facie and all-things-considered obligations have to do with moral dilemmas? If moral dilemmas are to be paradoxical things, then it's arguable that the competing moral claims involved must be equipollent—neither claim should be stronger than the other. This is not just the epistemic point that the competing moral claims seem equally compelling; this would give us only an epistemic dilemma. Rather, genuine moral dilemmas must involve metaphysical equipollence; neither claim can be weightier than the other. If so, moral dilemmas must involve *insoluble* conflicts of prima facie obligations. For there seems nothing very puzzling about the existence of conflicting prima facie obligations, one of which is stronger than the other.

However, not everyone thinks that moral dilemmas require insoluble conflicts. Consider a *soluble* conflict. There are moral reasons to do A and there are moral reasons to do B, but one cannot do both A and B. Moreover, we assume, though the reasons supporting A and those supporting B are both strong, there is in fact more reason to do A. Furthermore, to simplify, let's assume that the agent in question recognizes the greater stringency of A. Our traditional model implies that soluble moral conflicts have a perfectly straightforward analysis. What we have is one prima facie obligation being overridden or defeated by another; this weightier prima facie obligation is the agent's all-things-considered obligation. But some friends of dilemmas think that there is a genuine dilemma even in such a case, provided that the less weighty moral claim grounds compunction or regret on the agent's part when she fails to act on it in order to fulfill her weightier obligation. They take the appropriateness of attitudes such as regret or compunction toward B to show that the moral reasons supporting B do not disappear just because the reasons for B are defeated by the reasons for A.[15] And this must be incompatible with the traditional account, for such an account, as Williams claims, must "eliminate from the scene the *ought* that is not acted upon" and so remove the ground of any compunction or regret.[16]

Let us assume, for the sake of argument, that a kind of regret toward the fact of an unperformed obligation is appropriate.[17] The friends of dilemmas might have a reasonable argument against the traditional analysis of soluble conflicts if the traditional account relied on an epistemic or purely statistical reading of prima facie obligations. For then the weaker prima facie claim would or need be no real moral factor at all; indeed, on the epistemic reading, moral factors operate only when they win.[18] If the reasons supporting B do not operate when B is overridden by A, then regret or compunction could apparently be appropriate only for *instrumental* reasons. If the agent did not feel compunction about her failure to perform B (when this caused someone's suffering), perhaps she would become more callous and fail to do B-type acts even when they are (all-things-considered) obligatory.[19] This instrumental account of the appropriateness of compunction or regret may not seem to ring true.

But if we accept the metaphysical reading of prima facie obligations and view the function from prima facie obligations into all-things-considered obligation as moral factor addition, then we can explain regret for failing to perform defeated prima facie obligations. If prima facie obligations are moral forces that are at work even when they are overridden by competing forces, then the fact that an agent does not act on her prima facie obligation to do B explains the appropriateness of regret or compunction. Insofar as B is prima facie obligatory, it should be performed; if I do not perform it, whether A overrides B or not, then I am not responding to moral forces present in the situation. And this might be thought to be a cause for genuine regret and compunction. Perhaps a morally decent person should have moral attitudes, such as compunction or regret, that track moral forces or factors. If so, I can acknowledge that regret or compunction is appropriate toward my failure to do B while admitting that it is A that is all-things-considered obligatory. These reactions are sufficiently accounted for, on our metaphysical reading, by the assumption that I had a prima facie obligation to do B.[20]

III. A Recipe for Moral Dilemmas

For these reasons, we should deny that soluble conflicts are genuine moral dilemmas. Moral dilemmas must be insoluble, involving claims that are (metaphysically) equipollent. However, we need require only *broad equipollence*. It is not necessary that the competing claims represent the same denomination in a single moral currency. Between some currencies there may be no uniform exchange rate, with the result that we must recognize pockets of incommensurability. If two moral claims are incommensurably stringent, I assume that neither is greater or more stringent than the other. If so, the two claims are broadly equipollent.

If a genuine dilemma cannot be a mere conflict of prima facie obligations but must involve competing claims that are broadly equipollent, we might construe moral dilemmas as competing all-things-considered obligations. If so, the recipe for moral dilemmas appears to be something like this.

1. One has a prima facie obligation to do A.
2. One has a prima facie obligation to do B.
3. One is under an all-things-considered obligation to do x just in case one is under a prima facie obligation to do x, and there is no greater, simple or complex, competing prima facie obligation one is under.
4. One's prima facie obligation to do A is no greater than one's prima facie obligation to do B, and vice versa.
5. One is under no other prima facie obligation, simple or complex, that competes with A or B and that is as great an obligation.
6. Hence one has an all-things-considered obligation to do A. [1, 3–5]
7. Hence one has an all-things-considered obligation to do B. [2–5]
8. It is possible for one to do A.
9. It is possible for one to do B.
10. It is not possible for one to do A and B.

I trust that the recipe itself is reasonably clear. For now I just want to comment on the steps in the recipe that are less familiar and say enough to make them initially plausible. The less familiar steps are (3)–(5). Step (3) simply states the apparently traditional idea that an all-things-considered obligation is an undefeated prima facie obligation. Steps (4)–(5) describe the conditions that must be met if a prima facie obligation is to be undefeated.

Step (4) may seem to be the crucial step in the recipe. Once we distinguish the epistemic question of knowing or having justified belief that a prima facie obligation is defeated and the metaphysical question of its being defeated, we may wonder whether there are conflicting undefeated prima facie obligations. We may admit that it is often hard to decide which obligation is weightier but insist that the epistemic difficulty in settling conflicts is no evidence that they're insoluble.

Our belief in the frequency of insoluble conflicts is likely to depend upon what we make of the possibility of pockets of incommensurability involving moral claims of different kinds (for example, fidelity and nonmaleficence). Incommensurability presumably will exist only if there are different scales or dimensions of assessment. Let us say that there is *strong incommensurability* between types of acts x and y just in case no token of type x is comparable with any token of type y; and let us say that there is *weak incommensurability* between types of acts x and y just in case some tokens of type x are not comparable with some tokens of type y, but some are. Strong incommensurability is obviously more radical than weak incommensurability; weak incommensurability allows for substantial, though partial, comparability.[21] Even if we have different dimensions of assessment, strong incommensurability seems implausibly extreme.[22] However, weak incommensurability strikes me as fairly plausible. But while I'm sympathetic to the suggestion that pockets of incommensurability of this sort exist, I don't know how to argue for this claim and won't try.

A more secure route for the friend of dilemmas to take is to embrace the theoretical possibility of ties. The idea, as Ruth Marcus notes, would be to describe cases of symmetrically structured conflicting claims. We might imagine a parent who is equidistant between identical twins who are trapped in a burning building and can save one but not both. Make the case maximally symmetrical. The parent's duties conflict and their stringency is the same. Perhaps the choice that the Nazis force Sophie to make about which of her children to sacrifice involves such a conflict.[23] Narrow equipollence is not required, but it's more secure, because its theoretical possibility is harder to dispute.[24]

IV. Paradoxical Implications of Genuine Dilemmas

If we follow the recipe, then we have a conflict of all-things-considered obligations. We can then attach an obligation operator to both A and B. The reason for thinking that this is the structure of a genuine moral dilemma is that when we conjoin such a conflict with other initially plausible claims we get some very troublesome results. In fact, the existence of genuine moral dilemmas and the truth of these auxiliary claims generate contradictions.

In explaining these paradoxes, it will help to represent them symbolically. I adopt the following conventions. 'O(A)' means that one ought all-things-considered to do A or that A is all-things-considered obligatory. Indeed, unless otherwise indicated, I shall understand 'obligation' to refer to all-things-considered obligation. Where I have occasion to represent prima facie obligations symbolically I shall use the lower case 'o'; 'o(A)' means that one ought prima facie to do A or that A is prima facie obligatory. 'P(A)' means that A is permissible. '$\blacklozenge$(A)' means that A is in the relevant sense possible or within the agent's power—roughly, physically or psychologically possible.[25] For instance, in the example described above, it is not possible in the relevant sense, given familiar temporal and physical constraints, for the parent to save both of her twins from the burning building. Deontic principles or axioms (axiom schemata) are formulated using Greek letters (for example, 'α' and 'β'). These principles do figure as axioms or theorems in various systems of deontic logic. However, I am concerned only with whether they are intuitively compelling claims about the systematic relations among familiar moral and nonmoral properties (for example, the relations between permissibility and obligatoriness). If a principle is intuitively compelling, this is presumably (defeasible) reason to think that it should figure as an axiom or theorem in any reasonable system of deontic logic.

Paradox 1

One paradox has been widely recognized. It results from combining moral dilemmas with two standard deontic principles: a distribution principle, often known as *agglomeration,* and the principle that "ought" implies "can," which I'll dub the *voluntarist* principle. Agglomeration says that if one ought to do α and one ought to do β then one ought to do both.

$$(O(\alpha) \ \& \ O(\beta)) \longrightarrow O(\alpha \ \& \ \beta)$$

The voluntarist principle says that it is a necessary condition of one's being under an obligation to do α that α be possible or be within one's power.[26]

$$O(\alpha) \longrightarrow \blacklozenge (\alpha)$$

By combining agglomeration and voluntarism we get the following paradox.

1. $O(A)$
2. $O(B)$
3. $\neg \blacklozenge (A \ \& \ B)$
4. $(O(A) \ \& \ O(B)) \longrightarrow O(A \ \& \ B)$ [agglomeration]
5. Hence $O(A \ \& \ B)$ [1, 2, 4]
6. $O(A \ \& \ B) \longrightarrow \blacklozenge (A \ \& \ B)$ [voluntarism]
7. Hence $\blacklozenge (A\&B)$ [5, 6]
8. Hence $\blacklozenge (A\&B) \ \& \ \neg \blacklozenge (A \ \& \ B)$ [3, 7]

How impressive are the credentials of the auxiliary principles used to derive this paradox? A full discussion is not possible here; and, because the other paradoxes are more robust, a full discussion is not necessary. It is enough to explore some central worries and resources.

Consider agglomeration. Where there is no conflict between A and B, it seems harmless to recognize an obligation to do both as well as obligations to do each. But it also seems unnecessary; an obligation to do each seems adequate to explain the moral situation.

However, perhaps I rely on agglomeration in *avoiding* dilemmas. Assuming that I want to fulfill my obligations, I want to avoid doing things that will prevent me from doing so. If I believe that I ought to do A and that I ought to do B, not only will I try to avoid doing things that will prevent me from doing one or the other, I will try to avoid doing things that prevent me from doing both. Does this presuppose that I have an obligation to do both as well as obligations to do each? I don't think so. All it requires is that I have two obligations and a desire to satisfy each; it does not require a conjunctive obligation.

Now, I can think of one argument for compound obligations. Consider a case where the agent has an obligation to do A and an obligation to do B and *is* able to do both A and B. In such a case it seems reasonable to hold that it is impermissible for him to fail to do both.

$$\neg P(\neg(A \ \& \ B))$$

But it also seems reasonable to accept a *correlativity* principle according to which α is obligatory just in case it is impermissible not to do α.

$$\neg P(\neg \alpha) \equiv O(\alpha)$$

But these two claims imply that he has a compound obligation.

1. $\neg P(\neg(A \ \& \ B))$
2. $\neg P(\neg(A \ \& \ B)) \equiv O(A \ \& \ B)$ [correlativity]
3. Hence $O(A \ \& \ B)$

This argument establishes that there are conjunctive obligations where each conjunct is obligatory *and* both obligations can be performed. However, it does not establish, as agglomeration claims, that conjunctive obligations follow from the obligatoriness of each of the two conjuncts. Moreover, this particular route to conjunctive obligations won't work in the case of moral dilemmas. For, as I shall argue in Section V, in a genuine dilemma, in which one cannot do both A and B, what is impermissible is to perform neither; it is not impermissible to fail to perform both, provided one performs one of them.

$$\neg\neg P(\neg(A \ \& \ B))$$

If so, the correlativity principle does not allow us to generate a conjunctive obligation in dilemmatic situations.

Indeed, we might think that it is the correlativity principle that explains why there is a conjunctive obligation when there is one. If so, the existence of conjunctive obligations in nondilemmatic situations provides no support whatsoever for agglomeration or its claim that there are conjunctive obligations in dilemmas.

Nor does there seem to be any reason to assume the existence of conjunctive obligations in dilemmatic situations, as agglomeration would require. Why should we assume that there's an obligation to do both? Why not say, instead, that there is an obligation to do A, an obligation to do B, *and* an obligation to do A or B, but *not* an obligation to do both?

What about voluntarism? It seems more intuitively compelling. It may seem too harsh to require of people actions that they cannot perform; the voluntarist insists that it be up to us whether to be moral. Nonetheless some people claim that there are counterexamples to the voluntarist principle; they claim that there are impossible obligations. We will have more confidence in discarding the voluntarist principle if there are counterexamples in nondilemmatic situations.

Some of the counterexamples involve obligations that one is no longer in a position to fulfill. For example, it has been claimed that a debtor who is no longer able to pay his debt, whether through his own fault or not, is still under the obligation to repay his debt.[27]

But it seems that we can admit that the debtor remains under obligations to those whom he owes without assuming that he has an obligation to perform the repayment that he is incapable of performing. If the debtor is himself at fault for becoming unable to pay the debt at the appointed time, then when he fails to pay the debt he can be blamed, not for failing to pay the debt, but for allowing himself to become unable to pay the debt. Moreover, whether his inability to pay is his own fault or not, we can claim that, ceteris paribus, he has an obligation to pay back as much as he can until the original debt is paid, perhaps with interest or compensatory damages. These claims seem not to require positing impossible obligations.

However, it might be claimed that duties of restitution or compensation make sense only as a consequence of breaching an obligation. If so, a duty to compensate seems to imply that the debtor was obligated to do something he was unable to do. But this analysis is not mandatory. Some obligations get met; others lapse or end without being discharged. And obligations can end or lapse for a variety of different reasons. Some of the reasons an obligation lapses may bring no new obligations in its wake, as when a creditor chooses to release the debtor from his obligation. But other reasons for the lapse of an obligation may bring new obligations in its wake. If a debtor is unable to pay as agreed, then his old obligation lapses and, ceteris paribus, is succeeded by new obligations to repay according to a new schedule and to compensate for damages. The voluntarist can appeal to this view about the *succession* of obligations to recognize duties of compensation without recognizing impossible obligations. If so, it's not clear that we yet have a counterexample to the voluntarist principle.

Another possible challenge to voluntarism involves moral emotions. People often say that someone ought to have some moral feeling or attitude (for example, gratitude) in a particular situation even if the person does not have the attitude and seems incapable in the circumstances of producing it. Whereas emotional sensibilities may be intentionally cultivated or repressed, it seems they are not under our direct voluntary control in the required sense. If we have not cultivated or otherwise acquired the relevant background sensibilities, it may not always be within our power to experience the appropriate attitudes in the appropriate contexts. Yet it may nonetheless seem true to say that we ought to have these attitudes.

But we may question the counterexample without disputing the psychological assumptions upon which it relies. For one thing, it's not clear that this is a case of an impossible obligation. Although it may seem natural to say that the person in question ought to have these feelings, we need not be ascribing an obligation to him. We often say that something ought to be the case without ascribing obligations to anyone; here we usually mean that it would be a good thing if what ought to happen did, or perhaps that it would have been a good thing if what ought to have happened had. No one thinks that voluntarism must apply to these axiological uses of 'ought'. Moreover, we may think that the person in question has or had certain obligations, even if he does not have an impossible obligation. For if he does not have sensibilities that allow him to have the appropriate feelings in this situation, he may well be blameworthy for having violated an obligation, which was in his power to perform, to cultivate the relevant sensibilities and he may now have an obligation (to do what he can) to cultivate the relevant sensibilities. So, it's not clear that there really is any obligation in such cases that the voluntarist cannot recognize.

I haven't shown voluntarism to be immune to counterexample (and there are the usual problems about proving negative existential generalizations). But my analysis of these counterexamples suggests voluntarist strategies for dealing with other alleged counterexamples. To say that someone ought to have done something she was unable to do may reflect an axiological, rather than a deontic, judgment; if so, we can accept the judgment without recognizing impossible obligations. Moreover, we may recognize that the agent in such a situation has or had obligations without recognizing impossible obligations. There may have been an obligation the agent violated in getting into the predicament, and there may be obligations to mitigate damages and provide restitution. We need to test the adequacy of these strategies on a case-by-case basis.

Paradox 2

The second paradox also relies on two deontic principles. The first says that if you're (all-things-considered) obligated to do α, and β would prevent α or bring about not-α, then you're obligated not to do β.

$$(O(\alpha) \ \& \ (\beta \longrightarrow \neg\alpha)) \longrightarrow O(\neg\beta)$$

We might call this the *obligation execution* principle, because it obligates us not to do anything that would interfere with the execution of our (original) obligations.

The second principle simply claims that if it is obligatory to do not-β, then it is not obligatory to do β.

$$O(\neg\beta) \longrightarrow \neg O(\beta)$$

This statement of the consequences of an obligation is weaker than a third principle we are likely to find attractive.

$$O(\neg\beta) \equiv \neg P(\beta)$$

The third principle asserts a kind of *correlativity* of obligatoriness and impermissibility that is equivalent to the correlativity principle we've already discussed.

$$\neg P(\neg\alpha) \equiv O\ (\alpha)^{28}$$

This version of correlativity says that if not-β is obligatory, then β is impermissible, and vice versa. Because the second principle is weaker than this correlativity principle (and for lack of a better name), I shall call it the *weak obligation* principle. The weak obligation and obligation execution principles help constitute a second paradox of moral dilemmas.

1. O(A)
2. O(B)
3. $\neg \blacklozenge$(A & B)
4. Hence B $\longrightarrow$ $\neg$A   [3]
5. (O(A) & (B$\longrightarrow$ $\neg$A)) $\longrightarrow$ O($\neg$B)   [obligation execution]
6. Hence O($\neg$B)   [1, 4, 5]
7. O($\neg$B) $\longrightarrow$ $\neg$O(B)   [weak obligation]
8. Hence $\neg$O(B)   [6, 7]
9. Hence O(B) & $\neg$O(B)   [2, 8]

Now, the basis of the second paradox seems much more secure than that of the first paradox.

The obligation execution principle surely plays an important, although perhaps tacit, role in our moral deliberations. Consider some examples. I recognize an obligation not to kill innocent people; I know or learn that putting a certain substance (in an unlabelled spice bottle) in Oscar's food would bring about his death; so I conclude that I ought not to put the substance in his food. Or, I recognize an obligation to be with my son on his birthday; I receive an invitation to participate in a conference on that day; so I conclude that I ought to refuse this invitation. Or, I recognize an obligation to meet you at the time and place we agreed upon; I realize that the only way for me to do so is to catch the noon train; so I conclude that I ought to catch the noon train. These common inferences seem reasonable, because obligatoriness seems to be transmitted from the action that is the focus of the original obligation to those actions that are required, as means or necessary conditions, for the performance of the original obligation.[29] It's hard to imagine how we would find our way around in the world morally if we did not accept this principle.

And the weak obligation principle, as its name suggests, seems especially uncontroversial. If I'm obligated not to kill my neighbor, then surely it's not the case that I'm obligated to kill him. Indeed, as the stronger, correlativity principle asserts, if I'm obligated not to kill my neighbor, then it's impermissible for me to kill him. But our second principle is even weaker than this plausible third principle; so surely it must be acceptable.

Paradox 3

A third paradox results from combining the obligation execution and correlativity principles with a principle that claims that if β is impermissible then it is not the case that β is obligatory.

$$\neg P(\beta) \longrightarrow \neg O(\beta)$$

Because this is a very weak principle about the consequences of impermissibility, I will call it the *weak impermissibility* principle. These three principles and the assumption of moral dilemmas create the following paradox.

1. O(A)
2. O(B)
3. $\neg\blacklozenge$ (A & B)
4. Hence B $\longrightarrow$ $\neg$A   [3]
5. (O(A) & (B $\longrightarrow$ $\neg$A)) $\longrightarrow$ O($\neg$B)   [obligation execution]
6. Hence O($\neg$B)   [1, 4, 5]
7. O($\neg$B) $\equiv$ $\neg$P(B)   [correlativity]
8. Hence $\neg$P(B)   [6, 7]
9. $\neg$P(B) $\longrightarrow$ $\neg$O(B)   [weak impermissibility]
10. Hence $\neg$O(B)   [8, 9]
11. Hence O(B) & $\neg$O(B)   [2, 10]

We might also notice that the obligation execution and correlativity principles allow us to generalize the argument for (8) to the claim that in a dilemma, whatever the agent does, she does something impermissible. For these two principles imply that any action that leads to the nonperformance of an obligation is impermissible, and the impossibility of doing A and B ensures that whatever the agent does she will fail to perform an obligation. It follows that whatever she does, she does something impermissible. We might consider this result overly harsh; it is incompatible with the general voluntarist idea that it ought to be within our power to live up to our obligations and to avoid impermissible actions. In this sense, some may regard this result as a distinct paradox of dilemmas. However, this conclusion does not itself involve a contradiction and so is not paradoxical in the strong sense that the other results are.

Nonetheless, (11) is a contradiction. As with the second paradox, the auxiliary deontic principles in the third paradox seem especially compelling. We've already seen the plausibility of the obligation execution and correlativity theses. The new deontic principle is the weak impermissibility principle. But surely that must be true. If it's impermissible for me to torture my neighbor, then surely it's not the case that I'm obligated to torture him.

V. Reconsidering the Existence of Moral Dilemmas

Because the paradoxes are generated from the supposition that there are moral dilemmas, understood as conflicts of all-things-considered obligations, and various deontic principles, we must reject some of the deontic principles or the supposition that there are moral dilemmas. Which reaction is correct depends on the independent plausibility of the principles and the case for dilemmas. We must determine which reaction is least costly. The principles underlying the first paradox—agglomeration and voluntarism—strike me as somewhat uncertain. Rejecting one or both of them—especially agglomeration—may be a cost that we could bear. However, the second and third paradoxes rest on more secure deontic foundations. Obligation execution, weak obligation, correlativity, and weak impermissibility all seem to be fundamental or uncontroversial principles in our moral reasoning. If so, the second and third paradoxes make the costs of maintaining the existence of moral dilemmas greater than has generally been recognized.

We could simply restrict the scope of such principles to nondilemmatic situations in order to avoid paradox. But that would be ad hoc. We need a principled and independent account of why their scope should be limited in just this way. Moreover, if we restrict the scope of these deontic principles to nondilemmatic situations, then different principles will apply to obligations in dilemmatic and nondilemmatic contexts. But if the sense of deontic terms (such as 'obligation') is determined jointly by the various deontic principles in which the terms figure, then this response to the paradoxes appears to have the unwelcome consequence of requiring us to say that the term 'obligation' has different meanings in the two contexts. If so, it is better to reject such principles than to restrict their scope. But then we must find alternative mechanisms (of unrestricted scope) for generating their results in nondilemmatic situations. However, I see no such mechanisms to serve as alternatives to the principles underlying the second and third paradoxes.[30] If I am right, friends of dilemmas reject such principles at a high price.

These paradoxes suggest that we should examine the case for moral dilemmas more closely. Earlier, I presented a prima facie case for thinking that moral dilemmas are theoretically possible. And they need be only theoretically possible—people need never face a genuine dilemma—in order for ethical theory to contain paradox. Though I agreed that we should be skeptical about the frequency of conflicting undefeated prima facie obligations, I argued that we must allow for their possibility. They are possible either because of weak incommensurability between prima facie obligations or because of equal stringency of prima facie obligations, such as cases of symmetrically structured, conflicting obligations. As long as we accept the idea that an undefeated prima facie obligation yields an all-things-considered obligation, we must admit that moral dilemmas are possible.

It is this idea that we can and should reject. Ordinarily, an undefeated prima facie obligation does constitute an all-things-considered obligation. But not always. Where there is an undefeated competitor, we can conclude that neither obligation is an all-things-considered obligation. This may seem to leave the agent confronting an insoluble conflict with no all-things-considered obligations, and this may seem puzzling to some. But the agent does face an all-things-considered obligation; it is to perform one or the other of the conflicting prima facie obligations. We can see this better if we allow 'O' to stand for all-things-considered obligation (as usual) and 'o' to stand for prima facie obligation. In an insoluble conflict of undefeated prima facie obligations, the following claims seem true.

o(A)
o(B)
$\neg$(o(A) > o(B))
$\neg$(o(B) > o(A))
O(A v B)
$\neg$O(A)
$\neg$O(B)

If so, the only all-things-considered obligation in an insoluble conflict is this disjunctive obligation.[31] And the disjunctive all-things-considered obligation feels right. By correlativity, if the agent performs neither disjunct, she has done something impermissible. But she may perform either of the disjuncts in order to fulfill her all-things-considered obligation. Whichever disjunct she performs, she will leave a strong (indeed, undefeated) prima facie obligation unperformed, and this may be cause for a kind of regret or compunction for the moral force to which she does not respond. But as long as she performs one of the disjuncts, she will have done nothing impermissible.

This disjunctive analysis seems fairly natural as applied to narrowly equipollent moral conflicts; in the case of a tie, it seems permissible to perform either alternative. But the analysis can and should be extended to moral conflicts whose insolubility is due to incommensurability. For what makes the disjunctive analysis appropriate is just that when all the moral considerations about the alternatives have been exhausted neither moral claim is weightier than the other. And this is true for any insoluble conflict, whether the insolubility represents a tie or incommensurability.

If, as I believe, the disjunctive analysis of insoluble conflicts is perfectly adequate, then we should deny the possibility of moral dilemmas.[32] In particular, we should reject step (3) in the recipe for moral dilemmas and its claim that an all-things-considered obligation is simply an undefeated prima facie obligation. An all-things-considered obligation represents what one ought to do in light of *all* morally relevant factors, including alternatives. If so, then only prima facie obligations that are undefeated *and* defeat all competitors are all-things-considered obligations. In other words, to be an all-things-considered obligation, a prima facie obligation must be *overriding* and not simply not overridden. But there cannot be two incompatible obligations of this sort; it cannot be true that A overrides B and that B overrides A.

Recognition that insoluble conflicts generate only a disjunctive obligation itself provides a kind of solution to these conflicts. There is no all-things-considered obligation to do A or B, rather than the other. But there is an all-things-considered obligation to do one or the other rather than some third thing. In particular, there is an obligation to do one or the other rather than nothing. To fulfill this disjunctive obligation one must choose one or the other, though by hypothesis the choice cannot be guided by moral considerations about A or B. Instead, one's choice should be determined by the greater salience of one disjunct or by some (other) randomizing device. In this way, our analysis does not itself make the choice. But it does tell us that we have an unequivocal duty to do either A or B and that, as far as our duty goes, it doesn't matter which we do. This is itself a kind of guidance.

This parallels what I take to be the right response to another sort of insoluble conflict—the case of Buridan's Ass. Neither bale of hay is more desirable than the other, and so there is no reason for the ass to prefer one bale rather than the other. Nonetheless, there is a very strong reason for the ass to choose one of the bales, it doesn't matter which, rather than starve in indecision. The rational ass, therefore, should quit looking for reasons for choosing one, grounded in the desirability of the bales, and choose the more salient bale or employ a randomizing device to select one. Only in this way will he do what is rationally required of him, namely, to eat from one or the other bale. We give the ass a kind of guidance when we tell him it doesn't matter which bale he chooses so long as he chooses one.

However, this disjunctive solution to insoluble moral conflicts may seem to trivialize them. It is commonly thought that such conflicts present no-win situations, whereas the disjunctive solution may seem to treat such conflicts as no-lose situations. More generally, the disjunctive solution may seem to take the conflict out of moral conflict.

Now it is true that the disjunctive solution implies that in an insoluble conflict an agent does nothing impermissible as long as she performs either A or B, it doesn't matter which.[33] But, whatever she does, she will fail to perform a strong—indeed, undefeated—prima facie obligation, and this can be an appropriate object of compunction or regret. So the disjunctive solution allows that whatever the agent does, it may be appropriate for her to experience compunction or regret. In this way, the disjunctive solution can represent insoluble conflicts as no-win situations. Moreover, the disjunctive solution does not imply that it's easy to recognize genuinely insoluble conflicts. Indeed, if the broad equipollence of competing moral claims is rare enough and hard enough to identify reliably, it may never be reasonable for an agent to conclude that she is in an insoluble conflict to which the disjunctive solution applies (even if she is in one).[34] So the disjunctive solution preserves robust epistemic conflict for the agent in an insoluble conflict. If we bear these forms of residue in mind, I see no reason to find the disjunctive solution implausibly sanitary.

VI. Moral Conflict and Metaethics

Williams believes that moral dilemmas have metaethical implications as well as implications for deontic logic.

> It seems to me a fundamental criticism of many ethical theories that their accounts of moral conflict and its resolution do not do justice to the facts of regret and related considerations: basically because they eliminate from the scene the *ought* not acted upon. A structure appropriate to conflicts of beliefs is projected onto the moral case; one by which the conflict is basically adven-

titious, and a resolution of it disembarrasses one of a mistaken view which for a while confused the situation. Such an approach must be inherent in purely cognitive accounts of the matter, since it is just a question of which of the conflicting *ought* statements is true, and they cannot both be true, to decide correctly for one of them must be to be rid of error with respect to the other.[35]

Moral conflicts, he concludes, "are more like conflicts of desires than they are like conflicts of beliefs."[36]

Insofar as Williams's claim is simply that a cognitivist construal of conflicts of obligation cannot accommodate the phenomena of regret or compunction, his argument has already been addressed in section II. As long as we treat prima facie obligations as genuine moral factors or forces in the situations to which they apply, we can treat soluble conflicts as cases in which one prima facie obligation overrides another, and insoluble conflicts as cases of conflicting undefeated prima facie obligations. In either case, we can explain such regret as is appropriate for the prima facie obligation not acted upon.

But Williams also seems to be offering a somewhat different argument against cognitivism. He wants to compare conflicts of beliefs and conflicts of desire or attitude and argue that moral conflicts have properties more like those of conflicts of attitude than those of conflicts of belief. His argument seems to have the following form.

1. It is unreasonable to hold conflicting (contradictory) beliefs.
2. It can be reasonable to hold conflicting noncognitive attitudes toward the same thing.
3. In moral conflicts, it is reasonable for the agent to make conflicting judgments about her obligations.
4. Hence judgments and ascriptions of obligation in cases of moral conflict express attitudes, rather than beliefs.
5. There should be a uniform semantic treatment of judgments and ascriptions of obligation.
6. Hence judgments and ascriptions of obligation express attitudes, rather than beliefs.

Williams thinks that (2) is obvious, but I'm skeptical. It can be reasonable to hold different attitudes toward different aspects of the same situation. But it's less clear that it can be reasonable to hold different attitudes toward one and the same aspect of one and the same situation. There's no problem taking conflicting attitudes (for example, attraction and repulsion) toward an object if we take one attitude toward it *qua* F and take the other attitude toward it *qua* G. For then our attitudes take different objects—they are directed at *different aspects* of one and the same object—although at a superficial, coarse-grained level of description they both take x as their object. Thus, I can be both pleased and dismayed by my toddler's new resistance to being dressed: I am pleased insofar as this means that he is developing a sense of his own independence (*qua* F) but dismayed insofar as dressing him is now less pleasant and more time-consuming for both of us (*qua* G). Indeed, it is these different properties of the same event or object that *ground* the appropriateness of my conflicting reactions, presumably because our attitudes toward things are based on their properties. If so, this is not an example of having conflicting attitudes toward one and the same thing.

It's much less clear that it can be reasonable to hold conflicting attitudes toward x *qua* F—where this can't be explained away as having different attitudes toward different constituent properties of the complex property F. If it is aspects of a situation that ground or make appropriate certain attitudes toward it, then there is no reason to expect that it could be reasonable to hold conflicting attitudes toward one and the same aspect of a situation[37]—at least, not unless we've *already* been convinced of a noncognitivist thesis to the effect that one and the same natural property of a situation can make different responses appropriate.

What about (3)? Is it reasonable for the agent to make conflicting judgments about her obligations? If (3) is to support the noncognitivist conclusion, the conflicting judgments must endorse contradictory propositions about her obligations.

If my analysis is correct, it cannot be reasonable to accept contradictory propositions about the agent's all-things-considered obligations. There are no conflicting all-things-considered obligations. In soluble conflicts, there is only one all-things-considered obligation, and that is to perform the weightier prima facie obligation. In insoluble conflicts, the only all-things-considered obligation is the disjunctive obligation.

However, there can be conflicting prima facie obligations (in both soluble and insoluble conflicts). Do these conflicts yield contradictory propositions about the agent's prima facie obligations? A and B are each prima facie obligatory. Presumably we can accept an analogue of obligation execution for prima facie obligation.

$$(o(\alpha) \mathbin{\&} (\beta \longrightarrow \neg\alpha)) \longrightarrow o(\neg\beta)$$

Because A and B are incompatible, my prima facie obligation to do either (for example, A) generates a prima facie obligation not to do the other (for example, B). This allows one to argue as follows.

1. o(A)
2. o(B)
3. $\neg\blacklozenge$ (A & B)
4. Hence B $\longrightarrow \neg$A   [3]
5. (o(A) & (B $\longrightarrow \neg$A)) $\longrightarrow$ o($\neg$B)   ["obligation execution"]
6. Hence o($\neg$B)   [1, 4, 5]
7. Hence o(B) & o($\neg$B)   [2, 6]

But, of course, this conclusion falls short of the required contradiction

$$o(B) \mathbin{\&} \neg o(B).$$

Nor do I see how Williams can get the negation outside of the scope of the prima facie obligation operator. My having reason not to perform an act does not prevent there being reason to perform it. Indeed, more generally, analogues of weak obligation, correlativity, and weak impermissibility all fail when applied to prima facie, rather than all-things-considered, obligation. So premise (3) of Williams's argument is false.

This should be clear from our account of prima facie obligations. Recall that prima facie obligations represent the operation of moral forces or factors and that we can represent these moral forces as moral laws or generalizations. These generalizations imply that an action is obligatory *insofar* as it possesses a morally relevant property. In moral conflicts, one and the same action has more than one morally relevant property. Action A is obligatory insofar as performing it responds to one moral force, while it is not obligatory insofar as performing it fails to respond to another moral force. There is no contradiction here, because the logical form of our predications is

$$A \text{ is O insofar as it is F}$$

and

$$A \text{ is not-O insofar as it is G.}$$

Williams's problem is that he sees contradictory attitudes and obligations where there are none, and this is because he fails to see that the attitudes and obligations in question attach in virtue of different aspects of the same situation. Because of this fact, we can see that there is no contradiction. So we should reject this argument for noncognitivism based on moral conflict.

VII. Conclusion

There may well be insoluble moral conflicts, perhaps a great many. I have not addressed directly the frequency of such conflicts or the significance of their frequency.[38] But moral conflict of this sort does not itself have paradoxical implications for ethical theory, as friends of moral dilemmas have claimed.

Whereas the robust nature of the second and third paradoxes *motivates* a reexamination of the case for moral dilemmas, the argument against moral dilemmas is largely *independent* of the deontic paradoxes and the plausibility of the deontic principles. An all-things-considered moral obligation is what one ought to do in light of all morally relevant factors. To be an all-things-considered obligation, a prima facie obligation must not only be undefeated, it must defeat competitors; it must be overriding. And, indeed, familiar deontic principles, of the sort discussed here, are plausible only when applied to all-things-considered obligations, understood in this way. But there cannot be conflicting overriding requirements. So there cannot be conflicting all-things-considered obligations. In insoluble conflicts, neither of the conflicting obligations is an all-things-considered obligation; the only all-things-considered obligation is the disjunctive obligation to perform one or the other of the conflicting undefeated prima facie obligations. If we understand moral dilemmas as conflicts of all-things-considered obligations, to which familiar deontic principles apply, as many writers have, then we should agree that moral dilemmas would produce paradox in ethical theory but deny that there are or could be any moral dilemmas.[39]

We can deny the possibility of moral dilemmas without disputing any of the moral phenomenology to which friends of moral dilemmas point. Indeed, both the construction and the resolution of the paradoxes require us to understand better the distinction between prima facie and all-things-considered obligations and to do justice to prima facie obligations. Alleged dilemmas are really conflicts between undefeated prima facie obligations. Such conflicts can be unfortunate but are not paradoxical. Indeed, when we understand prima facie obligations as genuine moral factors or forces in situations, we will better understand why insoluble and even soluble conflicts can be unfortunate and even tragic.

Notes

This paper was written during a fellowship at the Center for Advanced Study in the Behavioral Sciences that was funded by an Old Dominion Fellowship from the Massachusetts Institute of Technology and by grants from the National Endowment for the Humanities and the Andrew W. Mellon Foundation. I would like to thank these institutions for their support. I would also like to thank Norman Dahl, Alan Donagan, Catherine Elgin, Ted Everett, Mark Johnston, Terrance McConnell, Alison McIntyre, Ruth Marcus, Gene Mason, Paul Pietroski, Peter Railton, Amélie Rorty, Alan Sidelle, Walter Sinnott-Armstrong, Robert Stalnaker, Peter Vranas, Susan Wolf, the editors of the *Philosophical Review*, and audiences at the University of Minnesota Conference on Moral Dilemmas, Princeton University, the University of Vermont, Brown University, the University of Wisconsin at Madison, the University of Arizona, Tufts University, the University of Virginia, the University of Southern California, and the University of California, San Diego for helpful comments and discussion.

1. See, for example, Nagel (1979) and Taylor (1982).

2. Notice three things about my discussion. First, I am discussing *moral* conflicts. There are comparable issues involving conflicting nonmoral oughts and conflicts between moral and nonmoral oughts, but these will not be my focus. Second, my focus is on conflicts *per accidens,* rather than conflicts *per se.* Most of my conclusions are easily carried over to conflicts per se. Third, I shall not distinguish between conflicts whose existence is the agent's own fault (*secundum quid*) and those that are not (*simpliciter*). These two sorts of conflicts are interestingly different. But these differences seem irrelevant to my main claims.

3. See Ross (1930), pp. 1–20, 28–29, and Ross (1939), pp. 84–86.

4. My views about the role of ceteris paribus clauses in laws and generalizations have been heavily influenced by Paul Pietroski (1990). Also see Pietroski (1993).

5. The factor addition model makes the *additive assumption* that the moral status of an act *sans phrase* results from adding the moral forces contributed by the various morally relevant factors. This may seem to involve the *atomist assumption* that the value or force of an individual factor is independent of the other factors in the situation. And the atomist assumption may be suspect. Perhaps certain factors (for example, pleasure) have positive moral force only when combined with other factors (for example, when they are innocent pleasures). If so, doubts about the atomist assumption may lead us to question the additive assumption and the factor addition model. See Kagan (1988). But the additive assumption does not require the atomist

assumption; we can reject the atomist assumption that the moral force of a factor is independent of all other factors and allow some moral factors to be specified relationally without giving up the additive assumption that moral status results from adding the values or forces of various moral factors. (Of course, we cannot specify moral factors in a *maximally* relational way if we are to preserve the distinction, essential to the factor addition model, between prima facie and all-things-considered duties or claims.)

6. Foot recognizes genuine obligations that may be overridden (type-1 obligations) and distinguishes them from the obligation associated with what there is the most moral reason to do (type-2 obligations) and so recognizes something like the distinction that I intend between prima facie and all-things-considered obligations. But she seems to treat prima facie obligations epistemically or statistically (see text below) and so does not want to equate the type-1/type-2 distinction with the prima facie/all-things-considered distinction. See Foot (1983), reprinted in Gowans (1987). Because I reject these readings of prima facie obligations, our distinctions are similar.

7. See Williams (1965), in Gowans (1987), pp. 125, 126; van Fraasen (1973), in Gowans (1987), pp. 141, 142; Marcus (1980), in Gowans (1987), p. 191; Foot (1983), in Gowans (1987), p. 257.

8. Ross (1930), p. 20.

9. On the metaphysical reading, a prima facie obligation expresses a *pro tanto* moral obligation or moral reason.

10. Ross (1930), p. 19.

11. Ross (1930), pp. 28–29.

12. Cf. Foot (1983), in Gowans (1987), p. 257.

13. Ross (1930), p. 29. The analogy is especially strong if moral factor addition *just is* moral vector addition. And perhaps it is. However, one apparent disanalogy is that in vector addition the output is rarely the same as any one of the inputs, whereas in moral factor addition the output is usually (always?) one of the inputs.

We might notice that Ross also connects prima facie obligations with ceteris paribus moral claims; see Ross (1930), p. 30.

14. We might also notice that our factor addition model of the relation between prima facie obligations and all-things-considered obligations does not imply consequentialism or utilitarianism. Although factor addition requires that we add the moral forces, positive and negative, associated with alternative actions in order to determine which action available to the agent is supported by the strongest moral force, this does not require assuming that the strength of a moral force is proportional to the amount of good or value that an action would realize. Thus, Ross can help himself to the factor addition model, and he is not thereby a closet utilitarian.

15. See Williams (1965), in Gowans (1987), pp. 122–25, 134; van Fraassen (1973), in Gowans (1987), pp. 147–48, 151; and Marcus (1980), in Gowans (1987), pp. 193 and 196–97.

16. Williams (1965), in Gowans (1987), pp. 122–25.

17. Is regret appropriate in soluble conflicts? First, we must distinguish the issue of whether it's appropriate to *harbor* or *express* regret from the issue of whether the thing in question is an *appropriate object* of regret. It is only the latter issue that is in question. Second, whether compunction or regret is appropriate depends, I think, on the *object* of such attitudes. We might distinguish some apparently different objects of regret. Regret might focus on (1) the circumstances that make some sort of conflict (now) unavoidable, (2) the consequences for others of the unperformed obligation, (3) the fact that one obligation remains unperformed, or (4) the fact that

one performed the action one did. (Cf. Foot [1983] in Gowans [1987], p. 257.) Though (1)-type and (2)-type regret are arguably appropriate, they do not threaten the traditional account; (4)-type regret seems clearly inappropriate; only (3)-type regret is potentially troublesome for the traditional account. Let me explain briefly.

The circumstances that make conflict unavoidable seem an appropriate object of regret. We wish the world were not such as to make it necessary to leave one of our prima facie obligations unfulfilled. But there also seems to be no basis for paradox here and nothing that the factor addition model of soluble conflicts cannot explain. Because we want to respond appropriately to all moral forces, we regret that circumstances require us to ignore some moral forces in order to attend to stronger ones.

More complicated is (2)-type regret. Indeed, one may even wonder if this is a distinct category of regret. Typically, though not always, failure to meet a prima facie obligation results in hardship to the person(s) to whom the obligation was owed. We may regret the fact that this person must suffer this hardship and the fact that we play a role in producing this hardship. But this regret seems perfectly compatible with recognizing that it is morally necessary to cause this hardship in order to avoid violating stronger moral requirements. Perhaps this regret just involves the wish that things could have been otherwise, such that causing this hardship was not necessary. If so, it involves no more than (1)-type regret.

The object of one's regret may be the unfulfilled, but weaker, obligation—(3)-type regret. One regrets not performing B. But it's also not clear that this is a distinct kind of regret. One's reason for regret at not performing B might be the fact that one would have liked to perform B. But this is regret that one was in a situation such that performing B was morally unavailable (because it would have been morally irresponsible to act on the weaker claim). This is (1)-type regret again, and poses no problem to the traditional analysis of soluble conflicts. Alternatively, this regret might involve more; it might involve the thought that in the actual circumstances one should have performed B rather than A. This is (4)-type regret. But it seems precisely inappropriate. Surely, if it is a soluble conflict in which there is a greater obligation to do A, then it *is* inappropriate to wish that one had performed B, rather than A.

However, perhaps (3)-type regret need not collapse into either (1)-type or (4)-type regret. It may be appropriate to experience regret or compunction at the fact of not fulfilling an obligation, even if it is an obligation that is overridden by others. I discuss this form of regret in the text.

18. Winning presupposes a contest, and a contest presupposes competitors. If so, the idea that a factor is a factor only if it wins may be incoherent.

19. This may be Hare's view about the sort of regret that is appropriate in cases of moral conflict; see Hare (1981), chs. 2–3.

20. Cf. Ross (1930), p. 28.

21. Where partial comparability applies, the relation *not worse than* is not transitive. Cf. Parfit (1984), p. 431. Suppose that A and C are items on one dimension of assessment and B is an item on another and that A is marginally greater than C. If both A and C are incommensurable with respect to B, then C is no worse than B, and B is no worse than A. But if A is greater than C, C is worse than A; thus, the relation *not worse than* is not transitive.

22. A very strong version of incommensurability would be needed to show that insoluble moral conflict is so pervasive as to threaten the possibility of systematic moral theory and moral knowledge. It is in part because I see no motivation for this kind of incommensurability that I think it more profitable to examine the structural issues about moral dilemmas that are independent of issues about their frequency.

23. Styron (1980). Of course, Sophie's choice is an insoluble conflict only if it is

false that her duty not to be involved in the sacrifice of any of her children is greater than her duty to save one of her children.

24. In this way I want to disagree with McConnell ([1978], reprinted in Gowans [1987]). He wants to reject moral dilemmas by arguing that once we distinguish epistemic and metaphysical issues, we should deny that there are or could be conflicts between undefeated prima facie obligations. But, while I agree that we should be skeptical about the frequency with which insoluble conflicts occur, I think that we must admit that they are possible, and the case of symmetrical but conflicting duties demonstrates this most clearly. I, too, will reject the possibility of moral dilemmas (see section V below), but because I reject (3), not because I believe insoluble conflicts are impossible.

Foot construes her type-2 oughts as claims about what there is most or best reason to do and concludes that there cannot be conflicts of type-2 oughts. See Foot (1983), in Gowans (1987), p. 256. But conflicting actions can both be best as long as the corresponding moral claims are broadly equipollent. If so, then Foot has no ground for denying type-2 conflicts.

25. Thus, we should distinguish the modality that '♦' signifies from the sort of metaphysical possibility that '◊' signifies. Moreover, insofar as we are concerned with impossibility, it is with specific kinds of impossibility, not with the sort of impossibility that, if determinism is true, characterizes an agent's relation to all actions she does not perform.

26. Common sense distinguishes between two kinds of modalities. Most of us assume that alternative actions can each be within my power even if it is causally determined which one I will perform. But some actions that are possible in this quite general way are nonetheless impossible or outside an agent's powers because the particular context imposes a sufficient physical or psychological disability (for example, as where the parent is unable to save both twins from the fire). These actions are impossible for the agent in question in a way different from the way in which, if determinism is true, all the actions the agent does not perform are impossible. In formulating voluntarism and construing a moral conflict as a conflict among duties such that one can perform each but not both, I am relying on a conception of possibility that includes both the more general and the more specific forms of possibility. So if determinism and compatibilism are both true, A and B will each be possible in both the general and specific senses, but it will be impossible in the specific sense to do both. In such a case, the voluntarist can accommodate obligations to do each, but not an obligation to do both. If incompatibilism and determinism are true, then there is no distinction to draw between the modality in which it is impossible for the parent to save both children and the modality in which it is impossible to act otherwise than one does. A voluntarist would conclude that there can be obligations to do only things one does. But we would face no moral conflicts; A and B are not each within the agent's power, and, according to voluntarism, there could not be two conflicting obligations.

27. See, for example, Stocker (1987).

28. The two correlativity principles are equivalent as long as we adopt a rule of extensionality allowing us to substitute logical equivalents within the scope of the deontic operators 'O' and 'P'. Then, if we treat either principle as an axiom schema, we can derive the other as an instance.

29. Similar principles are discussed by van Fraassen (1973), in Gowans (1987), and by Judith Thomson, in Thomson (1990), pp. 156–7.

It should be clear that this requires us to read the embedded conditional in the obligation execution principle as asserting some kind of counterfactual or nomological dependence between β and ¬α, rather than as a simple material conditional.

For instance, we might represent the embedded conditional with something like Stalnaker's "corner"; see Stalnaker (1975).

Someone might think obligation execution too strong a principle. By contraposition within obligation execution we get $(O(\alpha) \ \& \ (\alpha \longrightarrow \neg\beta)) \longrightarrow O(\neg\beta)$. But it may seem that some nomic consequences (for example, epiphenomena) of things we are obligated to do need not themselves be obligatory. For instance, suppose I am obligated to give a talk on a certain date at a certain university, one consequence of which is that I see something of the campus after the talk and before returning home. It might seem strange to suppose that I am obligated to see the campus as well as give my talk. Upstream consequences of our obligations may be obligatory, but downstream consequences do not seem to be. But I'm not so sure. If downstream consequences are genuine consequences, then failure to bring them about entails that one will not have fulfilled one's original obligation. Ceteris paribus, if I do not see the campus, then I will not have fulfilled my obligation to give my talk. So in one sense failure to realize downstream consequences of our obligations prevents our fulfilling those obligations much as failure to realize upstream consequences does. If so, perhaps both sorts of consequences are obligatory and obligation execution is defensible. Moreover, the friend of obligation execution can recognize an important *pragmatic* asymmetry between upstream and downstream consequences. Upstream consequences are or can be part of planning the execution of one's original obligations, as downstream consequences cannot.

Alternatively, of course, we might defend obligation execution simply by interpreting the embedded conditional as representing a narrower kind of nomological dependence between an obligation and its upstream consequences of the sort when β would prevent α from coming about.

30. In this connection, it is worth noting that my view about agglomeration is not that we should just restrict its scope to nondilemmatic situations. That would be ad hoc. I think that we should reject it and that we can identify a *different* mechanism for generating compound obligations in nondilemmatic situations, namely, the first correlativity principle. However, I do not see any similarly plausible alternatives to obligation execution, correlativity, weak obligation, or weak impermissibility.

31. Alan Donagan discusses some aspects of the disjunctive solution in Donagan (1984), in Gowans (1987), pp. 286–87.

32. This form of skepticism about moral dilemmas should sound familiar, because it is similar to my criticism of agglomeration. Here we deny the existence of genuine dilemmas by admitting only a disjunctive all-things-considered obligation. There we argued that if there were moral dilemmas, we might avoid the first paradox by denying agglomeration, and we might do this by conceding only a disjunctive obligation. We admit that an (all-things-considered) obligation to do A and an obligation to do B yields a disjunctive obligation to do A or B, but we deny that it yields a conjunctive obligation to do both A and B. But the present point is not simply the denial of agglomeration for prima facie obligations. We can see this symbolically. When we deny agglomeration we assert four main claims.

O(A)
O(B)
O(A v B)
$\neg$O(A & B)

If we denied the "agglomeration" of prima facie obligations we would assert four parallel claims.

   o(A)
   o(B)
   o(A v B)
   ¬o(A & B)

Instead, in denying the possibility of dilemmas, we make the following claims about insoluble conflicts.

   o(A)
   o(B)
   O(A v B)
   ¬O(A & B)
   ¬O(A)
   ¬O(B)

The explanation of these difference is that whereas agglomeration is a function that takes only all-things-considered obligations as arguments; premise (3) in our recipe for a dilemma takes prima facie obligations as input and all-things-considered obligations as output. So, though similar in part, skepticism about dilemmas and skepticism about agglomeration have different structures.

33. To be accurate, the only insoluble conflicts that the disjunctive solution must represent as no-lose situations are conflicts *per se,* in which A and B are mutually exclusive and jointly exhaustive alternatives; in such a case, whatever one does, one performs one of the disjuncts in the disjunctive obligation. Conflicts *per accidens,* in which A and B are mutually exclusive but not jointly exhaustive, are not no-lose situations; one does something impermissible if one performs neither disjunct.

34. For a rigorous statement of a similar claim about the judicial treatment of legal conflict, see Sartorius (1977), pp. 1269–75.

35. Williams (1965), in Gowans (1987), p. 125.

36. Williams (1965), in Gowans (1987), p. 121.

37. In a similar way, Greenspan appeals to emotional conflict to argue against a cognitive construal of the emotions; see Greenspan (1980). Although I do not accept the view that she calls cognitivism—the claim that emotions just are judgments or beliefs—I do think that this and other cognitivist views of the emotions are untouched by her argument. In particular, a cognitivist view that holds that emotions are and should be grounded in beliefs about the natural and evaluative properties of situations can readily accommodate conflicts of attitudes, because, as I indicated, these conflicting attitudes take different aspects of the same situation as their objects. The parallel between Greenspan's and Williams's arguments occurred to me during discussions with Tracy Isaacs.

38. Issues about the frequency of moral dilemmas need not be resolved by our conclusion that there can be no moral dilemmas, provided we do not understand 'moral dilemmas' univocally in both contexts. Whereas the structural debate concerns the existence of conflicting all-thing-considered obligations, and I have argued that there can be none, the frequency debate is easily understood as concerning the existence and frequency of insoluble conflicts between conflicting undefeated prima facie obligations. My own view about this, for which I have not argued

here, is that there can be and are such conflicts but that there is no good reason to think them so common as to be troublesome for ethical theory.

39. Sinnott-Armstrong represents himself as a friend of dilemmas; he construes them as conflicts among non-overridden moral requirements and denies that they have paradoxical implications for ethical theory. Sinnott-Armstrong (1988). Because non-overridden moral requirements just are undefeated prima facie obligations, I agree that *if* we understood moral dilemmas as involving such conflicts, then moral dilemmas would have no paradoxical implications. But Sinnott-Armstrong must deny what other participants in the debates (e.g. Williams, van Fraassen, Marcus, Foot, and McConnell) assume: that moral dilemmas involve conflicts of all-things-considered obligations, to which familiar deontic principles apply.

8

Dilemmas: Dithering, Plumping, and Grief

SIMON BLACKBURN

I

At the risk of lowering the tone of this volume, I am not going to start in concentration camps, the French resistance, or the hard world of Greek tragedy. I am going to start in the supermarket, and by introducing a distinction. Let us call a *quandary* any situation in which there are a number of alternatives, of which must adopt one and only one, but where you do not know which one to adopt. You do not know what to do. It is undeniable that there are quandaries. One spends a lot of time in supermarkets in quandaries. Buridan's ass was in a quandary. Now we can distinguish between an *objective* and a *subjective* or *agent's* quandary. An objective quandary is one where one does not know what to do, and there is no fact that would provide a reason that settles what to do: even a God's-eye view would not reveal that one alternative beats the others. For instance, one is undecided about which can of beans of the same price to buy, but, in fact, although packaged differently, they are of the same manufacture. There simply exists nothing that, if known, would provide a reason to settle the matter in favour of one can or the other. Suppose we say that some events vindicate a decision if, once they are known, the events make it apparent that the decision was uniquely the right one, and that events undermine a decision if they do the reverse. Then a quandary is objective if nothing would either vindicate or undermine either decision. A subjective quandary, or agent's quandary, on the other hand, is one in which one does not know anything that settles the matter, but in which there may be such a fact. It is because one fears that the beans inside one can may be vastly better than those inside the other that one dithers, and even if in fact they are just the same, one can be in an agent's quandary. We can notice in passing that an objective quandary as I have defined it need not be objective all the way down. A quandary will only be an objective quandary because of contingent profiles of preference and indifference.[1] If the packaging mattered—if your partner is made sick by blue cans, for example—then there would not be an objective quandary, although if you do not know this you may still be in an agent's quandary. Agent's quandaries typically feel bad partly because we fear that the quandary actually is not objective. We think that there is a right answer, again, contingent on the profiles of interest and desire in the offing, but we don't know what it is.

I now define a *stable agent's quandary* as one in which one does not know anything that settles the choice in favor of one alternative, and also where no practical investigation or further exercise of thought or imagination can reasonably be expected to alter this. The beans case is one (you may say that one could buy both cans, and taste the beans in both, thereby effecting a ranking unless the beans are in fact identical or equal in point of taste. But if buying both is an option, the case is not a quandary at all. A quandary only exists where just one option is possible, not both.) Whether an investigation is practical will typically depend on its cost, as opposed to the likely benefit of discovering an objective ranking. There may exist no further possible investigation, or its cost may be too great. In either case, the quandary is irremediable. You are in a stable agent's quandary in the supermarket because your available strategy is pretty much confined to just looking, and what you see does not rank the alternatives. Perhaps some neutron bombardment would provide information to rank the beans in one can above those in the other, but even if it were possible, it would certainly not be worth it to bring the equipment into the store. In such a case then we can be pretty sure that an agent's quandary is stable, even if we suspect that it is not objective. That is, we can be pretty sure that nothing we can do will rank the alternatives, even if in the outcome one would have been much better than the other. Faced not with cans of beans but with a choice between two cars, we may eventually decide that we are in a stable agent's quandary, although we can also be pretty sure that in the long run one car would prove to have been a better buy than the other.

The supermarket provides a clear case of a stable agent's quandary. But it is unusual in this. For in wider contexts it is very hard to know whether further investigation, or further exercises of thought or imagination will not discover an asymmetry resolving the quandary. Two cars may strike us as equally attractive, but we may fear that there is some practical test for ranking them, if only we could think what it is. Here too there is an objective/subjective distinction. There may indeed be a test, but if there is no effective way of knowing what it is, then the quandary is stable. Perhaps one car has hidden under its carpet a service record showing that it is a complete lemon, but if there is no way of suspecting this, it cannot help resolve the issue. The quandary remains stable. But the judgement that a quandary is stable is in general defeasible, and this has consequences for our behaviour. For because of this defeasibility, quandaries typically do not *feel* stable. It typically feels as if there must be one simple investigation, or exercise of just the right thought or imagination, that will provide the decisive reason for just one side. This is what we fear. But we might nonetheless know that the fear is irrational. It may really be quite predictable that the quandary is stable. One might offer the advice to someone never to treat a quandary as stable: always go on looking for the elusive decision procedure. This would be bad advice, fit only for Buridan's ass. But we are sometimes prone to behave as if it were good advice. Our dithering takes the form of running again and again at the issue, as if some secret ranking will reveal itself, long after we ought to know that it will not. And after a decision has been made we agonize over whether there were practicable tests that we didn't consider, so that we could have done more to remove the quandary. Sometimes such reflections will be merely neurotic, but sometimes not. I come back to this later.

There is a different notion of stability worth mentioning. Some quandaries have what I shall call a great deal of *inertia*. It is not just that one is in a quandary, but that even if some fact came along to favour one side, one would still be in a quandary. One is agonizing over which car to choose, and it will not settle the issue if the salesman offers you $1 to choose car A. Or even $10 or $20, although it might if he offered $1,000. The reason is that if weighty considerations are at stake, small incentives seem irrelevant. Some asymmetries may be inappropriate and even insulting. If you are torn between marrying A and B, it does not help if your parents, who prefer A, say they will throw in a holiday in Martinique if you choose to marry A. The amount of inertia in a quandary will affect the difficulty of solving it: there may be practical strategies for finding some asymmetry helping A against B, but none for finding a sufficiently important asymmetry to prevent one still being in a quandary. One of the problems with serious moral quandaries is that they have so much inertia that any asymmetries we are likely to establish between the possible courses of action will seem inadequate to solving them.

Once an agent's quandary is perceived as stable, both common sense and high theory tell us how to handle it. The agent has to *plump* for one alternative. I say "plump" deliberately, because saying that you have to choose carries a bad implicature. Choice is a process that invokes reasons. But the reasoning is all in *before* the case is describable as a stable agent's quandary. It is because the reasoning leaves no ranking of alternatives, and because this is seen to be irremediable, that there is nothing left to do but plump. Common sense tells us that this is so. It is because Buridan's ass could not plump that it lived up to its name. But theory tells us the same. Reasons fail to rank the alternatives and practicable investigation is expected to fail to do so as well. But a quandary was defined so that just one alternative had to be taken: in other words, there is a cost or other embargo attached to refusing to act at all, which makes this option worse than plumping.

Plumping sounds light-hearted, and some of the writings on moral dilemmas—which we have not reached yet, of course—speak of it with disdain, as if one were to recommend that great Agamemnon toss a coin. But as I use the term plumping can be done with a heavy heart, and under a heavy umbrella of doom, as one convinces oneself that the alternative one did not plump for will prove to have been the right one in time. In fact, it is often very unpleasant to have to plump, precisely because we would have liked reasons to determine a choice, and we fear that with hindsight one will see that they would have, if one had investigated, thought, or imagined better. In a situation in which you have to plump, it is true that as far as making the choice goes you *might as well* toss a coin. If the advice to toss a coin sounds unserious, inadequate to the gravity of some choice, this is, I believe, a cultural matter. Notice that the most serious quandaries, in which plumping for one side or another is almost unbearable, are often solved by drawing lots. Cards and straws have a history of deciding volunteers and victims, so they have a fateful gravity that coins, used mainly in sporting events, perhaps lack. Agamemnon might not be inclined to toss a coin, but a suitably solemn ritual of turning up a fateful card might be a good deal more appropriate.

Once we have a stable agent's quandary, then, we have to plump. Assuming, for the moment, that moral dilemmas are at least stable agent's quandaries, there is then something odd about one thought people sometimes have: a thought that seems partly to have guided the design of the conference from which this volume emerged, for example. One thing we were to discuss is "the possibility of rational strategies for solving" dilemmas. But there can be no rational strategy for solving a stable agent's quandary, except plumping. To repeat: the exercise of reasoning went on *before* the situation was so identified. Once it is accepted to be a stable agent's quandary, no further rational strategy is possible, except one that makes the process of plumping as painless as possible. There is, I agree, room for strategy and imagination in doing this. As I have said, knowing that you have to plump is typically an unpleasant state for most of us, so anything that hastens the event is good. On the other hand, there may be people who enjoy wallowing in indecision, and for them delay may be desirable. In the case of a very serious quandary we do not want to be hurried too much, although we also do not want to be debilitated by inaction, which may, of course, have other costs. Common-sense, practical rationality therefore knows that there is a time to dither, and a time to plump. Both come after the time to reason. They come when we are in a stable agent's quandary. But the real use of straws and cards suggests that in some cases plumping may be so traumatic that we need some kind of shelter, enabling us to see the matter as fated or decided by forces outside our control. In very serious cases we may have to tell ourselves a story afterward that makes our plumping an adequately dignified event. There may be need for grief, and for therapy for those who have had to plump.

Suppose now we imagine an attempt to codify practical rationality, at least as it applies to someone with my profile of preferences and priorities. The code should contain decision theoretic lore, and might give me advice to take shopping: never spend more than one minute working out calculations like whether a pint at 48 cents is better than 12 fluid ounces at 35 cents; do not spend time dwelling on cholesterol, because doing so causes hypertension; try not to think of how the food got there; and so on. This might be good advice for me, in the simple sense that by following it I avoid needless dissatisfactions and satisfy more preferences. Of course, I don't need such a code, because I shop by *phronesis* rather than by consciously following norms. This is partly because I am practiced at being a good enough trustee of my own interests, partly because I do not have to justify my decision to others. But we can imagine such a code, with norms determining how I should act at various choice points. Ought I to expect the code to remove altogether the need to plump? Of course not. Saving miracles, the code cannot possibly foresee the stable agent's quandaries I shall meet. All it can do is give me advice on how to act once a situation is so identified: how much time to spend dithering, how to plump. It will be *after* using the code that a situation is identified as a quandary. The code has then done its work, except insofar as it contains advice on how quickly to plump, whether to shelter from the responsibility (toss a coin, ask your spouse which one to buy), and so on.

Leaving opportunities for plumping is not the same as containing conflicting advice. A code might do that, in the strong sense: never buy the cheapest brand;

always buy the cheapest brand. This is a clear defect. More interesting is inconsistency in the weak sense of containing advice that, given a contingency, counsels conflicting action: never buy the cheapest brand; always buy the brand that Mother recommends. Good advice, until Mother recommends what is in fact the cheapest brand. An occasion on which this happens is one in which *these* bits of the code leave one in a quandary. But it does not follow that one is in a quandary tout court: there may be other factors that sway the choice decisively. If there are not, one will have to plump, and we have seen that it would be silly to promote as an ideal a code that never left you having to do this.

It is not so silly to promote as an ideal a code that cannot give rise to inconsistent advice, whatever the contingencies, but the form it takes needs some thought. Provided Mother seldom recommends the cheapest, each piece of advice might save me much dissatisfaction: perhaps it is better to have them in a simple form than have them hedged against the remote case, especially if there is no practicable way of seeing what might on occasion resolve the conflict. On the other hand, if we need to know where we stand, a code would do well to anticipate contingencies in which its advice conflicts with itself. A building code, for example, would not be defensible if it mandates one depth of footing for slopes and a different one for clay soils, even if (luckily) nobody ever starts to build a house on sloping clay. Might it be tolerable to have weakly conflicting norms or mandates, but qualified in a general way? The code would be headed by a rubric: remember that each piece of advice is to be thought of as hedged. There is a ceteris paribus clause, and other things are not equal if a weak inconsistency has arisen. Although we want this protection against weak inconsistency, we would not want it if, as a result, what ought to be swift choices become laborious. I return to this in the moral case below, when we consider requirements.

A final point before we turn to higher ground. Plumping resolves the merely practical quandaries I have talked about. But it need not resolve them without leaving a residue, akin to the residue that Sartre and Williams first highlighted in ethical cases. First, it can be hard to turn one's back on a choice made by plumping. Many people no sooner plump than they suffer a strong sense that they are bound to have made the wrong choice. The other car would have been better, this one will turn out to be a lemon. As we have already mentioned, people can believe, irrationally, that it was their fault that plumping became necessary: "If only I knew more about cars," they think, "I would have been able to spot the crucial reason for preferring one to the other." They can doubt whether the situation was really a stable quandary: "If only I had taken it for one more test drive," they think, "the crucial evidence would have been visible." A full set of norms for plumping would tell us to what extent these reflections make sense, and to what extent they are neurotic.

Second, in some cases the residue involves something like reparation: making it up to some proponent of the side for which you did not plump. Suppose each of two friends offers me use of their chain saws. It doesn't matter which I take, so I plump for Alice's. I then owe it to Bertha to make some friendly overture to show that I took her offer seriously, that I had no particular preference for Alice, and so on. Notice, however, that this might be so even if the situation never put me in a quandary. Perhaps it was easier for me to pick up Alice's chain saw, but I still owe Bertha some soothing noises. At the very least I have to show that I appreciated her offer. This is important, because it is sometimes argued that the need for reparation or apology to a side whose interests are not met after a dilemma shows that a genuine requirement has been violated. Here I simply point out that the phenomenon is more widespread, for similar apology and even reparation may be in order when no requirements have been violated, and even when no quandary ever existed. In fact, this issue of proper residue is quite independent of whether the situation is ever a quandary in moral cases as well, as we shall see below.

Third, some fortunate people may be able to contour themselves around the consequences of plumping in such a way that, in retrospect, the decision can seem to have been the only right one. They can think that the choice revealed their real preference. Having plumped for the Ferrari rather than the Plymouth, I live up to the role, so that after a time I cannot understand how I was ever at all drawn to the Plymouth in the first place. Some people are better at this than others. In spite of Sartre, we should not think that everybody can do it all the time. Nor should we always recommend it, although it may often be good advice, to ward off useless regret. If we admire it, we are admiring a lack of understanding of our past selves, and this seems to me to be a pity. Worse, as we shall see below, it may create intolerance of those who plumped the other way.

To sum up so far: We have seen the unproblematic, inevitable nature of stable agent's quandaries. We have seen that no codification of practical rationality could avoid them. We have seen that there can be no strategy for resolving them, beyond one making the experience of plumping as painless as possible. We see something of the defeasible nature of the judgment that a quandary is stable, and of the residue of more or less neurotic doubt that this can leave. We have seen, finally, how a protagonist of the choice that is plumped against may be offered apology or reparation, even when no requirement of any kind has been violated.

II

It would be pleasant to be able to say that morality brings in nothing new. If we can see moral dilemmas as simply juicy examples of stable agent's quandaries, there will be nothing puzzling about them. In effect, I think this is true, but there is much to be said to make it seem plausible.

First, then, what makes a quandary a moral one? In the cases discussed so far, the reasoning has been entirely cost-benefit. The pressures on each side may have been commensurable, but balanced, as in the beans case. Or they may have involve different considerations that ended up balanced, as when choosing between cars that offer different attractive features and different drawbacks. But in either case the pressures simply work through subjective desirability. We make a quandary a moral one by adding motivations from the territory of virtue, obligation, duty, and right and wrong. We can all accept that much without having an agreed-upon theory of what delineates that territory. We may think that it gets its identity from the presence of altruistic and social motivations, or from the existence of rational demands, or from some other source entirely, while agreeing that it is only when a pressure comes from that territory that a quandary has a moral element. Notice that there can be mixed quandaries, in which one of the factors making it a quandary is a moral one but the others are not. Much is going for the Ferrari, but it makes worse exhaust emissions than the Plymouth, and one feels under a duty not to contribute more than necessary to atmospheric pollution. Notoriously, some philosophers have suggested that as soon as a tincture of morality enters on just one side, as in this case, that settles it, so that if the agent remains in a quandary, this is because he is out of control or only using ethical terms in an inverted-commas sense, or is a hypocrite. This strikes me, as it has many others, as simply wrong. Nobody is out of control here, and the other diagnoses may be clearly inapplicable: it is only *because* the agent takes the moral issue seriously that he is in a quandary at all. Otherwise it would be a walkover for the Ferrari.

Mixed quandaries can be stable. There may be no practicable investigation or further exercise of thought and imagination that enables me to rank the alternatives. This will mean that I cannot place the moral ingredient, and whatever else is working for its side, above or below the total package of considerations on the other side. I will know, of course, that if I plump for the Ferrari, I will have to put up with whatever discomfort is produced by my perception of myself as polluting more than I should. A bad conscience on that score will be a cost. But so will knowing that I have foregone the pleasures of the Ferrari. A small amount of foreseeable guilt may be balanced by a large amount of foreseeable regret. In that case, as usual, I have to plump. And as usual there will be residues whichever way that is done. If the moral consideration was not impersonal but arose from the decision's effect on some identified person, reparation or apology may be in order. If the problem with the Ferrari was that it makes more noise than it ought to on starting up, I may feel obliged to make soothing remarks to my neighbor after I have plumped for it.

You may be thinking that even if mixed quandaries exist, good people would not get into them. For a good person the moral tincture would 'trump' or even 'silence' the others. If we are good, once we realize the moral objection to the Ferrari, its blandishments count as nothing. Partly this may be a matter of definition: a good person is one in whom ethical considerations trump or silence others, just as an economic person is one in whom economic considerations trump or silence others. But if it involves a recommendation that we should particularly emulate or admire people for whom there cannot be mixed quandaries, it needs a little critical attention. If their purity arms them against even seeing the blandishments of the world as blandishments, there may be costs of self-righteousness or self-pity, of limited imagination or sympathy. In this sense, there is nothing paradoxical about it being better not to be all that good.

Similarly, and perhaps more importantly, the sheer number of everyday quandaries, practical, mixed, or moral, casts doubt on one influential ethical ideal. This is the ideal of reflective equilibrium, if that is conceived of as strong enough so that the system in such equilibrium contains the rankings and principles necessary for solving all quandaries. I believe that we should not admire anything of that strength. It is not an ideal, for it would not be ideal to be equipped in advance with an algorithm preventing any choice's being seen as a stable quandary. It is essential to moral maturity that we get into stable quandaries. Being equipped in advance to award outright verdicts to one side or another is indeed to be armed against one kind of indecision, just as someone who always eats exactly the same brand of food is armed against indecision in the supermarket. But the cost is too great—the cost of limited sympathy, imagination, or sheer awareness of the possibilities that life has to offer.

Once we have mixed cases, we can play with the mix. We can add the same moral considerations to each side, or different considerations, and if we end up with a stable quandary all the remarks made so far apply. I conclude that if moral dilemmas involve something more puzzling than stable practical quandaries, it is not because of the addition of the moral to the practical. It must be because there is more to a dilemma than a quandary. What more?

The usual definition is in terms of *requirements*. It is when there is something more than a consideration or a practical pressure, or even a moral pressure, on each side that dilemmas exist. It is when there is a requirement to perform each alternative, so we can say that an agent is in a moral dilemma if he is in a moral quandary, in which there is a requirement to perform each alternative. The difference this brings is that whichever way the agent acts, he will have failed to do something that is required of him. Equivalently, we might think that he will have failed to do something that he was obliged to do, or had to do.

It is not at all obvious that any situation deserves being described like this. Consider that the language of requirements is at least sometimes the language of resolution of quandary. "What am I required to do?" is likely to be a request for an answer to a problem of choice, equivalent to asking, "What am I to do?" Only an answer picking out a unique choice satisfies the question. To identify a requirement is then to give an outright verdict. The requirement is to do whichever wins. If no choice wins, none is required. In other words, a demand may be matched by conflicting demands, but if one of them is issued as a requirement, then in this outright sense it brooks no competition. To sidestep this outright or verdictive logic, proponents of this way of looking at quandaries may choose to define a notion of a 'non-overriding' requirement: a requirement that can in principle be matched or beaten by another, more important requirement, or matched by another equally important requirement, as it is in a case of dilemma.[2] But it is not clear that the strategy is a good one. Races can be run in the knowledge that two runners may tie, and they may be judged to be 'first equal'. But suppose a race is in the nature of a play-off, run to determine an outright winner for some purpose. We cannot then use the concept of a matched outright winner. If a putative winner is matched by another putative winner whose claims are equally good, then neither is an outright winner. You cannot say that they both are. If the notion of a requirement shares this logic, as its use in giving a verdict suggests, then the notion of a matched or beaten requirement is contradictory. Sophie and Agamemnon are not required to do either thing, and whatever they do, they will not have transgressed a requirement. They will have done something awful, but in their situation they were not required not to do that awful thing. So the question of whether there are dilemmas as opposed to quandaries now becomes the question of whether we insist that the notion of a requirement be tied to a verdictive logic, or whether we allow what I am calling matched requirements. The one choice assimilates the logic of requirements to that of 'outright winner'; the other assimilates it to that of, say, demands, where we can perfectly well contemplate matched and inconsistent demands.

The question of whether 'requirement' in English means 'outright requirement', or permits matched requirements, might seem to be an empirical and possibly indeterminate one. The issue must be whether we ought to think in terms of matched requirements—whether we miss some important facet of moral quandaries if we fail to understand them in these terms. The only arguments I know for allowing matched requirements allege that some desirable feature of our reaction to quandaries is better preserved if we think of the quandary as involving a requirement on each side. Thus Sinnott-Armstrong argues that the goal of enabling people to live better together in society is better served when people

> recognize the worth and rights of others, and this is done when an agent displays regret or offers excuses, apologies or compensation after violating a moral requirement. Theories that exclude moral conflicts cannot serve this purpose as well, because they cannot justify such residue when the moral requirement was overridden.[3]

The idea is that if I see myself as having been subject to two requirements in my quandary, I will know that I have violated one, and this is *all* that justifies my display of excuses, apologies, and compensation. But I see no reason to accept this. We saw above that when I accepted Alice's chain saw rather than Bertha's, good behavior might demand making some excuse or apology or even compensation to Bertha, yet no moral issues, let alone moral requirements, were involved. In the weighty cases in the literature, *of course* a good person is going to feel awful about the side whose claims were not met. Having decided to go to war, Sartre's hero knows that he has not done things for his mother that he could have, so he will be motivated to proffer excuses, apologies, reparation, atonement. It makes no difference whether he filters his knowledge through the category of having failed in a requirement. If it appears to make a difference, this is, I suspect, because we are illegitimately importing something from the verdictive or 'outright' sense into the supposed matching sense. In other words, some of the importance of failing to respect an outright winner is supposed to rub off onto the case in which we plump against a first equal. Or even, which is more perturbing, when we rationally choose against a beaten competitor. For on the more liberal logic, a requirement can exist even though it is obviously outmatched by a more important and demanding requirement.

Notice especially that as far as reparation and compensation go, it may make no difference whether the choice is actually the outcome of a quandary at all. A coach may never be in doubt that he has to choose Rupert rather than Cedric for the team, but if Cedric had reason to hope, invested effort in the enterprise, and so on, the coach will still recognize an obligation to talk to Cedric, compensate him for dashed hopes, or remember to give his claims some priority next time around. The coach has violated no requirement made on him by Cedric or Cedric's claims to a place, but for all that may properly feel the residual obligation.

We have seen already that all quandaries are apt to leave residues. A serious moral quandary will leave more than others. Sometimes we look askance at someone who, having had to plump for one terrible course of action rather than another, sleeps perfectly easily. Suppose we not only understand but also admire or expect a residual guilt or sense of taint or curse, as in the Sophie and Agamemnon cases. Must we then be conceiving of the matter in terms of an unmet requirement? Again, I do not think so. Agamemnon and Sophie make a choice that condemns one of their children to death. Isn't that bad enough? It is not likely to make it much worse if we say: "P.S. You also failed to meet a moral requirement."

Another suggestion is that seeing quandaries in terms of matched requirements gives us a proper tolerance of persons making the other decision.[4] We do not have to see them as mistaken or defective. But, again, it is not apparent that this toleration is helped by conceiving the matter in terms of matched requirements. Once the situation is identified as a stable moral quandary, we know that we might as well toss a coin; we have to plump, and do so knowing that we can have no possible quarrel with those who plump the other way. It makes no difference whether we also conceptualize the issue in terms of competing matched requirements, or whether we just say that there were competing moral pressures but no requirement. The real enemy of proper toleration will be the Sartrean psychology that, having plumped, reformats its character and its view of the past so that its particular choice is thought of as the only possible one. Once that has happened, those opting the other way may get condemned. This is a reason we need to beware of that psychology.

I think, therefore, that there are no pressing reasons to insist on describing these quandaries in terms of matched requirements. Are there good reasons against doing so? Of course, there may be background reasons against thinking of morality in terms of requirements at all: reasons for thinking in terms of virtue and practical wisdom, rather than in terms of obligation and duty. But waiving that large issue, should we insist on an outright logic for the notion of a requirement? The best argument for doing so, apart from conceptual economy, is, I think, as follows. Think of morality as like the norms issued by some authority. If an authority issues outright requirements and penalties for disobedience, then well and good. But if it issues conflicting requirements with the same penalties, then things are not so good. As we saw above in the case of a building code, it seems like a defect, even an irrationality, in an authority that it should do this. If the conflict counted as no excuse, the authority would be unjust and arbitrary. A better authority would build in exception clauses, as legal codes do ('Unless a case is covered by subsection 7.35, then providing the regulations in 6.89 are met . . .'). If a morality issues conflicting, matched requirements, then it seems irrationally harsh, a taskmaster that can be feared but not really respected.

Although I sympathize with this train of thought, I do not think it speaks

decisively against conceptualizing quandaries in terms of matched requirements. The harshness or injustice has already gone into the situation when it is
recognized as a stable moral quandary. That is, things are already as bad as
could be for Agamemnon and Sophie. It is going to be hellish whatever they do,
but not because an unjust lawmaker has irrationally issued requirements that
match and conflict. It is the world that has landed them in a hellish situation. If
they had absorbed and internalized different moralities, they might not find the
situations hellish, but it is impossible to see how this could be without their being
severely defective, or scarcely human at all.[5]

The upshot is not, I think, that there is anything especially wrong about
conceiving of moral quandaries in terms of conflicting matched requirements.
It is just that there is nothing especially helpful about doing so. English is wise to
remain indeterminate over insisting on an outright logic, or allowing a matching logic, for requirements. If we allow the latter we have one set of descriptions, but if we insist on the former we can substitute others equally good.
Understood properly, no ethical or intellectual consequences follow from preferring one move to the other.

That leaves me inclined to recommend sticking with the outright logic, and
conceiving of moral quandaries as simply stable agent's quandaries in which
moral considerations favor each alternative, or stand in the way of each alternative, equally.

III

We saw that the best possible practical reasoning, codified as ideally as we could
imagine, would not ward off the possibility of stable agent's quandaries. The
same will be true of that part of practical reasoning that concerns our relations
with others, and situations in which we must think in terms of excuses, apologies, reparation, and even guilt and atonement: in short, moral quandaries. In
moral cases, as in wider practical ones, there is a time to reason, a time to dither,
a time to plump, and sometimes a time to mourn. Nevertheless, moral cases do
show some interesting differences from other practical cases, and I shall conclude by mentioning some of them.

Many practical quandaries are stable but not objective. That is, there may
well be a best choice, but it will only be revealed in the future, and there is no
way of foreseeing which it is. On the other hand, some moral dilemmas may be
objective. They are neither vindicated nor undermined by anything that happens. They may have sufficient inertia for the future not to bring in a ranking
consideration. There is simply no fact, nothing in the outcome, that shows that
Sophie made an outright uniquely right or an outright uniquely wrong choice.
There might have been, but there need not be. The war turned out reasonably
well for Agamemnon, but even if it had not, he might still look back on his
quandary as having been objectively insoluble. Perhaps his unfortunate home-
coming undermined his decision in our eyes, but it might not have in his.

If this is so, it might seem to make the actual experience of a quandary—its
phenomenology—difficult to understand. In his quandary the agent paces the

floor, asking again and again what he ought to do. Is he presupposing that there is a unique thing that he ought to do, an outright requirement? And, if so, ought he not recognize that this is likely false, for not only may his quandary be predictably stable, but it may also even be objective?

The phenomenology is understandable, however, even if we know that this is a possibility. In some practical cases, it is easy to conclude that a quandary is stable: in the supermarket, our only practicable strategy of inquiry was to look at the can, and that was not going to tell us what its contents tasted like. But we saw that even in purely practical cases the judgment that the quandary is stable is defeasible, and we may not be all that ready to believe it. We fear that we have overlooked something. We fear that putting the facts a new way, or turning the issue over in one light or another, ranks the alternatives. We do not know when we have exhausted all such strategies. We may suspect that we have, but the more momentous the choice, the more we twist and turn to escape the moment when we must plump. In moral cases the same is true, but frequently more so. The divergent sources of values and obligations, our awareness that we are prone to forget and overlook things that turn out to have mattered, all stand in the way of finally believing that the quandary is stable. So we twist and turn, and even if we come to believe it, we dither. And having plumped, we wonder whether we should have, and may grieve whatever values we had to trespass against when we did so. There is nothing difficult to understand in all of this, nor does any sensible theory of ethics need to suppose that there is. In other words, I accept neither the view associated with Bernard Williams that quandaries provide an argument for moral anti-realism, nor the rival view that they provide an argument for moral realism.

Earlier I raised a question over the ambition of providing rational strategies for solving dilemmas. Dilemmas, or quandaries, arise when rational considerations have all had their turn on the floor. Stable quandaries arise when we know that giving them another turn will not help. Someone might think that this makes the situation analogous to social decision theory, so that a rational strategy according different votes to different considerations, or producing an algorithm for turning the votes into a verdict, could be a useful thing to find. But this is misdirected. If considerations on one side are visibly weaker than those on the other, then there is no quandary in the first place. If they are not, then reason has had its day. Accepting that we are in a stable quandary, we can only dither and plump. There can indeed be decision-theoretic analyses of when we should accept that a quandary is stable: as we saw above, main variables will be the cost of further investigation, the cost of lost time, and the probability of a ranking emerging. We may also be aware of the long-term effects of cultivating a habit either of being too quick or too slow in accepting that a quandary is stable. We do not want people to take serious decisions too lightly or dither too long. Otherwise, it seems to me, there are only two places where there is room for rational strategy. One is in finding ways to make plumping painless. The main strategy we actually use is to shelter, behind excuses, false consciousness that a decision was forced, or behind devices for making fate play the decisive role, as when using cards or straws or self-imposed policies of random choice. The other place for rational strategy is in dealing with post-plumping grief. We do not expect Sophie and Agamemnon to bounce back, but people can wallow in guilt, become paralysed by turning the decision over and over in their imaginations, to no purpose, and so on. I suspect that the best the philosopher can do, by way of therapy, is to go over exactly the ground we have been covering. Once you see what practical reasoning is bound to be like, what morals add, and where requirements stop, then unless you actually know in retrospect that you got it wrong, you should be able to accept yourself for making any but the most hellish decisions.

Notes

1. I am not here entering on any grand debate about the objectivity of ethics, or the existence of Kantian reasons that have a life independent of agents' desires. I am simply pointing out that not all reasons have that kind of grand, superlunary independence.

2. Sinnott-Armstrong (1988), p. 29.

3. Sinnott-Armstrong (1988), p. 188.

4. Sinnott-Armstrong (1988), ch. 8.

5. Sophie's case is perhaps stronger than Agamemnon's here. Some might think that Agamemnon is only tragic because he puts too much weight on kingly and military duties.

9

The Diversity of Moral Dilemma

PETER RAILTON

We find ourselves confronted with situations we are inclined to call dilemmas. Some are theoretical: What truth value can we assign to the sentence "This sentence is false"? Others are practical: Buridan's notorious ass faced starvation because it sat poised between two equally attractive piles of hay, with no reason to favor heading toward one rather than the other. Famously, moral choices seem to present us with dilemmas, as, for example, when Churchill had to decide between evacuating Coventry (thereby giving the Germans evidence that the Allies had broken their code) and allowing a murderous air bombing of the city to proceed without warning the populace.

Dilemmas are often seen as calling into question the genuineness or reality of the subject matter for which they arise. Thus: If there were such a thing as truth as classically conceived, then mustn't a definite truth value be assignable to every well-formed, non-vague declarative sentence? The dilemmatic cases suggest otherwise.

However, dilemmas are sometimes invoked for a different purpose. That is not to suggest that some area of life or language is dubious, but rather to illustrate the folly of thinking that this area of life or language is amenable to thoroughgoing systematization. Thus Churchill's predicament is often taken to show not that ethics is unreal, but that it is unreal to expect that there will always be right or best answers to ethical questions.[1] Historically, the possibility of moral dilemma has been used to argue against the possibility of "moral theory" at various levels—utilitarian, Kantian, cognitivist, and realist.

One important class of philosophical responses to either use of dilemmas has been to turn the question by denying the genuineness of the purported dilemmas themselves, thereby attempting to rid oneself of the embarrassment of contending with them. Defenders of utilitarianism, Kantianism, cognitivism, and realism have therefore taken up arms against moral dilemma, arguing against its very possibility.

But there is an alternative response. One might admit the possibility of genuine dilemma, and yet deny that this possibility has the impressive implications alleged. The present paper began life in that spirit. I aimed to show that a Millian utilitarianism, under a fairly robust realist interpretation, could accommodate—even help to explain—the possibility of moral dilemma, at least as this possibility is often conceived. That task remains the focus of the first section of this paper.

However, the more I worked with the literature, the more concerned I grew that widely used interpretations of the notion of moral dilemma constrain in unfortunate ways our understanding of the issues at stake in the examples under discussion. So I needed to make a fresh start. In the second section of this paper I make this new start and begin to develop a different account of the nature and sources of moral dilemma.

Finally, in the conclusion, I use this alternative account to revisit briefly the question of the implications of moral dilemma for moral realism.

I

The Straightforward Argument

Consider the following line of argument, meant to show that the possibility of moral dilemma would rather straightforwardly preclude a realist interpretation of ethical discourse. Call it the "Straightforward Argument."[2] To formulate this argument we need to fix a sense for 'moral dilemma' and 'moral realism'.

Although no one conception of *moral dilemma* has gained universal acceptance, the following account has become something of a paradigm: We will say that an agent faces a moral dilemma just in case she is under conflicting, non-overridden moral obligations.[3]

It is yet more difficult to point to a standard conception of *moral realism.* Rather than defend a conception against rivals, I will propose an initial understanding of the term by giving it a stipulated meaning with three elements (later we will somewhat strengthen the definition).[4]

First, and at a minimum, the realist about morality believes moral discourse to be *cognitive* in its semantic character, in the following sense: statements involving moral concepts or expressing moral judgments purport to attribute genuine properties and are capable of truth or falsity. Many philosophical accounts of the semantics of moral language deny this, claiming instead that moral discourse is best interpreted noncognitively. According to noncognitivists, moral discourse has as its primary semantic function not the statement of facts but the issuing of imperatives or the expression of attitudes. We must be somewhat careful here. Virtually all noncognitivists recognize that moral judgments behave linguistically just like ordinary assertions and that we typically speak of moral judgments as true or false. No one questions whether moral discourse is cognitive *on its surface.* Controversy arises only at another level, when it is asked whether the underlying semantic character of the discourse reflects this surface cognitivism or, alternatively, affords a nonstandard explanation of it without appeal to notions of truth and falsity.[5]

If cognitivism about the underlying semantics of moral discourse is necessary for moral realism, is it sufficient? No, since cognitivism is compatible with two positions that seem clearly at odds with whatever anyone seems to have had in mind by 'moral realism'.

First, one could interpret moral judgments as capable of truth value and yet hold that they are uniformly false because the properties that moral predicates stand for are (either necessarily or actually) uninstantiated. John Mackie, for instance, interprets moral language as property-attributing, and hence cognitive. But what properties! They would possess a seemingly occult power of "objective prescriptivity," which, as far as he can see, nothing in this world has.[6] Despite its cognitivism, Mackie's "error theory" is surely not a form of realism.

Second, one could interpret moral language as genuinely property-attributing yet insist upon a minimalist, pleonastic conception of truth or propertyhood.[7] Defenders of minimalism about truth tend to see themselves as opposing the more familiar forms of realism, and sometimes prefer for themselves the label *anti-realist* or *irrealist*. Unlike noncognitivists, minimalists see the assertoric grammatical behavior of moral discourse as in itself sufficient to establish moral discourse as property-attributing or factual, without qualification. Minimalists find empty the allegedly more substantive notions of truth or propertyhood that non-minimalists invoke when asking whether moral language is cognitive "at bottom" rather than merely on the surface. At best, in their view, the non-minimalists' talk of more substantive notions of truth or propertyhood involves confusion of epistemic or metaphysical features of particular properties or areas of discourse with quite generic, lightweight notions of truth or propertyhood. Thus, for minimalists, a perfectly legitimate issue about whether ethical discourse is akin in method or aim—or reducible in substance—to scientific discourse has been illegitimately transformed into an issue about truth-aptness and (metaphysical) realism. Minimalists, then, can accept cognitivism about moral discourse without seeing it as bringing any serious form of realism in train.[8]

Let us then fix ideas as follows. We will for now take *moral realism* to involve, at a minimum, three theses: (1) moral judgments typically are capable of truth or falsity in a standard sense;[9] (2) at least some of the central, affirmative judgments of moral discourse are (quite possibly) true—or, at least some moral properties are (quite possibly) genuinely instantiated;[10] and (3) there is more to the notion of truth—or propertyhood—than merely the minimalist idea of an appropriately behaved assertoric practice. Theses (1)–(3) yield a very basic conception of moral realism, but suffice to enable us to state the Straightforward Argument.

It will help to have an example before us. Suppose that I am a recently graduated law student who has borrowed from two former classmates, Pico and Young, in order to make an overdue debt payment on my law school tuition. We are all just starting out and neither Pico nor Young has any particular wealth. Indeed, each needs to be repaid before the first of June in order to cover their rent, and so each asks for the strongest possible commitment on my part to repay promptly. That seems unproblematic, because I have been promised a large gift of money by an uncle upon graduation, and it should arrive within the month. But it turns out that my uncle's new scheme to sell high-fiber ice cream has bankrupted the family business, and he won't be able to make the promised gift after all. So the first of June is at hand and I am unable to repay both Pico and Young, though I am able to scrape together enough so that I could repay one in full. What should I do? If I split the money, neither will be able to pay his rent and both will be in serious trouble with their landlords. If I choose to repay only one, then I will voluntarily have decided not to repay the other, contrary to a solemn promise. Yet I am unable honestly to say to either one, "I simply *cannot* repay you." For I could repay *him* if I chose to do so. It seems I am in a moral dilemma: I ought to pay Pico, and I ought to pay Young. Neither obligation overrides the other, yet I cannot fulfill both. How might such a possibility be seen as problematic for moral realism?

According to the Straightforward Argument, the moral realist interprets moral judgments as fact-stating. This, *together with* her non-minimalism about truth, properties, and so on, requires her to view moral judgments as purporting to describe some or other "state of affairs." My being strictly obliged to repay Pico in full would appear to constitute one state of affairs; my similar obligation to Young to constitute another. Yet these obligations are in conflict. Now we come to the central question: How does the realist represent this conflict? The most direct way would seem to be by claiming that the two states of affairs are incompatible. But then there could be no *genuine* dilemma, since two incompatible states of affairs cannot simultaneously exist. Thus, according to the argument, a realist conception of moral discourse precludes the recognition of genuine dilemma.[11]

One might, however, question the Straightforward Argument's assumptions about how a realist must construe moral conflict. Consider a moral theory whose realist credentials, one would think, are impeccable: a utilitarianism of the kind pursued by John Stuart Mill. On this view, utility is equivalent to (what is claimed to be) a natural, psychological property: happiness.[12] For Mill, the state of affairs that constitutes an agent being under a moral obligation to perform act X in circumstances C is (roughly) this: failing to perform a token of X in circumstances of type C would be punished (either by explicit penal sanction or by the sanction of conscience and opinion) by the scheme of social rules and expectations, the general teaching of which would most promote overall net happiness in society at large.[13]

Here, then, we have a moral theory according to which the existence of an obligation does indeed consist in a robust state of affairs. But does this account have the result that conflicting obligations must involve *logically incompatible* states of affairs?

The question can be reformulated less abstractly for the example at hand. Might the optimal set of rules and expectations to be taught in a given society assign to someone in circumstances like mine *both* a non-overridden obligation to repay Pico in full *and* a non-overridden obligation to repay Young in full? The question is an empirical one, and the answer could well be yes. Whether optimal rules would treat any particular circumstances as excusing conditions for debt repayment will depend upon the overall social effects of teaching and internalizing such an exception. The existence of particular excusing conditions tends to lessen the pressure to repay, to create perverse incentives (incentives to put oneself in a position such that one cannot repay), and to undermine in general the willingness to make loans. Some excusing conditions will doubtless be recognized. But how many, and which? In some cases, a "strict liability" standard might be optimal: one is responsible and liable to punishment for failure to repay however hard one was trying to avoid this failure. So, the optimal set of rules and expectations to encourage might call for some measure of punishment or disapprobation for me *whichever* course I pursue with Pico and Young. Indeed, it might well be for the best if, thanks to my moral instruction, I am inclined in such circumstances to experience self-punishment in the form of guilt.

In general, it is no easy matter to determine when and to what extent a strict standard of holding oneself and others to task would be optimal. This is certainly not something we can settle a priori. A tendency to feel guilt, or to blame oneself and others, cannot be turned on and off at will. There is nothing psychologically incoherent about the possibility that one might feel some measure of guilt and impose some degree of blame *whenever* one's debts go unpaid. Moreover, this sort of "strict liability" might function to preserve appropriate incentives among lenders and borrowers alike. If so, then the unabashed realism of this Millian utilitarianism would be compatible with a dilemmatic interpretation of my situation.

Now it might be objected that it simply never would be optimal to have an established set of rules or expectations that permit dilemmatic situations to arise, since precisely what seems to happen in such cases is that the rules and expectations become in a way dysfunctional—they no longer give clear practical guidance in choice. This view, however, ignores the multiple functions of rules and expectations, and the many direct and indirect ways they shape our behaviors and feelings. Some degree of dysfunction or confusion in certain, perhaps relatively rare, cases might be a small price to pay for the social and personal entrenchment of strong norms against certain unfortunate but potentially very tempting behaviors. More intriguingly, there are cases in which the confusion or stalemate that results from conflicting directives could be advantageous in forestalling otherwise undesirable outcomes or in introducing a useful unpredictability.

Indeed, whichever way the empirical issues might resolve themselves—whether or not "strict liability" of this sort would prove optimal in practice—the bare possibility that it might does enable us to see that realist utilitarianism is not *in principle* incompatible with moral dilemma. There certainly is nothing outright inconceivable about the entrenchment of potentially dilemmatic norms in individuals and communities.

It might, in fact, be argued that *recognizably* dilemmatic norms now play a crucial role in our communities. For example, some philosophers of language have urged that we should understand the paradox of the Liar as a byproduct of our norms regarding the assignment of truth or falsity, norms which do not go awry in the common run of cases, but which lead to dilemma in certain special, self-referential cases.[14] Seen this way, the Liar paradox is a kind of cost resulting from our practice of truth-assignment, but perhaps the costs of adopting a practice not liable to this particular sort of dilemma would be greater still. In any event, the widespread practice of attributing truth and falsity has hardly come to a halt as a result of the discovery in ancient Greece of self-referential paradoxes.

I conclude, therefore, that the Straightforward Argument fails: a realistic (and moreover utilitarian) moral theory can recognize that there might exist *non-contradictory states of affairs* that nonetheless make true *conflicting, non-overridden claims of moral obligation.*[15]

Before leaving the Straightforward Argument, however, let us observe that there is some difficulty in seeing moral dilemma as even prima facie more problematic for moral realism than moral anti-realism. Consider, for example, noncognitivism. A simple emotivism presumably has no difficulty in saying that dilemma is possible, since, according to such a view, judgments of moral obligation are expressions of emotion, and there is nothing extraordinary about imagining that one might have conflicting emotions regarding one and the same situation or act. But simple emotivism is hardly the most plausible form of noncognitivism. Any noncognitivist who wishes to offer an interpretation of actual moral discourse, rather than a wholesale revision of it, must provide a non-propositional semantics for moral discourse that affords some explanation of the seemingly propositional behavior of moral discourse and argument. If moral discourse functioned only to express emotion, we would be without adequate explanation of the central role in moral argumentation of appeals to principles and consistency, or of hypothetical reasoning ("If X-ing in C is wrong, then X-ing in C' would have to be wrong, too. But it patently isn't."). These difficulties have long been recognized, and noncognitivists have attempted to develop such non-propositional semantics in various ways, among them the approaches of Blackburn and Gibbard.[16] Gibbard, for example, interprets moral discourse as expressive of commitment to norms of permission and prohibition, and then develops a semantics of "credal-normal worlds" in which a condition of consistency (in what is permitted or prohibited) plays an essential role. Whatever its merits, this non-realist semantics has the effect of furnishing the wherewithal to make the idea of genuine moral dilemma at least as problematic as it is for realism. An alleged moral dilemma could be seen as "straightforwardly" presupposing a credal-normal world in which doing X in C is both permitted and not permitted—but such a world would be a priori excluded. Gibbard no doubt could avail himself of other resources for accommodating moral dilemma. My point, however, is that the problem of giving an account of moral language that does justice both to ordinary demands of ethical consistency and to compelling intuitions about moral dilemma is one that faces cognitivist and non-cognitivist alike.

Similarly, one might argue that the question of moral dilemma need have no net import for the debate between realists and anti-realists within the cognitivist camp. The realist's picture of facts as robust states of affairs, as we have seen in the Millian example above, does not preclude dilemma; the anti-realist's picture of facts as (say) points of rational convergence within an assertoric practice does not obviously admit dilemma—without univocal convergence there might not be moral facts at all (and thus certainly no dilemmatic facts). The Straightforward Argument is useful primarily as a caution for those who would offer an interpretation of moral language: it would be wise not to settle upon a scheme for explaining conflicts among moral judgments or the notion of moral fact independently of asking what one thinks about the nature and possibility of moral dilemma.

This ends the first phase of our discussion of moral dilemmas, in which we presupposed a standard characterization of moral dilemma—as a matter of the existence of competing, non-overridden obligations—in order to ask whether this notion is incompatible with moral realism. But let us now consider some cases that call this characterization into question.

II

Commonsense discourse is remarkably promiscuous in its use of the expression 'moral dilemma'. Many of the circumstances we commonsensically describe as moral dilemmas do not involve clear conflicts of obligation. Are these simply marginal examples in a domain in which the central cases do involve conflicts in non-overridden moral obligations? Let us distinguish two classes of cases: First, cases in which the conflict involves *values* or supererogatory *ideals* as well as (or rather than) obligations; second, cases in which the seemingly dilemmatic character of the moral situation seems to arise from fundamental indeterminacies or incommensurabilities rather than along determinate lines of conflict. Of course, as we will see, a single case can fall into both classes.

Before turning to several widely discussed cases, it will perhaps be useful to consider a few more modest examples first. Let us begin with a case of the first of the two sorts just distinguished.

The Forum

You've been asked to participate in a television forum on an important subject, about which you feel you have something worthwhile, but infrequently heard, to say. The forum, which appears regularly, is something of a media phenomenon and is run by a telegenic fellow academic bent on propelling himself into public life. The wider public pays a surprising amount of attention to this forum, in part because of its reputation for handling tough issues and for representing "both sides." You and your associates, on the other hand, have long viewed it as tendentious at best in its framing of issues and its choice of participants. Indeed, you're a bit surprised to be invited, since your sort of viewpoint is seldom allowed to express itself there. You're pretty sure that if you participate you would reach people who would not otherwise be exposed to views like yours, and equally sure that if you don't agree to participate the next person to be asked would not be likely to represent your viewpoint. Moreover, if you refuse, you would give your self-aggrandizing colleague the opportunity to say in public that some of those vocal in criticizing the forum for lack of openness have actually turned down invitations to appear. At the same time, you're very reluctant to lend your name to this enterprise, and to lend to it whatever appearance of legitimacy and fair-mindedness this would yield. It also is well known that the forum pays a handsome honorarium, and that being in the good graces of its very influential host can boost a career. Even your associates— especially your associates?—are likely to be somewhat suspicious of your motives in participating. In truth, you know enough about yourself to recognize that these blandishments are not without appeal and would almost certainly have some effect on how you would conduct yourself. You would feel much less compromised never to have been involved.

In such a case you certainly might feel faced with a moral dilemma, but I doubt that you would feel yourself to be under two conflicting moral obligations—to participate and to decline. Indeed, I doubt that you are morally *obliged* either to participate or decline, although you might well feel a generalized obligation of public responsibility that itself dictates neither choice definitively. As the case has been described, either course strikes me as morally *permissible*. The man running the forum is an opinionated opportunist, but not a moral monster; the expression of your point of view on the subject of the forum would have various benefits, but it is not necessary to avert moral disaster. Though either choice seems morally permissible, all things considered, you feel strongly conflicted over what to do. Perhaps we should describe your quandary not in terms of obligation at all, but as being torn over what it would be best to do, or over what a decent person with political savvy would do in the circumstances.

Now consider a case of the first *and* second sort:

Violin Lessons

Let us suppose that developing true virtuosity at the violin requires sustained, intensive instruction at an early age. Absent this, we'll imagine, there is almost no chance of developing the highest order of talent. Your four-year-old child shows real interest in the violin, and truly startling promise. After some inquiries, you learn that Kelso is the premier teacher in town. Kelso auditions your child and, with visible excitement, proposes an intense regimen of private lessons. Your child takes to Kelso, loves playing the violin, and badly wants to take the lessons. Kelso strikes you as marvelously skilled and devoted, but also perhaps a bit too eager to enlarge his own reputation. On the other hand, a less ambitious instructor might not be willing to invest the extraordinary personal effort that developing a prodigy requires. And you know your child: she loves the violin and her lessons, and has real determination, but the required level of participation in lessons, practicing, and recitals week in and week out would try you both in a host of ways, and would powerfully shape the character of a large portion of the time you are able to spend together. Moreover, it would significantly affect her relations with her peers and, especially, her two older siblings. You would, of course, make every effort to keep in balance the time and attention received by all three of your children. But you know that this would not be entirely possible, given the constraints upon your own time and the special sort of recognition your youngest would doubtless receive from outside the family. Further, you see only too clearly that the intensive course of instruction and performance would throw *you* together with a different group of adults than you otherwise would have sought out, would preempt a number of activities normally part of your life, and so on.

In this case, too, you might feel that you are facing something of a moral dilemma—you are making a decision for someone else as well as yourself, a decision with potentially profound implications for her life and the lives of others. The dilemmatic character of your situation arises not because you see yourself as having clear, conflicting moral obligations to undertake and not undertake the intensive instruction. Your chief obligation here is to the well-being of your children, and it would be implausible to claim that either choice is mandated by that parental duty. So we may suppose that either choice is, all things considered, morally permissible. But what is the best or wisest thing to do?

Some of the difficulty in deciding might be attributable to lack of information: talent of the highest order is rare, and many prodigies do not flourish and develop into successful adult virtuosi. But one can imagine that your quandary would not be resolved even if you had much less uncertainty. Suppose yourself to have strong, convincing evidence that your child would, after prolonged and intense training, develop into a successful first or second violin in a major orchestra, with something like the ordinary mix of happiness and unhappiness in life, though with a persistent sense of a lost childhood, an unresolved hostility to an overbearing parent, and rather nonexistent relations with siblings who never fully overcame their jealousy. Suppose, too, that you have strong evidence that the alternative life for her would involve roughly comparable success and happiness in some other, more prosaic and less intensely engaging and rewarding area of endeavor, and better family relations overall, though not without occasional pangs of longing on her part at the thought of the violin career that might have been, accompanied by accusatory thoughts directed at the parent who let the talent go underdeveloped and the overly conventional family that held her back. In such a case, it is indeed no straightforward matter to ask "Which life seems to suit my child best?" since the choices one now makes will shape in important ways the sort of person one's child becomes.

In this case, your sense of dilemma (if I have succeeded in confronting you with such a sense) might stem less from a sense of conflicting, nonoverridden obligations than from a sense of conflicting, difficult to compare—perhaps even incommensurable—*values, loyalties,* and *ideals.* At stake are aesthetic values, values of parent-child or child-peer relationships, values of accomplishment and autonomy, relationships with specific individuals, and so on. You are deciding for others as well as yourself, and you know only too well that, whichever way you decide, something very significant will irretrievably be lost—a "normal" childhood, say, or an unusual talent. This sense of *inevitable loss* seems characteristic of much of our thinking about moral dilemmas, even when the loss or failing in question is not—or is not entirely—a matter of failure to meet moral obligations.

The Forum and Violin Lessons have as well at least two other features that are characteristic of much commonsense thinking about dilemmas. First, the agent is called upon *to choose rather than compromise or postpone*—not because of some specifically moral requirement, but by the sheer force of circumstance. That is, you are presented with alternatives that do not appear to admit readily of degree, and that cannot be postponed without de facto deciding the matter.[17] Had your child not been so talented and enthusiastic, or had the invitation to the forum not come, you would not face these hard choices. But you now do face these choices, and, unfortunately, some of the usual ways of "balancing" or "hedging" to reconcile conflicting pulls in decision making are not open to you. A half-hearted regimen of instruction would simply fail to promote the kind of development essential for virtuosity. And there is no intermediate level of involvement in a televised forum. Moreover, you are in no position to reshape the forum—it will take place on the scheduled date, with or without you, and postponement of the decision would only cause the invitation to go to someone else, who would almost certainly not be someone you yourself would have chosen. If you attempt to make a public spectacle of refusing to participate, it will only make you look somewhat ridiculous and attract negative publicity to your point of view.

Second, both examples illustrate, in somewhat different ways, the *expressive* aspect of moral dilemmas. To participate in the forum would appear to be making a statement you do not in fact endorse, but could not expect fully to cancel, a statement to the effect that the forum is quite open after all, and that you respect this activity on the part of your colleague. To fail to participate would appear to manifest an unwillingness to take a public stand to affirm one's principles in an open setting. In the second example, to commit yourself and your child to intensive violin instruction, a commitment that includes sticking with it even when it becomes a source of family conflict, also seems to be making a statement you cannot expect fully to cancel: that you attach greater importance to developing a prodigy than to fostering a "normal" childhood; and that this one child, because of her talent, deserves more of your time and attention than the other children.

We often find dilemmatic situations uncomfortable because they seem to lead us to act in ways we ordinarily would have quite sufficient grounds to criticize and avoid. They therefore "taint" or "compromise" us in ways we find destructive of the messages we ordinarily hope to convey with our actions. There is more to this than feeling regret or remorse at certain consequences in the aftermath of decision—though that, too, is important here. For one also feels as if circumstances prevent one from fully being, or from communicating to others by one's actions that one is, the sort of person one hopes to be.

Let me now add several more examples, some of them central cases in the literature. The first is perhaps the most famous.

Sartre's Student

During the Second World War, one of Sartre's students came to him with a dilemma.

> His father was quarreling with his mother and was also inclined to be a 'collaborator'; his elder brother had been killed in the German offensive of 1940 and this young man, with a sentiment somewhat primitive but generous, burned to avenge him. His mother was living alone with him, deeply afflicted by the semi-treason of his father and by the death of her eldest son, and her one consolation was in this young man. But he, at this moment, had the choice between going to England to join the Free French forces or of staying near his mother and helping her to live. He fully realized that this woman lived only

for him and that his disappearance—or perhaps his death—would plunge her into despair. He also realized that, concretely and in fact, every action he performed on his mother's behalf would be sure of effect in the sense of aiding her to live, whereas anything he did in order to go and fight would be an ambiguous action which might vanish like water into sand and serve no purpose. For instance, to set out for England he would have to wait indefinitely in a Spanish camp on the way through Spain; or, arriving in England or in Algiers he might be put into an office to fill up forms. Consequently, he found himself confronted by two very different modes of action; the one concrete, immediate, but directed towards only one individual; the other an action addressed to an end infinitely greater, a national collectivity, but for that reason ambiguous—and it might be frustrated on the way. At the same time, he was hesitating between two kinds of morality; on the one side, the morality of sympathy, of personal devotion and, on the other side, a morality of wider scope but of more debatable validity. He had to choose between the two.[18]

Now I suppose one might interpret this as a case of clearly conflicting obligations—an obligation to his mother colliding with an obligation to democracy or his countrymen—but that does not seem to me the most compelling diagnosis.

First, the cause of Free France really seems to be a *moral ideal* for the student, not a duty. Perhaps everyone in occupied France had some moral obligation to avoid or resist various sorts of collaboration so long as the personal cost were not too great. But it would be a singularly demanding moral conception that claimed that every young male in France had a moral *obligation* to undertake the perilous course of joining the Free French.

Second, even as a parent I rebel at the suggestion that an adult child has a clear moral *duty* to remain with a parent in these circumstances. It would be a supererogatory, not mandatory, act of filial devotion to remain with a parent in such a case. Here, too, there is a *moral ideal* at work, in this case, of "personal devotion," to use Sartre's phrase.

Now, it might be said that, whether or not *we* view this case as one of conflicting obligations, the student himself does. Both courses of action strike him as something that morally *must* be done, and that is what accounts for the poignancy of his case. I am not sure this is right, or that every moral 'must' is the 'must' of obligation.[19] Nonetheless, what seems most important here is that even if one imagines oneself in such a situation without seeing the alternatives as obligatory—seeing them rather as reflecting ideals to which one's life has been or could become strongly devoted—the sense of being in a moral dilemma does not seem to go away. One can, for example, imagine oneself saying of each alternative, "Could I really do *that* (abandon my mother/leave the dangers of freeing ourselves from the Nazis to others) and still be the sort of person I want to be?"

It certainly seems as if Sartre himself favors understanding the student's dilemma in terms of competing ideals rather than conflicting obligations. He describes it as "hesitat[ion] between two kinds of morality," directed at (or devoted to) different ends. Indeed, we know from Sartre's philosophy in general that he is more likely to see choice as inexorably staking out one's identity rather than as a response to objectively given duty.[20] Sartre's philosophy draws our attention especially to the expressive and self-defining characteristics of choice and commitment, and this certainly seems to capture something important to our commonsense experience of moral dilemmas.

Sartre's Student shares with The Forum and Violin Lessons several crucial features, already mentioned. First, all three involve circumstances in which whatever we do—even if we remain "inactive"—a choice concerning what common sense would regard as the nub of the matter will de facto have been made. Second, all three make it clear that a sense of uncancellable moral cost can accompany not only violation of duty, but also decisions (or failures to decide) that have the effect of foreclosing the realization of certain values. And, third, all three draw our attention to the expressive aspect of choice. Making certain choices involves making a statement the meaning of which (like the meaning of the sentences we utter) belongs in part to a public arena and cannot be stipulated at will. Indeed, we can no more stipulate the meaning of our actions than we can stipulate their consequences.

Consider the following thought. Perhaps Sartre's student does not face quite the dilemma it seems. After all, there are many clandestine ways of helping the Free French while remaining in France and attending to most of his mother's needs. To be sure, she might not approve of his running this risk, so a pure ideal of filial devotion might point to avoiding all entanglement with anti-Vichy forces. But it is not improbable to assume that he could keep her in the dark about this sort of activity while still doing virtually all a devoted child would to provide his mother comfort, companionship, and so on. Yet we can readily imagine that Sartre's student would not want to hear of this Solomonic solution. His state of mind finds him torn between two poles of pure commitment, and it is a choice of *that* sort—rather than a compromise—that he might feel he must make. I would suggest that the felt 'must' here, if indeed there is one, has much to do with the expressive dimension of choice—with what an action says or seems to be saying about the agent—and little to do with the notion of duty. Some confirmation for this is to be found in the student's worry that if he leaves the country to join the Free French he might be "put into an office to fill up forms." Any war effort requires form-fillers as well as combatants. Fulfillment of his duties, reassertion of the "national collectivity," and even revenge for his brother's death could all be advanced materially by hard work in a London office. What office work—or, for that matter, somewhat compromised clandestine work in France—might lack is not so much efficacy in achieving certain moral or quasi-moral ends as the vivid, expressive power the student needs in order for his actions to speak with the voice he seeks.[21]

That the plight of Sartre's student, described as Sartre describes it, has been seen as paradigmatically dilemmatic is some reason for broadening our understanding of dilemma to include conflicting ideals and to recognize that we can be as torn by meanings as by duties.

The expressive dimension of choice seems especially prominent in the following example, which was called a moral dilemma by no less an authority on conventional norms than the *New York Times*.

The Governor

According to the *Times,* Governor Mario Cuomo of New York faces a "moral dilemma." A federal court has ruled that an inmate on death row in Texas must be returned to New York to finish a twenty-years-to-life sentence for murder. The inmate, Thomas Grasso, prefers death over imprisonment, and wishes to stay in Texas, where he will soon be executed. Cuomo, as governor, is legally permitted to waive the return to New York, which would spare Grasso many years in prison—although it would cost him his life. Alternatively, Cuomo can insist that Grasso spend two decades imprisoned in New York anticipating a return to Texas, where he would subsequently be executed. Waiving the return might seem at first to be the humane thing to do, but it would involve sending a man directly to his death. Moreover, Cuomo is a well-known opponent of the death penalty, and very likely would be seen by the public to be—and perhaps would feel himself to be—acquiescent to, even complicitous in, a system that administers the death penalty, were he to waive Grasso's return. Of course, there is some chance that Texas (of all places) will eliminate the death penalty during the next twenty years, or that through some entirely unforeseen development the condemned man will be shown to have been coerced into a false confession, or that Grasso will die in prison in New York of natural causes before his return to Texas (imagine seeing *this* as a possible silver lining!). Most important, there is the chance that Grasso is mistaken, and that living the next twenty years—albeit in a prison in upstate New York, and always awaiting execution—would be a substantial benefit to him.

It does not seem that Cuomo faces obvious, competing, symmetric *obligations.* One might say that he has both an obligation to the prisoner to be humane and an obligation to the citizenry to be just. But sheer justice would appear to permit either course. And, although there are humanitarian considerations on both sides of this question, the (imperfect) duty to be humane does not appear to be sufficiently symmetrically disposed to explain the sense of dilemma. One feature this case shares with those that have gone before is that it is not hard to imagine feeling guilt or remorse in the aftermath of either decision. Has one assisted in the execution of a fellow human being? Or, is one subjecting a fellow human being to years of suffering simply in order to keep one's own hands clear of any taint of involvement in an execution?

To understand this dilemma, I suspect we must pay attention not only to effects on the prisoner's well-being, but to a public figure's special role in declaring, by his or her actions, allegiance to principle. What would Cuomo be saying, were he to make either choice? Perhaps he opposes the death penalty partly on humanitarian grounds. Would it be an advertisement for the humane treatment of prisoners to require a man to live some twenty years of a life he does not want, only to be put to death, as opposed to granting his wish to have done with it? Perhaps the *Times* is right in calling this a moral dilemma rather than a mere political quandary, in part because expression is so intimately tied to evaluation. As we noted earlier, part of what is unsettling about moral dilemmas is that we find ourselves facing a situation in which the case for either action, though perhaps somewhat imponderable, is one that normally would be morally sufficient. To act in a dilemma is therefore to act contrary to what one is accustomed to regarding as sufficient grounds, grounds that anyone alive to the values or obligations at stake would ordinarily take to be determinative. How, then, to manifest in action one's respect for these values or obligations?

However, the problem cannot be quite so easily captured, as the following cases suggest. We will begin not with a moral dilemma but a prudential one.

Buridan's Ass

Consider the following principle of prudence:

(i) Always choose the best act, from the standpoint of one's own interests.

Buridan's ass finds himself in a situation in which (i) yields a dilemma. Even though the ass clearly has sufficient ground—hunger and the ready availability of good fodder—to go for either the north shock or the south, he seems to have no sufficient ground for preferring one over the other. This case has been seen as a paradigm of the practical dilemma, but there would be some justice in saying that although the situation poses a dilemma for principles such as (i) that do not envision ties, it does not pose a dilemma for the ass himself. All the ass need do is to break the symmetry in some way or to hit upon a principle more like (ii):

(ii) If there is a uniquely best act from the standpoint of one's own interests, choose it; if there are equal-best acts, choose one of these using a random method.

Principle (i) might leave Buridan's ass forever in suspense between the two shocks of hay, but principle (ii) would eliminate stalemate. Equipped with (ii), the ass will confront an *embarras de richesses,* not a dilemma. But let us suppose that the ass sticks stubbornly to (i), and is able to begin eating only by violating its own principle and simply starting with one shock first. Would there be any "prudential residue"? The ass's goals will have been well realized after eating the two hay shocks, and it would be puzzling at best for the beast to feel any regret over a "road not taken" (i.e., eating the other shock first).

The cases of moral dilemma we have considered above all involve the thought that, whichever path is taken, there will be a "moral residue"— morally intelligible grounds for guilt or remorse over what one has done, given what one has forsaken. But mere conflict in obligation, or the presence of conflicting, normally sufficient reasons need not leave a residue. To the extent that we are inclined to think of residue as a central feature of dilemma, the presence of conflicting duties thus is neither necessary nor sufficient. Consider next a case similar to one discussed by Philippa Foot.[22]

Overbooking

You have made an appointment to meet Winkle in a park on the West Side at noon on the sixteenth and to meet Squires in a park on the East Side at noon next Monday. You have, however, made an honest mistake: misreading the calendar, you failed to notice that next Monday *is* the sixteenth. But now you have made two promises that cannot both be kept. Unfortunately, you learn of the mistake only at the last minute—there is no time to ask either Winkle or Squires to rearrange his schedule, and one of them must be left hanging (or both, I suppose, if one has a principle concerning obligation akin to [i] rather than [ii]!). You flip a coin and head for the West Side. There you meet Winkle, explain the difficulty, and apologize for having to reschedule. Winkle is, surprisingly, pleased—an old friend of his turned up unannounced that morning and talked his ear off, and he'd love to have his noon hour free to finish some work needed by that afternoon. You rush to take a cab to the East Side, and, thirty minutes late, seek out Squires. Unforeseeably, Squires, too, was late for the appointment, and feels some measure of relief when you come charging up to him in the park in an apologetic state. At least, he thinks, he didn't miss you and offend you by being late himself. The two of you quickly sort out what has happened, each laughingly dismisses any apologies from the other, and you head off for a somewhat abbreviated lunch.

You were under conflicting obligations in this case, and did not really live up to both fully. Yet in the circumstances your conduct seems to have left no moral residue. So it would to that extent be odd to think that you genuinely faced a moral dilemma rather than a practical problem.

Emboldened by this example, let us return to an example discussed in the first section of this essay that affords a somewhat more serious case of conflicting duties. Perhaps it will reveal something about the oversimplified view of obligation we have thus far relied upon.

Two Loans

Recall that I had contracted debts with Pico and Young, and now find myself unable (though not through any genuine negligence or bad faith) fully to repay. I could repay each half of what I owe, or, because each needs the money to make a rent payment, could chose one by lot to repay in full. At the same time, I could also commit myself to some suitable plan for further repayment, plus compensation for the special difficulties my failure to repay has caused. Indeed, I could myself undertake to arrange with one or both of the landlords a scheme for extended payment, with interest, of that month's rent. If I did so, then although I would have failed to live up to all of my non-overridden obligations, I would also have shown *respect* for the obligations and for those to whom they were incurred. We speak, in such cases, of taking "full responsibility" for one's actions and obligations.[23] Part of full-blooded regret for one's special role in causing harm is the desire to take such steps when they are available.

The idea of a genuine dilemma cannot be captured, however, by the idea of being led by circumstances into acting in a way that inevitably produces regrettable harm. For this is a feature of many cases in which there is no dilemma, real or perceived. Thus, when a stronger obligation overrides a much weaker one, for example, when someone stops to aid a fallen bicyclist even though this makes her late for dinner, the agent faces no real dilemma, and it would be morally inappropriate for someone else to blame her morally or for her to spend time in self-blame. And should it happen that the agent feels only regret at the inconvenience she knowingly has caused, rather than guilt or remorse, there would be nothing to say against this morally.

Similarly, if I do all I can to respect equally my equal obligations to Pico and Young, it might not seem appropriate for them to blame me morally. Would either be on good moral ground in claiming that I *should* have paid him and only him? Moreover, it would not appear to be an intrinsic character defect in me were I to feel regret but not true guilt for the difficulties I have caused one or both of them. Most of us *would* feel guilt in the circumstances, and, to follow out the Millian line of thought discussed earlier, it might even be the case that anyone with sufficiently strong moral motivation in general inevitably would. But this is in part an empirical question, and it is not impossible to imagine someone of strong moral motivation who would feel nothing other than acute regret at causing like inconvenience to her creditors. Moreover, we might also say that Pico and Young are, in circumstances, under something of a moral obligation to release me from the original agreement and accept the renegotiated arrangement without trying to heap guilt upon me. In this respect, Two Loans lacks the wrenching character sometimes associated with moral dilemma—although it involves regret at harm inevitably caused by failing to live up to symmetric, non-overridden obligations, there appear to be ways of "domesticating" the moral residue within our ordinary notions of respecting obligations and those with whom we incur them. Indeed, the very symmetry of Two Loans, and many other similar examples, facilitates the domestication of moral residue because it makes the solution of choosing by lot so salient. A pair of examples involving a more serious, and not obviously compensable, harm will help illustrate this.

Paramedical Promise I

Suppose that I live in an isolated rural community with two friends, Parke and Davis. Years ago, in the army, I served as paramedic and performed a number of life-saving procedures on my own when my unit was engaged in combat. Both Parke and Davis know of this experience, and, aware of the remoteness of our small community, each has asked me to agree that I would assist him, should a life-threatening medical emergency arise. I readily promised to come at any hour and do whatever I could, although I insisted that my formal training was slight and my experience well out of date. By bizarre coincidence, and without any fault, the cars driven by Parke and Davis collide at high speed near my house. Each is in critical condition and will surely die unless a long and desperate procedure—at the very limit of what I could possibly hope to do—is performed at once. Two simultaneous procedures are out of the question, and both Parke and Davis are young, in good health, and have families. It would seem that there can be no question of compensating the individual whom I do not treat. If I draw straws to determine who will receive the procedure, have I violated any real moral obligation? The case is wrenching, but would we think there to be any *moral* merit in a complaint, lodged against me by the family of the one who dies without the procedure, that I failed to live up to my moral obligations? At the same time, wouldn't we think it true that, given the impossibility of anything like full compensation, I would fail to show full respect for the promise I made or the individual to whom I made it if I thought I had washed my hands of the matter and took no interest at all in finding ways to assist the family or children left fatherless?

Human psychology being what it is, I doubt any of us would find it incomprehensible were I to feel significant guilt over my failure to aid a friend in dire need. Yet were I, and the bereaved family, to see matters more in terms of regret than guilt and blame, this would not seem morally damning. Again, it is doubtful that we have fully described the situation if we speak solely in terms of fulfilling or failing to fulfill obligations without seeing that we have various practical and expressive means of showing respect for obligations we cannot carry out. The most dire moral dilemmas, then, would seem to be ones in which virtually all avenues of conciliation or expression are unavailable or blocked— or, indeed, in which some quite different expressive content seems unavoidable.

Paramedical Promise II

Suppose that the cases of Parke and Davis are *not* so symmetric. Suppose, for example, that Parke is my nephew—to whom I have made no special promise— while Davis is, as before, a close friend to whom I have made an explicit promise.[24] Would the solution of drawing lots now seem so salient? Is the obligation of a promise to a friend greater, weaker, or comparable to the familial obligation to a nephew? Or suppose that Parke and Davis are equally close friends, although as it happens I have made a promise only to one of them to render emergency aid. Should the fact of a promise matter at all in a case like this? When certain formal symmetries and contractual features are removed from the case, a symmetric, formalistic solution such as drawing lots comes to seem less salient and less appropriate. Indeed, it might seem to trivialize a friendship to allow the question of whether or not an explicit promise has been made to enter into such deliberation. But then it would also seem to trivialize a solemn promise—the weight of giving one's word—simply to draw straws. When a choice presents asymmetries that nonetheless do not prevent the case for both sides from being (roughly) equally compelling, resort to the lot seems to say something that one does not wish to say at all. For choices like these involve not only a choice between actions but a choice between important values and sources of obligation: family vs. friendship, friendship vs. fidelity to one's word. We view opting among such important species of value and obligation as something that calls for direct personal assumption of ultimate choice, even if the two actions are equally compelling morally, and even if we do not think that choice could be free of arbitrariness. A wrenching situation seems to become more strikingly dilemmatic precisely because it seems inappropriate to displace any responsibility for the choice onto a formal or random procedure. This inability to displace responsibility can bring with it a greater residue—in choosing, one will have in effect committed oneself as between values and sources of obligation, a potential source of regret or remorse that is absent when the kinds of value or obligation at stake are truly symmetric. This, too, is an expressive aspect of moral dilemma. It is something like a demand for full *authorship* of the action, and full recognition thereof.

Let us then turn to a final set of cases.

Sophie's Choice

This example, like Sartre's discussion of his student's quandary, has taken on a life of its own in the literature on moral dilemma, somewhat independent of original work that inspired it.[25] So I will describe it only briefly, in what I take to be its canonical form.

Sophie is imprisoned in a Nazi concentration camp, and a guard forces upon her the following choice. If she will select one of her children to be killed, the other will be allowed to live. If she refuses to select one, both will be killed. We will assume—contrary to the original—that the children are as nearly alike as possible in any dimension one might take to be relevant.

Sophie is obliged to protect the well-being of each child, and in this case it would appear that her obligation to each is equally strong, neither commitment overriding the other. Her situation thus appears to fulfill the standard characterization of a moral dilemma. Moreover, any choice she makes would appear to leave a dreadful residue: it would be, for Sophie, grounds not only for regret, but for lasting and deeply justified remorse. But compare:

Ruth's Choice

Ruth is a single parent who has given birth to Siamese twins. The hospital doctors tell her that both will die unless a complex and uncertain surgical operation is performed at once that will disconnect the two, after which only one will have the requisites for survival. Ruth is asked whether she consents to this procedure, which will involve selecting one of the two twins to emerge (if the operation is successful) capable of sustained life. Assuming that the surgeon discovers nothing new on the operating table, this could be done by lot if Ruth so wished. Her obligations to each child, again, seem equally compelling, and neither commitment overrides the other. Thus she faces a dilemma in the standard sense.

But what of residue? Would it be a sign of morally defective character were she not to experience lasting guilt at having made a choice, for example, to consent to the operation and use of the lot? Suppose that Ruth resolves not to dwell upon her choice in the future, but to prevent it from casting a cloud over her life with her new child by seeing it as nothing more than a regrettable way of having done what was necessary to save his life. And suppose this resolve proves highly successful. Would anyone think she *ought* to feel greater regret or remorse, with the inevitable effects this would have upon her psyche and her child's?

Several differences between the two cases stand out for our attention. First, in Ruth's case, quite unlike Sophie's, entry into the process of choice does not itself involve an act expressive of complicity with grave moral wrong. Second, in Ruth's case, again unlike Sophie's, the children have not lived long enough to develop established relationships with their mother or distinctive individual identities. Third, for various reasons, the most psychologically salient aspect of Ruth's Choice is the saving of a life, while the most psychologically salient aspect of Sophie's Choice is the taking of a life. These three considerations do *not* have to do with whether Sophie or Ruth face conflicting, non-overridden obligations to promote the life and well-being of each of their children. Presumably, both have such obligations if either does. That Sophie's Choice would have greater moral remainder is therefore not a consequence solely of its involving conflicting obligations—Ruth's Choice is not different in that regard. Indeed, given the cases as described here, it might even be obvious that both Ruth and Sophie should follow the same course: to accept the need to choose and to choose by lot. If common sense is much more likely to regard Sophie's Choice as an archetype of moral dilemma, I suspect that is due instead to the different expressive significance of choice in her circumstances and, perhaps above all, to the greater depth of her relationship to her individual children.

But there is also a symmetry to be found in both Sophie's and Ruth's Choice, at least as we have described them here. And if the remarks made above about symmetry are correct, then this symmetry should have a mitigating effect, and we should be able to modify the cases to create situations in which symmetry is not present and in which it therefore is even less obvious that there is a morally acceptable choice. Thus, consider a modification of the case in which each mother must choose not between two of her children, but between a single child of her own and the children of five others, or between the death of a single child and the destruction of a document that is the only source of information on the whereabouts of thousands of children who have been separated from their families. In these modified cases, a decision to use the lot no longer seems appropriate; an exercise of direct personal choice seems expressively appropriate, even if we recognize that any personal decision in such circumstances is going to be little more than desperately arbitrary.

We should be able to apply this thought about symmetry, finally, to help explain why the first moral dilemma mentioned above—that faced by Churchill regarding Coventry—has the force it does. Suppose Churchill's choice had been more symmetric. Suppose he had been forced, by a shortage of ways of sending secure messages, to decide which of two equally large and important English cities to warn of an approaching German bombardment. Here, choice by lot would seem expressively appropriate, as would the displacement of responsibility this involves—not *displacement of responsibility for deciding to warn either city A or city B*, which deciding to use the lot already presupposes on Churchill's part, but *displacement of responsibility for deciding to warn city A as opposed to city B*. In Churchill's actual situation, choice by lot does not seem appropriate. Some philosophers locate this difference in part in an asymmetry: the people of Coventry are identifiable, whereas the individuals who will be spared future Nazi attacks owing to the shortening of the war are not.[26] If Churchill is to take the terrible step of sacrificing the people and city of Coventry to help protect indeterminate future gains that would arrive from preserving (at least for now) the secret of the broken code, then it will seem to those who see an asymmetry here as if this should not be determined by the flip of a coin.

Conclusion

Characterizing Moral Dilemmas

If it is not amiss to describe The Forum, Violin Lessons, Sartre's Student, The Governor, Paramedical Promise II, and Sophie's Choice as moral dilemmas, and if Overbooking, Two Loans, Paramedical Promise I, and Ruth's Choice strike us as less genuinely or profoundly dilemmatic, then it seems inadvisable to make conflicts between non-overridden moral obligations the foundation of our thinking about dilemma. Moreover, we might begin to draw some very preliminary conclusions.

First, the possibility of moral dilemma does not seem to depend upon some or other controversial principle in deontic logic—dilemmas can arise apart from the framework of obligation or in cases in which obligation is indeterminate.

Second, even moral schemes—such as certain forms of utilitarianism—that evaluate kinds of action in terms of what is best need not preclude genuine dilemmas or "residues" that would justify remorse or guilt.[27]

Third, the alternatives that face us in cases commonsensically seen as dilemmas have typically been restricted by circumstances or human agency in a special way: ordinarily available means of compromising among alternatives or temporizing are not open to us. The one kind of obligation (almost?) universally present in commonsensically recognized dilemmas is not a *moral* obligation as such at all—it is the "obligation of circumstance." Choice has become de facto inescapable because one is aware that circumstances will irreversibly select among alternatives if one attempts to evade choice. To be sure, every choice forecloses *some* alternatives. Therefore it matters not only that some alternatives are foregone, but which.

Fourth, the existence or appropriateness of a "moral residue" does not in itself force upon us the notion of dilemma as a conflict of non-overridden obligations. Such residues can arise in cases in which a good must be foregone or an ideal compromised, but no obligation violated.[28] And one can fail to meet non-overridden obligations without creating a moral residue.

Fifth, despite its independence from obligation as such, the existence or appropriateness of residue does play a significant role in commonsense thinking about the genuineness or profoundness of dilemma. This is suggested by the fact that residue is more or less absent in the cases considered that do not strike us as deeply dilemmatic—Buridan's Ass, Overbooking, and Two Loans. We must, however, be careful with the discourse of "depth": residue and dilemma can be compelling even in cases that do not involve life or death matters—as, perhaps, in The Forum.

Sixth, obligation, and especially "living up to" our obligations or respecting those to whom they are owed, are complex and partly symbolic matters, with many routes to reconciliation and the mitigation of moral residue.

Seventh, although the literature on moral dilemma often emphasizes symmetry as a way of generating dilemma, because it can lead to conflicts among equally compelling alternatives, symmetry as such might actually lessen the dilemmatic character of choice because it can make certain procedural solutions seem obviously favored and appropriate. Asymmetries in the species of value or obligation at stake can, by contrast, make a choice seem more dilemmatic—at least if this involves the idea of a circumstance in which no choice or manner of choosing seems morally appropriate. As a result, asymmetry can yield both greater expressive significance and greater residue.

Eighth (and this is but a consequence of the conclusions already listed), a taxonomy of moral dilemmas better able to register their full import for moral theory must be multi-dimensional, taking into account not only obligation but also values or ideals, not only types and magnitudes of harm but also expressive force. Indeed, my suspicion is that expressive force and its relation to an agent's self-concept would play a central role in an improved taxonomy.

Ninth and last (for now!), it appears that the relevance of moral dilemma to moral realism is a good deal less straightforward than some "refutations" would suggest. In the first section of this essay we considered a robust moral realism that accommodated—and perhaps helped to demystify—the possibility of moral dilemma, understood as the existence of conflicting, non-overridden obligations. But in the second section of this essay, we broadened our search and considered various sources of moral dilemma. It remains to ask: Did we come across anything anathema to moral realism? Here are a few unsystematic comments.

Moral Dilemmas and Moral Realism

I have tried to suggest how a genuine moral realism might accommodate genuine moral dilemmas.

Yet there might be a counter-thought. Perhaps dilemmas indeed suggest the existence of hard-to-deny yet conflicting values or responsibilities. But however much this might point toward a kind of realism about *particular* values or responsibilities, it appears to run contrary to an important presupposition of *morality* as such—the presupposition that there is a certain "moral order" in which the most important values and duties fundamentally cohere, an order that makes possible a certain intelligibility in the realms of value, choice, and character. Historically, at least, philosophers as different as Aristotle and Kant seem to have supposed that morality would lose any rational foundation if such a moral order could not be assumed.

One can detect at least two distinct elements in this long-standing idea that some degree of moral order must be presupposed if morality is to be well founded. The first of these is one we are tempted nowadays to take less seriously. This is the notion that there must be a definite path of duty by which one can win divine approval and that affords one corresponding rewards—if not in this life, then in an afterlife. Here the idea of "rational foundation" is closely allied with "enlightened self-interest." Such a notion certainly holds out some incentive to morality, but it now seems clear that the incentive invoked is really an external one as far as morality is concerned.

But there is a second conception of "rational foundation" that must be taken more seriously and that depends upon no theistic or teleological assumptions. Moreover, if it involves "self-interest" at all, it is in a very broad sense of the term—the sense in which the unity of the self is, for an agent, always an issue. In order for the idea of a "moral life" to be an organizing principle for the development of individual character and the guidance of choice, it must be possible that this life afford (at least in the general run of circumstances) certain kinds of coherence: it must involve some degree of self-support motivationally and some degree of intelligibility cognitively. To take an extreme case, if fundamental clashes of value and obligation were the stuff of daily life, such that moral principles seldom provided any definite guidance—except perhaps to license unremitting guilt for what one cannot avoid—there would be little prospect for the moral life as a source of allegiance or as a way of understanding oneself and one's place in the world. Ordinary moral thought would seem to leave one abandoned, and one would have to plunge ahead on one's own. Many thoughtful people would doubtless seek other ways of understanding who they were and what they were doing. Thus described, this looks like a practical rather than a theoretical matter. But it might bear directly on moral realism.

For example: Elsewhere I have suggested an approach to the meaning of moral terms in which we understand them as embodying a structure of truisms about morality, paradigm cases, and so on.[29] This approach is similar to a strategy employed in giving definitions of terms in empirical theorizing.[30] Consider a natural-kind term such as 'water'. Arguably, among the truisms about water are these: that it is a chemically unified substance; that it is found in our rain, lakes, and rivers; that it is potable and necessary for life; that it can freeze, thaw, and evaporate; that it dissolves various other substances, such as sugar and salt; and so on. But suppose we cannot find any substance, or even any fairly unified family of substances, that plays all or most of these roles. Empirical inquiry discovers instead an incredible array of different substances found mixed together in rain, lakes, rivers, and so on. The mixtures vary around the globe and over time, so that rain over Athens in the time of the ancient Greeks, say, has little in common chemically with rain over San Francisco today. Some of these individual substances can play some of the roles of water, some mixtures can play others, and yet none play anything like all the roles of water. The substances can also occur separately, and often have done so in the natural environment in the past. Then we would be inclined to say that there is no such thing as water, really, just complex blends of other substances. This would make water much like "vital fluid." Even though there are lots of fluids that play essential roles in sustaining life, there is no particular, privileged fluid that distinguishes the organic from the inorganic or the living from the dead.

In a similar way, we might be led to an error theory of moral properties if no unity or practical coherence could be found among the various values or principles of choice that are central to our ordinary moral thought. The truisms we would associate with morality—that it contributes to the conditions for social harmony and the promotion of individual well-being, that it affords practical guidance in choice, that the various virtues it recognizes are compatible or even self-reinforcing, and so on.[31] In such a world, ordinary moral thought would not express a coherent evaluative or directive point of view, since any course of life, or set of choices, or internalized dispositions or standards that would fit some significant number of commonsense values or truisms would also fail to fit significantly many others, equally central. It is perhaps in this way that we can understand those who have claimed that if there is no moral order (such as an order created or sustained by God), then there can be no real distinction between right and wrong.

So what looked like a merely practical problem for morality can perhaps become a theoretical problem as well: it is not just a question of what to do, but of what to think. Thus, pervasive dilemma might lead us to think that there is no unified set of phenomena fit to play the role of moral properties, properly so called. But this sort of argument must be handled with care.

First, there is a danger of reification—of treating the circumstances in which we happen to find ourselves as merely "given." The theoretical problem that we are trying to identify for realism does not arise from the bare possibility or existence of moral dilemma. In the first section of this essay, we saw that dilemma as such need not create a contradiction for realism, and nothing we've canvassed in the second section of this essay would tend to call that discussion into question. Rather, we have perhaps seen—somewhat surprisingly?—that the theoretical bearing of moral dilemma might turn instead on *how much* dilemma we face.

But how much dilemma we face is not a given. For it depends as well upon *how much* we might do as agents to shape our acts, institutions, and circumstances in ways such that dilemmas do not become endemic. Many of the seemingly dilemmatic situations we now face—for example, regarding the conflicting claims on scarce resources or the division of one's responsibilities between family and the wider world—are perhaps the result of morally bad, but also morally alterable, institutions and practices. It might be an unalterable fact of life that the world does not support the sort of coherence that morality presupposes. But this cannot be shown by finding a handful of examples of striking moral dilemmas, especially if we fail to ask how many of the sources of moral dilemma might be in some measure within our control—if not as individuals at a moment, then socially over time.

The second danger concerns the need for coherence in a moral life. Some degree of coherence certainly is needed. Morality is a system not only of values and injunctions, but of meanings as well. It is in part a *perspective* on action and the world, and as such requires a certain amount of structure, coherence, and ordering if it is to confer distinctive and intelligible meanings upon actions and actors. Perspectives, as the metaphor suggests, presuppose a unity of vision, an integration of sorts of the sensory field. Sustaining a perspective, like sustaining any system of meanings, requires certain stabilities, uniformities, and univocalities. Absent these, the ambiguities, vaguenesses, and playfulness of language and vision would not be possible. Dilemma, in effect, prevents actions and actors from assuming a univocal character—even when choice is made of something good or right, so is choice made of something evil or wrong. Such a possibility is not unintelligible, as I tried to suggest in the first section of this essay. But its intelligibility presupposes a relatively well-structured, well-behaved background of moral significance.

Still, surely there is a danger of overstating the need for coherence as the source of intelligibility. In matters of language, prudence, and belief formation we face enormous amounts of dissonance and complexity, without letting go altogether of the idea that there are things to be said and better or worse ways of proceeding. We should not be quick to write off morality because our world is complex, although perhaps we should write off moralities that would represent it as otherwise. The semantic paradoxes are certainly at least as striking as any found in morality. Yet they do not so much destabilize the significance of ordinary language as depend upon it in order to formulate their own problematic content. We see the paradoxes as having significance, and we can understand the different ways in which they are paradoxical, because meanings in fact have enough inertia to carry us that far, given the relatively stable background of linguistic significance afforded by language as a whole. Discussions of moral dilemma often serve to illuminate just how much of our fine-grained scheme of moral distinctions can be brought to bear in understanding precisely the sorts of conflict and loss that are in question.

I would modestly propose that the debate over moral dilemma spend more time with the question "How much?" than it has in the past. This question faces us from several directions: How much irreconcilable conflict is there? How much could this be affected by changing human institutions and practices? And how much unity or coherence really is presupposed by the idea of a moral life or a moral point of view? My sense is that we tend to over-estimate this last, and that as a result we tend to downplay various quite real conflicts. This in turn leads us to downplay the quite substantial amount we might do to eliminate them.

We want our actions and institutions to say something about ourselves, typically something positive or at least not manifestly negative. We build monuments, hold celebrations and solemn rituals, and cover our conduct and history with explanations. Dilemma threatens to interrupt this impressive spectacle, however, since it makes it inevitable that our actions also say something negative, no matter what we try. Yet this reveals an unexpected affinity between dilemma and realism, for both contain the idea that the moral significance of our actions is no mere invention.[32]

Notes

An earlier version of this paper was presented at a conference on moral dilemma held at the University of Minnesota. I am grateful to my co-participants at that conference, and also those at an *Ethics* conference held on moral pluralism at Rollins College, for much helpful discussion. I am also especially indebted to Ronald Dworkin, Thomas Nagel, and Walter Sinnott-Armstrong for comments on earlier versions. As editor and colleague, Gene Mason has suggested many improvements—too many for individual citation. I hope that I have done them justice.

1. Ronald Dworkin has urged that we see Churchill's choice as a paradigm of a

real dilemma, and that it can be understood as having forced him to choose among two impermissible possibilities. Dworkin does not, however, see this as undermining all possibility of morality, only of specific moral theories such as utilitarianism (personal communication).

2. This argument is inspired in part by Bernard Williams's discussion in Williams (1966), reprinted in Williams (1973), pp. 204–5. See n. 11 for further discussion.

3. Later in the first section of this essay, we will strengthen this idea to include as well the possibility of "moral residue." The formulation here is borrowed, with slight modification, from Walter Sinnott-Armstrong ([1988], pp. 4–5). Sinnott-Armstrong's book seems to have played an important role in promoting shared understanding in debates about the nature of moral dilemma. There is one respect in which his usage has not been followed: Sinnott-Armstrong speaks of conflicting, non-overridden moral *requirements*, whereas most discussions of moral dilemma proceed in terms of moral *obligations*. I will follow the more common usage, in large measure because I seldom hear people characterize their moral situations in terms of *requirements*, although talk of *obligations* is fairly common. In particular, I seldom hear people characterize situations that strike them as dilemmatic in terms of competing *requirements*—perhaps in part because we tend to use 'morally required' only for an action-guiding conclusion of moral deliberation.

4. This conception receives some defense in Railton and Rosen (1995). For a further catalogue of dimensions associated with moral realism, see also Railton (1986a), pp. 164–5.

5. For an example of a nonstandard explanation, see Simon Blackburn, *Spreading the Word* (Oxford: Clarendon, 1984). Some theorists who have been associated with the label 'noncognitivism', such as R. M. Hare, insist that their view should be understood otherwise. They think that moral discourse is capable of truth or falsity in the ordinary sense, but deny that such discourse is *descriptive*, and thus deny that moral statements are made true or false by the instantiation of properties or states of affairs.

6. See Mackie (1977), ch. 1. Mackie himself apparently holds that it is only as a matter of fact, and not of necessity, that moral predicates are not instantiated. For although "objective prescriptivity" seems at first blush strictly incomprehensible, Mackie suggests, although without much explanation, (p. 48), that in a world with the right sort of deity, there would be objective prescriptivity and at least some moral judgments would be true.

7. For an example, see Schiffer (1990). However, Schiffer's view has complexities that I will pass over here.

8. For discussion of minimalist and somewhat-less-than-minimalist conceptions of truth, with special reference to the question of realism, see Wright (1993).

9. It is important to note that any cognitivist—realist, anti-realist, or irrealist—can acknowledge: (*a*) that in nonstandard contexts moral judgments might function merely to express attitudes, and (*b*) that in typical contexts moral judgments have multiple functions: both the expression of a proposition and the prescription or licensing of some attitude or behavior.

10. The qualification '(quite possibly)' is inserted to avoid the unwanted implication that realism about a subject matter excludes fallibilism about its central claims. Most realists, I would venture, are fallibilists on the following "scientific" model: although previous theories have often come to be rejected or massively revised, this has been a process of correction and improvement in the direction of truth; no doubt current theories will also be superseded, but they are on to something.

11. Here is a related passage from Williams (1973). In it, he is developing the suggestion that a realist explanation of moral conflict and the pressure toward "moral consistency" must differ from a practical, non-realist account:

It is obvious, and agreed by all, that the general run of ethical discourse has some features in common with assertions or descriptive discourse. . . . These features, together with other and very familiar considerations, notoriously led some philosophers to take the view that moral judgements were assertions reporting moral states of affairs. . . . [O]n a realist view, the significance of consistency, and the explanation of it as an aim, are going to come down to the simple point that moral judgements being straightforwardly assertions, two inconsistent moral judgements cannot both be true, and hence (truth being the aim of assertions) cannot both be acceptable. (p. 204)

Since Williams comments on the incompleteness of his discussion, we shouldn't attribute the Straightforward Argument to him.

12. Of course, Mill's conception of happiness is complex. For the sake of simplicity, let us understand it as the satisfaction of preferences one would have for the course of one's own life if one were widely experienced. Considerable argument would be needed to establish that this is (as I blithely claim) a naturalistic, psychological property. For some discussion, see Railton (1986b). To be sure, the question of realism is a separate issue from naturalism. For although realism does involve the idea of moral language referring to robust states of affairs, these need not be *naturalistic* states of affairs. Naturalism figures in the present argument only as one way of making credible the idea of a robust state of affairs.

13. This particular utilitarian characterization of obligation is incomplete: it does not tell us how to assess or amalgamate happiness, or whether to count the costs and likely success rate of inculcating any given set of rules and expectations, or what to say if more than one set—which might differ in whether they include punishment for failing to X in like circumstances—would be maximally happiness-promoting, and so on. Still, let us assume that sufficiently definite answers have been given to such questions, without undercutting the realism of the view.

14. Stephen Yablo explores an idea of this kind in an unpublished manuscript.

15. It might be claimed that while an *indirect* utilitarianism of the broadly Millian kind considered here is consistent with the possibility of moral dilemma, a direct utilitarianism is not. However, this does not appear to be so. A realist act-utilitarian (for example) who does not want simply to explain away all moral dilemmas can surely note the possibility of equal-best courses of action. Unless some care is taken in defining act utilitarianism, this possibility will arise immediately from the fact that more than one course of action might be ranked first. For further discussion, see Railton (1992).

16. See Blackburn (1984) and Gibbard (1990).

17. Of course, it is true in general that whenever one makes or postpones a decision one forgoes *some* opportunities irrevocably. What presses us in the direction of a sense of urgency or dilemma has more to do with the *kinds* of opportunities that will be foregone—for example, they have very important benefits, or others like them will not reoccur, or they are of a kind one would never otherwise pass up—and the *difficulty of offsetting or compensating* for the lost opportunities.

18. The case appears in Sartre (1956), in Solomon (1974), pp. 203–4.

19. Perhaps there is a French cultural norm at work here as well, assigning to adult children greater responsibility for their parents.

20. Sartre writes:

The existentialist is strongly opposed to a certain type of secular morality which seeks to suppress God at the least possible expense . . . [and introduces the idea that] it must be considered obligatory *a priori* to be honest, not to lie, not to beat one's wife, to bring up children, and so forth; . . . the existentialist, in the contrary, finds it extremely embarrassing that God does not exist. . . . Everything is indeed permitted if God does not exist. (1956), in Solomon (1974), pp. 201–2.

21. I am indebted to Elizabeth Anderson for helpful discussion of the expressive aspects of choice and action.

22. See Foot (1983), p. 387.

23. A sidelight on the case of Overbooking: Although it would be odd if there were any moral residue in the case, it would also be odd were I not to apologize to both (even though everything worked out well). The need to manifest respect for the promises, and for those to whom they were made, is not solely derivative from the inconvenience caused. It has, one might think, a symbolic but nonetheless indispensable character—which is to say that symbolism is by no means always a trivial matter, but rather is often one of the important dimensions of social practices. It would be very surprising were either Winkle or Squires to think it inappropriate for me to say "I'm sorry about the mix-up on my part," but more surprising still were either to think I should feel genuine *sorrow* in this case.

24. This case is modeled on an actual example described to me by Thomas Nagel.

25. Styron (1980), with apologies to the author.

26. A suggestion of this sort was made to me by Frances Kamm.

27. And not simply because of "ties" for best, as our Millian example in the first section of this essay showed. The *mere* fact of a tie for best might yield only a moral Buridan's Ass case rather than a genuine dilemma.

28. For a defense of the opposite view, see Sinnott-Armstrong's argument that the only plausible reason for feeling remorse is the violation of a moral requirement, Sinnott-Armstrong (1988), pp. 41–51.

29. See Railton (1993) for some discussion of this approach.

30. See David Lewis's discussion of "How to Define Theoretical Terms," reprinted in Lewis (1983). His approach uses the whole empirical theory (suitably Ramsified) for definitional purposes, but can also be adapted to give special weight to truisms.

31. Richard Boyd (1988) suggests a similar kind of concern in his discussion of "homeostatic clusters."

32. Of course, however congenial this idea might be to the realist—however little it might point us away from realism—it is not the unique possession of realists.

10

Moral Dilemmas, Gaps, and Residues:
A Kantian Perspective

THOMAS E. HILL, JR.

No one, I suspect, accepts everything that Kant said about moral matters, but many remain hopeful that Kant's ideas, suitably modified and supplemented, might be developed into an ethical theory that meets most familiar objections and remains worthy of serious consideration. The project of developing such a Kantian theory, however, faces formidable obstacles. Prominent among these are problems concerning conflicts of duty. Alan Donagan has addressed at length the most familiar problem of this sort: the charge that Kantian principles generate unresolvable moral dilemmas.[1] Although correct and important in its main thesis, I think that Donagan's defense of a Kantian position concedes too much in one way and too little in another. Moreover, the objection to which Donagan responds is not the only problem Kantians must face regarding moral conflicts.

For example, even if Kantian moral theory does not absolutely command incompatible courses of action, it is hard to deny that the theory has *gaps*. If so, it may leave us to face tragic moral conflicts without guidance and without reason to expect that there is, even in theory, a best option. What is worse, Kantian theory seems to give conscientious moral agents the wrong message *after* they had to make such choices. If they had "good wills," why should they have any personal regret or special concern for those they have harmed? We commonly expect people to feel bad when they knowingly cause harm to others, even if there was nothing morally better they could have done. But does this make sense from a Kantian perspective? How, in fact, can a Kantian say that they "should feel" anything at all?

In what follows, I explain these problems more fully and sketch some lines of response that I think are reasonable and compatible with Kantian ethical theory, broadly construed. My discussion will be divided as follows. (I) I mention a variety of reasons why philosophers have been interested in cases of moral conflict, distinguish some different issues raised by such cases, and identify the questions that will be my main concern. (II) I summarize some common features of theories that, for purposes of discussion, I shall count as "Kantian." (III) I review critically Alan Donagan's response to the objection that Kantian theory generates unresolvable moral dilemmas. (IV) I grant that Kant's moral theory has gaps, but suggest that such indeterminacy may be better than the alternatives. (V) I describe what I take to be common and reasonable views about how conscientious persons should feel *after* they have acted in cases of tragic moral conflicts. (VI) I respond to the suspicion that Kantian moral theory is deeply incompatible with these common expectations. I conclude that Kantians should agree that those forced to make hard choices in practical moral dilemmas have grounds for agent-regret and special concern for those they have harmed, even if they acted with good will. In a sense, this is just how they should feel.

I. Questions about Practical Moral Dilemmas

Conscientious people at times find themselves in situations I shall call *practical moral dilemmas*. That is, they confront situations in which important, and apparently decisive, moral considerations seem to demand incompatible courses of action, condemning all their options, and they see no reasonable way to resolve the conflict. In the most dramatic cases they know that they will cause grave harm whatever they do. Through no fault of their own, principles and values that they assumed could never be compromised pull at them from opposite directions, threatening to tear apart that unity of soul long supposed to be the only indestructible reward of virtue.

There are some moral conflicts that we cannot resolve simply because we lack relevant information. Often we must act under uncertainty, sometimes almost in darkness, with regard to facts that, if known, would leave us in no doubt about what we should do. But in the conflict situations on which I want to focus here, the moral tension that the conscientious person experiences is not due to missing information. The problem is that, even given the facts as we see them, the moral values and principles to which we are committed seem to draw us strongly to opposing conclusions without offering any non-arbitrary way to choose between them. What we need is not more facts, it seems, but a better way to think about the facts we have.

Literary and religious classics offer a rich array of stories to illustrate the problem. Antigone, for instance, felt that she must either dishonor her brother or disobey the king, and Abraham thought (before being told otherwise) that he must sacrifice his son or disobey God.[2] Films and novels suggest further dramatic examples: in the film *High Noon,* the sheriff's bride must abandon either her pacifist convictions or her husband and his just cause; in the film and novel *Sophie's Choice,* Sophie must lose both her children or accept the fiendish Nazi demand that she select which child is to die; and in John Fowles's novel *The Magus,* a mayor can save eighty villagers from Nazi atrocity only by personally beating to death two guerillas whom he regards morally innocent. Philosophers, of course, have invented a further range of now-familiar stories having to do with runaway trolleys, fat men stuck in caves, and so on. Ordinary life offers more mundane but still significant cases of moral conflict that are encountered as having no reasonable, or even acceptable, resolutions.

Philosophers have had a special fascination with such cases, for various reasons. *Teachers of ethics* like to use dramatic cases of moral conflict to capture the

attention of lethargic students, perhaps unintentionally luring them into philosophy with the false hope that what is practically difficult becomes easy after
one has studied a bit of moral theory. Those doing serious work in *applied ethics*
are often called upon to give moral advice on real and urgent cases of moral
conflict, and so, understandably, they want to discuss past and hypothetical
cases in an effort to stimulate the thinking of professionals who must soon face
such decisions.

For *moral theorists,* the examples of apparent moral dilemmas offer a challenge, testing the resources of their theories as well as their skills as casuists. As
advocates of particular theories, they typically want to defend and confirm their
theories by showing how the theories can resolve apparent moral dilemmas. As
critics, they often hope to expose the limitations of other theories by demon-
strating that the theories remain silent on cases that clearly call for a moral
response; and, more ambitiously, they may try to prove a theory incoherent by
arguing that the theory yields contradictory prescriptions in hard cases. Some
conclude from the prevalence of practical moral dilemmas that what we call
"morality" is a fragmented cluster of incommensurable ideals and principles
that in ordinary circumstances serve well enough, but in crisis situations lead to
nothing but ambivalence and tragedy. Others see apparent moral dilemmas as
colorful entries into some intriguing metatheoretical questions, such as whether
admitting the existence of genuine moral dilemmas is compatible with moral
realism and a satisfactory deontic logic.

Questions about practical moral dilemmas, of course, are not merely of interest to professional philosophers. On the contrary, they are prompted by concerns that any conscientious person might have when facing such moral conflicts.

The first concern naturally is the immediately practical one, (1) *How can I
find a way to resolve the dilemma?* That is, a conscientious person will want to
continue to ask whether there are new options, previously overlooked facts, and
alternative perspectives on the conflict that favor one course of action over the
other, thus revealing the dilemma to be merely apparent.

If this effort fails repeatedly, despite one's best efforts, the tension and
frustration of the search may well prompt the more abstract question, (2) *Can it
really be, as it seems, that I will be morally wrong whichever option I take?* Could this
be so, one might well wonder, even after all things are considered, including the
extraordinary circumstances of the case and the fact that one has searched so
hard to find something morally permissible to do?

An affirmative answer may seem too paradoxical to accept. But even so, if
efforts to resolve the dilemma continue to fail, the conscientious agent might
still wonder, (3) *Can it really be, as it seems, that morality pulls me so strongly in
opposite directions and yet lacks the resources to determine which way, all things
considered, I should go?* Is it possible that there simply is no resolution, that no
further facts or reflection can help me, and so I must make an arbitrary choice?
The question here is not whether morality prescribes too much but whether it
prescribes too little. That is, the concern is not whether morality makes demands that we cannot meet but whether it is silent when we want advice.

Now suppose that, though still unable to find a morally satisfactory resolution to the conflict, the conscientious agent decides that to delay action longer would be even worse than embracing other options, and so simply seizes one horn of the dilemma, causing, as expected, grave harm.³ Imagine that even afterward, despite more reflection and consultation with others, the agent finds no reason to change his initial assessment of the conflict. Now further questions arise, questions about "moral residues." Most obviously, there is a new practical question to face about how to *act* in the aftermath of the dilemma. That is, (4) *What should I do now? For example, must I make reparation, compensate, or apologize to those I have harmed or to their survivors? Do I have a special obligation to comfort or ameliorate the plight of the injured?*

No matter how they decide these questions concerning residual obligations, conscientious agents who have seriously harmed others by the stand they have taken in a practical dilemma may feel regret and experience painful guilt, or guilt-like, feelings. Then they may well wonder whether these painful feelings are morally important responses or merely insignificant side effects that they would do well, if possible, to ignore or be rid of. More generally, they may ask, (5) *Now that I have taken a stand in an unresolved practical moral dilemma, what should my attitudes and feelings be about myself and those I have harmed?*

This last question is not about what one should *do,* either in confronting a practical moral dilemma or afterward; rather, it is about how one should *be* after having made a hard choice in a situation of serious moral conflict. It concerns the *attitude* one should take, how one should *feel,* and how one should *regard* oneself and those one has harmed when, despite one's best efforts, one has had simply to seize one horn of an unresolved practical moral dilemma. This question may be prior to the preceding question about what one should do, and it would remain significant even if there was nothing compensatory or ameliorative one could do, for example, because the injured parties died without survivors.

For present purposes I set aside the controversial topic of how Kantian principles and procedures can determine what we ought to *do* in various situations. That is, I address questions (2), (3), and (5), but not (1) and (4). In sum, the issues are: Can one, within a broadly Kantian perspective, acknowledge that there are genuine moral dilemmas, tragic gaps in moral theory, and morally significant residues of feeling and attitude?

II. Some Features of Kantian Moral Theory

Since our project is to investigate how Kantian moral theory can respond to questions about practical moral dilemmas, we need at least a preliminary account of what is to count as "Kantian" for purposes of our discussion. Theories that are called Kantian vary widely, and there is room for reasonable disagreement about which of Kant's beliefs a theory must preserve in order to use the label without disrespect. Here I merely stipulate some main features of "Kantian theory" as I intend to understand it in my subsequent discussion.

1. Kantian ethics is primarily *addressed to concerns we have as rational moral agents,* as we deliberate conscientiously about what we ought to do. Morality

must make sense from this first-person, deliberative point of view. Standards of how we evaluate, praise, and blame others are secondary, derivative, and of less practical importance. It is not the task of moral philosophy to give third-person perspective, empirical explanations of moral phenomena (e.g., how we talk, behave, and feel). Although presumably such explanations are possible, moral principles and the conception of the agent that they presuppose are not reducible to these.

2. Moral "oughts" purport to express categorical imperatives or judgments based upon these.[4] At least this is so in paradigm cases of moral "oughts" that strictly prescribe or prohibit specified actions. These *express rational requirements on choice* that are not grounded in either the need to take necessary means to one's particular contingent ends or one's general desire for happiness. If I have a strict ("perfect") duty not to do something, then no matter what the competing reasons, I must not do it; for me to choose otherwise would be wrong and contrary to reason.

3. Categorical imperatives and the moral judgments derived from them express rational prescriptions *in a vocabulary of constraint* ("must," "bound," "obligatory," "duty," "Do it!") that reflects how recognizing a rational moral requirement is experienced by those ("imperfect wills") who know that they can satisfy the requirement but also know that they can and might violate the requirement and choose instead to pursue some conflicting desire-based end. To acknowledge that one is morally bound to do something goes beyond thinking that it would be "a good thing to do *if possible.*" Rather, it expresses a sense that this is the course of action, *among those open to the agent,* that is rationally and morally demanded.

Acknowledging a moral duty is also more than believing that one is under an actual command of some person or group. Moral duties are "commands *of reason,*" that is, "oughts" based on considerations generally recognizable as reasonable, whether actually commanded by someone or not. Individual and group authorities can, and at times do, issue commands that are so demanding that their subjects cannot obey them in all circumstances, and they may have reasons for refusing to accept "I could not comply" as an excuse.[5] But Kantian "commands of reason" are essentially directives for deliberating agents that tell them *how to choose among options* presumed to be available to them in their situation. Kant opposed the facile use of "I can't" as a bad-faith excuse; for example, presuming without adequate grounds that one is inwardly too weak or frail to do what (Kant believed) duty requires. But his concept of duty implies that what is manifestly physically impossible for a person to do cannot be that person's duty, all things considered, to do or even to "will" to do.[6]

4. Moral "oughts" express a deep, self-identifying, and inescapable disposition of moral agents, who have reason and autonomy of will, to acknowledge certain considerations as overridingly authoritative and so internally binding.[7] Therefore, if I am a moral agent, I cannot be indifferent to what I judge I morally ought to do in the way I might be indifferent to what I believe conforms to prevailing social norms or maximizes general utility. For fully developed moral agents, then, the first and virtually inevitable penalty for moral failure is self-condemnation: one identifies oneself, in a sense, as moral law maker and

judge as well as law breaker, and so it is painful to acknowledge "*I* should have, *I* could have, and yet *I* chose not to."

5. It is a fundamental moral principle that humanity in each person is to be regarded as an end in itself. We are to attribute dignity, an unconditional and incomparable worth, to all human beings, insofar as they are presumed to have the capacity for rational and moral living.[8] In part we acknowledge this dignity by trying to restrict our personal policies to those we judge, in reasonable and appropriately impartial reflection, to be policies that would be rationally accept-able for anyone to adopt for relevantly similar circumstances. We can think of the policies and acts that would be acceptable for everyone, in the relevant sense, as just those policies and acts that would conform to the "universal laws" that moral legislators would accept if trying to work out a reasonable system of moral principles under certain ideal conditions ("the kingdom/realm of ends").[9]

6. These general principles are supposed to establish a strong presumption against willful deception and manipulation. For example, trying to motivate people to avoid practical dilemmas by cultivating in them a false sense of guilt would not be an option for Kantians.

7. When thinking from a practical moral perspective rather than an empiri-cal scientific perspective, we conceive typical human actions as done inten-tionally—for reasons—by agents presumed capable of choosing to act differ-ently. We understand or explain an action from this point of view by attributing to the agent a rationale. A rationale is not a *causal* explanation, as this is usually understood, but a reconstruction of the beliefs, intentions, aims, policies, and deepest commitments that (we suppose) made up the agent's *normative* reasons for ("freely") choosing to do what he or she did. Thus, we think of actions as typically done intentionally on the basis of agents' judgments as to what they had good reason to do, given their perceived options, aims, commitments, and implicit norms of rational choice. A person's judgment can be unreflective, clouded, and perhaps suspended under pressures of various kinds, but, at least in serious moral cases, we still typically attribute to the agent the final capacity and responsibility to use and follow judgment. ("He *let* his feelings overpower him," we say.) Conscientious agents, when acting to do what duty requires, are conceived as acting on their *judgment* that the particular act was (overridingly) good to do, based on a *rationale* that includes both their deep disposition (*Wille*) as rational moral agents acknowledge the moral law as authoritative and their commitment to a personal policy (maxim) of conforming to it.[10]

8. In human beings practical judgments and feelings are not usually sepa-rable.[11] Our moral judgments have an impact on our sensibility. For example, we *feel* respect for the moral law because we acknowledge its validity, we *feel* respect for people because we judge their acts to exemplify the moral law, and we *feel* moral contentment or remorse because we judge ourselves to be inno-cent or guilty. Normally, when we make a moral judgment we experience a corresponding affective response, and this is so familiar, expected, and deeply human that, barring special explanation, we are very reluctant to believe a person who claims to make a moral judgment but altogether lacks the usual corresponding affect. For example, we would naturally doubt the sincerity (or self-awareness) of someone who said, "It is wrong to humiliate women, I know,

but I love to do it and I have no bad feelings about doing it." Feelings of constraint or revulsion are not the ultimate *grounds* of the judgment that it is wrong for one to treat others with disrespect, but, given normal human sensibility, such feelings are among the expected signs that one genuinely recognizes that such treatment violates the basic norms of morality and reason to which one is committed.

III. Are Genuine Moral Dilemmas Possible?

What makes this question particularly challenging for Kantians is that Kant held that ethics is based on reason and that a rational moral system cannot admit genuine conflicts of duty, and yet despite this Kant presents principles in his *Groundwork* and *The Metaphysics of Morals* that, when applied to hard cases, seem to yield conflicting prescriptions. I begin with a few remarks about this second point.

The first natural question upon confronting a practical dilemma is, "How can I find a way to resolve the (apparent) dilemma?" The Kantian answer to this, although long and complex in detail, is easy to summarize: Review the facts of the case, explore your options, and be guided by the ideas expressed in the various versions of the Categorical Imperative. Alternatively, if you are convinced (as I am not) that Kant's system of principles in *The Metaphysics of Morals* is derivable from his fundamental principles, then the answer is: Use that system, with casuistry and good judgment, to work out what to do in your conflict situation. Unfortunately, it has seemed to many that these procedures not only leave some apparent dilemmas unresolved but also that they themselves *generate* dilemmas.

The Metaphysics of Morals, for example, includes many unqualified principles that apparently can conflict: they include not only prohibitions of adultery, murder, and slavery but also "perfect" duties against lying, rebellion against lawful government, and any form of disrespect for others. Also, at least one form of the Categorical Imperative (if thickly interpreted)[12] seems more liable to generate practical dilemmas than to solve them. This is the Formula of Humanity, which attributes an unconditional and incomparable value to each person. The problem is that sometimes it seems that one cannot fully respect the value of humanity in one person without violating it in another.

Alan Donagan has argued ingeniously against the facile assumption that Kant's principles *actually* generate unresolvable conflicts in *real* cases. The stories offered as posing dilemmas, he argued, often turn out to overlook distinctions between "doing" and "letting," between the consequences of one's acts and the consequences of others' responses to one's acts, and so on.[13] To the same end, I suggested in an earlier paper one way a Kantian could try to resolve moral conflicts that stem from the Formula of Humanity.[14] The basic idea is to take the Formula of Humanity as prescribing a basic moral attitude, not a decision procedure to be applied case by case. If it is understood as expressing a value that can be incorporated into procedures for moral reflection on how *general principles* of conduct should be specified, what exceptions they should allow, and so on, then at this higher level of deliberation we may find reasons for adjudicating apparent (first-order) moral conflicts one way or another.

Unfortunately, neither Donagan's procedures for resolving apparent moral dilemmas nor mine guarantee success in all cases. What one must do, in either case, is to examine each apparent dilemma, with the background facts and arguments that seem to generate it, as it arises. Donagan had remarkable confidence that, with an exception to be considered later in this essay, such ad hoc investigations could resolve all the apparent dilemmas generated by Kant's Formula of Humanity and the system of moral precepts derivable from it. Here I think Donagan conceded too little to Kant's critics; for, despite all Donagan says, it seems to me that extraordinary circumstances can put one in a situation, through no fault of one's own, in which one has to break a promise or tell a lie even though doing so would be forbidden by the rigorous precepts accepted by Kant and Donagan.[15] But I shall not press the point here, as it is incidental to my main project.

Instead, let us consider what follows if Kant's actual principles and precepts sometimes unequivocally prescribe incompatible courses of action.[16] Must Kantians then concede that genuine moral dilemmas are possible? The answer, as Donagan has made clear, is, No, because there are other theoretical options.

To see this, consider the following propositions that Kant himself held: (*a*) to have a moral duty is to be under a practical command of reason; (*b*) reason cannot issue incompatible practical commands, and so (*c*) there can be no genuine conflict of duties; (*d*) the moral principles presented in Kant's works are correct, as stated, without need for further qualification; and (*e*) these principles, judiciously applied, will not in fact impose incompatible demands on anyone.

If, as suggested above, we suppose that Kant's principles sometimes lead to incompatible demands, we reject (*e*). Contemporary Kantians can still hold on to Kant's central tenets (*a*)–(*c*) if they are willing to deny (*d*). In other words, Kantians can still deny the possibility of genuine moral dilemmas if they are willing to modify the particular principles in Kant's moral system that generate the apparent dilemma. Many contemporary Kantians would grant that Kant's particular precepts, for example, those about lying and disobedience to civil authorities, need to be modified to allow more exceptions, regardless of whether the precepts generate dilemmas.[17] Even Donagan, who believed that Kant's principles do not need much modification to avoid troublesome dilemmas, conceded that the principles *would* have to be revised *if* they generated incompatible prescriptions to *innocent* persons.

Given that apparent conflicts resulting from Kant's principles leave them a choice, Kantian theorists, in my opinion, will preserve more of the central and distinctive features of Kant's ethics by rethinking the arguments leading to apparent dilemmas and, if necessary, revising Kant's system of principles than by taking the alternative course, which would be to abandon the rationalist conception of duty that refuses to tolerate moral dilemmas. That is, assuming (*e*) above is false, it is better to abandon (*d*) than (*a*)–(*c*).

A revision of Kant's system of principles to avoid dilemmas, we should note, need not be undertaken in a piecemeal fashion. Rather than trying to modify each particular principle separately, a Kantian revisionist might insure the whole system of principles against dilemmas by a qualification: if the principles, as so far stated, unequivocally prescribe incompatible courses of action, then take that judgment as only provisional and count both courses, or at least one, as permissible in the special circumstances.[18]

To summarize: Is it *possible,* then, that I can be in a situation in which I will be *wrong no matter what I do?* The answer Kantians should give, in my view, is *No.* The reason lies in the Kantian conception of moral judgments discussed in section II, (1)–(3). The primary function of moral judgments (expressed by "ought," "duty," and "wrong") is to express rational demands on our *wills* as deliberating agents, telling us which among our (perceived) options to choose to take. If all options seem to be morally condemned and yet we cannot avoid taking one or another of them, then we must rethink the issue, for we cannot coherently judge, from this Kantian point of view, that every choice we could make would be strictly wrong, such that doing it in that actual situation would be contrary to duty, all things considered. If rethinking yields no practical resolution, we can conjecture that Kant's system permits a resolution that we have been as yet unable to see, or we can admit that Kant's principles need to be amended. In either case, however, we must concede that, despite appearances, at least one available option must be permissible.

My remarks here obviously draw from Donagan's admirable discussions of moral dilemmas, but there is an important difference between his position and the Kantian position I have just described. Donagan argued that rationalist ethical theories must reject the possibility of genuine moral dilemmas *except when the agent got into a dilemma situation through his own fault.*[19] Suppose, for example, I promised a person to do something and then wrongly promised someone else that I would do what I knew was incompatible with my fulfilling the first promise. On Donagan's view, rationalist ethics can concede that at this point *I will do wrong no matter what I do.* He held, however, that even if all my options are contrary to duty, one option may still be morally *worse* than another and, if so, I should *do the lesser evil.*[20] The lesser evil, as well as the greater, remains condemned by inflexible moral principles, and so I cannot avoid doing wrong; but I can and should try to control the damage and minimize the offense.

Donagan found in Thomas Aquinas's work a precedent for his idea that rationalist ethics can tolerate moral dilemmas *when (but only when) the agent is already at fault,* but he had at least two further motives for making this exception to his general denial of moral dilemmas.

First, Donagan wanted to defend a system of quite rigorous moral precepts modeled on (but not identical with) Kant's system in *The Metaphysics of Morals.* Donagan thought that he could show, with subtle casuistry and attention to detail, that most cases alleged to be dilemmas resulting from his own precepts turn out to be spurious. Cases in which guilty agents themselves generated the problem, however, he acknowledged to be more intractable. To argue that moral dilemmas do not arise even in these cases, he would have had to admit many more exceptions into his system of moral precepts than he thought tolerable.

Second, if we allow no exceptions to our denial of moral dilemmas, then the following objection arises. Suppose I make a promise and then wrongfully make a second promise knowing that I cannot keep both. If I keep the first and not the second, supposing this to be morally best in the circumstances, then neither "I could not keep both" nor "I was wrong to have made the second promise" is an adequate defense when the second promisee complains, "But, nonetheless, you did wrong in breaking your promise to me." By conceding that there can be moral dilemmas resulting from the agent's misconduct, Donagan could grant the objector's judgment, "Having wrongly made the second promise, you would have then done wrong, no matter what you had done."[21]

Whatever his motives, by conceding that there can be genuine unresolvable conflicts of duty Donagan abandoned a feature of Kant's ethics that seems to me quite central. What is lost is the idea that moral principles and precepts can guide the decision making of every deliberative agent, the guilty as well as the innocent, to choices they can make without further wrongdoing. So conceived, morality acknowledges that human beings are imperfect and often guilty, but it calls upon each at every new moment of moral deliberation to decide conscientiously and to act rightly from that point on. No matter how guilty in the past, each person is respected as now able to do and responsible for doing only what duty permits and always what duty requires, all things considered, in her or his situation.[22] To say that every option is wrong—strictly contrary to duty—in fact makes no sense if *duty* is understood in the Kantian way described earlier. It would be like saying that practical reason, after due reflection, unequivocally directs you now to refuse to take any of your available options, including doing nothing. A perverse secular authority might "demand" this and then pretend to justify punishment by citing your noncompliance with his orders; but no one should confuse his orders with the voice of practical reason.[23]

Let us reconsider the motives mentioned above that inclined Donagan to grant that there can be moral dilemmas if the agent is at fault. One was the desire to maintain, without further modification, a quite inflexible system of moral precepts. Donagan saw that to deny moral dilemmas without qualification, a Kantian would have to modify his system of moral precepts, as needed, to ensure that, whatever the situation, agents have at least one permissible option. For Donagan and others fully confident of his system of strict precepts, this consideration makes sense; but its appeal is quite limited. For example, to those who share my sense that modifications in the Donagan/Kant systems of precepts are needed *even apart from worries about dilemmas,* a wish to avoid modifying the precepts is not a very compelling reason for tolerating moral dilemmas.

Consider, then, the second motive that inclined Donagan to grant that there are moral dilemmas created by the agents' misconduct: Donagan's belief that this concession is necessary to make moral sense of the second promisee's complaint in the two-promise story. It is arguable, however, that our moral intuitions about this case can be accommodated by less drastic measures. Assuming that in this case the second promise was wrongly made and breaking it would have been morally worse (or no better) than breaking the first, we do not need to say that the promisor was morally *wrong,* or *ought not,* to have broken the second promise. We can say, instead, that the agent is to blame *for making* the second promise and that in breaking the promise he *incurred further obligations* to the second promisee. He incurs these further obligations not because he was *wrong* to break the second promise, but because in doing so he disappointed legitimate expectations that he knowingly and wrongfully raised. Now he must apologize and try to make up for the damage he caused, for, although his breaking of the second promise was the right thing to do, it was foreseeable as the (morally) necessary extension of his earlier moral offense: the making of the second promise. By denying that the promisor was in a genuine moral dilemma, then, we do not provide him with a blanket excuse from liability to blame and compensation. The complaining second promisee was right to suggest that breaking a promise is a *kind* of act that is *normally* wrong, but not to suggest that the agent's choice to break that promise, in the actual situation, was wrong, all things considered. When morally *required* to do what is called "the lesser of two evils," we must be *permitted* to do it and thus doing it, from the best motives, is not really an "evil." If we created the problem, however, we are to blame for that, and consequently we are obligated to compensate for the damage we do in response to the problem.

Now one might argue on Donagan's behalf that there may be less substantive difference than at first it seems between his view and the Kantian position as I have presented it. The differences, and apparent incompatibility, may be partly due to matters of terminology. For example, when Donagan says that in a moral dilemma (of the sort he allows) the agent cannot avoid doing something *imper-missible, wrong*, and *contrary to duty*, he may be using these words in a special way. Perhaps what he *means* is just that given his situation, the agent cannot avoid doing something contrary to a set of rules that morality and reason pre-scribe to all *in an initial position of innocence* as rules that *at that initial point* they should resolve to follow, and can follow, without exception. Perhaps, too, "im-permissible" and "wrong" for Donagan imply the undisputed point that the agent may be liable to compensate for damages and subject to blame (at least for prior choices leading to the moral necessity to do "wrong"). If he were to interpret the relevant terms in this special way, Donagan *could* say, without incoherence, that in some situations morality and reason demand that a person do something "wrong" and "impermissible," namely the "lesser evil."[24] Then, so construed, his contention that there can be fault-generated moral dilemmas would not be in conflict with the *substantive* Kantian point that, whatever the situation, there is something a conscientious person can then choose to do without being blameworthy *for that choice*. Donagan's point in saying that there can be fault-generated moral dilemmas, then, would be simply to say that if we act badly, we may incur blame and further liability by putting ourselves into situations in which everything we can then do is incompatible with what *innocent* people can and should do. So understood, the contention would no longer be one that a Kantian, as characterized here, need deny; but I suspect it also falls short of what most people understand when they say that there are genuine moral dilemmas.

But even if it turns out that there is no deep substantive *incompatibility* be-tween our Kantian view and Donagan's position, as construed above, nonethe-less the way each uses "duty," "wrong," and so on seems to reflect a significant difference in focus and attitude. What I have in mind is that the Kantian use of these terms, and its corresponding refusal to admit moral dilemmas of any kind, seem especially suited to express an attitude of respect for persons, conceived of as Kantian moral agents.

Here, somewhat simplified, is the familiar Kantian picture. Moral agents are in general conceived of as knowing the moral law and acknowledging its authority, as capable of following it for the right reasons, and as responsible for bringing themselves to do so. Although we know that the effects of our choices are not entirely up to us, we must never suppose that external natural forces or other human beings could prevent us from having a good will, the sole source of moral worth. No matter what crimes and moral offenses they have committed, moral agents should be viewed as capable of radical reform at any time. All human beings have a dignity grounded in these capacities, and by realizing them they can become worthy of the highest moral esteem. We carry responsibilities incurred by past commitments and offenses, and we are responsible for having the right intentions regarding the future; but these are only aspects of our primary responsibility, which is to make our present choices at each moment as directed by morally informed reason.

Now my thought is that the Kantian position on dilemmas respects and highlights this conception of a person in a fitting way insofar as it allows that, no matter how grave their past crimes and moral offenses, a person *can choose* at any time to be fully conscientious and *to do no further wrong*. Neither nature, nor other persons, *nor one's own past failures*, on this view, can rob one of the opportunity, and responsibility, to "go and sin [i.e., violate duty] no more."

For example, suppose, as an unlikely but possible occurrence, that a gang member has a fundamental change of heart while taking part in a kidnapping and robbery. Though now eager to do what is right, he may be so deeply entangled in the web of crime that the only way for him now to save innocent lives is to carry on for a while, even receiving stolen goods, driving the getaway car, and helping to hold the hostage until he can reveal his intentions without further endangering innocent people. He has no moral choice, I am supposing, but to do further *illegal* things that also violate moral precepts that, in all *normal* conditions, everyone should abide by. Undeniably, he can be justly punished, and he may owe compensation. He will also have a credibility problem, for he has no way to convince others that he had a moral conversion in the midst of the sequence of crimes. Nevertheless, assuming he really acted for moral reasons from the moment of his change of heart, the Kantian position respects his ability to reform by refusing to count his post-reform conscientious acts as, all things considered, *morally wrong* in the context.

Now, as I granted, one *can* understand "wrong" (as Donagan may have) in a sense that allows one to coherently describe the case quite differently, but the Kantian refusal to use "wrong" in that way and thus its categorical denial of moral dilemmas serve to call attention to the conception of a person as primarily responsible to govern himself as reason directs at each moment, regardless of past errors. By saying that after his change of heart the kidnapper, acting in good conscience, did not violate moral duty or do anything "evil" (not even a "lesser" one), we highlight the Kantian ideas that morality never demands more than one can do, that one is always able and responsible to will conscientiously, and that, if one acts with a good will, one has thereby a moral worth undiminished by other features of the act and situation, however regrettable these may be.[25]

IV. Are There Gaps in Kantian Theory?

A theory has gaps if it provides no way, even in principle, to determine what one should, or even may, do in some cases. That is, even given all pertinent facts about a case, a theory with gaps lacks the resources to determine for all acts whether they are obligatory, forbidden, or neither. The idea is not just that the theory's decision procedures are somewhat abstract and complex, and that therefore reasonable people might occasionally apply them differently. This would be true of virtually any action-guiding theory. When a theory has gaps, it simply has no procedures for deciding some issues. An example of a theory with (many) gaps is Ross's intuitionism, which asserts there are several basic prima facie duties and no theory-governed way to judge what to do when these prima facie duties conflict. An example of a theory that (in principle) has no gaps is hedonistic act utilitarianism, which holds that acts are *permissible* if they produce at least as much balance of pleasure over pain as any alternative, *obligatory* if they produce a greater balance than any alternative, and *wrong* otherwise.

Some theoretical gaps may be practically unimportant, whereas others may prove to be deeply troubling. If a consequentialist theory grants that some personal goods are incommensurable, it will have gaps; but these may not in fact make the theory significantly harder to apply than standard consequentialist theories. Gaps make an important practical difference, however, when they stem from a claim that very basic moral values are incommensurable and yet also virtually absolute. Consider, for example, the idea that each human life has a sacred, incalculable, and incomparable value. This is not a minor incommensurability. It urges us most strongly, and without any explicit qualification, to try to preserve every human life, and yet it forbids us to adjudicate conflicts by comparing and weighing the worth of some lives against the worth of others, or more lives against fewer. A theory that said this, and no more, would repeatedly expose us to tragic conflicts: cases in which, although the outcomes are vitally important, basic incommensurable values pull relentlessly toward incompatible choices and our moral guidelines fail to determine what we should (or even may) do.

Does Kant's ethical theory have gaps? If we concentrate on Kant's famous universal law formula of the Categorical Imperative, scholars may disagree, but there are many reasons at least to suspect gaps. Kant himself seemed at times to think that he had offered a procedure for testing maxims by which an agent could determine, for all cases, whether proposed acts would be morally forbidden, required, or (merely) permissible. But the procedure requires selecting a maxim for each act and determining what one "can will" as universal law, and these requirements, especially the first, introduce considerable indeterminacy into the procedure. Critics have often charged that applying the universal law procedure results in conflicts of duty; and even if, following Kant, we stipulate that this can only be a conflict in the "grounds" of obligation, it is not clear that Kant's universal law procedure can always determine which ground should override in these *apparent* conflicts of duty.[26] Some say that the procedure is only a negative test, condemning some maxims as wrong without certifying every maxim that passes as not wrong; and if so, again, we have gaps. Kant's defenders have addressed some of these problems with remarkable ingenuity in recent years, but few, if any, are bold enough to defend Kant's universal law formula as successfully offering a determinate ("gapless") moral decision procedure.

Consider Kant's formula that humanity in each person is always to be treated as an end in itself. On some interpretations the formula is "thin" or completely "formal," yielding no practical conclusions independently of other considerations. So viewed, the formula neither introduces nor closes "gaps" in Kant's theory. On a more common substantive reading, however, the humanity formula declares that persons, or "rational nature" in each person, has an unconditional and incomparable worth. Unlike "price," this value "admits of no equivalent." Although not the same as "human life," "rational nature" is supposed to be a basic and incommensurable value, just as "life" was for the "sanctity of life" advocates mentioned earlier. What is required by valuing *humanity* as an end is more complex and indefinite than what is required by regarding human *life* as sacred, and it is not so evident with Kant's formula as it is with the sanctity of life theory that we will be driven to acknowledge many unresolvable, tragic conflicts.[27] Nevertheless, it seems hard to deny that, when interpreted substantively, Kant's idea of the incomparable value of humanity in each person could sometimes draw us powerfully toward opposing courses of action, without telling us definitively "Do this," "Do that," or even "You may do either."

Sophie's choice and my earlier example from John Fowles's *The Magus* seem to illustrate the point, and one can also think of examples in which the conflicts involve degradation, deprivation, and deceit rather than loss of life. Any particular example may be questioned, but the general point that the humanity formula (on a substantive reading) is liable to generate more conflicts than it can resolve seems more obvious than any particular example can demonstrate. Acknowledging that *each* person (or something "in" each person) has a (substantive) value naturally leads to prima facie conflicts, just as virtually any recognition of multiple values does. But then counting these potentially conflicting values as *unconditional, incomparable,* and *without equivalent* prevents us from resolving conflicts by the familiar methods of weighing, balancing, and trading off one value against another. Kantians can propose other procedures for deciding what to do in these cases, but the proposals go beyond the humanity formula itself. So, in sum, although the extent of the problem remains open, it seems only reasonable to grant for now that Kant's ethical theory has "gaps," even gaps that can leave us without help regarding some tragic choice problems. The same will hold for any Kantian revisionist theory if it has not shown how it plugs the gaps.

Is it a serious objection to a theory that it has gaps of this sort? Several considerations suggest that even the best moral theories may need to admit gaps. Moreover, we may even have reasons to welcome them.

First, it is not necessarily a theoretical virtue of an ethical theory that it eliminates gaps. Life itself is complex and often tragic. Ethical theories represent the efforts of various limited human beings to highlight important recurrent values; to articulate, organize, and inevitably simplify the results of many generations of moral experience and moral thinking. The theories are constructed by individuals with different hopes, purposes, and theoretical ideals. Thus they are bound to be imperfect and limited in what they can do for us. Theories that satisfy ideals of neatness, completeness, and elegance may serve some purposes less well than theories that unabashedly highlight the moral conflicts we experience. Theories that offer precise unequivocal decision procedures help to satisfy philosophical yearning for neatness and closure, but the cost is often ignoring or distorting the deeply felt value conflicts that originally led us to moral theorizing. Having gaps, then, is not unqualifiedly a defect in a theory. Gaps may reflect important features of our moral experience that closure would distort.

Second, insofar as our interest in theories is practical, it makes a significant difference how frequent and important the cases are in which its gaps expose us to tragic conflicts. Fortunately, we are not forced every day to face choices like those of Antigone, Abraham, Sophie, Bernard Williams's "Jim," the fat man in the cave, and so forth. If our best theory abandons us only in these extreme cases, then perhaps we can live with this. In any case, merely closing gaps in theory does not necessarily help us settle our perplexities in practice. For example, theological and consequentialist theories can avoid gaps in theory by stipulating what counts as "duty," "wrong," and "permitted" in terms of God's rational commands or sums of intrinsic value; but this is no practical advantage if we have no effective ways to discern God's rational will or to identify and calculate with intrinsic values.

Third, the incommensurable values that open gaps in Kantian theory may help to explain why we should strive to avoid tragic moral conflicts. The background thought is this: Whatever their position on dilemmas and gaps, everyone should agree that we ought *generally* to avoid getting ourselves into tragic situations in which we have no further choice but to cause severe harm and to contravene the normal constraints of decent conduct. The point needs to be qualified, for at times the only way to avoid tragic choices is to refuse positions of power, to disengage from political struggles, and to retreat into a less challenging private world in which tragic conflicts are avoided by isolating oneself from the major world problems. Some means of escaping tragic conflicts, then, are cowardly and not to be encouraged, but the general point stands: we should want to *use all honorable means* to avoid creating or falling into tragic dilemma-like situations.

What moral motives do we have to avoid these situations? What will deter us from simply welcoming dilemma-like conflicts as an opportunity to enjoy with impunity the exercise of powers that one is normally forbidden to use? Some have thought that seeing tragic conflict situations as *genuine moral dilemmas* gives us the moral motivation we need to prevent such situations from arising. Because we want not to do wrong, we would be motivated not to fall into real moral dilemmas; for these are seen as situations in which we cannot avoid doing wrong, no matter what we choose. Ruth Marcus suggests that this is an advantage of holding that there are genuine moral dilemmas.[28]

But tolerating moral dilemmas is not necessary to provide a strong motivation to avoid tragic situations of moral conflict.[29] The Kantian position also provides a strong motivation, and yet it denies the possibility of genuine moral dilemmas. By attributing an unconditional and incomparable worth to rational nature in each person, Kant's humanity formula affirms that we have powerful moral reasons to not destroy, damage, dishonor, or discount any person, which is what we would be forced to do if we allowed ourselves to fall into tragic conflict situations.[30] Obviously, we have a strong reason in advance to do everything that we permissibly can to avoid later being forced to do what we have powerful moral reason not to do.

In sum: Although the incalculable worth of humanity in each person opens a gap in Kantian theory, leading us to admit that there may be some unresolvable tragic moral conflicts, the same idea directs us in the strongest terms to abhor what we would need to do in such conflict situations and so to use all permissible means to prevent those situations from arising.

Fourth, it is not always a good idea to try to settle potential conflicts before one faces them. There may be psychological and moral costs, and no practical need, to have them settled in advance. This seems obviously so in many mundane cases, but my conjecture now is that even in developing general normative theories it may be better to leave some questions open.

The conjecture is suggested by an analogy. Think of individuals who are utterly devoted to their children, their partners, their vocations, and their personal standards of how people should treat each other. If they guide themselves by their commitment to these highest values in a realistic and flexible way, in favorable conditions they are likely never to face a situation in which they must *sacrifice* any of the values for another. Of course, they will need to compromise, adjust their schedules, and live with the fact that they wish they could do more than they can. But they do not need to rank their values. They do not have to ask in advance what their priorities would be if, through horrible misfortune, they could not continue to live a life that expresses their full respect for all of these values. Treating their several values, for all practical purposes, as supreme and yet incommensurable serves to frame a way of life for them, and so they reasonably confess that if forced to make a radical choice they "would not know what to do."[31] Living in the faith that they can reconcile the things that they most cherish enables them to live with a virtually unqualified, self-defining commitment to each value. This, we can imagine, energizes their pursuits and motivates them to anticipate and forestall crises in which the values could not be reconciled. Also, importantly, it enables them to enjoy special relationships that are built upon the similar and reciprocal commitments of others.

If actually forced to make the hard choice to sacrifice one of their highest values, they might in fact cope and eventually restructure a new life, as people often do when their normative world collapses. Then again, they might not; but even in this worst case, they would not necessarily have been better off to have ranked their values in advance. Doing so would probably not have prevented the loss or made them immune to the pain, and it would have robbed them of benefits of unqualified, wholehearted commitment. To try to make a *serious* decision in advance as to which basic values they *would* sacrifice *if* faced with various imagined crises seems not only unnecessary but also potentially self-destructive. Like Sophie, but without any evident need to do so, they would make a self-fracturing choice, in effect forcing themselves to put a price on commitments that in their hearts they regard as priceless.

Parallel considerations are worth considering when we reflect about whether moral theories should provide determinate answers for all possible contingencies. Moral theories are constructed for different purposes, but let us consider their practical function. Insofar as they are meant to be normative, or action-guiding, for *that* purpose, it is undeniably a merit that they offer guidance for the significant moral decisions we actually face, the more the better, if *other things are equal*. To provide answers to purely hypothetical questions about imaginary cases or extremely rare cases is not crucial for practical purposes, although *how* a theory answers such questions, if it does, can confirm or shake our confidence in its acceptability. There is, then, a presumption for determinacy in normative theories, but this is only a limited presumption. To give no guidance, for example, is better than giving clearly unacceptable guidance. The question now is whether the analogy with incommensurate personal values suggests a further way the presumption might be rebutted.

Suppose that, as Kant thought, we hold some of our basic *moral* values as incommensurable and virtually absolute. Imagine further that although the effort to reconcile tensions and prima facie conflicts among these values sometimes requires us to adjust, balance, and reinterpret these values, we rarely, if ever, face situations in which we must make the radical choice to abandon, sacrifice, or permanently subordinate any of the values for others. Refusing to rank these values, let us suppose, helps to motivate us to anticipate and circumvent situations in which we would be forced to make such radical choices. As with personal values, imagine that our unreserved commitment to these moral values energizes us to realize them more fully and provides the foundation for special relationships with those who have similar and reciprocal commitments.

Given this situation, a moral theorist who insisted that we must treat our basic values as commensurable and subject to ranking would be in some ways like someone who thinks that we should prioritize all of our personal values in anticipation of the horrible choices that extreme circumstances could force upon us. In *both* cases, closure comes with costs: we would have to put a price on what previously we held, for all practical purposes, as priceless. Moreover, relative to the Kantian view, the shift to commensurability *in moral theory* seems to involve an *extra* cost, for if we are not to view others as having an incomparable worth we cannot claim any such value for ourselves. Thus, adopting a price model for all evaluations would require not merely a change in one's self-conception but also a lowering of one's self-esteem.[32]

V. Residual Feelings and Attitudes Commonly Expected

Our final issue concerns whether the Kantian position about residual feelings and attitudes is compatible with what we ordinarily expect. What are these expectations? For present purposes and tentatively, I suggest the following.

1. *Nonmoral responses.* Some responses we might expect are worth mentioning only to separate them from the morally significant responses that are my main concern. We would commonly anticipate, for example, that those who made hard choices in practical moral dilemmas might have various personal concerns, the absence of which might be unusual but would not mark one as morally defective. These might include *fear* that those whom one injured might retaliate, *anger* at whomever or whatever caused one to be in the dilemma, *regret* that one's social image has been tarnished, *desire for reassurance* from friends, distasteful *memories,* and *worries* that similar problems will disturb one's peace of mind again.

2. *Judgment of "not guilty" for the choice.* By hypothesis, the agents did not create the problem by previous wrongdoing, they deliberated conscientiously, they honestly concluded that they had no better option, and they have not changed their minds in retrospect. I imagine that most people, understanding all this, would not expect the agents to judge themselves to be morally *guilty* or blameworthy *for what they chose to do.* For the agents to judge that, in the fullest sense, they were *guilty* and so blameworthy, they must, I assume, believe that they did wrong, all things considered and without excuse. Admittedly, in advance and in retrospect, our agents saw the option they chose as *apparently* wrong, that is, *as far as they could discern,* condemned by moral considerations no less (or more) than an alternative they had. But this is not to say that they concluded, then or later, that what they did, or their choosing it in the situation, was actually wrong, all things considered. We may expect that, if duly modest, they will admit that they *might* have chosen to do otherwise if they had *known* more, had more *time* to think, or had a more developed *capacity* for moral judgment. Thus, they might admit that what they did could have been "wrong" in a sense that abstracts from the agents' knowledge, opportunities, and capacities; but moral guilt and blameworthiness are commonly understood to be determined by how well one conducted oneself given one's available knowledge, opportunities, and capacities, not by whether one did wrong in the sense that abstracts from these factors.[33] *Even* when using the latter sense, modest agents only have reason to say, "I *might* have done what was wrong," not "I *did* what was wrong."

It seems unreasonable, then, for our agents to judge themselves to be guilty, and so we can suppose other people who understand the agents' situation would not expect them to judge themselves to be guilty. Of course, we often blame people who *claim* to have acted in practical dilemma, but this is usually because we do not believe them. That is, we suspect that, contrary to what they say, they did not try hard enough to find a better option or did not honestly believe their options were morally equivalent. In saying that we would not "expect" them to judge themselves as guilty for what they have done, I mean that we would not suppose that they *should* judge themselves as guilty and we would not look down on them for regarding themselves as not guilty. We might, of course, *predict and anticipate* (i.e., "expect" in another sense) that some would *regard* themselves as guilty, even while admitting they could have done no better; for we know that at times people make irrational, even inconsistent, judgments, especially concerning innocence and guilt.

3. *Guilt for other things and quasi-guilt feelings.* Although not expecting agents to regard themselves as guilty *for what they chose to do* in a practical dilemma, we should not be surprised if they had some other genuine and appropriate feelings of guilt. They may realize, for example, that even though they were not to blame for *what* they did, the *manner* in which they acted was callous, clumsy, or weak. They may suspect themselves of *mixed motives,* even of having enjoyed causing grave harm to innocent persons. The episode may cause them to reflect on their character, calling to mind past neglects and misdeeds; or it may reveal how arrogant and self-righteous they have been in posturing as too "pure" ever to do the sort of thing that they have just done. But whether it is appropriate for a person to feel guilty about these further matters will depend on the special features of the particular case.

Besides all this, our agents may experience *displaced* guilt, *natural* guilt, or *associated* guilt. That is, in thinking of what they did in the practical dilemma, they may *feel* bad, even quite awful, about themselves in a way they say "feels like guilt," but the feeling is explained by something other than their judgment that they were at fault in their decision. *Displaced guilt feelings* are genuine but misdirected, perhaps unconsciously, to something other than that for which the person is really guilty. *Natural guilt feelings,* if there are any, would be emotional discomforts and dispositions not stemming from self-regarding *moral judgments* and not rooted in social learning to turn against oneself after behaving in certain ways. A tendency to feel bad and act self-destructively after knowingly killing a parent or companion might be thought to be an example. *Associated guilt feelings* are similar in that they do not reflect the agent's actual moral judgments, but are feelings we have because our emotional responses do not discriminate finely enough between morally distinct but otherwise similar behaviors. For example, although one may not actually *judge* oneself morally guilty after killing a loved one (purely) by accident, the horror may be so intense that one cannot help but feel as if one is to blame.[34]

Although we should not be surprised if, after facing practical moral dilemmas, our agents experience guilt-like feelings (displaced, natural, and associated guilt), I doubt that we would "expect" such feelings, that is, think that this is how the agents *should* feel. Strong feelings of *displaced* and *associated guilt* in conscientious people who are not at fault are typically seen as regrettable psychological problems, invoking sympathy rather than blame; and *natural guilt,* if it exists, must be acknowledged as a universal and inevitable tendency, for good or ill, rather than a reaction that moral agents "should" have and can be disparaged for lacking. The tendency to feel these kinds of quasi guilt to some degree may be socially useful, but when felt by those who have conscientiously faced practical moral dilemmas, they seem to be an *undeserved* or misplaced burden of suffering. If we found someone who was free from these tendencies but who felt guilty when and only when *appropriately judging* himself to *be* guilty, then probably most of us would count that person *fortunate and healthy* rather than lacking in something that a good person must have.

4. *Moral responses expected of everyone.* We expect that morally good people who are aware of the dilemma and its aftermath will have various moral feelings and attitudes toward those who have suffered, toward the community, and

toward the agent in the practical dilemma, considered simply as persons involved in a situation of this kind. For example, we expect everyone to regret the fact that someone had to face the agonizing choice and that some innocent persons suffered. Everyone, we suppose, should hope that such choices can be avoided in the future. We might expect, too, that anyone would want the victims and the community not to misunderstand what has occurred, for example, to realize that, although it may appear otherwise, the agent was conscientious and could find no better option. The event may have ruptured normal moral relations, provoked powerful desires for vengeance, and contributed to a general climate of suspicion and moral skepticism. If so, we suppose that a good person, knowing all this, would deplore the outcome and want to change it. We anticipate and allow that the *intensity* of responses will vary with persons' relations to the problem; for example, depending on whether they were players, immediate witnesses, or simply people who read about the problem in the papers. But to respond to some degree in the ways I have suggested seems normally expected of people independently of their role in the dilemma situation or their special relations to the individuals in question.

5. *Personal, or individual-relative, moral responses.* The agent in a practical moral dilemma is not just anyone. There are special responses that we expect of the person who faced the choice and caused the harm. We expect the agents to have deep personal regrets about what they have done to the *particular individuals* they have harmed. The appropriate attitude is *not just* regret that *someone* was harmed, especially not merely that someone was harmed *by someone*. The agents need to acknowledge that their actions, although justifiable in the extraordinary circumstances, put them in a special relation to the actual victims in the situation. This is *not* to say that they should feel *more regret* for harming that individual than they *would have had* if they had injured a different person in a comparable situation, but they should deplore the fact that they injured *that very person*, not just that they injured someone (or someone like him).[35]

Agents often feel, and are expected to feel, a special deep sadness, if not horror, that they themselves have done what they have done, even though they were unable to find anything morally more acceptable to do. We may call this *agent-regret*, but must remember that it does not imply that the agent wishes she had done something different, *given the options*. It is not simply wanting to avoid the *appearance* of having done wrong, nor need it be a part of self-righteous obsession with the purity of one's moral record compared to that of others. The regretting agents need not be so presumptuous as to think that from an *impartial moral point of view* it would have been better if someone else had to make the tragic decision, but *personally* they cannot be indifferent to the fact that they themselves, rather than someone else, were the agents. As in serious cases of causing harm accidentally or in the course of duty, agents often feel their lives somehow *marred, tainted, made worse* than they would have been.[36]

What is puzzling is not so much that people react to tragic choices this way, but that they are expected to. That is, we seem to think that, in some sense, people *should* have the attitudes and feelings that typically they do. Recall the tragic choices posed by *The Magus* or *Sophie's Choice*, and Truman's decision to use atomic bombs to end the Second World War. Or, if you doubt that these were really practical dilemmas, then construct your own best example. Then imagine that, having knowingly caused many deaths as they "plumped" for one horn of the dilemma, the agents said sincerely, not masking deeper feelings:[37] "There was nothing better to do, as far as I could tell. It's a pity that someone had to do this (or something as bad) and people died. But I am content, even proud, that I wanted to avoid doing anything wrong, and I did. My life is no worse for doing what I did, I have no more reason to feel concern for the people I killed than you do, and, other things being equal, I would happily take up the job of making the hard choice again if someone had to do it." Something seems missing here: attitudes and feeling we suppose any decent person would have.

VI. A Kantian Perspective on Residues of Attitude and Feeling

What should Kantians say about the attitudes and feelings one should have after facing a practical moral dilemma?

1. *Should a conscientious person who takes a stand in an unresolved practical dilemma feel guilty?* Here Kantian theory coincides with reflective ordinary opinion (as described above). That is, both agree that the agents should not feel guilty in the robust sense that implies a *judgment* that they are in fact guilty. Since there are no *genuine* moral dilemmas, at least one of the agents' options must have been permissible. For example, Sophie must have been morally permitted either to save her daughter, to save her son, or to refuse to select between them. Since practical dilemmas are only apparent dilemmas, it is still conceivable that more fully informed or subtle moral judges could see that *only* one of her options is "permitted," the rest being "wrong" in a sense that abstracts from the agent's perspective. But the agents facing practical dilemmas must choose within the limits of their perspectives or, as Kant would have it, on a "maxim" that reflects how they see the problem. Now, taking this into account, *what they do*, described as is now morally relevant, is *to "plump" for one option with a good will but with a nonculpable inability to discern that one option is morally preferable to another.* Described in this way, what they do is not *wrong* in the primary sense that takes into account the agent's perspective (knowledge, intention, and motive).[38] Therefore, there is no warrant for the judgment "I *am* guilty for doing it" that is normally implicit in the self-description "I *feel* guilty for doing it."[39] "Displaced," "natural," and "associated" guilt feelings may be experienced, but one can have these feelings without thinking that what one did was wrong, all things considered.

The first conclusion, then, is that Kantians should agree with ordinary opinion that agents *should not, strictly speaking, feel guilty* when they act conscientiously in practical moral dilemmas.[40] The argument, in sum, is that *feeling bad* about what one has done does not amount to *feeling guilty* in the fullest sense unless it reflects the *judgment* that one *is guilty*, and Kantians should not judge that conscientious agents who act in practical dilemmas are in fact guilty. The argument for this negative conclusion does not presuppose the dubious general thesis that because feelings cannot be called up and extinguished at will, it is *always* inappropriate to make "should" and "ought" judgments about feelings. This general thesis is clearly incompatible with common opinion. Unfortunately, the general thesis is strongly suggested by many of Kant's remarks, which is why we must now turn to the following question.

2. *How does it make sense to say that a person "should feel" one way or another?* Common opinion holds that certain special regrets and concerns for the injured should be felt by anyone who has made the hard choice in a practical moral dilemma. But in Kantian theory this cannot be understood in a straightforward way.

Why not? The Kantian primary moral "ought" or "should" is a command of reason, addressed to the will of imperfect moral agents, who can follow it but might fail. Addressed to the deliberative agent, it says, "Choose this from among your options, whether you feel like it or not." But substitute "to feel regret" for "this" here and the result seems to be nonsense. We cannot simply choose how to feel at the moment, whereas obligation and duty are the moral "necessity of a free action under a categorical imperative of reason."[41] Thus Kant says, "There can be no duty to have a moral feeling or to acquire it." It is a self-contradiction, for example, to suppose that we have a duty to have feelings of love, respect, or even "hatred of vice."[42]

The point here does not depend on a "two worlds" picture of feeling as caused and human behavior as uncaused. Kant does assume that, from a practical point of view, we must view our actions as freely chosen in a way that our feelings are not. The point, however, is not that feelings fall under empirical causal laws whereas human behavior does not; for, on Kant's view, everything that occurs is in principle subject to causal explanation when viewed empirically. Kant relies on his idea that we can and must view the same phenomena from two different perspectives, empirical and practical, depending on our purposes, even though neither perspective is reducible to the other and they seem incompatible. Assuming this, Kant granted that from the empirical point of view both feelings and behavior are subject to causal explanation; but he thought, as most of us do, that from the practical point of view we consider what we do, or at least *will* to do, as immediately "up to us," whereas how we feel is not. For example, a doctor can simply choose whether or not to clean her patient's festering wound, but not whether or not to enjoy the task. From my deliberative standpoint, my feelings are like other things over which I lack direct practical control, for example, your choices and attitudes, and my headaches, heart rate, and dreams.[43] Hence, Kant thought, moral imperatives can only command actions, not feelings, and so "should feel" never expresses a direct requirement of duty.

One might imagine that Kant's view can be reconciled with common opinion by emphasizing our capacity to develop our sensibilities and so *indirectly* influence the feelings we have at later times. But this strategy does not seem promising. Granted, we can sometimes and to some extent control our feelings by circuitous means—for example, by distracting ourselves when we are angry and putting ourselves into environments in which friendly feelings typically grow. In fact Kant in *The Metaphysics of Morals* says that it is a conditional and indirect duty to cultivate affections as a means of promoting active benevolence.[44] But when common opinion *expects* agents to feel regret and says that they *should* feel it, the main point, surely, is not that they should now do things to cause senti-ments of regret to well up in them, for example, visit the morgue or the family of their victims.[45] Nor is the point that they should take steps to develop a disposition to regret on later occasions, for example, through psychotherapy or association with more sensitive people. They should feel regret *now*.

Given that they cannot interpret "should feel" as a moral command, the best strategy for Kantians is to construe the "should" here as one of normative expectation. Consider, for example, the parent who tells a child just returning from the store, "You should have a dollar in change!" or a doctor who tells her patient, "You should have a higher red cell count." Both express disappoint-ment at finding something less than expected or normal. This may not in itself be a problem, but as a symptom of deeper trouble it causes concern. Absence of expected *feelings* may be symptomatic of problems too. Suppose, for example, after a husband or wife happily departs to Hawaii for what he or she professes to be the funeral of an old friend and then a week of "nothing but tedious work," the spouse left behind remarks suspiciously, "He [or she] should have felt sad." The point is not that the departing spouse should have tried to work up some sad feelings or to cultivate a disposition to sadness on such occasions in the future. Rather, if there was nothing amiss with the spouse's aims, attitudes, commitments, and value judgments, he or she *would* almost certainly have felt sad; and so the absence of sadness was a bad sign.

Similarly, the thought that those who harm others in practical dilemmas, or even accidentally, should feel regret or sorrow may be interpreted as the idea that such feelings are normally to be expected in moral agents who have the aims, attitudes, commitments, and value judgments that they should have. Ab-sence of the expected feelings would not be morally bad in itself but merely symptomatic of moral defects in the agent. The expectations would rest upon the Kantian point that in human beings, as a matter of fact, our moral judg-ments and commitments are *typically* accompanied by corresponding feelings. Normally, we might add, we find these virtually inseparable: that is, we experi-ence and express our judgments and commitments in an emotional way. We are to blame, if at all, not for the absence of affective responses per se, but for culpable defects of judgment and will of which lack of affect is a typical symptom. These defects, on the Kantian view, are seen as directly "up to us," unlike the affective aspect of our feelings. Thus it is our responsibility to alter our defective will and judgment immediately, not later. If we do, we can expect that, as a rule, corresponding changes in how we feel will eventually follow.

Kantians, then, can understand claims about how we "should feel" as ex-pressing the "should" of expectation rather than of obligation. What makes such claims *morally* significant is that the defects signaled by the absence of the expected affective responses are *moral* defects. Let us think of *attitudes* broadly as including the aims, policies, value judgments, and commitments that express the agent's "will" and so are, in the appropriate sense, within the control of the agent. Then we can say that feelings are morally significant at least insofar as they are expressions of morally relevant attitudes. Thus the more moral basic question underlying "How should we feel?" is "What attitudes should we adopt?" We can understand our remaining problems then as concerned directly with attitudes, and only indirectly with feelings.

3. *Why should the agents, or even bystanders, care about the outcomes of practical dilemmas?* Why, for example, should I think that it is a bad thing that someone was injured or killed by someone? After all, by hypothesis, the agents in our practical dilemmas maintained a good will, which is supposed to be the only unconditional good and the condition of all values. Also, by hypothesis, agents did what was right, given the situation as they perceived it, and they were not acting from culpable ignorance. So the Kantian reason for deploring the resulting injury or death cannot be a general opposition to immorality. Further, Kantian theory denies that there are "intrinsic values," natural or nonnatural, that exist prior to and independent of the will of rational agents. So Kantians cannot say that the pain, or even death, that was caused by the agent is *in itself* a bad thing in the way utilitarians might understand this. How, then, is it bad?

Here it may help to distinguish what I shall call the extreme hard-line Kantian position from a moderate one.[46] The extreme hard-line Kantian insists that only immoral choices (or "willings") are to be considered objectively bad, strictly speaking; everything else is considered bad only in a derivative sense or relative to individual tastes and preferences. On this view, although as individuals we tend to find such things sad and distasteful, the pains, injury, and death of others *must* be regarded as "bad things" *only* in the sense that they are "things we would normally be wrong to choose to bring about."[47] When these misfortunes occur naturally, result from accidents, or are caused in the performance of duty, the hard-line Kantian (with the Stoics) tries to maintain the attitude, "What is that to me?" for he sees such things as not in themselves bad and sees no reason to indulge his own empathetic suffering when it can do nothing for the victims.[48] On the hard-line view, morally good persons as such need only be concerned with their own acts and motives. Some of their duties, to be sure, direct them to aim to promote certain effects and to try not to cause others; for example, they must try to aid the needy and avoid killing innocent people. Perhaps, too, as Kant said, they should cultivate some sympathy to counterbalance the selfish and malicious inclinations that commonly tempt people from the path of duty. But apart from such concerns, which are derivative from a commitment to do one's duty, the hard-line Kantian says that morally good persons may have an attitude of indifference to the pains, injuries, and deaths of human beings when these result from natural causes, the unpreventable behavior of others, or their own dutiful acts.

This hard-line Kantian position seems so clearly opposed to common opinion that Kantians who hope for some reconciliation with common opinion have good reason to find, or develop, a more humane position on these matters. The roots of this more moderate view are in Kant's idea that humanity in each person is an end in itself. Like other formulations of the Categorical Imperative, Kant's humanity formula expressly addresses how we should act, but in explaining the grounds for this act-guiding principle Kant expresses the broader requirement to conceive of humanity in each person as an end in itself.[49] The required conception is really an *evaluative attitude*, for it means regarding each (rational) human being as "something whose existence is in itself of absolute value," as having "dignity," as above all "price." The basic disposition to acknowledge this evaluative stance as morally and rationally appropriate is not something we choose, but is supposed to be inherent in all moral agents.[50] What we are required to do, can do, but might fail to do, is to affirm and adopt this attitude as our own overriding commitment. To do so, I suggest, is to let the idea of human dignity guide not only our actions and policies but also our judgments about what is good and bad among the things not under our control.

Suppose, for example, some people have just suffered horrible deaths from some natural or accidental disaster. Upon learning of it, those with the right moral attitude will no doubt do what they can to aid secondary victims and to minimize the risk of recurrences. But they will also regard it a very bad thing that the people suffered and died needlessly; and this is a judgment that is more than a morally optional "wish" or personal preference. The right attitude leads one immediately to see and deplore the tragic fate of the victims and not merely to focus on one's own future-oriented tasks. Even if the tragedy was utterly beyond human control, the moral attitude is reflected in the "will" that it not be so, were this possible.[51]

Returning to the issue at hand, the moderate, but not the hard-line, Kantian can agree with common opinion that we should have concern for those who suffer as a result of how someone acts in a practical dilemma. In deploring these misfortunes as well as other tragedies and outrages that are not our fault, we are expressing the basic moral attitude that counts each human being as having a special value. We may at the same time, of course, express *personal* grief and sympathy for the victims, but this goes beyond the attitude that can be morally expected of everyone. What is required of all is at least the judgment that it was a bad thing, even apart from further consequences, that human beings were injured and killed. This is not to say that the injuries and deaths had a property of "intrinsic badness" that is independent of our wills. On the contrary, in saying that these were bad things to happen, we *express* our will, broadly construed: "Would that such things not occur!"

4. *Why should Kantians care particularly about the individual victims?* Assuming now that Kantians can explain why we should regret that *someone* was injured or killed, how can they explain why we should have a *particular* concern for the *very individuals* who were harmed?[52] After all, the formula of humanity tells us to treat persons with dignity because of something quite general: their rational nature. Is it not enough, then, that I regret that *a person,* considered abstractly as a rational being, was injured? Why need I care, beyond that, about *the individual victim*—Harry, Tanya, or whoever?

The answer requires a closer look at what it means to value a person, or a person's humanity, as an end. Humanity, for Kant, is in part a rational "capacity to set ends, any ends whatsoever." Apart from the "obligatory ends" that all rational agents are supposed to share, each person freely adopts certain personal ends as his or her own. We are naturally inclined to pursue various goals, but our inclinations do not finally determine what our ends are. We each shape our own vague conception of happiness as we select our particular goals and policies. Unless our ends are immoral, by endorsing personal ends we are, in a sense, creating (person-relative) values. That is, we confer a new status on something that may have previously been of no value to anyone: now it gives *us* reasons to value various means, and it gives *others* moral reason not to hinder arbitrarily our achievement of those particular ends. To value humanity in persons, then, is not simply to favor rational decision making abstractly or to promote ends that *every* rational agent *must* endorse. It requires *valuing* persons *as the authors of their own personal ends*, which means that these ends must have weight with us simply because they are permissible ends that the individuals have endorsed.[53]

Having reason, inclinations, will, and freedom are supposed to be the shared general features of all moral agents, but individuals are in large part identified as "the very individuals they are" by the different sets of ends (or "projects," as some say) that they choose to endorse. So, we must conclude, the formula of humanity itself implies that we must acknowledge and give appropriate weight to the individuating, special ends of each person.

Since we obviously cannot, and need not, give attention to the individuating features of every person on earth, this moral imperative must be understood as applicable relative to context. In practice, we must pay special regard to the particular, self-defining ends of those with whom we most closely interact, the people related to us in ways that make our individual attention most relevant. For example, it is important for me to be alert and responsive to the special projects and aspirations of my family and students who come to me for advice; but it is surely not required that I probe into personal matters as I check out a library book, pay for my groceries, or greet a passing stranger. Even in these routine exchanges, however, there are subtle but important ways of acknowledging the other person as an individual. A pleasant comment, a sincere "Thank you," or even just a friendly demeanor can signal recognition of a person as an individual, suggesting a readiness to deal on a more personal level if circumstances should call for this.

These considerations establish a presumption that the agents in practical dilemmas, and perhaps even close witnesses, have moral reason to concern themselves with the victims as individuals and not simply as abstractly conceived moral agents. What needs to be done to express this varies with the case; but the minimal attitude of "regretting that *someone* was harmed," which may be an appropriate response to a news report of injuries in a foreign war, seems obviously insufficient for the agents in the tragic practical dilemmas we have been considering. By knowingly doing what causes someone serious harm contrary to all normal moral expectations, the agents put themselves in a non-routine relationship to their victims, a relationship in which the personal concerns of the individuals harmed become highly relevant.

5. *Why should the agents in practical dilemmas have any special personal regrets?* Why should the *agents* regard the forced choice as a tragedy for themselves as well as for those they harmed? Why should they think of their lives as marred or made worse by what they have done? Why regret being the agent rather than merely a bystander? After all, the agents are not guilty; and they have no reason to think that it would have been morally better to have done something different. The idea of a "moral stain," that is, a metaphysical property that can attach to a person (like social stigma) no matter how good the person's will, has no

place in Kantian ethics. Moreover, from a general moral point of view, it is not worse that the particular agents, rather than others, caused the harm. Our conscientious agents who act in practical dilemmas are, by hypothesis, spotless within the limits of their knowledge and abilities. They may even have had a good will throughout their lives. What more does it take to have an unmarred, regret-free moral life?

To see why agent-regret is to be expected we need to take a broader view of our lives as moral agents situated in a dangerous world. On the Kantian view, we must be committed to the unconditional value of every human being, but we know that everyone is highly vulnerable. If we are to honor the commitment, we must make it a permanent life project to do all that is physically and morally possible to avoid causing serious harm to people. Although a good person typically accepts this project without much explicit thought, it requires steady vigilance in daily activities (such as driving) and extraordinary efforts in crisis situations (such as responding to crime, medical emergencies, and threats of war). Realizing that we cannot altogether avoid causing harm to others, we need to think hard about which harms are justified in various contexts; and we need to try to avoid situations that would force us to cause harm in the line of duty. For similar reasons, the moral project requires us to try hard to avoid falling into practical dilemmas, for these, again, leave a conscientious person no alternative to causing serious harm.

This background provides a natural explanation of why morally conscientious persons feel their lives made worse by what they must do in practical dilemmas. When forced to cause serious harm to others in a practical dilemma, they have to that extent failed in a fundamental life project. By hypothesis, the failure is not their fault, but it is bound to bring disappointment, frustration, and regret. Agents who did not regard their personal lives as made worse by causing serious harm in a practical dilemma would give strong evidence of not having been deeply committed to the moral project. The attitude of personal regret, although not in itself morally required, is morally significant insofar as it is a natural expression of conscientious agents' deep and self-identifying commitment to preserve and respect humanity in each person. The regret is (normatively) expected because lacking it is a symptom that one does not take one's basic moral responsibility seriously. If we understand that agents were conscientious in facing their practical dilemmas and guiltless in falling into them, we should not lower our moral esteem for them; but we should be able to see how, from the agents' perspective, their lives fall short of what they deeply hoped for.

An analogy may be helpful here, although analogies are also liable to mislead. The view of most players and avid fans of a sports team is that it is not enough for players to have the attitude, "I will do my best but I don't care about the outcome of the game." They want players to make winning an end, something they care about beyond their own performance or any rewards. This attitude motivates players to play harder, but the attitude is valued, apart from this, as an expression of a shared commitment that binds them together. But if players strive to win with all their hearts and yet fail, then, even though it is no fault of their own, they will almost inevitably experience disappointment, regret, and unhappiness about that brief part of their lives. The liability to regret is inseparable from whole-hearted commitment, in sports and in the attempt to live morally. But there is a crucial disanalogy. In both cases, absence of regret signals weakness of commitment; but only in the latter case is it cause for *moral concern*. Commitment to the goals of a sports team is optional; but, at least on the Kantian view, we "ought" to be wholeheartedly committed to moral ends. This is because the moral commitment, unlike the other, is supposed to be the full expression of our nature and common bond as reasonable and autonomous human beings. It is necessary, so to speak, to be true to ourselves and to others.

One final note. Consequentialists have their own answers to the questions raised here, and I have not argued that the Kantian position is superior. Indeed, for the most part, the challenge has been just to find Kantian answers that are more plausible than the completely untenable answers it might seem at first that Kant was committed to. However, one comparative point is worth mentioning: the Kantian position presented here does *not* appeal to the idea that it is *useful* to foster feelings of agent-regret *as a means* to make people more reluctant to cause harm and violate useful norms *on other occasions*. All the more, Kantians could not endorse a policy of encouraging people to feel guilty when they are not really guilty, even if this would be useful. Perhaps some utilitarians also reject these strategies in the end, but for Kantians the systematic manipulation and deception required would be immediately repugnant.

Notes

I want to thank Gene Mason, Henry West, Martin Gunderson, Andrews Reath, David Cummiskey, Geoffrey Sayre-McCord, Terrance McConnell, Walter Sinnott-Armstrong, and David Weber for their comments. I am also grateful for helpful discussions at the Minneapolis and Duluth campuses of the University of Minnesota, and the University of California, Riverside.

1. Donagan (1977b), Donagan (1984), Donagan's paper in this collection.
2. The cases I mention have often been cited to illustrate the moral conflicts of the sort I describe, but it is not important for my purposes that the reader sees these particular examples as practical moral dilemmas.
3. Although there are serious moral conflicts of other kinds, to simplify I will assume that in the "practical dilemmas" to be discussed here the agents know that they will cause serious harm to someone, no matter what they do.
4. See Kant (1956), and, for more interpretation, Hill (1992a), ch.1, pp. 1–37. Bracketed pages in the references to Kant's writings in the bibliography refer to standard Prussian Academy edition pages, cited in most translations.
5. The possibility of moral dilemmas in command moralities is noted by Donagan in his paper in this volume.
6. In some cases, Kant thought, the rational case for doing or achieving something if it were an option is so compelling that we should assume on faith that it is an option, even though empirical evidence suggests otherwise. For example, unlike more typical cases, regarding "perpetual peace" and the "highest good," we are apparently to determine our duty first without being constrained by prior empirical assessments of what is possible for us and our likelihood of success. Even here, though, duty is seen as the rational choice among options presumed to be open.
7. Kant (1956), pp.108–16 [440–48], Hill (1992a), ch. 5, pp. 76–96.
8. See Kant (1956), pp. 95–8, 102–3 [427–30, 435–36].

9. For a fuller account of my interpretation of these points, see Hill (1992a), ch. 2, 3, 10, and 11, and Hill (1992b).

10. Kant's view contrasts with Hume's in that "reason" does "move us," but this is not to deny Hume's point that judgments and beliefs motivate only when combined with an underlying disposition to act that is part of the character of the person. Kantian "reason" is not merely the cognitive capacity for discerning "relations of ideas" and "matters of (empirical) fact" that Hume stipulated. To attribute reason to a ("free") agent is, in part, to attribute a deep disposition (*Wille*) to acknowledge as authoritative (and so to follow) certain very abstract, higher order norms, which (Kant argues) are the Hypothetical and Categorical Imperatives. This disposition, presupposed in moral agents as an invariable background fact is part of human nature, but an aspect characterized as "rational" rather than "sensuous." Moral judgments move us because they subsume particular cases under these basic norms (toward which we are all presumed to be motivationally disposed). It may be doubted that "reason," in this strong sense, should be attributed to everyone, but the idea is not as mysterious as contemporary Humeans like to suppose.

11. Kant conjectured that there could be purely rational ("holy") wills who lacked sensibility (and thus moral feelings) and yet could still discern by reason the same basic propositions about what is good to do that we imperfect human beings experience as categorical imperatives. He also thought that the core of our capacity for moral judgment is logically independent of our disposition to have certain feelings. He held, for example, that we can discern the most general principles that reason prescribes without relying on our feelings as either data or "sensors." Kant's critics are no doubt right to suspect that moral feelings, judgments, and behavioral dispositions are connected in more complex ways than Kant realized, but my discussion does not presuppose Kant's most extreme views about the separability of rational judgment and feeling.

12. By "thick" interpretations I have in mind quite substantive, action-guiding readings, like that of Donagan in Donagan (1977b) and mine in Hill (1992a), ch. 2. I discuss the distinction between "thick" and "thin" interpretations in Hill (1993).

13. Donagan (1977b).

14. Hill (1992a), ch. 10.

15. Kant's intermediate moral precepts are in *The Metaphysics of Morals*, Kant (1991). Donagan's comparable system of (first order) moral precepts, which is somewhat less rigoristic than Kant's, is in Donagan (1977b), ch. 3. Donagan comments on Kant's system in Donagan (1985).

16. Note that even Donagan concedes this, since he thinks that Kant's principles allow genuine moral dilemmas that are created through the agent's prior wrongdoing.

17. See Kant (1991), pp. 225–7 [429–31] and 129–33 [318–23].

18. If the particular principles in irreconcilable conflict each strictly follow from the basic principle (the Categorical Imperative), under some interpretation, then the qualification amounts to a concession that the basic principle itself (as so interpreted) is not absolutely binding but must be understood as leaving a permissible option in dilemma-like cases.

19. See Donagan (1977b).

20. See Donagan (1977b) and (1984).

21. See Donagan (1977b), pp. 284–5.

22. Note that Donagan's ideal system of precepts will require those in a self-generated dilemma to take whichever option is a violation of a duty of lesser gravity, even though it blocks the conclusion that the option is a permissible act. Some might

think that this is guidance enough, but, as I suggest below, there is something positive and attractive about a Kantian system that respects each person as able at each time to act rightly for the right reasons, not merely to conscientiously choose a less offensive way to continue to do wrong.

23. This is not to deny that the perverse commander might have good reasons from his perspective for giving the orders he knows you cannot fulfill. The point is that for Kant, and for a long tradition before and after, "reason" refers to what is conceived as a common faculty that guides us to conclusions (in logic, in science, and in morals) that are not so agent-relative. It is conceived as a faculty that demands consistency among the beliefs and norms that it endorses, that has a purpose of guiding its possessors to think and act well, and that does not in the end frustrate its own purposes. Normally we must presume its verdicts are just what we ourselves conclude in our own best reflections, but conceptually these are not identical. If, in considering theoretical paradoxes or apparent moral dilemmas, our reflections stop with "Believe and don't believe" or "Do and don't do," we have to admit we have not yet found what (if anything) reason directs, for these are not really choice-guiding directives. Kant, of course, famously insisted that "reason" in its speculative use disposes us to seek more and more unconditional explanations and so drives us towards "antinomies." But Kant does not leave us with the antinomies as the final verdict of reason; instead he uses these apparent conflicts of reason as grounds for accepting the noumenal/phenomenal distinction that supposedly dissipates the conflicts.

24. Note that "lesser evil" will have to be defined with a special spin, too, to avoid the implication that the agent is somewhat evil in choosing it. It will be, perhaps, the option that does less harm (an "evil") to others or the option that, were the agent not in the dilemma, would be a less grave offense than the other option. Some cases are discussed in Hill (1994).

25. I fully understand and share, but set aside here, doubts about whether this conception of persons as moral agents actually fits every sane adult human being. Kant had a faith regarding this that was not uncommon for his time, but those of us who doubt it need to reflect seriously on how a more realistic assessment would require limitations in the application of Kantian theories.

26. See Kant (1991), p. 50 [224].

27. See Hill (1992a), ch. 2, and 10.

28. See Marcus (1980), in Gowans (1987), esp. pp. 188, 197–9.

29. Terrance McConnell has been helpful on this point, as well as others.

30. Here I am conceding that the strong moral prescriptions implicit in the humanity formula, such as to preserve lives and avoid deception, are defeasible, but not that the humanity formula itself is a defeasible or prima facie principle. It affirms absolutely that one must always treat humanity in each person as an end, but the idea of valuing humanity as an end is complex, many-sided, and indefinite enough to permit some flexibility of application. It encompasses many strong moral presumptive considerations that in crisis situations cannot all be satisfied. Note, too, that I rely here on a "thick" interpretation of the humanity formula, as opposed to a "thin" or formal reading that Kant also suggests. These are distinguished in my "Donagan's Kant," Hill (1993).

31. We may disapprove of this refusal to rank values if the conflict is of a particular kind, say, between one's family and one's vocation (e.g., Gauguin) or between one's vocation and one's integrity; so my point is more intuitive if we focus on conflicts in which the choice is between the various persons one loves.

32. This is a theme of "Social Snobbery and Human Dignity," Hill (1991),

pp. 155–72, esp. p. 171. My point is not that theorists should pretend, for pragmatic reasons, that basic values cannot be ranked despite strong non-pragmatic argument that they can, but rather that, lacking such argument, we need not necessarily deplore the gaps opened by leaving certain basic values unranked.

33. One can, of course, be culpable for acts and omissions that result in one's ignorance, limited opportunities, and stunted capacities, but this general point is not relevant here because we are assuming that our agents are in the practical dilemmas through no fault of their own and so their limited knowledge, opportunities, and capacities are not the result of their wrongdoing or vice.

34. So-called "residual guilt feelings" are perhaps a special case of associated guilt feelings. One feels residual guilt for behavior that one was earlier socialized to accept as wrong but no longer thinks wrong. Here our feelings fail to take note, as it were, of a change in intellectual judgment about the same behavior.

35. Perhaps one should feel more regret for harming, say, one's brother than a stranger, but the concern should be particularized in either case. The regret that one killed this stranger may be of the same degree as the regret that one would have had for killing that stranger, but in neither case should it be merely regret that "I killed someone."

36. I say more about this in "Moral Purity and the Lesser Evil," in Hill (1991).

37. I borrow the label "plumping" for these choices from Simon Blackburn.

38. This allows, however, that what they did, described independently of their inability to discern a morally better option, was (unbeknownst to them) in fact "wrong" in a sense (e.g., a rights violation) that detaches from knowledge, motives, and circumstances. Practical dilemmas, on the Kantian view, are only apparent dilemmas; and what follows from the denial of genuine dilemmas is that at least one option must be permitted (in the "detached" sense), not that both are. What makes the conscientious agent in a practical dilemma guilt free is not that his act was not wrong in the detached sense, but that he did his best and so was not wrong to choose it, given his understanding and motive.

39. "But when a man is aware of having acted according to his conscience, then as far as guilt or innocence is concerned, nothing more can be demanded" Kant (1991), p. 202 [401]. What is needed to accord with conscience, Kant says, does not require actually satisfying "the objective judgment of whether or not something is a duty," in which "one can sometimes be mistaken," but only satisfying "my subjective judgment as to whether I have compared something with my practical . . . reason for the sake of such a judgment," which (Kant says) is a matter about which one cannot be mistaken (ibid).

40. "Acting conscientiously" in a practical dilemma, of course, must be understood not as "acting as conscience dictates" but as "acting without contravening conscience after conscientiously reflecting on what to do."

41. See Kant (1991), p. 48 [222–3]. "Duty" is "the action to which a person is bound," the "matter" of "obligation."

42. Kant (1991), pp. 203–4 [402–3].

43. Qualifications are needed here. I may find that I feel sad every time I play a certain piece of music while looking at old photos of a deceased friend, and so I could try to make myself feel sad by this means, predicting success as well or better than many things I decide/choose/will to do, for instance, finish a paper by the deadline. I might even say, "Tonight I choose to be sad," and then set about to make myself sad by the music and pictures. But this possibility of choosing our feelings seems of little help when we return to our problem of making sense of the common expectation that I feel guilt, remorse, sympathy for the injured, and so on. If I had

to use devices analogous to the music and pictures to work up the expected feelings (on the appropriate occasions), I would not be meeting those expectations but rather still showing myself morally defective (by the standards of common opinion). So the fact that I cannot do this with regular success is only part of the story.

Ordinarily, I think, we want the appropriate moral feelings in agents who have done wrong and caused harm, and so on, not as an end in itself but as expressions of the agent's genuine moral commitments. Compare: We want our friends to grieve our death not because we value for its own sake their suffering on our account but because absence of grief, given human nature, would be a rather sure sign that they lacked the sort of attitude, commitment, preferences, and dispositions that we hoped and expected them to have.

44. Kant (1991), pp. 250–1 [456–8].

45. Even Kant says that we have a duty not to avoid places of suffering where sympathetic feelings are likely to be aroused, but what common opinion expects is not just these indirect future-oriented measures but appropriate feelings at the time they are called for. Kant (1991), pp. 250–1 [456–8].

46. The moderate position, in my opinion, is a plausible and more sympathetic reconstruction of Kant's views; but the hard line at least echoes some of Kant's remarks. Both are compatible with the basic Kantian position sketched earlier.

47. Note that this is not exactly the idea of prima facie wrong made familiar by W. D. Ross. There may be absolutely nothing against doing something "normally wrong" in an atypical case; but there is always something against doing what is "prima facie wrong" in Ross's sense.

48. Kant expresses admiration for the Stoic wise man's refusal to suffer for the fate of a friend he could not rescue, but nonetheless urges the cultivation of compassionate natural feelings. See Kant (1991), p. 250 [457].

49. Kant (1956), p. 96 [429].

50. This is important if we are to make sense of the claim that people "ought" to commit themselves fully to the attitude in question. If sociopaths totally lacked the basic disposition to acknowledge other persons as ends, then one could not say, in a Kantian sense, that they ought to so regard and treat them. Moral "oughts" are meant to express the sense of being bound because of principles that agents themselves are deeply disposed, as moral agents, to acknowledge as rationally authoritative and so see as (in a sense) expressive of themselves. A too-seldom noted consequence is that if one thinks that Kant's faith that virtually all sane adult human beings have such dispositions is unwarranted, then one should also see Kant's ground for attributing moral duties, rights, and dignity to *all* human beings as undermined.

51. The hard-line Kantian supposes that we can will only our own actions, but the moderate view allows that, in a broader sense, one can have a "will" toward other possible states of affairs. Here one's "will" expresses what one is prepared to hope and cheer for, to plead and pray for, to welcome openly, or to dread and bemoan, to protest and cry out against, to resist becoming "resigned" to, whether these can affect outcomes or not. Note that to be so "prepared" is not merely to "wish" to "feel" passively, without judgment or choice. Kant seems to endorse the less narrowly restricted idea of "will" in Kant (1991), p. 42 [213–14].

52. Note: I do not assume that common sense says that one must care more for that person than one would care for another person who was injured, as might be the case if the person was one's mother, but only that a personalized, individual-directed caring is in order.

53. See Kant (1956), pp. 95–96 [427–9] and Korsgaard (1986).

Moral Theory, Moral Dilemmas and Moral Responsibilities

CHRISTOPHER W. GOWANS

Discussion of the possibility of moral dilemmas has coincided to some extent with debate about the viability of moral theory. In fact, it is sometimes suggested that the assertion that there are moral dilemmas is a key element in the critique of moral theory, alongside claims concerning the significance of the plurality of moral considerations, the need to focus on particulars, the impossibility of a decision-procedure in moral deliberation, and the like.[1] As a means of exploring connections between these two issues, I will begin by distinguishing two styles of moral reflection I call *rationalism* and *experientialism*. These correspond at least approximately with the respective contentions of proponents and opponents of moral theory. I will then consider the supposition that many of the arguments for and against moral dilemmas can be seen as a dialectic between experientialism and rationalism, and more generally that the insistence on the part of some that there surely are dilemmas evidences an experientialist outlook, while the equally strong conviction on the part of others that there cannot possibly be dilemmas reflects a rationalist temperament. My conclusion will be that this interpretation is revealing, although it cannot be considered a fully accurate or complete account of the moral dilemmas debate.

From this standpoint, it may appear that the debate about moral dilemmas is at a stalemate, with the two sides divided by fundamental differences in moral sensibility. Though there is a measure of truth in this, I will not attempt to resolve the issue at this deeper level. Rather, I will simply acknowledge my qualified support for a form of experientialism and argue that the case for dilemmas needs to be, and can be, advanced beyond its current stage. In particular, I will suggest that the argument for dilemmas has relied too heavily on the description of moral experience, and that more attention needs to be paid to providing an adequate explanation of this experience. With this end in view, I will develop an understanding of normative value that focuses on the idea of moral responsibilities to persons, and I will argue that this account helps make sense of those experiences that experientialists have taken to imply dilemmas. No doubt this will not convince rationalist opponents, but it will provide a more compelling response to counter-arguments rooted in rationalism.

Styles of Moral Reflection

Rationalism and experientialism both aim to achieve philosophical understanding of moral practice and sometimes to modify that practice. But to this common enterprise they bring radically divergent approaches. For purpose of contrast, I will present rationalism and experientialism on the pattern of Weber's "ideal types."[2] They are highly simplified, general models, defined not in terms of necessary and sufficient conditions, but around familiar characteristics commonly conjoined. It may be that no philosopher perfectly exemplifies either type. Moreover, it should not be supposed that these are the only forms of moral reflection, nor that every moral philosopher could be classified as one or the other. Nonetheless, it is useful to sharply distinguish these models as a means of bringing into focus recognizable dispositions of philosophical reflection on the moral life. Many moral philosophers clearly are drawn to one type or the other, at least in important respects.[3] Moreover, these types are not mere conceptual possibilities. They have a history. For each style of thought, there are significant historical figures who serve as role models. Thus rationalists are likely to identify with philosophers such as Plato, Kant, or Sidgwick, while experientialists may be expected to feel more kinship with the likes of Aristotle, Montaigne, or Hume.

Rationalism regards moral practice primarily as a form of human rationality, in which the nature of rationality is defined by a prominent tradition in western philosophy. In this tradition, reason is understood as requiring system and order, as necessitating commensurability and hierarchy, as insisting on the importance of generality and abstraction, and as demanding fully articulate, explicit, and precise formulation of concepts and principles. Although rationalism seeks to understand moral practice, it often finds its paradigm of rationality elsewhere. In the Platonic tradition, mathematics has served as the ideal case of rationality, whereas in the Enlightenment tradition the model has usually been the natural sciences. Rationalism is inclined to see disciplines such as these as definitive of human rationality at its best, and it strives to understand and critique moral practice in light of this conception. It judges the moral life, ideally considered, as an exemplification of practical reason so conceived and hence as embodying the aforementioned characteristics. When actual moral practice fails to meet these standards, rationalism argues that it should be corrected by reference to them. As a result, rationalism is prepared for the possibility that our present moral practices are fundamentally flawed, and may require radical transformation from the standpoint of rationality as it understands it.

As a consequence of this orientation, the rationalist suspects strongly that all moral considerations are ultimately based on a single, universal, abstract principle, and that any specific action-guiding moral judgment may be deduced from this principle, along with factual premises specifying the relevant generic features of the situation. Deliberation so understood puts a premium on exact description of these features. Conversely, the rationalist is deeply skeptical about the philosophical value of concrete moral experience. It is not denied that our encounter with particular moral situations is important, whether in our personal lives, in histories and biographies, or in the imaginative creations of literature and the arts. But with respect to philosophical reflection, the rationalist is inclined to think these encounters are at best illustrative and at worst more likely to impede than advance our understanding. For they are encumbered by a wealth of idiosyncratic detail concerning background, context, personality, and the like, and we are likely to react to them with extraneous and unpredictable emotional responses. In both respects, these are obstacles to philosophical understanding on the rationalist model. Although inescapable features of life, these are features that practical reason seeks to overcome: it looks to the universal features of situations as the proper basis of rational evaluation, and it seeks to carry out this evaluation from a perspective free from the inevitable biases and distortions of emotional involvement.

Experientialism stands in sharp contrast to the rationalist approach. It seeks to understand moral practice primarily from the standpoint of the moral experience of persons. Experientialism gives priority to observation and reflection on what it is like for a person embedded in a particular social context to live a life constituted by values and commitments, to encounter circumstances of perplexity and choice, to deliberate and determine a course of response, and to carry out this decision and live with its consequences. What it feels like to live life from the inside, to live a human life as a moral agent, is for experientialism the principal source of comprehending moral practice. That life so lived is enmeshed in idiosyncratic detail and charged with emotional response is no obstacle to understanding for experientialism. To the contrary, experientialism believes the perception of the particularity of actual moral situations is essential to a proper appreciation of moral deliberation, and it regards our emotional responses to specific persons as an important and perhaps indispensable source of moral knowledge. As a result, experientialism looks to history, biography, literature, and the like, not as (at best) a storehouse of possibly useful illustrations of points already established by philosophical analysis, but as a significant resource for expanding the horizons of our own personal experience, and hence as having an important role to play within philosophical analysis.

Experientialism begins by giving prima facie authority to what it finds in moral experience, and what it finds is usually not what rationalism supposes rational moral practice should comprise. Thus experientialism typically supposes that moral deliberation involves reflection on a plurality of diverse and relatively concrete moral considerations, that it looks as much to the distinctive features of a situation as to its generic properties, and that these considerations and features do not always lend themselves to precise and full articulation. For these reasons, experientialism sees little plausibility in the rationalist conception of deliberation as deduction from an abstract first principle by reference to exactly stated universal properties.

This is not to say that experientialism is opposed to reflection on what is revealed in moral experience, nor that it accepts uncritically what is so revealed. It is rather that experientialism rejects the rationalist model of reflection and criticism. In particular, experientialism sees no basis for thinking that models of reason drawn from other disciplines have authority with respect to moral deliberation, and it is deeply suspicious of the idea that actual moral practice should be reformed by reference to these models. For experientialism, there is no higher authority for judging moral practice than what is found in moral experience itself. Hence the reform of moral practice must come from within, from reflection on difficulties revealed by moral experience—whether this be one's own experience or that of other persons. For experientialism, it is conceivable that reflection on these difficulties might lead to extensive revisions of moral practice, but the idea that something altogether outside moral experience could establish that moral practice as a whole is fundamentally flawed is regarded with acute skepticism. Experientialism does try to "save the appearances" presented by moral experience, but when it is forced to abandon some of these, this is only on account of attempting to preserve others.

II. The Moral Dilemmas Debate

With these two models of moral reflection in hand, I will now consider the thesis that it is informative to interpret the debate about moral dilemmas as a dialectic between philosophers with rationalist propensities and those with experientialist inclinations. I will begin by presenting the argument for the thesis and will then note some obstacles to it. As the two models are themselves idealizations, the reconstruction of the debate is necessarily highly simplified. Still, it purports to be illuminating in its reading of the sources of some of the main considerations on both sides of the discussion. Moral dilemmas are standardly defined as situations in which an agent morally ought to (and can) do one thing, and morally ought to (and can) do another, but cannot do both. Later I will need to discuss exactly what this might mean, but for the present purpose this definition may be taken at face value.

It is evident that the debate does not begin with rationalism. Sometimes it is pointed out that traditional moral philosophers were not much concerned with moral dilemmas,[4] and this is certainly the case if we look to those figures regarded as canonical in the rationalist tradition (conversely, it is arguably not the case if we consider philosophers, such as Aristotle or Montaigne, favored by experientialists). Left to its own perspective, it is unlikely to occur to rationalism that there might be moral dilemmas. This is not to say that rationalism is unaware of the appearance of conflict in morality. But its theoretical commitments to system, order, commensurability, hierarchy, and the like encourage it to regard whatever moral conflict might appear in moral practice as mere appearance, as a betrayal rather than a manifestation of reason, and as something that reason properly understood would reveal as such. From the standpoint of rationalism, the possibility of genuine moral dilemmas hardly seems an issue worthy of discussion. Apparent moral conflicts are taken as phenomena to be eliminated. The only question for the rationalist is how to achieve this.

It is only from the point of view of experientialism that the question of moral dilemmas is likely to arise as a serious issue, for it is only by paying close attention to concrete moral experience that the possibility of genuinely conflicting 'oughts' is apt to present itself. In fact, it is doubtful whether anyone would have ever suggested there might be moral dilemmas in the absence of reflection on

examples drawn from moral experience. For this reason, the role of the rationalist in recent debates has been mainly to react: it has been to explain why
claims for dilemmas rooted in experientialism are misguided.

To turn to specifics, the assertion that there are moral dilemmas begins with
a particular argument from moral experience.[5] The argument describes some
concrete situation in which moral considerations conflict, and it suggests that in
such a situation, whatever was done, the person involved would feel, and would
find it appropriate to feel, an emotion such as regret, remorse, or guilt. It then
proposes that this emotional reaction would make sense only if the person were
in a moral dilemma, and from this it concludes that there are dilemmas. This
argument may be referred to as "the phenomenological argument."[6] As its
underlying assumption is that we can learn from reflection on our moral experiences, it looks to be a quintessential expression of experientialism.

Among the numerous critics of this argument there is a recurrent thought:
its conclusion *must* be wrong. There is something about the idea of moral dilemmas that strikes these critics as deeply and indeed as obviously mistaken.
One important source of this reaction is a tacit, if not expressed, allegiance to
some form of rationalism. Evidence of this is found in the explanations advanced to show *why* the conclusion must be wrong. One standard line of response is that it conflicts with various principles of classical deontic logic, such as
"'ought' implies 'can'" and agglomeration, principles that prior to this debate
were mostly unquestioned among deontic logicians.[7] The suggestion is that our
knowledge of moral concepts as articulated by deontic principles shows that
there cannot be moral dilemmas. Conceptual understanding, traditionally
taken as the preserve of the a priori, undermines whatever might be suggested
by moral experience.

There is no denying that these deontic arguments against dilemmas may be
given valid formulations. Hence proponents of the idea of moral dilemmas
have focused on their soundness by challenging the a priori authority of their
underlying principles. In particular, they have claimed that deontic principles
ought to be answerable to moral experience rather than the other way around.
For example, Bernard Williams maintained with respect to the agglomeration
principle that "it is not a self-evident datum of the logic of *ought,* and that if a
more realistic picture of moral thought emerges from abandoning it, we should
have no qualms in abandoning it."[8] The "more realistic picture" is that suggested by our moral experience in the phenomenological argument. Thus it is
the perspective of experientialism that is being brought to bear on this rationalist objection.

A second line of objection is that the persons referred to in the phenomenological argument must be involved in some cognitive deficiency. Thus it has
been variously proposed that these persons must be uncertain about what to do,
must be making a mistake, must be confusing something or another, or perhaps
must simply be irrational.[9] These claims, too, seem to evidence a rationalist
mentality. Since on the rationalist account both moral dilemmas and our emotional responses are viewed with suspicion, it is natural to suppose that persons
whose feelings imply dilemmas must be failing to understand something. In
response, proponents of the phenomenological argument have questioned why

there has to be some cognitive deficiency in the experiences of these persons. Without denying that this is a possibility, they have wondered why we should not just take these experiences as being what they appear to be: manifestations of moral dilemmas.[10] Once again, it is experientialism that appears to be at work here. For experientialism, there is no standard external to moral experience that dictates what moral practice ought to look like. In the absence of this, it sees no basis for assuming there has to be some kind of error in these experiences.

There is, however, a further line of objection that may appear more persuasive. It purports to explain *why* the person in the phenomenological argument mistakenly feels as if there is a dilemma. According to this objection, which may be developed inter alia along Kantian as well as utilitarian lines,[11] moral deliberation is ultimately based on a first moral principle that, it is supposed, cannot generate conflicting conclusions. Still, from this first principle it is possible and helpful to derive a plurality of secondary principles that pertain to specific kinds of circumstances, and it is these latter principles that ordinarily are applied to particular moral situations in our lives. On occasion, according to this objection, these secondary principles conflict. Various explanations for this may be given. For example, it may be said that the secondary principles are strict corollaries of the first principle, but that they are often imperfectly formulated. When so formulated they may conflict, but when correctly stated this cannot happen. Or it may be said that secondary principles should be understood not as corollaries but as prima facie guides, as useful rules of thumb for applying the first principle. On this view, conflict among secondary principles may be permanent, but since they carry no authority in themselves this is no evidence of dilemmas; the real authority lies in the first principle, and it cannot justify conflicting conclusions. Either way, this account explains why the person in the phenomenological argument is mistaken: the person's emotional response is a predictable reaction to an encounter with conflicting secondary principles, but a proper understanding of these principles shows that there are no genuine moral dilemmas.

This conception of deliberation is naturally suggested by rationalism. In view of the widespread acceptance of Kantian and utilitarian variations of the conception, it is not surprising that this critique has appeared persuasive to many. By way of rejoinder, those who believe there are moral dilemmas have questioned the viability of this account of moral reasoning. For example, they have challenged the idea that the plurality of moral considerations that appears to us in moral experience can plausibly be reduced to a single factor, or they have contested the claim that our actual deliberations can reasonably be seen, even in principle, as conforming or aspiring to the model of deduction from a first principle.[12] Once again, it is a propensity toward experientialism that seems to motivate these arguments. Experientialism is likely to see little in moral experience that suggests this understanding of deliberation and to suspect, moreover, that it is based on a notion of rationality that is foreign to moral practice. As such, experientialism is likely to be unimpressed with this explanation of the feelings of persons in the phenomenological argument.

Such is the argument, in brief, for the interpretation of the moral dilemmas debate as rooted in disagreements between philosophers with experientialist tendencies and those with rationalist ones. Though this reading captures a good deal of the exchange between those who are and are not sympathetic with the idea of dilemmas, two considerations suggest the need for a more complex account.[13] First, the plausibility of the explanation depends more on the arguments given than the overall profile of those who have given the arguments. It is certainly possible to identify prominent figures on both sides of the debate who show affinities with rationalism and experientialism respectively. For example, the anti-dilemmas arguments of R. M. Hare and Alan Donagan reflect the role of the rationalist in the dialectic outlined above, and both describe themselves as "rationalists" while questioning the evidentiary value of moral intuitions.[14] Conversely, among those on the other side of the dialectic several, such as Martha Nussbaum and D. Z. Phillips, have clear affinities with experientialism, while others, such as Williams and Michael Walzer, may be said to have at least some tendencies in that direction.[15] On the other hand, in other cases, especially among the pro-dilemma forces, these characterizations cannot be made. It is interesting to observe, however, that even here the arguments offered for dilemmas often depend crucially on appeal to examples. In the context of a more traditional analytic idiom, moral experience is being given its due.

The second limitation of this interpretation is that other explanatory factors look to be at work, especially among opponents of dilemmas. Some may have normative commitments, to a deontological or consequentialist account, for example, that preclude dilemmas, without these commitments themselves being expressions of rationalism. Elsewhere I have suggested that opposition to dilemmas may be rooted in an ideal of moral innocence or purity, and the belief that this could not depend on factors beyond our control.[16] In some cases, religious beliefs may play a role, though with respect to Christianity at least there is disagreement about the implications of these beliefs for dilemmas.[17]

A full account of the debate about moral dilemmas would need to consider a variety of factors, allowing for diverse and even conflicting considerations on each side. It remains the case, however, that much of the debate as it has so far developed has centered on issues that are approximately marked out by the opposition between experientialist and rationalist tendencies. Insofar as this is true, it may appear that the debate has reached a standoff, with each side *from its own perspective* having reasons for its position and grounds for rejecting that of the other, a standoff that would be resolved only by facing the deeper questions that divide experientialism and rationalism. Though this may indeed be the case, I believe it is possible to advance the discussion without directly confronting these questions. In particular, I think it is possible to say a good deal more on behalf of the experientialist's defense of the phenomenological argument than has been said thus far.

With this end in view, it is helpful to distinguish between two propensities *within* experientialism. On the one hand, there are those (for example, some Wittgensteinian writers) who are content mainly to describe moral experience, to let it speak for itself largely in its own terms. But there are others (such as Nussbaum and Charles Taylor) who believe it is important to go beyond mere description and to develop explanations of moral experience, explanations that may involve concepts and ideas that are not immediately evident on the surface of unreflective moral practice. This second approach is not a move in the direction of rationalism, for it remains skeptical about the value of rationalism's conception of reason for moral deliberation. But it is a move in the direction of a more reflective and critical stance than the first approach. Although it insists on taking its bearings from moral experience, it also sees the need to stand back and develop a general explanatory account of this experience.

I believe the second form of experientialism is more adequate than the first, and that defenses of the phenomenological argument have suffered from a tendency to follow a more descriptive and less explanatory approach. Specifically, they have usually been content merely to describe situations in which persons inescapably feel some form of moral distress, and they have been less inclined to go on to give a general normative account that explains why these feelings make sense. In the absence of such an account, objections rooted in rationalism have greater credence because it is then plausible to say that the mere description of moral experience has little weight. But a description accompanied by an explanation would provide a much more powerful response to the rationalist objections: it would show that there is a substantial alternative to the rationalist position. In the current climate of philosophical discussion this would be a significant advance. My aim in the remainder of this paper is to develop such an alternative.[18]

III. Inescapable Moral Wrongdoing and the Phenomenological Argument

As a preliminary, it is important to clarify the meaning of 'moral dilemmas' and the nature of the phenomenological argument. The debate about dilemmas has actually concerned two issues. The first concerns the possibility of irresolvable moral conflicts. In my view, no serious philosophical problems are raised by this issue. On the one hand, it is obvious that there can be conflicting moral reasons, neither of which overrides the other, for these reasons may be perfectly symmetrical (what could guarantee that this would never happen?). On the other hand, in these situations the correct all-things-considered conclusion of moral deliberation is surely that one or the other action ought to be done (the choice as to which being left to nonmoral or arbitrary grounds). To say that the correct decision is to do one *and* the other, when both cannot be done, would be incoherent.[19] The second issue pertains to the possibility of inescapable moral wrongdoing. The question here is whether or not there are moral conflicts in which whatever the agent does he or she will do something morally wrong in the sense of transgressing some moral value. This is independent of the first issue. For one thing, the fact that conflicting moral reasons did not override one another would not entail that moral wrongdoing is inescapable. It might be said, and sometimes is, that in such situations as long as the agent does one action or the other he or she will do nothing wrong in any sense.[20] In addition, even when one conflicting reason does override the other, so that the correct conclusion of moral deliberation is to act on that reason, it may nonetheless be the case that moral wrongdoing is inescapable. It might be said, and sometimes is, that an agent who acted in accordance with the correct deliberative conclusion would still do something morally wrong in the sense of violating the moral value expressed by the overridden reason.[21] If this is so, since it is obvious that it would be wrong to violate such a conclusion, wrongdoing in some sense will be inescapable.

In my view, the second issue is the important one in the moral dilemmas debate: it is the claim that moral wrongdoing is sometimes inescapable that I propose to defend. As I will understand it, the phenomenological argument for this claim begins by declaring that there are moral conflicts in which persons find it natural and appropriate to feel moral distress no matter what they do. As an example, consider the events of Herman Melville's story *Billy Budd, Sailor (An Inside Narrative).*[22] Billy Budd, a young, virtually childlike sailor on board an English naval ship in time of war (in 1797, with France), is falsely accused by an evil officer of plotting mutiny. In order to test this accusation, the captain of the ship, Vere, compels the sailor to face his accuser and respond. But the innocent sailor is afflicted with a speech impediment, which is activated in times of stress, and he cannot speak. In frustration, he strikes the accusing officer, who drops dead to the deck. Captain Vere orders an immediate trial of Billy Budd for this insubordinate act. Before the court, Vere grants that Budd was falsely accused, and he acknowledges that justice and compassion compel leniency. But he argues that the court's higher obligation is to enforce the law, which requires execution, and that no mitigation of this penalty can be allowed in view of the fact that the navy has recently suffered two mutiny attempts. The court reluctantly agrees, and the following morning Billy Budd is hanged.

My contention is that Vere, insofar as he is a morally responsive agent, would find it natural and appropriate to feel moral distress in this situation, whether he set out to execute Billy or to let him live.[23] By 'moral distress' I mean a feeling of moral pain in response to the fact that one has done something morally wrong—not necessarily in the sense of having transgressed the correct conclusion of moral deliberation, but in the sense of having violated some genuine moral value—and that one ought if possible to apologize or compensate in some way for this wrong.[24] The phenomenological argument should not be interpreted as regarding contentions such as this as incorrigible sources of moral insight. Rather, they should be thought of as references to significant albeit fallible data of moral experience. Of course, it is possible to deny the data, to maintain that people would not find moral distress unavoidable in such situations. But it is noteworthy that most critics of the argument have not denied that people would have some such feeling. They have claimed instead that these reactions can be explained without supposing that wrongdoing is inescapable (for example, in terms of misunderstandings of secondary principles). For the experientialist, however, this is a telling concession. It suggests that these experiences are deeply rooted in our moral sensibility.

Nonetheless, it would be a mistake to conclude straightaway from this data that wrongdoing is inescapable. The phenomenological argument requires as its second premise the claim that the best explanation of the fact that people feel this way is, at least often, that there are conflicting moral values, each of which it is wrong to transgress. Only then would we be entitled to conclude that moral wrongdoing is sometimes inescapable.[25] To the extent that proponents of this argument have offered such an explanation, it has generally involved the idea that there is a plurality of types of moral value (in contrast with the monism implicit in most rationalist objections).[26] As moral experience strongly suggests a multiplicity of kinds of moral value, I am not inclined to reject moral pluralism in this sense. Nevertheless, in my view this is not an adequate explanation of all, or even most, cases of unavoidable moral distress appealed to in the phenomenological argument. First, in some cases the conflict involves a single type of value, as when a mother must choose between saving the life of one child and saving the life of another.[27] More important, the distress is typically focused not simply on the wrong of violating a type of moral value (as in "I was wrong to be disloyal"), but on the wrong of violating a particular person (as in "I was wrong to be disloyal *to him*"). Both points suggest that what is centrally important here is not the plurality of types of values per se, but the plurality of moral responsibilities to specific persons. It is this idea I wish to develop.

IV. Moral Responsibilities to Persons

An explanation offered in defense of the second premise of the phenomenological argument has to make clear what it means by 'moral wrongdoing'. In ordinary usage, there is moral wrongdoing when there is a transgression of some moral value. It need not be supposed, as philosophers often do, that these values must be understood only as whatever is required by correct moral deliberation about what to do, and hence as something that cannot conflict. Deliberation is constrained by the need to act and hence by the possibilities for action. But moral values, though obviously concerned with action in a general way, reflect a more complex set of considerations. It is with this in mind that I propose to speak of what I call *moral responsibilities,* a set of moral values that have a standing independent of particular conclusions of moral deliberation. These responsibilities do figure prominently in deliberation: they are grounds of deliberative conclusions. But their significance is not exhausted by their contribution to the deliberative process. Moreover, although it is wrong to transgress these responsibilities, they can conflict. It is in this sense that wrongdoing is sometimes inescapable.[28]

The place to begin is with our particular, concrete relationships with persons with whom we are, to a greater or lesser extent, and in various respects, intimate—especially relations of kinship, friendship, and love. I take these to be the paradigmatic (though not the only) location of moral responsibilities. All of us suppose we have, with respect to various persons with whom we are so related, a set of more or less well-defined specific moral responsibilities. These responsibilities are rooted in two kinds of consideration. The first is the perception that each of these persons is both intrinsically and irreplaceably valuable. The second is the recognition that some connection or another obtains between oneself and these intimates.

To say that persons are intrinsically valuable means that they are valuable, but not merely because they have instrumental value as means to some valued end or as parts of some valued whole. Hence, even if they were not valued in this way, which of course persons often are, they would still be valuable. The idea that persons are valuable in themselves is, of course, a common idea in moral philosophy. For example, it is related to Kant's notion of respecting persons as ends in themselves. On the other hand, to say that persons, taken individually, are irreplaceably valuable is a less familiar notion. The common assumption that equality is the supreme moral value has obscured the importance of the irreplaceable value of persons, since equality can seem to imply fungibility. As a result, there has not been much discussion of this idea among contemporary moral philosophers.[29] On this view, each person is not only intrinsically valuable, but has a value that cannot be fully replaced by the value of another person.

That persons are irreplaceably valuable is a pervasive feature of our moral experience: it is revealed most poignantly in our attitudes toward the death of a loved one. When such a person dies there is an irreplaceable loss. We regard the deceased person as someone who cannot be fully replaced by another person, no matter how valuable he or she may be. By contrast, if your CD player stops working, and the warranty provides you with another one, then you have been fully compensated for your loss. CD players, unlike persons, can be replaced without loss of value.

Kant's insistence on the fundamental moral difference between persons and things is helpful in this regard. Only persons, Kant says, have a value that "admits of no equivalent."[30] The basis of this value is our autonomy, our capacity for choosing on the basis of reasons, independently of external causes. But insofar as what is important is simply our common autonomous nature, this is not sufficient to explain our intuitions concerning irreplaceability. Distress in the face of the loss of a loved one does not focus merely on the fact that *an* autonomous person is now gone, but that *this* person is now gone; hence replacement by another person does not fully compensate for the loss. Kant himself was more concerned with what we have in common than with what distinguishes us from one another. Yet there are resources in the Kantian conception of autonomy for understanding our intuitions about irreplaceable value.[31]

For Kant, as autonomous beings we freely create our life and character. This is a source of irreplaceability. Only you can possess the particular worth you merit for what you have created. Although others may have similar or greater worth, no one else is entitled to *this* specific worth, since no one else created this life and character. In addition, for Kant, as autonomous creatures we freely undertake actions for which we are responsible. This is a further source of irreplaceability. If you have been generous to me, only you can be the object of my gratitude for your action. If I have broken my commitments to you, only I can be the object of your forgiveness for my action. These autonomy-based phenomena explain our intuitions concerning irreplaceable value. By showing how such values are necessarily attached to particular persons, we come to understand the irreplaceable loss we feel upon the death of a loved one.[32]

Of course, the irreplaceable value of persons can play different roles in our lives. In some cases, especially familial or romantic love, the specific ways in which a particular person is irreplaceable are vitally important: we strive to respond to those specific features of *that* person. But in other cases we are in less of a position to recognize or appreciate what is irreplaceably valuable in a person. At the opposite extreme, that of the virtual stranger, we can hardly respond to anything specific about the person at all. Here we respond not so much to what is irreplaceably valuable per se as to the fact of irreplaceable value. We try to respond as one should respond to any irreplaceably and intrinsically valuable person. In this respect, of course, there is a kind of equality. But precisely because each person is irreplaceably valuable, that persons have equal value cannot be taken to imply that they have interchangeable value.

That we regard persons as being intrinsically and irreplaceably valuable is one of the most significant features of our understanding of ourselves. Because we regard persons in this way, we suppose they are in various respects deserving, in and of themselves and irrespective of circumstances. For example, a child suffering from malnutrition is deserving of food. But to say that a person is deserving in this sense does not immediately entail that anyone has moral responsibilities to this person. Which persons have responsibilities to feed this deserving child depends upon a variety of factors.

Being intrinsically and irreplaceably valuable merely creates the potentiality for responsibility: it establishes that this is a kind of being for whom one can have moral responsibilities. These responsibilities arise only when some connection is established between persons, for example, through family relation, friendship, love, nationality, ethnicity, agreement, proximity, knowledge, common background, commitment, interest, and the like. There is a great deal of diversity here, both with respect to the nature of these connections and the degree of their relative dependence on choice and unchosen circumstance. On the basis of these various kinds of connections, relationships among persons are formed, and inherent in such relationships there is typically an understanding of mutual (but not necessarily symmetrical) responsibility.

These responsibilities are constitutive of meaningful and worthwhile human lives. On this account, one's identity as a particular person is explicable only by reference to the network of these responsibilities. One's well-being depends not only on the responsiveness of others, but on being properly responsive to others. Although specific responsibilities can sometimes be irksome, a life comprising responsibilities, far from being onerous, is essential for human flourishing.

Though I have suggested that moral responsibilities are paradigmatically located in more intimate relationships with particular persons, it is important to extend this account to other contexts. First, there may be responsibilities rooted in relationships with less endurance and depth. At the outer limit, there may be responsibilities among strangers, so long as there is some connection among them, even if only a momentary encounter. Second, there are responsibilities to social entities that consist of individual persons brought together through some common interest, purpose, origin, need, belief, aspiration, hope, and the like. Thus there may be responsibilities to one's community, nation, government, ethnic group, race, family, church, company, profession, labor union, political party, and so on. These social entities clearly have a life of their own that transcends the individuals who make them up. Our relationships with social entities, and their concomitant responsibilities, play an important part in human life. Though different in many respects from relationships with individual persons, they can inspire their own forms of intimacy and passion. Human flourishing requires participation in collective forms of activity as well as individual relationships.

In both cases—relationships with more casual acquaintances and those with social entities—there is also an appreciation of something intrinsically and irreplaceably valuable with which one has some connection. However, the diversity of relationships makes it clear that the nature, scope, and importance of our responsibilities to persons and social entities varies considerably, depending on the characteristics of the relationship in question. Some responsibilities are likely to be attached to almost any relationship. Others are clearly quite specialized in that they occur only in very particular kinds of relationship. In all cases, we do not suppose our responsibilities to be unlimited, in the sense that we are prepared to do anything at all, to anyone, at any time for the person or group with whom we are related. A given relationship will imply an understanding of the specific features of the responsibilities that are constitutive of it. In general, we have an ongoing but open-ended sense of the general shape of our moral responsibilities, of their nature, extent, and significance. However, although we can certainly discuss these responsibilities, there is no reason to suppose that we can be fully articulate about them. Nor, in particular, is there any reason to think that they can be expressed in a set of more or less simple rules. Deliberation involving moral responsibilities may be facilitated by the use of guidelines, but responsibilities should not be thought of as corresponding to the secondary principles in the rationalist understanding of deliberation.

In this connection, it is worth contrasting the bases of deliberation on the responsibilities to persons account with that of rationalist approaches. Moral responsibilities do figure prominently in deliberation: they provide us with prima facie reasons to act. But these responsibilities are a product of the multiplicity of relationships with particular persons which make up our lives. We cannot plausibly be thought to enter into these relationships, and thereby acquire these responsibilities, by deliberating about what to do on the basis of some abstract first principle as applied to the circumstances of our lives. Rather, it is through the specific, concrete experience of encountering this person in these circumstances, or of being connected in these ways, and also of recognizing the intrinsic and irreplaceable value of this person, that a relationship is formed in which responsibilities are recognized. This is not to say that no reflection is involved in their formation or development. Surely it is. But reflection often takes the form of a careful elucidation of the meaning and implications of the relationship in question, a process not helpfully understood on the model of inference from abstract first principle.[33]

V. Responsibilities to Persons and Inescapable Wrongdoing

It is now possible to see how the responsibilities to persons account provides an explanation of inescapable moral distress as a reasonable response to conflicts of responsibilities both of which it is wrong to transgress. It should be emphasized at the outset that we do have reason to seek a life in which conflicts of responsibilities are not common and constant. The value of the relationships that establish our responsibilities depends on our being able to fulfill these responsibilities a good deal of the time. It would be self-defeating to enter into a set of relationships knowing that it will be impossible to fulfill most of their responsibilities. However, to acknowledge this does not entail that we have an overriding reason to avoid conflicting responsibilities altogether. Avoiding conflict is one concern among others. If it were our only or highest concern, our best hope of fulfilling it would be to take on as few responsibilities as possible. This would also be self-defeating, for it is the relationships constituting these responsibilities that make life worthwhile in the first place.

The principal reason we sometimes have conflicting responsibilities is that these responsibilities originate in responses to the intrinsic and irreplaceable value of the particular persons (and groups of persons) with whom we are connected. It is the recognition of the value of, and hence the appropriateness of our specific response to, each of these persons that generates our various moral responsibilities. Although these responsibilities arise in the context of circumstances that preclude taking on unlimited responsibilities, they are nonetheless driven primarily by the acknowledgment of the value of each particular person with whom we are related. It is because they develop out of these separate responses to distinct persons that conflicts cannot plausibly be eliminated.

Of course, reflection on apparently conflicting responsibilities may lead to the conclusion that they do not really conflict or that they should be modified so as to avoid conflict. But this is only one possibility. For reflection may equally reveal no misunderstanding or basis for modification of responsibilities. In fact, it may make it all the more evident that in this situation responsibilities really do conflict. In these cases, deliberation is not the occasion for determining that our relationship with one or another person must now be sharply curtailed. Rather, it is a time for determining how best to fulfill the responsibilities we continue to regard ourselves as having. And it is a time for acknowledging, to ourselves as well as to those involved, the persistence of these unfulfillable responsibilities. Such acknowledgment is an affirmation of the particular value of these persons and of our standing with them. It is a way of maintaining the network of relationships that constitutes our moral identity and sustains our well-being.

When in the face of conflicting responsibilities we do what is best, we nonetheless often feel morally distressed. We feel that we have done something wrong, not in the sense of violating a sound deliberative conclusion, but in the sense of transgressing a responsibility to someone. We feel that we have not responded in a manner that is required by the worth of that person and the value of our relationship. This pains us morally, and we feel that we should try in some way to make up for our failure to fulfill this responsibility, if only by apologizing. In this sense, it is not necessarily enough that we have acted for the best. For we have a more fundamental concern: to be properly responsive to each particular person with whom we are connected and to whom we have responsibilities.

To return to the example from *Billy Budd,* it is reasonable to suppose that, in the wake of Billy's killing of the officer, Vere has both a moral responsibility to his king and country to uphold the rule of law and the order of the state, and a moral responsibility to Billy to show justice and compassion. Vere himself acknowledges the distinct value of each of these—king and country on the one hand, Billy on the other—and he recognizes that there is an indisputable basis for his responsibilities to each. On the one hand, he has sworn to enforce the law of the state, and that law requires execution. For a person in Vere's position, to refuse to carry out the law would be tantamount to disloyalty. On the other hand, although Billy did strike the officer, the circumstances were extraordinary: Billy was practically a child, he had been impressed into the Navy, he was the object of an evil plot by the officer, he acted under extreme provocation, he suffered from a speech impediment, and he had no intention to kill. Under these circumstances, whatever Billy might deserve, he could not be said to deserve execution. He was as much a victim of a crime as a perpetrator of one. As the agent of his punishment, Vere could not responsibly bring about Billy's death. To do so would be to commit a manifest and serious injustice to this person in these circumstances.

In view of this, the fact that one of these responsibilities is determined to be most important (whatever it may be), and hence is the one to be acted on, does not thereby eliminate the other responsibility. Hence, whatever Vere does, he will violate one of these responsibilities, and in this sense he will do something morally wrong no matter what—if not to Billy, then to his country. As a morally sensitive agent, Vere would find moral distress inescapable because moral wrongdoing is inescapable. This distress may be expected to have two elements: mental anguish in response to the recognition that he has violated a responsibility to someone, and the felt need to apologize or in some way make up to the person for this wrong. Hence, even in acting for what he believes to be the best in executing Billy, it would be appropriate for Vere to feel such anguish as a manifestation of his understanding of the continuing reality of his responsibility to Billy. It would also be appropriate for Vere to attempt to apologize to Billy. For such compensatory action, although in one way woefully inadequate, is still an important expression of his acknowledgment of Billy's value as a person and the fact that he did not deserve this fate.

I have argued that the inescapable feelings of moral distress referred to in the phenomenological argument may be explained as a reasonable response to situations of genuinely conflicting responsibilities, each of which it is wrong to violate. It may be said, by way of objection, that there is nothing wrong per se with violating moral responsibilities as I have defined them, and hence that conflicts among these responsibilities do not establish that wrongdoing is inescapable. The assumption that gives force to this objection is allied with the rationalist understanding of deliberation. It is that there are only two possible kinds of moral consideration relevant to the debate about moral dilemmas: all-things-considered conclusions about what is morally best, and the appearance of these in merely prima facie obligations.[34] Although it is wrong to transgress the former, on this view, there is nothing at all wrong about transgressing the latter, so long as they do not rise to the status of the former (like an unsigned contract, they have no binding force whatsoever).

The import of the responsibilities-to-persons account is to challenge the validity of this exhaustive dichotomy. For moral responsibilities are neither mere prima facie duties nor rules of thumb for the determination of actual duties. Although they provide premises for deliberative conclusions, their importance does not depend only on their contribution to deliberation. In particular, they are not merely appearances, which may or may not be veridical, of sound deliberative conclusions. They are constitutive features of our relationships with persons that it is wrong to violate even when they conflict. In my view, if we attend to our moral experience, to what our life looks like from our perspective as moral agents, it is natural to suppose that we have such responsibilities. We should not allow rationalism, nor any other standpoint extrinsic to moral experience, to persuade us otherwise.

Notes

Portions of this paper, especially in the second half, have been taken from Gowans (1994).

1. See, e.g., Clarke (1987); Louden (1992), ch. 5; Railton (1992); and Walker (1989).

2. The historical connotations of 'rationalism' are close enough to what I will be calling 'rationalism' to warrant use of the term. But the connotations of 'empiricism', the term usually opposed to this, are quite different from the contrasting position I will be describing. Hence, for this position I use the term 'experientialism' instead.

3. We might think of these types as constituting the endpoints of a continuum on which many moral philosophers may be arrayed, with some drawn toward one end and others toward the other.

4. See, e.g., MacIntyre (1990).

5. For the classic statement of this argument, see Williams (1965). There is now a sizable literature concerning it.

6. I borrow this phrase from Santurri (1987).

7. There is a substantial literature concerning these deontic objections. For extensive discussion of them, see Sinnott-Armstrong (1988), chs. 4, 5.

8. Williams (1965), in Williams (1973), p. 182.

9. See, e.g., Conee (1982); Levi (1992); MacIntyre (1990); McConnell (1978); and Santurri (1987), p. 51.

10. See, e.g., Phillips and Mounce (1970), pp. 100–1.

11. For an example of each, see Donagan (1984) and Hare (1981), chs. 2, 3. It is usually supposed that Kantianism and utilitarianism are incompatible with moral dilemmas, although there is now some dissent from this. See, e.g., Louden (1992), pp. 110-11; Railton (1992); and Slote (1985).

12. See, e.g., Nussbaum (1990), ch. 2.

13. I am indebted to Gene Mason for urging the importance of considering these complexities.

14. They identify respectively with the Enlightenment traditions of utilitarianism and Kantianism, in which moral rationality was often modeled on scientific rationality. In his paper in this volume, Donagan compares moral theory to physical theory.

15. Williams is obviously the animating figure in the debate. Writing about philosophers who insist on "moral theory," he asks, "What authority is theoretical

tidiness or simplicity supposed to have against the force of concerns which one actually finds important?" He adds that there may be "no, or few, purely theoretical pressures to reduce the conflicts in our value-system" (Williams [1978], p. xvii).

16. See Gowans (1994), ch. 9, sec. I.

17. For other explanations, see the papers by Dahl and Donagan in this volume.

18. A full defense of this alternative would require consideration of epistemological issues concerning the cognitive status of moral experiences and their ability to reveal "moral truth," as well as examination of the various objections rooted in rationalism just described. I discuss these issues in Gowans (1994).

19. We can see this even in nonmoral cases of deliberation. There would be no point in deciding to see this play and that one, knowing that I cannot see both. In Gowans (1994), ch. 4, I argue that the incoherence of conflicts between all-things-considered conclusions of deliberation helps to explain the intuitions behind the deontic objections to moral dilemmas.

20. See, e.g., Donagan (1984), p. 307, and Feldman (1986), p. 201.

21. See, e.g., Nussbaum (1986), p. 27, and Stocker (1990), p. 28.

22. Melville (1962).

23. In saying this, I am not suggesting that the conflict is irresolvable nor that Vere's decision is morally for the best.

24. Oftentimes in discussions of this argument terms such as 'guilt', 'remorse', 'shame', and 'regret' are employed. But these terms are poorly understood, and there is little agreement about their meaning and implications. Hence, I prefer to speak of moral distress as defined.

25. It might be objected that the second premise begs the question or renders the first premise idle. But this objection misconstrues the experientialist approach as I understand it. On this approach, it is crucial that we have these experiences, but it is also important that we find a way to make sense of them. The experience and the explanation are individually necessary and jointly sufficient for the conclusion.

26. See, e.g., Nussbaum (1990), ch. 2, and Taylor (1989).

27. This point has been emphasized in Marcus (1980).

28. In his paper in this volume, Mason also emphasizes the importance of moral responsibilities for understanding moral dilemmas.

29. There has been some discussion. For example, see Blustein (1991), ch. 17; Nozick (1981), pp. 452–7; Nussbaum (1986), ch. 6, and Nussbaum (1990), ch. 13; and Vlastos (1973).

30. Kant (1956), p. 102.

31. This is a modification of my view in Gowans (1994); I discuss this further in Gowans (forthcoming). In drawing on Kant's conception of the person, I mean to appeal to certain intuitive features of it; I do not mean to endorse the critical apparatus generating the phenomenal-noumenal distinction nor the deeply rationalist outlook permeating Kant's moral philosophy.

32. In my view, other phenomena often associated with irreplaceable value, such as a common history of intimacy, must also be explained by reference to autonomy. For a discussion of the value of particular persons in Kant, see Hill's paper in this volume.

33. Nor is this to say that every relationship with a person is valuable or immune to critique. There are obviously many relationships that are unjust, oppressive, and destructive of people's lives.

34. For an example of this assumption, see Conee (1982).

Responsibilities and Principles: Reflections on the Sources of Moral Dilemmas

H. E. MASON

Moral conflict has long been prominent in the attempts of philosophers to understand morality. It was recognized by Plato, celebrated by Hegel, and, more recently, taken as a commonplace by a variety of non-cognitivist moral theorists. Moral dilemmas are no more than a special case of moral conflict, but they are of particular interest because they exhibit the possibility of conflict within the moral consciousness of a single individual. It is one thing for a person to recognize that others might fundamentally disagree with his moral stands, quite another to experience apparently irresolvable conflicts in his own mind. In recent years, philosophers have given a good bit of attention to moral dilemmas. Taking dilemmas as standing in the way of a well-conceived and practically useful moral philosophy, they have wondered how a genuine dilemma could be possible. In this paper I will take another tack. Taking dilemmas as a fundamental fact of moral life, I will ask what their possibility can teach us about that form of life. I will give special attention to some of the varying circumstances in which they arise, and the form they take in those circumstances. I will in light of those reflections offer several general speculations about the concept of morality assumed in much of the controversy over the possibility of moral dilemmas.

Specifications of the form of a moral dilemma are prominent in philosophical discussions of the problems posed by the possibility of moral dilemmas. That is quite appropriate when the problems in question are paradoxes or comparable conceptual difficulties for careful and principled moral thought. A casually framed paradox is unlikely to pose serious problems for any form of systematic thought. Prominent formulations tend to focus on conflicts of obligation. Bernard Williams wrote simply of conflicting *oughts,* but he treated those conflicts as of a sort with the conflicts of duties or obligations W. D. Ross had described.[1] In subsequent discussions, it has become common to speak of conflicting obligations or conflicting moral requirements. A person facing a dilemma is said to be morally obliged to do each of a pair of incompatible things, or is morally required to do each of them. Because one obligation is sometimes said to take priority over another, it is, in stricter specifications, said that a person facing a dilemma is obliged or morally required to do each of a pair of incompatible things in a situation in which neither of the obligations is overridden by the other.[2] To allow for the fact that in the course of deliberation a standing obligation may be qualified in the light of circumstances, Dahl has argued that the obligations forming a dilemma must be all-things-considered obligations, adjusted to the particular circumstances in question.[3]

Difficult moral choices commonly regarded as dilemmas are seldom so explicitly formulated, and they are not necessarily couched in terms of paired obligations or requirements. Choices among obligations to comply with conflicting promises or assurances in circumstances in which there are no clear reasons for thinking that one takes precedence over the other provide the most plausible cases. But even among conflicts over the obligations created by promises, vows, and assurances, there are many conflicts that would not pass muster. There must be a great many conflicted marriages, for example, in which the obligations of fidelity play a role without framing the difficult choices to be made. The concerns over children and profession often involved are seldom as definite as the obligations created by explicit promises, but they can create difficult choices described by participants and sympathetic observers alike as dilemmas.

Dilemmas of public policy also tend to resist prevailing philosophical conceptions. A nation or an international agency imposing an arms embargo in hopes of maintaining peace may face a terrible choice between, on the one hand, maintaining the embargo and permitting continuation of genocidal destruction on the part of well-armed combatants, and, on the other hand, lifting the embargo and thereby facilitating a general escalation of warfare. Public action to relieve widespread suffering often promises to bring even greater suffering in its wake. A readiness to ransom hostages jeopardizes other potential victims, while efforts to rescue them may place the rescuers in great danger. There are many comparable examples.

These and similar dilemmas undoubtedly involve a wide diversity of moral considerations. In hope of casting light on some of the ways in which distinct moral considerations can figure in forcing moral conflict, I will turn to a familiar form, dilemmas that occur at the intersection of overlapping spheres of responsibility: familial responsibilities, professional responsibilities, civic and public responsibilities. They tend to illustrate in a fairly accessible way both the complexity and the diversity of moral considerations bearing on hard moral choices and the difficulty that causes. The independence and relative autonomy of the various responsibilities provide some reason for regarding moral conflict as a fact of life to be expected in the natural course of things.

Suppose that a parent in an official post is called upon to undertake a demanding task in circumstances in which there is some reason to believe that the stability of her young family may be jeopardized if she agrees. If she is particularly well qualified for the task, the request is likely to create a difficult choice for her. Depending on the importance of the mission and the gravity of the possible harm to her family, the question of what she should do may be a question with no completely satisfactory answer. It is quite possible that, whatever she does, there will be people who will have reason to think she has failed them.

Cases of this sort exhibit two features common to a great many of the hard choices commonly spoken of as dilemmas. The responsibilities that give rise to the dilemma are somewhat indeterminate, and the responsibilities themselves are, in a way, disparate, the accountings they call for taking divergent directions. These two features, which are common to a great many dilemmas, provide some explanation for the difficulty they often present. They also cast some doubt on the monolithic conception of morality often assumed in philosophical discussions of moral dilemmas. I will say a word about each of them in turn.

The Indeterminacy of Common Responsibilities

Suppose that the parent mentioned earlier is a physician and that she is asked by her clinic to undertake extraordinary duty attending a group of gravely ill patients in need of the care of a person with her special skills. Thinking of the needs of the patients and the absence of anyone else capable of meeting their needs, she might feel it her responsibility to agree to the clinic's request. But if her children are going through a difficult time and need continuing attention, she may wonder how she can agree to an assignment that could easily turn out to be very demanding. Her conflict arises out of distinct responsibilities that require incompatible commitments of time and attention. In thinking through the situation, she would undoubtedly try to work out some compromise. Failing that, she might come to think either that she had to accept the special assignment, or that she could not leave her children at such a crucial time. Either of the conclusions might be put in just that way, the necessities introduced in saying that she *had to* accept the special duty, or that she *could not* leave her child. Necessities introduced in that way in the conclusion to a line of deliberation express a judgment of the comparative weight of the opposing considerations. Contrary to common philosophical expectations, they can seldom, if ever, be supported by principles explicitly embodying the necessities in question.[4] Where carefully argued, the reasons might be complex. The physician would have to compare the seriousness of her children's need for attention with that of her prospective patients, and consider how essential her own ministrations would be in either case. She would have to consider her general responsibilities as a physician, as well as any special commitments she had made to the clinic and any expectations she might have created that she would be willing to undertake extraordinary duty in such a case. In explaining why she had to take one course or the other she might mention a salient feature as decisive, but any number of contextual features not easily enumerated would also play a role.

I want to stress the complexity of even a deliberation like this, which is, in its way, fairly straightforward.[5] There is a temptation to think that the judgments forming a dilemma are no more than applications of ruling obligations or responsibilities. But the complexity of circumstances and the specific indeterminacy of ruling responsibilities stand in the way of that. The *conclusion* to a moral deliberation may be couched in terms of what the obligations or responsibilities require in the circumstances at hand, but those obligations or responsibilities are not normally understood in a way that allows the deliberation to be simply a matter of applying their specification to a case at hand.[6] Social and institutional arrangements frame the issue but conscientious judgment is bound play a role.

It tends to be assumed in philosophical discussions of moral dilemmas that the judgments forming a genuine dilemma must be entailed by general principles explicitly incorporating the moral necessities that formulation of a dilemma commonly requires. That is the view of moral rationalists like Alan Donagan,[7] but it is a view shared by many others as well. Philippa Foot goes so far as to say that the conflicts discussed in the recent philosophical literature are not conflicts in the mind of a person torn between alternatives, but conflicts between principles such as *keep promises* and *save lives*. In situations of moral conflict thus understood, "one principle enjoins one action and another another, and it is impossible that the agent should do both."[8] Other writers treat the conflicts as conflicts of a person torn between alternatives, but explain the conflicts as arising out of the acceptance of principles enjoining incompatible actions. The conflicting requirements forming a conflict are entailed by accepted principles, the moral necessities in question explicitly specified in the engendering principles.

It may be true that there are hard or impossible moral choices reasonably understood in this way. That is, there may be instances in which, upon reflection, explicitly formulated principles that are commonly acknowledged can be said to give rise to a dilemma requiring incompatible actions of those who honor them. But it is a striking fact that that does not appear to hold true of a great many of the moral conflicts that arise out of acceptance of responsibilities of the sort mentioned above. It cannot be said that in accepting an official post with its responsibilities, or, for that matter, parenthood with its responsibilities, a person will thereby have accepted ruling principles explicitly determining what her responsibilities would require in a particular situation. Each of the responsibilities will almost certainly be understood in a fairly general way, leaving open just what in particular they require in many situations. That is unquestionably true of the responsibilities of parenthood, and it is probably true as well of most of the responsibilities attached to official positions.

The responsibilities of those public officials entrusted with directing a nation's foreign policy work in a similar way. Although there may be wide agreement on the overall direction of policy an official is expected to carry out, that seldom leads to specific agreement over particular courses of action. Where an official's responsibility seems to require incompatible courses of action, it is seldom true that the judgments that those courses of action are required can be said to be entailed by principles outlining his responsibilities. To take a somewhat extreme if real example, it is probably true that, whatever judgment an official finally comes to in trying to decide how to deal with terrorists, those judgments will not be entailed by general understandings normally governing the work of that office.

It is not surprising that specific responsibilities should work in this way. Responsibilities are commonly understood in terms of tasks. An architect designs a building or a landscape and shepherds its construction; a hospital orderly attends to the needs of the patients in the ward; a river pilot keeps a boat on its course, guiding it through a variety of hazards. Successful performance of these various tasks imposes its own requirements, as does the social venue within which the responsibilities come to be accepted. But what the tasks may require in specific circumstances is seldom determined by general specifications of the task directly applicable to the case at hand. Practitioners will have come to recognize what a task requires in a range of varying circumstances, and will exhibit their sense of that in judgments of what must or can't be done in a case at hand. The fact that such judgments are often subject to critical controversy serves as a reminder of the indeterminacy of those general understandings governing the tasks in question.

The question what a responsibility requires in a particular circumstance is sometimes rephrased with the question of what can be reasonably expected of a person bearing that responsibility; what can be reasonably expected of a parent, a teacher, or a judge, for example. That way of phrasing the question has the merit of focusing attention on the expectations of those whose interests are at stake, but it cannot be said to introduce a more determinate basis for judgment. Where a policy or a specific action is praised as reasonable, it is normally its judicious balancing of relevant considerations and competing interests that earns that praise. Accommodation is often in question. In that respect, the question of what can be reasonably expected of a citizen or a teacher acknowledges that there may be a variety of considerations to be taken into account, and it asks for a balanced judgment in light of those considerations. It does not ask for or promise a more fundamental way of looking at a difficult question.

If relatively specific responsibilities are governed by somewhat indeterminate general understandings, that is even more likely to be true of many of the more comprehensive responsibilities with respect to which moral conflicts commonly arise. Familial and civic responsibilities, broad professional responsibilities, and the responsibilities of public office may be governed by common general understandings, but both those understandings and their application to specific cases are subject to critical controversy, and their discharge is often a matter of individual judgment. The considerations relevant to such judgments are commonly varied and diverse; the sense of what considerations are salient, controversial.

Diverging Directions of Moral Accountability

It is assumed in a great deal of writing on moral philosophy that there is a more or less uniform point of view from which human conduct is to be morally assessed. The circumstances of human life may vary greatly, but where justifications are in question they must take a common form and satisfy uniform and commonly available moral standards. That idea is cast into doubt by moral conflicts arising out of relatively specific and distinct spheres of responsibility. A physician, a teacher, or a parent may all, on occasion, be held accountable by those they serve, and, varying with practices in place and with circumstances, they can be expected to explain themselves to both the people they serve and to others affected by their actions. Where familial duties are allowed to take precedence over civic or professional duties, for example, a parent must be ready to explain himself to his fellow citizens or his clients and hear out their objections. When a professional's practices adversely affect others in the population, he may be expected to justify them to those affected. Human relationships being what they are, the ensuing lines of justification might be dogmatic and perfunctory, or they might be excessively conciliatory. If they are to be at all responsive, they must be cast in terms of the specific social relationships in question, but directed to the objections brought by the people affected.

I want to stress this point. Moral responsibility is sometimes thought of as a kind of diffuse accountability owed to no one in particular. Philosophers have given a good deal of attention to the conditions under which a person can reasonably be held responsible for his actions, but they have said little or nothing about the question of whether there are circumstances in which there are people to whom a person is particularly responsible for what he does. In the celebrated cases of moral dilemmas, there is a place for an accountability that is pointed and direct. Agamemnon must sacrifice his daughter, Captain Vere must condemn Billy Budd, and Sartre's young countryman faces the prospect of abandoning his aged mother. In *Fear and Trembling*, Kierkegaard[9] exhibited the place of a more pointed and direct accountability. With a striking contrast between Abraham's readiness to sacrifice his son Isaac and Agamemnon's sacrifice of his daughter Iphigenia, he sought to remind his readers that an ethical consciousness requires that a person explain himself to those affected by his actions. In the early pages of *Fear and Trembling*, Kierkegaard offered a number of abortive attempts to reconstruct the story of Abraham's trial in a way that makes the story, as he put it, humanly understandable. With a series of successive versions, each an attempt to make sense of the story, each equally unsatisfactory, Kierkegaard exhibited the difficulty Abraham might have encountered had he searched for a way of explaining to Isaac his readiness to sacrifice him. As the reconstruction proceeds, no thought is given to the possibility that there might be no need to explain the undertaking to Isaac. It is assumed that a wish on Abraham's part to explain himself, even some recognition of a kind of obligation to do that, is a constraint on the intelligibility of the story.

In the view taken in *Fear and Trembling*, there is nothing Abraham could have said that would have made his readiness to sacrifice Isaac understandable to Isaac. In contrast, Agamemnon's sacrifice of his daughter is said to be a terrible but ethically unavoidable deed. The sacrifice must be carried out to serve the ends of state: the becalmed fleet must be permitted to sail, whatever the cost.[10] But, while arguing that Agamemnon's act serves a "higher" ethical end, Kierkegaard insists that that justification must all the same be tried by the tears of Clytemnestra and Iphigenia. He goes so far as to say that Iphigenia ought to be permitted to weep for two months at her father's feet. Why should Agamemnon submit himself to the argument from Iphigenia's tears? Kierkegaard says that Agamemnon must shirk no argument "from outside." His justification must be tried in face of the strongest objections, the objections of those directly affected. Kierkegaard offers little suggestion as to how the objections are to be judged, and he gives no thought to the utter unresponsiveness of anything Agamemnon might say. His interpretation proceeds on the assumption that the sacrifice would have been justifiable, Agamemnon's action heroic.

But in arguing that Agamemnon's readiness to hear Iphigenia's objections is a measure of his tragic heroism, Kierkegaard gives special standing to the objections of people adversely affected by an action.

This feature of moral deliberation must be familiar to everyone. If a private physician learns that a bisexual patient is unwilling to inform his wife that he is infected with the HIV virus, the physician owes the wife an explanation of his own failure to warn her if she becomes infected. She may be ready to accept the physician's explanation, but that seems unlikely if he simply stands on the rule that confidentiality must be maintained at all costs. In these situations, a responsible person does not simply ask the abstract question what is the ethical thing to do, or the rational thing to do. He asks how he can explain himself to those affected by his actions. He recognizes his responsibility to those affected in one way or another by what he does or fails to do, and deliberates in the light of that. It is, of course, true that the responsibility goes in many ways. The physician must be ready to explain himself to the husband as well as the wife. If he departs from accepted rules of confidentiality he may be called on to explain his departure to fellow professionals. But the resulting complexity of his responsibility is no more than a condition of the moral problem the physician faces.

If responsibility can go in many ways, the task of justifying a course of action takes on a somewhat different appearance. The context in which justification is sought will determine the task of justification in a manner reminiscent of the way in which the context in which a scientific explanation is offered determines its task. What needs to be justified in a course of action will vary with the specific objections likely to be brought, just as the specific features of a natural phenomenon that call for explanation will vary with the specific perplexities at hand. Suppose that the physician does stand on the rule that a physician must respect the confidentiality of any information about a patient he acquires in the course of his normal duties. His responsibility to the wife to justify his failure to warn her that she is in jeopardy will not allow him to simply cite the rule, or affirm its importance. If he responds conscientiously he will address her objection, explaining, for example, the importance of abiding by the rule even in the face of a case with the difficulty of hers. The likely pattern of argument may seem little different from the familiar treatment of hard cases. But if the task of justification is framed by the physician's responsibility to explain himself to the affected person, and set by her objections, it takes on a different character. The justification must be thought of as offered to the affected person. If it is successful, it must be reasonable to expect her to accept it and unreasonable of her to reject it.

In a fairly cohesive society, such conditions might be satisfied. It is altogether possible that a person objecting to her treatment might find sufficient satisfaction in the justification she was offered that she would withdraw her objections. Or it might be beyond question that it was unreasonable of her to reject the justification. But it is important not to make too much of that. In saying that consideration of the objections of those adversely affected is a constraint on moral practices, I do not mean to suggest that it promises a determinate resolution. That would be at odds with the degree of uncertainty conscientious and responsible persons often experience in the face of difficult moral questions.

The question of whether it would be reasonable to expect an adversely affected person to accept a proffered justification, and unreasonable of her to reject it, is at best a question of judgment. What force the constraint has does not lie in a promise to settle issues that appear beyond settling, but rather in its setting a task for justification that will in many instances broaden the range of consideration and sharpen its focus. What it stands against is a tendency to rely on standing principles or practices in place to the exclusion of a consideration of objections that might be brought by or for people likely to be affected by a course of action.

In response to actual or anticipated objections, there is an important role for the formulation of principles. Should the physician break his rule of confidentiality, he might reasonably be asked by his patient or his fellow physicians in just what cases he believes he could justifiably do that. He might be asked, that is to say, for the principle of the decision. Such principles are commonly specific to a case, and in that way ad hoc, but they serve to articulate operative judgments of critical considerations, and focus lines of criticism. Saying that a rule of confidentiality can be broken when a third party would be placed in serious jeopardy by standing on confidentiality focuses critical consideration on the degree of likely harm as the salient feature, and in that way invites mention of comparable but slightly different cases. The fact that in a case of the sort mentioned confidentiality would have been exploited by the person protected by the common rule is a salient feature which might equally well have been cited in the principle articulating the judgment in question. Its likely introduction serves as a reminder of the dialectic typical of the critical consideration required by responsible judgment in a difficult situation. It is tempting to think that generalization is a necessary condition of justifiable judgment in such cases, but the complexity of even the simplest cases stands against that thought. The difficulty of fully specifying relevant contextual conditions restricts generalization to an important but limited role in moral justification.

Generalization of a judgment or decision taken in the face of the objections of those affected by a course of conduct may articulate a common understanding exhibited in normal responses to comparable cases. Extraordinary cases are more to the point. Where recognition of the force of an objection is groundbreaking, the principle articulating the response may become a matter of moral commitment and commitment to the principle may become testimony to the force of the objection. Such testimony plays a crucial role in moral change, but, as in more ordinary cases, the principles themselves have no independent justifying authority. It is only to the extent to which they are responsive to the objections of the people affected by a course of conduct or a practice that they must be given weight.

The constraint on moral justification I have described bears some resemblance to the contractarian idea that justifiable moral and political principles are those that would be accepted by suitably described members of a society. It thus shares with contractualist views what Rawls called recognition of the distinction of persons. It differs in its application to specific actions and practices, and in its crucial reference to the people actually affected by an action or a practice. It also differs in that it is no more than a constraint on the justification of those actions and practices. Whether the constraint applies in a particular case will obviously depend on the circumstances and the type of moral considerations in question. There are questions of personal virtue that have no apparent bearing on the lives of others, for example. I have stressed its application in cases of distinct spheres of responsibility, but it does have application to some hard decisions arising out of the acceptance of a single principle or practice. Where I have agreed to support you in your campaign, your readiness to release me from that promise relieves me of that burden in a way that another friend's advice to forget the promise does not.

Where the constraint I have described is recognized, it is sometimes said that it must rest upon some more fundamental idea—recognition of the autonomy of persons, for example, or recognition of their intrinsic worth.[11] Tempting as they might seem, neither of these ideas provides an explanation of why we should feel it important to listen to a person's objections in one sort of situation but not another. Misplaced claims of authority are reasonably and understandably challenged with reminders of autonomy, but we have little sense of how in general we should treat a person who is autonomous. Similarly, it may be important in the face of practices in which humans are treated like chattel property to give testimony that humans have intrinsic worth. But it is difficult to know how that testimony could stand in the way of a harsh refusal to acknowledge the objections of people placed at risk or disenfranchised by a policy or course of action. Where responsibility to those affected by an action is recognized and their objections heard, it is probably more accurate to say simply that that is a fundamental feature of moral practice, and that it lives by the testimony of faithful practice. There are times when testimony is more to the point than argument.

Features of Moral Practices Said to Exhibit Common Recognition of the Possibility of Moral Dilemma

The possibility of moral dilemmas is said to be recognized both in the recognition of moral failure exhibited in feelings of remorse, and in recognition of some obligation to make amends in one way or another. Those observations tend to be borne out by the treatment of dilemmas arising in the context of common responsibilities. Williams and others have argued[12] that the regret sometimes exhibited by a person for his failure to take the rejected one of a pair of conflicting judgments of what he ought to do where he has no doubt that he has taken the right course exhibits his continuing acceptance of the judgment rejected. Criticisms of the argument have tended to focus on the ambiguity of an undifferentiated feeling of regret or guilt. Although accepting the appropriateness of a kind of regret or even remorse in situations of the sort Williams had in mind, critics have argued that those feelings can be given an interpretation consistent with denial of the possibility of genuine moral dilemmas. What appears to be regret or remorse over failure to take the rejected course, it is said, may be simply regret over the effects of an unavoidable failure to take the other course. If responsibility in a dilemmatic situation is directed in the way I have suggested, any regret exhibited may arise out of a sense of failing the person not served. Suppose the physician described earlier decides to accept the request that she attend to the group of special patients. Having decided not to give full attention to her child, any regret she may exhibit will almost certainly focus on her failure to stay with her child, evidencing her sense that although she may have done the right thing, she may also have failed her child. Her regret might focus, that is to say, on her failure to serve the child and not simply on the effects of that failure. That would be some evidence that, by her lights, the moral difficulty she faced was a genuine dilemma.

It must be said that arguments of this sort are bound to be inconclusive. Williams's initial argument appealed to a reader's judgment that regret over the course not taken would be appropriate. Without that judgment, even explicit signs of remorse can be reasonably interpreted as misdirected. The indeterminacy of common responsibilities is a further complicating matter, introducing some uncertainty over concluding decisions to fulfill one responsibility at the cost of not fulfilling the other. Signs of regret in such a situation may be as much a matter of uneasiness over the choice made as over the course of action not taken.

Williams and others have also argued that the recognition of an obligation to apologize or to make amends for a course not taken sometimes exhibited by a person who has taken the best course in an apparently dilemmatic situation shows his sense that the rejected judgment of obligation still stands. That interpretation makes more sense if moral responsibility and moral failure are understood as directed in the way I have suggested. If a person's responsibility for moral failure is to those he has failed and not to the world at large, it is much more reasonable to take his apologies and efforts to make amends to the person affected as a sign of his sense that he has failed that person morally. The obligation to apologize or make amends is not merely an incidental obligation; it is a recognition of the responsibility he bears to the person affected.

Prominent Moral Dilemmas

Both the indeterminacy of commonly assumed responsibilities and the diversity of lines of responsibility tend to cast a somewhat different light on prominent examples of moral dilemmas. Commonly assumed responsibilities figure in most of those cases. Agamemnon's dilemma is created by his responsibilities as a head of state and a father; Captain Vere's by his responsibilities to the Royal Navy and the men who serve under him; the dilemma of the young man Sartre describes by his responsibilities as a son and a Frenchman. Sartre treats the dilemma he offers as a test case of various moral principles, and, indeed, for the viability of appealing to moral principles to resolve such dilemmas. But neither the responsibility of a son to his mother nor the responsibility of a patriotic national to his country and countrymen are well conceived as matters of determining principles. In the situation offered by Sartre, the choice is made difficult not by a clash of principles but by responsibilities that appear to require incompatible lines of conduct.

In the case as Sartre describes it, specific responsibilities are paramount. If a young man's mother is old and ailing and cannot fend for herself, he may believe it his responsibility to arrange for her care in one way or another; and if his country has been overrun and his brother killed by an occupying force, he may believe it his responsibility to join countrymen in resistance. It is obvious that the plausibility of the choice presented depends on the details of the case: in normal circumstances, the call to join a cause is commonly less urgent, and there may be many ways to arrange for the care and support of an aging parent. In conditions of occupation, joining a resistance force may be sufficient to jeopardize a relative; in more benign circumstances that may not be true. What each of the responsibilities requires will accordingly be a matter of judgment. Conscientious people with no general reservations about either of the responsibilities may well differ in their sense of what each of the responsibilities requires.

The diversity of lines of responsibility adds another dimension to complicate the choice. Whatever course of action he takes, it seems likely that the person Sartre describes would find it necessary to explain himself to his mother or those who speak for her,[13] and to people in the resistance who speak for his country and his people. The responsibilities that create the difficulty are associated with distinct persons, and the choice requires of him that he give one of those responsibilities priority. There is no dearth of ways of assessing the priorities. But where none of them has a standing reasonable for the affected persons to accept, the choice is best conceived as a choice to give one of the responsibilities priority. In that case, the choice is a choice among conditional requirements. In light of his responsibilities to his mother, Sartre's young man must not join the resistance forces. But in light of his responsibilities to his country and his people, he must join the resistance. However he chooses, he will fulfill one set of responsibilities to the exclusion of the other. I believe that this way of thinking of the choice explains why the choice can seem impossible. Where the governing responsibilities are independent of one another and not contingent on some more fundamental responsibility, there is no way of honoring the rejected responsibility while choosing to fulfill the other.

Happily, not every choice posed by distinct responsibilities is so harsh. In a great many cases of conflict, it is reasonable to expect accommodation of one sort or another. A conscientious judgment of what a responsibility requires will be made in the light of countervailing considerations, and with the expectation that the parties involved will understand. Where there are competing responsibilities, a conscientious person may make a judgment of what he must do in the light of some primary responsibility, but he will almost certainly attempt to adjust that judgment in light of any competing responsibilities and hope for understanding on the part of the people affected. A physician called to special duty in an emergency will ask how critical it is that she accept the duty, and whether her patients and co-workers would understand if she begged off to attend to the needs of her child. In some circumstances, it might be reasonable to expect accommodation; in more desperate circumstances, perhaps not. I would guess that in the terrible circumstances created by the ethnic conflicts in the Balkans, for example, there must have been a great many hard moral decisions much more harsh than that described by Sartre.

The Form Taken by Dilemmas Arising out of Common Responsibilities

Dilemmas that arise out of a conflict of responsibilities pose some difficulties for accounts of moral conflict prominent in the philosophical literature. Where a moral dilemma is said to be occasioned by a conflict of principles, it is natural to think of the resulting dilemma as framed by judgments of what the respective principles require in the situation, and as resolved, if at all, in a concluding judgment taking into account the competing considerations. Faced with a situation in which an honest response to a friend's question would be extremely painful to him, I must decide whether to respond honestly or in some more gentle and sympathetic way. In the language W. D. Ross used to describe such conflicts, I have a prima facie duty to respond honestly and a prima facie duty to respond beneficently, and I must determine my actual duty in the situation; the morally right thing to do.

This schema is ill suited to dilemmas arising out of conflicts of responsibilities. The judgments framing such a dilemma are not judgments of the general requirements of moral duties such as fidelity or beneficence, but relatively specific judgments of what a responsibility requires in a particular situation, taking into account relevant peculiarities of the situation. In the absence of conflict such judgments of what ought to be done serve in much the same way as Ross's judgments of actual duty, specifying what ought ultimately to be done in the situation. Unlike Ross's judgments, they are conditional, specifying what ought to be done in light of the responsibility in question. In the absence of conflict, mention of that condition does no particular work. In a situation of conflict, in contrast, acknowledgment of the competing responsibilities is necessary if the choice presented is to be understood. In a conflict between friendship and professional responsibility, the conclusion that one ought to take a certain course of action but cannot do that is left opaque if the conditions of the respective judgments are not specified.

So long as their conditional provenance is understood, the judgments that frame a dilemma arising out of conflicting responsibilities stand as what are sometimes regarded as all-things-considered judgments. Each represents a person's best judgment of what ought to be done in light of its respective responsibility, taking into account relevant considerations. What partiality it may exhibit derives from the opposition of the governing responsibilities. It stands, moreover, in the same relationship to the action that is to be done as does the concluding judgment in a situation without conflict: it specifies what ought to be done in a way leaving no room for further evaluative judgment.

I want to stress this last point. It is tempting to think that in any case of conflict there must be a place for a concluding evaluative judgment, taking all things into account. But where each of the framing judgments already represents a person's best judgment of what ought to be done in light of the responsibilities in question, there is no further consideration to take into account. Where deliberation has been exhausted, a person facing a conflict of considered responsibilities must simply decide which to honor.

This way of regarding a person's best judgment of what he must do in a situation of conflict may seem to rob the conflict of its pain. Treating the judg-

ments of what must be done in a situation of conflict of responsibilities as
conditional in the way I have suggested may seem to disallow their incompatibility. If the practical judgments framing a dilemma are to make conflicting
demands, it may be objected, they must be offered unconditionally, by saying
flatly, for example, that a given course of action both ought and ought not to be
taken. The objection is misconceived. It is as possible that a pair of responsibilities may make conflicting demands as it is that a pair of parents may do
that, and in deciding in either case what to do, a person will be at the same time
deciding which to honor, which responsibility or which parent. It is true that the
conflict occurs because not both of the demands can be fulfilled, but they may all
the same be understood as offered conditionally in the way I have suggested.
Their practical incompatibility is not inconsistent with their conditional provenance.

There are dramatic cases in which the diversity of lines of accountability is
primarily responsible for the difficulty of a dilemma. A minister of state whose
task it is to secure the safety of hostages taken by terrorists faces an uncommonly difficult dilemma. If he refuses to enter into negotiation for their release,
he may endanger their lives, but if he shows a willingness to negotiate he may
encourage the taking of other hostages for whose safety he would be equally
responsible. Whatever he does, he is likely to be held to account by those people
placed at risk by his actions. If he negotiates the release of the hostages and
other innocent people are taken hostage, he may be held to account by those
who speak for the newly taken hostages; if he refuses and the hostages are held
indefinitely or even killed, he will almost certainly be held to account by those
who speak for the original hostages.[14] In the situation it would, I think, be
otiose[15] to ask what course it would be right for the minister to take, which
course is his moral duty. At best, he could seek a more benign alternative to
negotiation, or some reliable reason for thinking that negotiation would not
have the consequences commonly feared. If there is no more benign alternative, he must simply choose, knowing that, whichever course he takes, he may be
held to account by those placed at risk by his action.

Conditions of the Possibility of Moral Dilemmas

It is not surprising that moral dilemmas should arise in circumstances in which
more or less independent and autonomous responsibilities overlap. Considering the variety of purposes served by the various practices and social institutions
in which responsibilities take shape, and the variety of historical forces under
which that happens, it would be surprising if moral conflicts of varying degrees
of intensity did not result. I would speculate that among factors tending to
ameliorate moral conflict, moral conflict itself would be prominent: endemic
conflict stands in the way of the normal functioning of most social institutions.
But because common responsibilities of the sort I have been discussing tend to
be historically local, their susceptibility to ameliorating transformation is bound
to vary widely. That is amply illustrated in the cultural variation in susceptibility
to change often observed in local conceptions of intrafamilial responsibilities.

There is a natural objection to the main drift of this line of thought. I have been arguing that moral dilemmas arise at the intersection of overlapping spheres of responsibility and that the independence and autonomy of those spheres of responsibility make it likely that they will arise there. I have mentioned commonly cited examples of moral dilemmas as instances of moral conflicts that do arise in this way, and I have noted the tendency of the indeterminacy of common responsibilities and the particularity of their accountability as factors contributing to the difficulty of those dilemmas. It would be natural to object that while moral questions may upon occasion arise over the responsibilities I have described as common responsibilities, they are not, as such, *moral* responsibilities. They are no more than conventional expectations, customarily established, and expected of people in virtue of their participation in the practices in place in a given society. The fact that dilemmas may occur when those expectations conflict is no better indication of the sources of moral dilemmas than the fact that a participant may occasionally be perplexed about what common practices or customs demand of them.

The objection is misconceived, but in a way that casts light on philosophical perplexities over the possibility of moral dilemmas. That the objection is misconceived is indicated by the fact that the examples of moral dilemmas discussed above are commonly acknowledged as examples of moral dilemmas. All of them involve conflicts among common responsibilities of the sort I have considered. In the same spirit, it must be said that the subject matter of most of the examples is the substance of many philosophical treatises on morality: familial responsibilities, responsibilities to those who are ill or suffering, the responsibilities of office, and other public responsibilities. Although the common notion of morality is perplexing in many ways, common usage does not stand with the objection.

All the same, the objection is tempting. The prominence of practices in place in determining common responsibilities calls for some more fundamental explanation of their difference from the requirements of custom or fashion. How does the analogy go wrong? Philosophical practice leads one to look to a general specification at this point, but I doubt that there are any candidates that could go beyond our sense of a difference in cases as offered. But there are differences already mentioned or implied. The most critical is that matters of custom tend to be settled with authoritative mention of what is done and where. That is not true in the cases of the common responsibilities I have been discussing. The physician's responsibilities to her patients and her children are not simply a matter of what is in fact expected of a physician or a parent in such a case. How her responsibilities are commonly understood does figure, but so too do the particular needs of her children and her patients. That the care of children falls in large part to a parent is a matter of existing practices. If it were commonly accepted that an extended family or the immediate community had an equal share in the care of children, or, for that matter, if the care of the seriously ill did not sometimes depend on the willingness of professionals to make sacrifices, the physician's choice might be less difficult. But although arrangements in place do figure, so too do the needs of the people to be served, and the physician's concern to serve them. A conscientious parent would not simply ask whether she was expected to stay with her children. She would ask how they would fare if she did not, and as a physician she would doubtless ask a similar question about the patients. Because of that sort of concern, the situation might pose a dilemma for her even if it were commonly understood that the extended family had an equal share in the care of the children. Although her care would not normally have been expected in such a situation, she might, in light of their present need, have reason to think her care sufficiently important to create a dilemma.

There is another distinctively moral dimension sometimes present in dilemmas of the sort I have been considering. The dilemma might be made difficult for the physician by the fact that professionals in her generation were in her view all too ready to give professional responsibilities priority over family responsibilities. In that circumstance, her decision to attend to the patients might be all the more difficult because it could be seen as further testimony to a priority she questioned. To alter the case, let us suppose that there is some social stigma attached to the patients. She might in that case think it particularly important to go to their aid, despite the cost to her children. Her doing that would be testimony to the importance of going to the aid of persons in need in circumstances in which that was stigmatized. She would be giving aid, but at the same time exhibiting the importance of doing that against the conventional views of her peers. Honoring in her judgment and action the responsibility to give them aid would in that way have a kind of expressive force.

I want to stress this point. The indeterminacy of common responsibilities is bound to leave a place for some variation in judgments of responsibility, and accordingly for dissenting judgments. Where a responsibility is deeply felt but not commonly acknowledged, it is to be expected that exhibiting the importance of accepting the responsibility will itself often provide further reason for taking a dissenting stand. That is particularly true in cases in which there are conflicting responsibilities, and commonly accepted judgments of the priorities to be given them. Where I dissent from your judgment of the relative importance of a particular set of accepted responsibilities, the testimony of committed practice is often the only form of argument open to me.

It is not a part of my argument that conflicting common responsibilities must necessarily issue in dilemma. I have in fact emphasized the occasional mediating role of mutual accommodation among affected parties. What I have wanted to argue is that it is reasonable to expect that there will be circumstances in which conflicting common responsibilities will issue in difficult and sometimes impossible dilemmas. But where accommodation of one sort or another is desirable, intractable circumstances can also figure prominently. American difficulties in responding to the war in Bosnia clearly exhibit the sometimes painful role of circumstances in causing moral dilemma.

As the war in Bosnia developed, many people came to believe that the United States had a moral responsibility to take action with some promise of ending the wanton destruction and widespread human suffering caused by the Bosnian Serbs in the prosecution of often overtly genocidal policies. Where that responsibility has been alleged, it has been commonly supported by citations of the power and international standing of the United States, the desperate need for independent intervention made evident by the Serbs' blatant defiance of international efforts toward amelioration, and the importance of effectively exhibiting condemnation of cruel and inhumane policies. Doubts have tended to take the form of a dilemma: they acknowledge a responsibility to take some action, and they focus on the human cost of any course of action with some prospect of being effective and on the responsibilities for those human costs incurred with a possibly effective course of action.

There is no mystery about the difficulty this dilemma has caused for the last two American governments. The prospects for effective military intervention in a situation with a tangled history and a difficult terrain would be uncertain at best, and have been made more uncertain by a lack of European support. In that circumstance some alternative to military action would have been desirable. But historical analogies like that with Munich amply exhibit the costs of a continuing readiness to negotiate without a clear threat of the use of force, and forcing negotiation on the aggrieved parties tends to compromise condemnation of cruel and inhumane policies.

The moral this situation poses for the American government is quite different from most of the dilemmas I have discussed. It is not framed by conflicting responsibilities or obligations, but rather by a single, dominant responsibility whose implementation is morally uncertain. Any policy of military implementation would carry with it a certain responsibility to the affected people of the countries involved, and to those American and allied participants who carried out the policies. Because of the terrain and the patchwork distribution of people on all sides of the dispute, any attempt to restrict the use of force to air power would almost certainly entail extensive civilian casualties. Other modes of implementation would carry comparably difficult responsibilities. As the war proceeded, members of the U.N. peace-keeping mission became virtual hostages of the Bosnian forces, making their security itself a concern. Recounting these and other stubborn facts clearly exhibits the role of intractable circumstances in forcing the dilemmas confronting American policy.

Dilemmas in which intractable circumstances play such a prominent role support Ruth Marcus's contention that recognition of the possibility of moral dilemmas can have a kind of dynamic force, reminding us that there is sometimes compelling reason to seek the transformation of the conditions that give rise to impossible moral conflicts. It is the underpinning for a principle to the effect that we ought to conduct our lives and arrange our institutions so as to minimize predicaments that make it impossible to fulfill acknowledged responsibilities.[16] At a personal level, a prudent care to avoid incurring obligations that cannot be fulfilled is a fundamental feature of social life, and at broader social and institutional levels there are analogous concerns. There are a great many social programs that serve, among other things, to make it possible for people to fulfill potentially conflicting responsibilities without having to make impossible choices among them. Although that does not show an aversion to conflict itself, as Marcus's language suggests, it does show a recognition of the tendency of social circumstances to force the conflicts dilemmas exhibit. That stands against the thought that genuine dilemmas are a sign of moral misconception, and call for conceptual reconstruction.

Moral Dilemmas and the Deliberative Conception of Moral Theory

At the outset of this paper I mentioned prominent discussions of the possibility of genuine moral dilemmas. I want, in conclusion, to return to that question. In my discussion of dilemmas arising out of common responsibilities, I have offered some reasons for expecting that those responsibilities would on occasion impose conflicting demands issuing in moral dilemmas, and I would expect that conflicts among moral virtues and ideals would similarly lead to dilemma. In many of those instances there may be, on reflection, no reason to take the avowed moral difficulties seriously. The operative considerations may be morally questionable national loyalties, for example, or doubtful ideals of honor. What I find puzzling is a *general* doubt of the possibility of moral dilemma. Considering all the variety of things offered or withheld under the cloak of morality, and the equally various parts of life affected, how could it be that difficult conflicts should not arise? Or, to mention the other partner in moral dilemma, how could it be that circumstances forcing difficult conflicts should not sometimes arise? I want to consider briefly two routes to the general doubt, the first turning on a certain conception of morality, the second on a certain conception of an adequate moral theory. I believe that both lines of thought figure prominently in philosophical resistance to the possibility of dilemma.[17]

Faced with a difficult problem of choice, it is natural to seek some basis for choice. "What is the right thing to do?" one may ask, or "What am I morally obliged to do?" Where that question is allowed in the face of a pair of carefully deliberated alternatives, it is assumed that there must be a rule of priority or some other comparable basis for determining the morally appropriate course of action in the circumstance. But in thinking about the wide range of cases in question it is difficult to know what such a rule of priority could introduce.[18] Where a moral dilemma involves conflicting standards of decent and humane behavior, for example, it is natural to ask which should take precedence. In most such cases, the terms used to raise the question of which course to take introduce no further considerations and have no specific content. It is significant that those questions of precedence are often answered with emphatic assertion that takes the place of further argumentation: "You have to be fair!" or "You may feel sorry for her, but you ought to give her an honest answer!" The not uncommon inarticulateness exhibited in such answers is a good indication that reasoning has run out.

Consider, for example, the various attitudes taken toward shoddy work within an academic community. It is easy to imagine both fiercely honest responses and extremely kind responses, and fairly easy to imagine how people taking each of those attitudes would explain their taking the attitudes they did. It would be reasonable to expect, moreover, that a person trying to decide how to respond to the work, what to say, and how much and how little to say would give some thought to each of those quite different attitudes toward the work.[19] But the issue is not likely to be advanced by appeal to general moral considerations. The respective merits of candor and kindness and their failings are well understood, as, normally, are the particular responsibilities of candor in an academic setting. Where a person has some doubt as to whether to offer an honest opinion or a gentler one, that may be the most perspicuous description of her choice available. As in the case of a person facing a decision among competing responsibilities, she may simply have to choose which of the competing virtues to allow to rule her response.

Resistance to the notion that there may be no more telling way to discriminate among alternatives in cases of this sort is likely to come from those who suppose that the concept of morality carries with it its own criteria of morally justified conduct. I doubt that. Considering the wide range of things commonly said to be morally significant in one way or another, it is extremely unlikely that there could be a form of justification sanctioned by morality itself. It is no accident that philosophers undertaking to specify the content of morality tend to say fairly innocuous things that could by no stretch of the imagination be supposed to apply to all the variety of questions, concerns, and considerations commonly said to be moral matters. Saying of an issue that it is a moral issue may distinguish it from a legal or a political issue, but it carries with it no normative content. At most, it places an issue in a broad and diverse group of issues, sharing no single distinguishing characteristics but each distinguished in a variety of ways from political, legal, and aesthetic issues.

The second route to a general doubt of the possibility of moral dilemma is more programmatic. Common morality is viewed as a broad set of intertwined practices burdened with accretions from the past, parts of it enlightened and other parts in need of critical reconstruction. The resulting task for moral theory is a systematic reconstruction of the principled basis of moral judgment and deliberation, crafted to serve moral deliberation. Allowing that there may be a variety of moral considerations that bear upon deliberation in one way or another, it proposes to provide an ordering of relevant considerations or some general criterion or set of criteria sufficient to determine the right course of action in a difficult situation.

I doubt that common acceptance of particular moral conflicts as difficult or even impossible must stand in the way of the project when it is conceived in this way. Where the competing considerations can be simply regarded as recalcitrant intuitions, it may be no more than reasonable to dismiss them. There is often less reason to honor intuitions in moral philosophy than elsewhere in the subject. They may be simply the residue of a moral training that has long since lost any genuine moral force. But where they are considered judgments of what a responsibility requires in a situation, they suggest a more formidable constraint on moral theories that aspire to serve deliberation. Moral theory crafted to serve practice bears the same responsibilities as the practice it would serve. Dilemmas that arise out of common but disparate responsibilities stand as a reminder that hard and even impossible moral choices are not necessarily an anomaly, but sometimes to be expected. Where that is true, philosophical reconstruction may be a diversion. What is called for may be simply conscientious and responsible judgment.

Notes

I am grateful to Peter Koller, Thomas Hill, Jr., Martin Gunderson, Henry West, Norman Dahl, and Joan Mason for comments on earlier versions of this paper.

1. Williams (1965).

2. See the contributions by Brink, Dahl, McConnell, and Sinnott-Armstrong, all in this volume, for detailed discussions of the form a genuine moral dilemma can be supposed to take.

3. Dahl (this volume), pp. 92–3.

4. It is assumed in many discussions of moral obligations that where necessities are introduced in the conclusion of a line of moral deliberation, they must be entailed by general principles specified in terms of the necessity in question. There are cases in which that is borne out. But, in a great many cases, the necessities are introduced in a conclusion in which no such principle is in play. Speaking of such cases, Blackburn says that to identify a requirement is to give a verdict. Blackburn (this volume), pp. 134–7. Williams speaks of the assumption that obligations introduced in the conclusion of a line of deliberation must be entailed by general principles specifying the obligation as the *obligation-out, obligation-in* principle. Cf. Williams (1985), p. 181.

5. The qualification "when carefully argued" is critical to this point. It is sadly true that there are a great many people who respond to some of the concrete moral problems they face without a sense of their difficulty. Their deliberations may well lack the complexity I stress at this point. That fact underlines the range of difference any comprehensive account of moral deliberation must acknowledge in one way or another. I return to this point later in the paper.

6. Another example taken from an earlier paper illustrates the complexity I have in mind in this paragraph: Even the simplest of moral questions will share this complexity to some degree. Suppose you wonder whether you can ask a friend or neighbor to care for your dog while you are away on vacation. You have no right to expect him to do it, you may be told. You know that, but you wondered whether it would be an imposition to ask him to do it as a favor. Told that it would, you wonder why it would be an imposition to ask him to take the dog, but not an imposition to ask him to feed the cat or water the plants. That is a matter of relative inconvenience and likely bother, you may be told. Granting that, you may wonder whether the friend might not welcome the opportunity to be of some help and even feel somewhat offended if he knew that, in the belief that it would be an imposition, you had refrained from asking him to care for the dog. If you were in serious difficulty he would surely be offended if you didn't turn to him for help. True enough, it may be said, but this is only a matter of your own convenience and surely not a matter of serious difficulty. The ensuing judgment that you couldn't ask him to take the dog is one that might be questioned, but not without some recognition of the force of all these diverse considerations. Even in a case so little fraught with telling consequences, the relevant considerations are both diverse and diversely related to the question at stake. Mason (1988), p. 420.

7. Donagan did not believe that genuine moral dilemmas are possible, but he supposed that any candidate must meet this condition. Donagan (1984).

8. Foot (1983), p. 380.

9. To be faithful to the text, I must point out that the treatment of the stories of Abraham and Agamemnon offered in *Fear and Trembling* should be attributed to Kierkegaard's pseudonymous author, Johannes de Silentio. The discussion is sup-

posed to exhibit a distinctive point of view and not a general account of the peculiarity of an ethical view of life. Kierkegaard (1983).

10. In framing the choice Agamemnon faces in terms of the ends of state, Kierkegaard naturalizes the situation as conceived by Agamemnon, and treats the role of the gods as no more than natural forces. As a result, the gods play no essential role in the priority given to the ends of state over Agamemnon's familial responsibilities.

11. I am grateful to Christopher Gowans for his criticisms of the doubts expressed in this section. Cf. Gowans (this volume), pp. 208–11.

12. Williams, (1965).

13. For quite a different view of the young man's obligations to his mother, see Railton (this volume), p. 150.

14. These distinct lines of accountability were dramatized in testimony offered in the course of the recent campaign of Oliver North for a seat in the U.S. Senate. The hostage released as a result of his covert negotiations testified that apart from North's efforts he would not have been freed. Another hostage held in Beirut, Terry Anderson, campaigned for North's opponent, and argued that North's actions had contributed to his own continued captivity and jeopardized other hostages and potential hostages as well.

15. This may be a bit harsh. Asking of a politician if he is doing the right thing is sometimes a useful way of reminding him that moral considerations are involved. It need not show the assumption of some overarching rule of priorities.

16. Marcus (1980).

17. There are other prominent philosophical reasons for the doubt mentioned in the text, some discussed at length in this volume.

18. It is sometimes a way of asking for reconsideration. But it tends as often to be a wishful way of avoiding a hard decision. Cf. Blackburn (this volume).

19. Cf. Mason (1988) for a more extensive discussion of this sort of case.

References

Anderson, Elizabeth. 1993. *Value in Ethics and Economics*. Cambridge: Harvard University Press.

Aquinas, St. Thomas. *De Veritate. Quaestiones Disputatae de Veritate*. In vol. 9 of *Sancti Thomae Aquinatis Opera Omnia*. Parma: P. Fiaccadori, 1859. Reprint, New York: Musurgia Publishers, 1949.

———. *Summa Theologiae. Summa Theologica*. In vols. 1–4 of *Sancti Thomae Aquinatis Opera Omnia*. Parma: P. Fiaccadori, 1852–54. Reprint, New York: Musurgia Publishers, 1948.

Baier, Kurt. 1958. *The Moral Point of View: A Rational Basis of Ethics*. Ithaca, N.Y.: Cornell University Press.

Benditt, Theodore. 1982. *Rights*. Totowa, N.J.: Rowman and Littlefield.

Berlin, Isaiah. 1978. *Concepts and Categories: Philosophical Essays*. New York: Viking Press.

Blackburn, Simon. 1984. *Spreading the Word*. Oxford: Clarendon Press.

Blustein, Jeffrey. 1991. *Care and Commitment: Taking the Personal Point of View*. New York: Oxford University Press.

Boyd, Richard. 1988. "How to Be a Moral Realist." In *Essays in Moral Realism*, ed. Geoffry Sayre-McCord. Ithaca, N.Y.: Cornell University Press.

Brink, David. 1994. "Moral Conflict and Its Structure." *Philosophical Review* 103:215–47.

Chellas, Brian. 1980. *Modal Logic*. Cambridge: Cambridge University Press.

Chisholm, Roderick M. 1963. "Contrary-to-Duty Imperatives and Deontic Logic." *Analysis* 24:33–36.

Clarke, Stanley G. 1987. "Anti-Theory in Ethics." *American Philosophical Quarterly* 24:237–44.

Conee, Earl. 1982. "Against Moral Dilemmas." *Philosophical Review* 91:87–97.

———. 1989. "Why Moral Dilemmas Are Impossible." *American Philosophical Quarterly* 26:133–41.

Dahl, Norman O. 1986. "Obligation and Moral Worth: Reflections on Prichard and Kant." *Philosophical Studies* 50:369–99.

Davidson, Donald. 1970. "How Is Weakness of Will Possible?" In *Moral Concepts*, ed. Joel Feinberg. Oxford: Oxford University Press.

Decew, Judith Wagner. 1988. "Moral Rights: Conflicts and Valid Claims." *Philosophical Studies* 54:63–86.

Donagan, Alan. 1977a. "Sidgwick and Whewellian Intuitionism: Some Enigmas." *Canadian Journal of Philosophy* 7:447–65.

———. 1977b. *The Theory of Morality*. Chicago: University of Chicago Press.

———. 1980. "A New Sidgwick." *Ethics* 90:282–95.

———. 1984. "Consistency in Rationalist Moral Systems." *The Journal of Philosophy* 81:291–309. Reprinted in Gowans (1987).

———. 1985. "The Structure of Kant's Metaphysics of Morals." *Topoi* 4:61–72.

———. 1993. "Moral Dilemmas, Genuine and Spurious: A Comparative Anatomy." *Ethics* 104:7–21.

Daube, David. 1965. *Collaboration with Tyranny in Rabbinic Law.* London: Oxford University Press.

Dworkin, Ronald. 1978. *Taking Rights Seriously.* Cambridge: Harvard University Press.

Feinberg, Joel. 1978. "Voluntary Euthanasia and the Inalienable Right to Life." *Philosophy and Public Affairs* 7:93–123.

———. 1980. *Rights, Justice, and the Bounds of Liberty.* Princeton: Princeton University Press.

Feldman, Fred. 1986. *Doing the Best We Can: An Essay in Informal Deontic Logic.* Dordrecht: D. Reidel Publishing Co.

Foot, Philippa. 1983. "Moral Realism and Moral Dilemma." *Journal of Philosophy* 80:379–98. Reprinted in Gowans (1987).

———. 1994. "Moral Dilemmas Revisited." In *Modality, Morality, and Belief,* eds. Diana Raffman, Nicholas Asher, and Walter Sinnott-Armstrong. New York: Cambridge University Press.

Forster, E. M. 1939. *Two Cheers for Democracy.* London: Edward Arnold.

Fried, Charles. 1978. *Right and Wrong.* Cambridge: Harvard University Press.

Gibbard, Allan. 1990. *Wise Choices, Apt Feelings.* Cambridge: Harvard University Press.

Goldman, Holly S. 1976. "Dated Rightness and Moral Imperfection." *The Philosophical Review* 85:449–87.

Gowans, Christopher W., ed. 1987. *Moral Dilemmas.* New York: Oxford University Press.

———. 1994. *Innocence Lost: An Examination of Inescapable Moral Wrongdoing.* New York: Oxford University Press.

———. Forthcoming. "Intimacy, Freedom, and Unique Value: A 'Kantian' Account of the Irreplaceable and Incomparable Value of Persons." *American Philosophical Quarterly.*

Greenspan, Patricia. 1980. "A Case of Mixed Feelings: Ambivalence and the Logic of Emotion." In *Explaining Emotions,* ed. Amelie Rorty. Berkeley: University of California Press.

———. 1983. "Moral Dilemmas and Guilt." *Philosophical Studies* 43: 117–25.

———. 1988. *Emotions and Reasons.* New York: Routledge.

———. 1992. "Subjective Guilt and Responsibility." *Mind* 101:287–302.

Hare, R. M. 1952. *The Language of Morals.* Oxford: Oxford University Press.

———. 1981. *Moral Thinking: Its Levels, Method, and Point.* Oxford: Clarendon Press.

Hart, H. L. A. 1958. "Legal and Moral Obligation." In *Essays in Moral Philosophy,* ed. A. I. Melden. Seattle: University of Washington Press.

Hart, H. L. A., and A. M. Honoré. 1959. *Causation in the Law.* Oxford: Oxford University Press.

Herman, Barbara. 1993. *The Practice of Moral Judgment.* Cambridge: Harvard University Press.

Hill, Thomas E., Jr. 1991. *Autonomy and Self-Respect.* Cambridge: Cambridge University Press.

———. 1992a. *Dignity and Practical Reason in Kant's Moral Theory.* Ithaca, N.Y.: Cornell University Press.

———. 1992b. "A Kantian Perspective on Moral Rules." *Philosophical Perspectives* 6:285–304.

———. 1993. "Donagan's Kant." *Ethics* 104:22–52.

———. 1994. "Kant on Responsibility for Consequences." *Jahrbuch für Recht und Ethik.* Vol. 2:159–76. Berlin: Duncker & Humbolt.

Hilts, Philip J. 1991. "The Imanishi-Kari Case." *New York Times*, March 31, 1991.

Hohfeld, Wesley Newcomb. 1919. *Fundamental Legal Conceptions*. Ed. Walter Wheeler Cook. New Haven: Yale University Press.

Kagan, Shelly. 1988. "The Additive Fallacy." *Ethics* 99:5–31.

Kant, Immanuel. 1956. *Groundwork of the Metaphysics of Morals*. Trans. H. J. Paton. New York: Harper & Row.

———. 1965. *The Metaphysical Elements of Justice*. Part 1 of *The Metaphysics of Morals*. Trans. John Ladd. Indianapolis: Bobbs-Merrill.

———. 1991. *The Metaphysics of Morals*. Trans. Mary Gregor. Cambridge: Cambridge University Press.

Kierkegaard, Sören. 1983. *Fear and Trembling*. Trans. Edna Hong and Howard Hong. Princeton: Princeton University Press.

Knox, Ronald, trans. 1963. *The Holy Bible*. London: Burns & Oates.

Korsgaard, Christine. 1986. "Kant's Formula of Humanity." *Kant-Studien* 77:183–202.

Lebus, Bruce. 1990. "Moral Dilemmas: Why They Are Hard to Solve." *Philosophical Investigations* 13:110–25.

Lemmon, John. 1965. "Deontic Logic and the Logic of Imperatives." *Logique et Analyse* 8 (29):39–61.

Levi, Isaac. 1992. "Conflict and Inquiry." *Ethics* 102:814–34.

Lewis, David. 1983. *Philosophical Papers*, vol. 1. New York: Oxford University Press.

Louden, Robert B. 1992. *Morality and Moral Theory: A Reappraisal and Reaffirmation*. New York: Oxford University Press.

McConnell, Terrance. 1978. "Moral Dilemmas and Consistency in Ethics." *Canadian Journal of Philosophy* 8:269–87. Reprinted in Gowans (1987).

———. 1988. "Interpersonal Moral Conflicts." *American Philosophical Quarterly* 25:25–35.

———. 1993. "Dilemmas and Incommensurateness." *The Journal of Value Inquiry* 27:247–52.

MacIntyre, Alasdair. 1990. "Moral Dilemmas." *Philosophy and Phenomenological Research*, supp. vol. 50:367–82.

Mackie, J. L. 1977. *Ethics: Inventing Right and Wrong*. London: Penguin Books.

Malcolm, Janet. 1993. "Annals of Biography: The Silent Woman." *The New Yorker* August 23, 30.

Mann, William E. 1991. "Jephthah's Plight: Moral Dilemmas and Theism." *Philosophical Perspectives* 5: 617–47.

Marcus, Ruth Barcan. 1980. "Moral Dilemmas and Consistency." *Journal of Philosophy* 77:121–36. Reprinted in Gowans (1987).

Mason, H. E. 1988. "Realistic Interpretations of Moral Questions." *Midwest Studies in Philosophy* 12:413–32.

Melville, Herman. 1962. *Billy Budd, Sailor (An Inside Narrative)*. Chicago: University of Chicago Press.

Mill, John Stuart. *Utilitarianism*. Excerpts reprinted in Gowans (1987).

Moore, G. E. 1962. "A Defence of Common Sense." In G. E. Moore, *Some Main Problems of Philosophy*. New York: Collier.

Nagel, Thomas. 1979a. "The Fragmentation of Value." In *Mortal Questions*. Cambridge: Cambridge University Press. Reprinted in Gowans (1987).

Nagel, Thomas. 1979. *Mortal Questions*. New York: Cambridge University Press.

Nozick, Robert. 1974. *Anarchy, State, and Utopia*. New York: Basic Books.

———. 1981. *Philosophical Explanations*. Cambridge: Harvard University Press.

Nussbaum, Martha C. 1986. *The Fragility of Goodness: Luck and Ethics in Greek Tragedy and Philosophy*. Cambridge: Cambridge University Press.

———. 1990. *Love's Knowledge: Essays on Philosophy and Literature.* New York: Oxford University Press.

Parfit, Derek. 1984. *Reasons and Persons.* Oxford: Clarendon Press.

Phillips, D. Z., and H. O. Mounce. 1970. *Moral Practices.* New York: Schocken Books.

Pietroski, Paul. 1990. "Meaning Naturally: A Partial Defense of Covariation Semantics." Ph.D. dissertation. Massachusetts Institute of Technology.

———. 1993. "Prima Facie Obligations, Ceteris Paribus Laws in Moral Theory." *Ethics* 103:489–515.

Pincoffs, Edmund. 1971. "Quandary Ethics." *Mind* 80:552–71.

Quinn, Philip. 1991. "Critical Notice of Sinnott-Armstrong, *Moral Dilemmas.*" *Philosophy and Phenomenological Research* 51: 693–97.

Railton, Peter. 1986a. "Moral Realism." *Philosophical Review* 95: 163–207.

———. 1986b. "Facts and Values." *Philosophical Topics* 14:5–31.

———. 1992. "Pluralism, Determinacy, and Dilemma." *Ethics* 102:720–42.

———. 1993. "Noncognitivism about Rationality: Costs, Benefits, and an Alternative." *Philosophical Issues* 4: 36–51.

Railton, Peter, and Gideon Rosen. 1994. "Realism." In *The Blackwell Companion to Metaphysics,* ed. Jaegwon Kim and Ernest Sosa. Oxford: Basil Blackwell.

Rawls, John. 1971. *A Theory of Justice.* Cambridge: Harvard University Press.

Roberts, R. C. 1988. "What an Emotion Is: A Sketch." *Philosophical Review* 97:183–209.

Ross, W. D. 1930. *The Right and the Good.* Oxford: Clarendon Press.

———. 1939. *The Foundations of Ethics.* Oxford: Clarendon Press.

Rousseau, Jean-Jacques. 1958. *The Confessions.* Trans. J. M. Cohen. London: Penguin Books.

Santurri, Edmund N. 1987. *Perplexity in the Moral Life: Philosophical and Theological Considerations.* Charlottesville: University Press of Virginia.

Sartorius, Rolf. 1977. "Bayes' Theorem, Hard Cases, and Judicial Discretion". *Georgia Law Review* 11: 1269–75.

Sartre, Jean Paul. 1956. "Existentialism is a Humanism." Trans. Philip Mairet. In *Existentialism from Dostoevsky to Sartre,* ed. Walter Arnold Kaufmann. New York: Meridian Books. Reprinted in Solomon (1974).

Schiffer, Stephen. 1990. "Meaning and Value." *The Journal of Philosophy* 87:602–11.

Schneewind, J. B. 1977. *Sidgwick and Victorian Rationalism.* Oxford: Clarendon Press.

Sidgwick, Henry. 1907. *The Methods of Ethics.* London: Macmillan.

Sinnott-Armstrong, Walter. 1988. *Moral Dilemmas.* Oxford: Basil Blackwell.

———. 1992. "An Argument for Consequentialism." *Philosophical Perspectives* 6: 399–421.

Sinnott-Armstrong, Walter, Diana Raffman, and Nicholas Asher, eds. 1994. *Modality, Morality and Belief.* New York: Cambridge University Press.

Slote, Michael. 1985. "Utilitarianism, Moral Dilemmas, and Moral Cost." *American Philosophical Quarterly* 22:161–68.

Solomon, Robert, ed. 1974. *Existentialism.* New York: Random House.

Stalnaker, Robert. 1968. "A Theory of Conditionals." In *Studies in Logical Theory,* ed. Nicholas Rescher. American Philosophical Quarterly Monograph, no. 2. Reprinted in *Causation and Conditionals,* ed. Ernest Sosa. New York: Oxford University Press, 1975.

Stocker, Michael. 1987. "Moral Conflicts: What They Are and What They Show." *Pacific Philosophical Quarterly* 68:104–23.

————. 1990. *Plural and Conflicting Values*. Oxford: Clarendon Press.

Styron, William. 1980. *Sophie's Choice*. New York: Bantam Books.

Taylor, Charles. 1982. "The Diversity of Goods." In *Utilitarianism and Beyond,* eds. A. K. Sen and Bernard Williams. New York: Cambridge University Press.

————. 1989. *Sources of the Self: The Making of the Modern Identity*. Cambridge: Harvard University Press.

Thomson, Judith Jarvis. 1986. "Rights and Compensation." In Judith Jarvis Thomson, *Rights, Restitution and Risk,* ed. William Parent. Cambridge: Harvard University Press.

————. 1990. *The Realm of Rights*. Cambridge: Harvard University Press.

Toulmin, Stephen. 1950. *Examination of the Place of Reason in Ethics*. Cambridge: Cambridge University Press.

van Fraassen, Bas. 1973. "Values and the Heart's Command." *Journal of Philosophy* 70:5–19. Reprinted in Gowans (1987).

Vlastos, Gregory. 1973. "The Individual as Object of Love in Plato." In Gregory Vlastos, *Platonic Studies*. Princeton: Princeton University Press.

Walker, Margaret Urban. 1989. "Moral Understandings: Alternative 'Epistemology' for a Feminist Ethics." *Hypatia* 4:15–28.

Williams, Bernard. 1965. "Ethical Consistency." *Proceedings of the Aristotelian Society* suppl. vol. 39: 103–24. Reprinted in Williams (1973) and Gowans (1987).

————. 1966. "Consistency and Realism." *Proceedings of the Aristotelian Society* suppl. vol. 40:1–22. Reprinted in Williams (1973).

————. 1973. *Problems of the Self*. Cambridge: Cambridge University Press.

————. 1978. Introduction to Isaiah Berlin, *Concepts and Categories: Philosophical Essays*. New York: Viking Press.

————. 1979. "Conflicts of Values." In Bernard Williams, *Moral Luck*. Cambridge: Cambridge University Press.

————. 1985. *Ethics and the Limits of Philosophy*. Cambridge: Harvard University Press.

Wright, Crispin. 1993. *Truth and Objectivity*. Cambridge: Harvard University Press.

Zimmerman, Michael J. 1987. "Remote Obligation." *American Philosophical Quarterly* 24:199–205.

————. 1988. *An Essay on Moral Responsibility*. Totowa, N.J.: Rowman and Littlefield.

————. 1990. "Where Did I Go Wrong?" *Philosophical Studies* 59:55–77.

Index

act utilitarianism, 25, 40, 165n15
Agamemnon, 18, 136
agglomeration, 51, 70, 80, 203
all-things-considered obligations, 36, 79, 92, 102–4, 115–16, 118, 227–28
Anderson, Elizabeth, 166n21
Antigone, 24
Aquinas, St. Thomas, 13, 16, 71
Aristotle, 202
autonomy, 74, 97, 148, 171, 209, 217, 224

Baier, Kurt, 22n18
Billy Budd, 207, 212–13, 221
Blackburn, Simon, 8, 93, 98n9, 164n5, 234n4
blame, 31, 96, 97, 99–100n25, 100n26
blameworthiness, 96–98, 99–100n25, 100–101n26
Brink, David O., 5, 63n4, 63n10, 88, 93

Chellas, Brian, 29
Chisholm, Roderick, 13, 47n28
Christian moral theory, 13
Churchill, Winston, 140, 158
classical moral theories and moral dilemmas
  act utilitarian, 25, 179
  communitarian, 16–17
  divine command, 15–16
  ideal utilitarian, 88, 96–97
  intuitionist, 18, 179
  Kantian, 14–15, 167–98
  Millian utilitarian, 143–44
  rationalist, 14–15, 66, 68, 69
  utilitarian, 18, 19, 25–26, 43, 73, 88, 140, 143, 144, 159, 179
common responsibilities, 218, 219–20
compensation, 42, 94, 135–36
conceptions of morality, 12, 76–77
  lifestyles and the sphere of morality, 35

moral codes, 23
moral principle defined, 23
  as not fully understood, 88–90
  as socially constructed, 87–88, 98n2
  sphere of morality, 29, 34, 229–30
Conee, Earl, 70, 62n1
conflicts of common responsibilities, 217–220, 229
consistency
  of a set of rules, 26–28, 98n3
  of moral codes, 14, 80–83
  of moral theories, 14
  of sentences or propositions, 26, 80
contrary-to-duty imperatives, 13

Dahl, Norman, 7, 64n17
Davidson, Donald, 25, 74
deontic logic
  in arguments for or against dilemmas, 69–71, 159, 203
  and ordinary moral reasoning, 79
  principles of, 29–30, 70; agglomeration, 108, 124n30, 124n32; obligation execution, 111, 123n29; obligatoriness and impermissibility, 112; voluntarist, 108, 110, 123n26; weak impermissibility, 113
  systems of, 29–31, 203
deontological theories, 97
dirty hands, 29, 33
diverging directions of accountability, 221–24
Donagan, Alan, 5, 9, 40–42, 47n29, 63n2, 80, 84n1, 86, 101n27, 195n15, 195n16, 195n22, 205
Dworkin, Ronald, 35, 163n1

egalitarian principles, 34
egoism, 14
emotion, 24, 38, 46n16
equipollence, 106
ethical theory and moral problems, 73

243

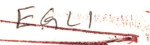